ARAB CULTURE AND THE NOVEL

Arab Culture and the Novel explores the status and role of the novel in modern Arab culture. It postulates the historical experience of modern Egypt as largely representative of the general condition of other Arab, Islamic, and postcolonial nation-states, especially as these wrestle with the perennial quest for a viable sense of personal and collective identity in modernity.

One of the book's major theses is that certain generic properties of the novel, such as its constitutive interest in the individual as an autonomous agent of moral, ethical, political, and sexual choices and desires appear incompatible with entrenched beliefs and norms of traditional Arab society and culture. How the Egyptian novel reconciles this proactive, discursive agency with the aesthetic imperatives of the literary genre is a major concern of this study.

The book tackles such broad questions through sustained textual analysis and close reading of a significant number of Egyptian novels. It thus consciously situates the literary text at the heart of the critical performance. Ultimately, the will of the Arabic novel is to imagine the unthinkable and to reinstate in the Arab public debate topics long banished from there, such as the body, sexuality, religious difference, and political dissent may bespeak the absence of a viable Arab civil society and a crippling cultural impasse. Could the Arabic novel be the harbinger of such a civil society and the cultural lever to transport it across, and beyond, the historical impasse?

Muhammad Siddiq is Professor at the Department for Near Eastern Studies, University of California, Berkeley, USA.

ROUTLEDGE STUDIES IN MIDDLE EASTERN LITERATURES

Routledge Studies in Middle Eastern Literatures is a monograph series devoted to aspects of the literatures of the Near and Middle East and North Africa both modern and pre-modern. It is hoped that the provision of such a forum will lead to a greater emphasis on the comparative study of the literatures of this area, although studies devoted to one literary or linguistic region are warmly encouraged. It is the editors' objective to foster the comparative and multi-disciplinary investigation of the written and oral literary products of this area.

1. SHEHERAZADE THROUGH THE LOOKING GLASS
Eva Sallis

2. THE PALESTINIAN NOVEL
Ibrahim Taha

3. OF DISHES AND DISCOURSE
Geert Jan van Gelder

4. MEDIEVAL ARABIC PRAISE POETRY
Beatrice Gruendler

5. MAKING THE GREAT BOOK OF SONGS
Hilary Kilpatrick

6. THE NOVEL AND THE RURAL IMAGINARY IN EGYPT, 1880–1985
Samah Selim

7. IBN ABI TAHIR TAYFUR AND ARABIC WRITERLY CULTURE
A ninth-century bookman in Baghdad
Shawkat M. Toorawa

8. RELIGIOUS PERSPECTIVES IN MODERN MUSLIM AND JEWISH LITERATURES
Edited by Glenda Abramson and Hilary Kilpatrick

9. ARABIC POETRY
Trajectories of modernity and tradition
Muhsin J. al-Musawi

10. MEDIEVAL ANDALUSIAN COURTLY CULTURE IN THE MEDITERRANEAN
Three ladies and a lover
Cynthia Robinson

11. WRITING AND REPRESENTATION IN MEDIEVAL ISLAM
Muslim Horizons
Julia Bray

12. NATIONALISM, ISLAM AND WORLD LITERATURE
Sites of confluence in the writings of Mahmūd al-Masadī
Mohamed-Salah Omri

13. THE ORAL AND THE WRITTEN IN EARLY ISLAM
Gregor Schoeler
Translated by Uwe Vagelpohl
Edited by James Montgomery

14. LITERATURE, JOURNALISM AND THE AVANT-GARDE
Intersection in Egypt
Elisabeth Kendall

15. THE THOUSAND AND ONE NIGHTS
Space, travel and transformation
Richard van Leeuwen

16. ARAB CULTURE AND THE NOVEL
Genre, identity, and agency in Egyptian fiction
Muhammad Siddiq

ARAB CULTURE AND THE NOVEL

Genre, identity, and agency in Egyptian fiction

Muhammad Siddiq

LONDON AND NEW YORK

First published 2007
by Routledge
2 Park Square, Milton Park, Abingdon, Oxon OX14 4RN

Simultaneously published in the USA and Canada
by Routledge
52 Vanderbilt Avenue, New York, NY 10017

Routledge is an imprint of the Taylor & Francis Group, an informa business

Typeset in Times New Roman by
Newgen Imaging Systems (P) Ltd, Chennai, India

British Library Cataloguing in Publication Data
A catalogue record for this book is available
from the British Library

Library of Congress Cataloging in Publication Data
A catalog record for this book has been requested

ISBN13: 978-0-415-59743-2 (pbk)
ISBN13: 978-0-203-96114-8 (ebk)

IN MEMORY OF MY BELOVED WIFE, AMĪNA;
AND FOR THE BRAVE WRITERS OF EGYPT

CONTENTS

PREFACE

The subject of this book changed drastically in the long process of its gestation. Initially, it had a much narrower focus: I intended to study the writings of the younger, "post-Mahfouz" generation of Egyptian writers as a distinct species of Egyptian fiction. The operative title of that project was symptomatic of its limited scope, and perhaps also of its implicit sympathies. It was: "New Directions in the Egyptian Novel."

But the more I reflected on the underlying causes of the younger writers' predicament, especially their acute alienation from the structures of power and the institutionalized modalities of identity, the more general these causes appeared and the less amenable to the specific dynamics of intergenerational conflicts and differences. To be sure, such differences abound, and they do figure in the overall picture. But they seem to operate on a secondary, rather than a primary level of cultural production. During what appears to have become a regular pattern of periodic crises, serious fiction, and the literary imagination itself, rather than any specific variety thereof, appear to be the real target of an abiding animus.

A series of portentous events during the last quarter of the twentieth century—the very period in which the "new generation" and the "new directions" were presumed to have come fully into their own—motivated and reinforced this realization. The following are only a few of the most salient among these events: the international uproar over Salman Rushdie's novel, *The Satanic Verses* (1986); the favorable mention by the Nobel Prize Committee (1988) of Naguib Mahfouz' most controversial novel, *Awlād Ḥāratinā* (1959); the calamitous consequences of this approbation, which culminated in the attempt on Mahfouz' life in 1994; and the spate of attacks on writers and books that followed, and is yet to subside.

Equally unfathomable was the cataclysmic vehemence that accompanied these convulsions. Why, I wondered, does a work of imaginative fiction, however contorted or grotesque its representation of religion, history, or "reality," stir up such deadly passions in people who have not even read it? In other words, what makes a work of fiction so threatening as to warrant killing and being killed for? A corollary and equally baffling question flowed directly from this quandary: Why do Arab and Muslim writers, who are only too intimately familiar with the raw emotions and hypersensitivities of their fellow-patriots and co-religionists to certain tabooed subjects, why do they risk so much to revisit, dramatize, and problematize these very subjects in their fiction?

Irrespective of whether these events were intrinsically connected or orchestrated by an invisible, world-embracing master plan, they were causally related in the act of interpretation. Thus, while Imam Khomeini was issuing his religious decree (*fatwā*) against Rushdie's life in Iran, Shaykh 'Umar 'Abd al-Raḥmān was elaborating the case of direct causality in Egypt. "Had Naguib Mahfouz been killed when he wrote *Children of our Alley*, Salman Rushdie would not have dared write *The Satanic Verses*," he is reported to have said. In both instances, as in many others, the novels were read allegorically, in flagrant disregard for their other constitutive literary and aesthetic attributes. As "disguised" theological heresies, the literary texts were readily indicted for infringing a fundamental tenet of Islam. Accordingly, the outraged "Islamic" response appeared duly uniform and universal.

Though ever present, the possibility of cynical manipulation of religion for political ends cannot detain us here. Suffice it to say that no two responses could have been more dissimilar than those of official Iran and official Egypt. Whereas the Islamic Republic of Iran appeared to stand solidly behind its supreme leader, the Ayatollah, the Arab Republic of Egypt seemed to speak in a cacophony of voices. Thus, while the government embraced Mahfouz without reservation and sheltered him like a precious national treasure, the religious establishment was sharply divided, and the Egyptian public appeared baffled and dismayed, but withal remained largely impassive. The merits of the respective positions aside, it is the boundless ability and willingness of the nation-state to insinuate itself as supreme arbiter of values in all domains of public life that warrants attention here. The point was crudely driven home to me in a brief conversation with the director of the Cairo office of a major American scholarship in 1986. "Beware of mingling too much with writers," the director said, "they are a bunch of trouble makers, and the authorities are weary of their constant threat to public peace."

I can no longer ascertain whether it was this curious casting of the nation-state as custodian of public safety and morality against novels and novelists that triggered the drastic reorientation of the present study. The effect, whatever its sources, is not in doubt. The paramount objective of the study shifted from the focus on a single generation of Egyptian writers to the far more complex and problematic relationship between the novel and the nation in modern Egypt. More precisely, the book explores the complex relationship between the novel and the major constituents of identity in modern Arab culture against the backdrop of the Egyptian national scene. It presents a close look at the multifaceted subject of identity across a broad spectrum of imaginative and discursive formulations. What makes the fictional treatment of this explosive and perennially topical subject particularly relevant is a simple fact: The novel gauges the effects of the identity crisis that has afflicted Arab culture during the last two centuries more accurately and extensively than any other literary or discursive genre. This is so, in part, because the difficulties the Arabic novel has experienced in acclimatization since its controversial emergence in modern Arab culture are in many respects analogous to (and symptomatic of) the endless vacillation of this culture between two seemingly polar orientations: one traditional, conservative, Arab-Islamic, and therefore deemed indigenous and authentic; the other modern, secular, and, consequently, "foreign," and "inauthentic."

Also, like Arab modernity, the Arabic novel continues to suffer from the congenital stigma of its putative origins in the West and its subsequent importation into Arab culture under the auspices of Western colonial domination. Many classics of Egyptian (and Arabic) fiction go to great lengths to dramatize the psychological and intellectual paralysis that grips fictional characters who venture into the hazardous terrain of encounter with the cultural "Other." Ominously, all attempts to imagine a credible reconciliation or workable synthesis between these alleged binary opposites have so far proven futile in fiction as in reality. Even so, the quest continues unabated in the Arabic novel as the theme of cultural encounter between "Self" and "Other" takes everchanging forms and directions. I trace the workings and permutations of this major theme through detailed analysis of a significant number of outstanding Egyptian novels.

As a former colony, Egypt shares many fundamental characteristics with most postcolonial nation-states in the Arab-Islamic world, as well as the Third World. The extent of this overlap allows for extrapolating more general conclusions from the imaginative treatment of the problematic of identity in the Egyptian national setting. But Egypt also exemplifies the historical predicament of contingent nationhood perhaps better than most such nation-states for two important reasons. The first concerns the country's rich history, particularly for purposes of the novel, its Islamic heritage, so vividly represented by the presence on its soil of the oldest institution of higher Islamic learning in the world: the Azhar university. The possibility of causal linkage between the curriculum of the traditional religious schools, including the Azhar, and certain character traits and personality types is an abiding preoccupation of Egyptian fiction. As I try to show, many Egyptian novels often defy an automatic or mechanical correlation or reciprocity between rote memorization of religious texts and genuine knowledge, public display of religiosity and genuine piety, official religious status and ethical conduct and spirituality. Such anomalies abound in the works of Mahfouz, for example, where they figure, often prominently, in both characterization and plot.

The second reason why Egypt exemplifies so graphically the historical predicament of contingent nationhood arises from the country's location at some of the world's major crossroads, and its attendant strategic centrality to Western interests in the Near East, and beyond. Physical proximity to different climes and cultures creates alternative horizons (or the illusion thereof) for contemplating different modalities of identity and cultural hybridity. The Egyptian novel retains a vivid record of the ravages visited on Egyptian identity by this powerful intersection of overladen history and fortuitous geography. To cite only one example here, the steady dwindling of the "European" communities of Alexandria after the Suez war of 1956 drives some of the Alexandrine (Muslim) characters of Ibrahim Abdel Meguid's novels to utter distraction.

But the novel is by no means a hapless victim in the often-violent drama it repeatedly stages and critiques. Though primarily a literary genre, it nonetheless doubles as an agent of cultural and historical change. Bound by generic imperatives to the principle of representing circumstantial reality and ordinary experience, the novel routinely intervenes in the discourses of identity, often against entrenched authoritarian and hegemonic narratives. Just as often, and under the same literary artistic mandate, the novel habitually questions sacrosanct religious, social, and cultural taboos in contemporary Arab culture. The status of religious minorities in the (Arab/Islamic) nation-state, the rights of women, the question of the body, sexuality, difference, and political and intellectual dissent, are frequently raised and addressed themes in this imaginative fiction. The attempt on the life of Egypt's foremost writer and Nobel laureate Naguib Mahfouz in 1994, like the constant harassment of unorthodox writers and the periodic bouts of censorship and banning of works of fiction (including such classics of world literature as *The Arabian Nights*) measure accurately the perceived danger implicit in this role of imaginative fiction as a countervailing force in modern Arab culture.

In other words, I want to argue that the Egyptian novel does not merely reflect a preexisting Arab cultural reality, but rather posits a reciprocal pattern of relations between culture and literature, in which the novel plays a performative and dynamic role. This perception, in effect, turns the Egyptian novel into a subversive genre that circumscribes a space in which the conflicts and crises that animate contemporary Arab/Islamic culture take imaginative shape. In "imagining the unthinkable" the Egyptian/Arab novel reflects this crisis because of its mimetic–reflective deportment, yet exacerbates it at the same time because of its constitutive–performative power.

The structural division of the study attempts to canvass this intricate relation between the novel and the nation from several crucial angles. Chapter 1, "A Genre at War: Literary Form and Historical Agency," doubles as a general introduction. It presents an overview of what seems to be a fundamental incompatibility between the dialogic, secular, and pluralistic commitments of the novel and the totalitarian, sectarian, and exclusionary modes of thought and practice in the national polity of modern Egypt. In addition to the conceptual and terminological confusion about the genre, the chapter examines manifestations of politically and culturally imposed limitations on the novelistic imagination. It illustrates this general problematic by identifying and describing representative instances of the precarious situation of writers, scholars, and intellectuals in Egypt at present. This situation often produces social and cultural crises that make it absolutely impossible to write about Arabic fiction exclusively in literary or aesthetic terms. The chapter also examines some telling examples of how the interlocking politico-cultural discourses that often converge at the site of the novel impact the poetics of the Arabic novel in Egypt. Noting the increasingly more frequent phenomenon of censorship and the fact that many of the works under attack are not recent, the chapter postulates a general working hypothesis about a recurrent, underlying pattern that operates at the formative level of modern Arabic literature and Arab culture.

In Chapter 2, "Tangents of Identity: The Poetics of Space in the Egyptian Novel," I examine the poetics of fictional space in relation to the thematics of personal and national identity. Here, as elsewhere, I draw on insights from the works of theoreticians and scholars of both nationalism and imaginative fiction to interrogate how different configurations of the same bounded space assume telling symbolic significance and discursive agency. As it maps the fictional representations of the "imagined community" of the nation-state, the chapter shows how the deployment of symbolic space in highly elaborate and calculated ways enables the novel to question modes of power relations on the national scene. Many Egyptian novels seem to plot space so as to question the ethical, moral, and political legitimacy (and value) of the artificial construct designating the nation-state and the arbitrary exercise of power wielded in its name. In addition to examining the various strategies through which the Egyptian novel foregrounds formative tensions that inhere in the Egyptian national space—for example, between the center and the periphery, the city and the countryside, the indigenous space of the self and the alien space of the "other," or, as is often the case, the space of the (alienated) "other" within, this chapter also compares the widely divergent treatment of Egyptian space by Western and Egyptian writers. Especially instructive in this regard is the sharp contrast between Lawrence Durrell's and Edwar al-Kharrat's depiction of Alexandria.

In Chapter 3, "Divining Identities: Religion and the Egyptian Novel," I investigate the various modes and strategies of representing religious themes, issues, and motifs in the novel. No other "fictional" intervention in the dominant discourses of identity has aroused as much controversy and hostility as has the Egyptian novel's treatment of religion. The chapter begins by noting the apparent incompatibility between commitment to Islam (and religion in general) and imaginative fiction. It examines this phenomenon through specific examples of several Egyptian novelists who, upon re-embracing Islam after being estranged from it, abandoned their novelistic (and other artistic) careers altogether. Its particular circumstances aside, this "recanting" phenomenon is uncannily consistent with—perhaps even constitutive of—the recurrent pattern of false starts and discontinuous modernity projects that vitiate the quest for a viable individual and national identity in modern Arab culture.

Two major thematic strands inform much of the discussion in this chapter. The first revolves around the psychoanalytic content that often underlies the treatment of religious themes and motifs in Egyptian fiction. This is particularly true of Mahfouz' novels where the God of institutionalized religion, the stern father, and the taboo against incest often appear inextricable. Mahfouz' magnum opus, *The Cairene Trilogy*, best illustrates this valence of the literary text as psychodrama in which unconscious processes, be they aesthetic or psychological, balance each other out in the creation of plot and character. This reading posits a creative role for culture in the dynamics of the plot. The second strand in Chapter 3 traces the novel's preoccupation with the evolution of constitutional thought in Egypt, especially as concerns the status of religious minorities, against the backdrop of the increasingly more pronounced advocacy of making Islamic law (*sharī'a*) a major—if not *the* major—source of legislation.

Finally, in Chapter 4, "Questionable Subjects: Individuality, Representation, and the Egyptian Novel," I take up the subject of the individual in its simultaneous capacity as the quintessential prerequisite of civil society, the nation, and the novel. The chapter examines fictional representations of this crucial concept, and its multiple permutations in ancillary terms such as individuality, personality, character, type, and stereotype. It interrogates the novel's treatment of this complex subject against the entrenched religious, political, social, and cultural constraints on the one hand, and traditional conventions and ideas about the writer, the author, literary genres, and norms of representation in Arabic literature and Arab culture, on the other.

The relationship of the novelist to his character lies at the heart of a major difficulty in the criticism of the Arabic novel, namely, that of disengaging the novel from autobiography, or from outright advocacy. The problem here concerns the autonomy of the art form itself. Similarly, the ready availability of prototypes of the "exemplary Islamic personality" in the popular imagination and the attendant imperative of reproducing additional, customary versions of this ideal personality in literary form—for both aesthetic and moral edification—immensely complicates the novel's constitutive interest in "ordinary" individuals. How the Egyptian novel negotiates these immense complications to "smuggle" into modern Arab consciousness and Arab culture fictional versions of the emergent private subjectivities of "typical," often demonstrably anti-heroic, ordinary individuals and quotidian experience is an overriding concern of this chapter, indeed of this study.

Collectively, the four chapters treat complementary issues of Arab identity and culture as represented in fiction. The opening and closing chapters provide overviews of foundational concepts of literary genres, perimeters of their interplay in modern Arab culture, and built-in constraints on the literary imagination. The second and third are more directly concerned with questions of literary representation. In all instances I try to supplement literary criticism (understood as analysis of text, *explication de text*) with the more general discourse of cultural criticism, which, considering the subject matter of the book, is perhaps more appropriate to the study of the Egyptian/Arabic novel.

A procedural/polemical overture

It may be useful to interpolate here a brief description of some of the operative theoretical premises, writing strategies, and organizational principles that inform this study. Such a clarification is all the more imperative in light of the irreducible complexity of the book's ambitious—perhaps overambitious—objective and mutiple foci. To recapitulate briefly: My objective is to examine major areas of contestation over individual and collective identity in modern Arab/Islamic culture as that contestation unfolds against the ubiquitous narrative of the nation in the biggest Arab nation-state, Egypt, and is variably refracted through the prism of the novel.

Ideally one would want to attend simultaneously and in equal measure to all the interests that bear on this study. In reality this ideal is seldom, if ever, attainable. What this means in practical and procedural terms is that one perforce has to select, and, by selecting, also to deselect. Thus, only a limited number of novels from the huge body of Egyptian fiction can be adequately discussed; and within that limited corpus, only those that bear directly on the defining discourses of identity and the nation. Similarly, only the most immediately relevant discussions of literary theory, nationalism, religion, psychoanalysis, and representation can be mobilized to contextualize the novel's treatment of, and interaction with, the dynamic constituents of identity.

Of all the general, overriding questions with which I had to wrestle continuously in this study none was more difficult than that of selection. For it applied equally to the primary and the secondary sources; and it always involved several paramount criteria. Thus, for example, in the selection of novels (and authors), I sought to reconcile artistic and aesthetic quality with relevance to the "master" narrative of the nation, or, barring that, to any of its ancillary discourses. And since the works discussed had also to be "representative," whatever one thinks of this notoriously volatile term, the major works of the "canon" could not be sidestepped without serious repercussions to the novel's claim to "comprehensive" mapping of the nation, however illusory that claim may also be.

Directly related to this matter is the question of repetition. Because the study seeks to canvass the fictional representation of the nation from multiple thematic, spatial, and temporal angles several major novels could not but figure in more than one perspective, such as space and religion, or religion and individuality. The temporal range of the study contributes its share to this compounded predicament. The formidable question of beginnings—of both nation-state and novel—periodization, literary generations, and the ever-present "anxiety of influence," are all deeply implicated in the intertwining trajectories I seek to uncover and unlock here.

To minimize redundancy and diffusion, I engage the extensive critical literature about such works and authors, especially Mahfouz, only sparingly—that is—only when that literature intersects directly and significantly with the primary interests of this study. To cement the disparate foci and thrusts of the study into a semblance of coherent whole, I try to harness whatever originality my reading of the novels has to the discursive function of these novels in that other realm, the overarching narrative of identity.

Understandably, texts written in one language about narratives of identity inscribed in another tend to involve a large measure of cultural translation. The danger of misreading and mistranslating in such transactions often lurks below the surface. One way to safeguard against such pitfalls is to engage the primary texts and the scholarship produced by the scholarly community within the original culture of the translated texts; in this case Arabic. In addition to performing this task, the preponderance of Arabic secondary sources in this study bespeaks a tacit assumption, namely, that most of the fundamental issues involved in the construction, and the crisis, of identity in modern Arab culture are internal to Arab culture itself. But contemporary Arab culture also has deep, unshakable roots in Islamic culture and civilization. Either way, to the extent that these issues find expression in literary form they concern, first and foremost, Arab writers, critics, intellectuals, and the Arab intelligentsia in general. How the dynamics of identity play out in the Egyptian cultural scene itself is paramount to my project.

In modern history, the quest for identity, whether individual, communal, or national, in Egypt as in other Arab and Islamic states and societies, has unfolded against an increasingly more troubled (and troubling) awareness of the cultural "Other." In the case of Egypt this has always been the West in general, and, at least since 1882, Great Britain in particular. At the present moment of global American hegemony, English, the language of both former colonial and present empires, has become the privileged vehicle of exchange in the debate over identity between modern Arab/Islamic culture and its "Other." To pretend otherwise in the post 9/11 reality is nothing short of being disingenuous. I state matters in such broad and categorical terms to delineate the boundaries and perimeters that frame this study. In reality, as I hope this study will show, the situation is immeasurably more complex and more nuanced. My decision to include here only relevant secondary sources in English is thus motivated by a dual objective: to economize, and to highlight this fateful historical entanglement.

Also notable for its absence from this study is a full-fledged feminist perspective on the novel's representation of the nation. Initially, I had planned a separate chapter for this purpose. But as the study unfolded, a number of realizations rendered that intention increasingly less practical. For one thing, the Arabic novel, like the nation, has always been highly gendered. Until recently, the Egyptian novel, perhaps not unlike the novel (and the nation), in other national cultures, has been predominantly a masculine affair. For another thing, the representation of women in this "imaginative" male enterprise readily lends itself to deconstruction. Rightly or otherwise, I felt that deconstructing the male perspective on the gendered narrative of national identity prefigures, and is a prerequisite for, a thorough feminist critique of that narrative. In any event, more *bona fide* feminist critics than myself have already undertaken this valiant task with evident zeal and competence. Wherever appropriate, I draw attention to their significant contribution to illuminating this crucial aspect of the novel's staging of (national) identity.

I argue in this study that the novel's embrace of reality, however awkward, flabby, and cumbersome it often appears, is nonetheless a defining characteristic of the Egyptian novel. Hovering as it often does between symbiosis and cringing dependence, this relationship renders the concept of closure in this study less urgent than the case might have been otherwise. Hence my decision to leave the study open-ended, that is, without a concluding chapter. Such a choice, it seems to me, is more apt to translate the metaphor of embrace into a structural feature of the text: For if fluid reality, like its representation in many Egyptian novels, has no closure, why should—indeed, how could—a critical study dealing with both have closure? After all, like the nation-state itself, and even more so civil society, the Egyptian novel is still a work-in-progress.

Finally, a word or two about the formidable task assigned to juxtaposition in this study. To situate the novel's staging of the nation in historical context requires constant attention to the other formative discourses of identity operating simultaneously on the national cultural scene. These, in turn, can be invoked collectively only by means of anecdotal juxtaposition. The risk of fragmentation inherent in the constant shifting and shuttling back and forth among these various discourses and foci is too self-evident to warrant further elaboration. But it is equally unavoidable if the study is to evoke the ambience of the times and to maintain its panoramic view of the cultural role of the novel in defining and representing the nation. In deference to the reader's critical aptitude and reading skills I have refrained as much as possible from insinuating my own "mediating" subjectivity between the reader and the dynamics of the text at such junctures.

ACKNOWLEDGMENTS

This book owes great many friends, colleagues, and students, more than sincere words of acknowledgment can express. Even though only a few read parts of the work while in progress, and still fewer read the entire text, my gratitude is not constrained. Help, like grace, works in mysterious, and not always perceptible ways. I am as indebted to those who extended intangible and indirect help as I am to those whose help was more concrete and material. The evident shortcomings of the book reflect my inability to benefit more fully from the insights and advice of these friends. It would have been all the poorer without their input.

I wish first to thank the many Egyptian and Arab writers and critics who gave generously of their time and attention during numerous meetings and interviews, both formal and informal, in Egypt, London, Washington, and Berkeley. The late Yahya Haqqi, Fathi Ghanim, Magda al-Nowaihi, and Ghali Shukri; Sonalla Ibrahim, Abdu Gubeir, Ibrahim Aslan, Bahaa Taher, Edwar Al-Kharrat, Ibrahim Abdel Meguid, Naguib Mahfouz, Gamal Al-Ghitani, Muhammad Yusuf al-Qa'id, Radwa Ashour, Siham Bayyoumi, Ferial Ghazoul, Samia Mehrez, Sabry Hafez, and Farouk Abdel Wahab, deserve special thanks.

At a slightly greater remove from the scene of literary production, but far closer to the pulse of the study, stand remarkable friends and colleagues: Daniel Boyarin, Hamid Algar, Robert Alter, Cathy Gallaghar, Abdul R. JanMohamed, Ibrahim Muhawi, and Satyel Larson of UC Berkeley; Jack Miles of the Pacific Council on International Policy; Roger Allen of the University of Pennsylvania; Ato Quayson of the University of Toronto; Molly Rotherberge, Ray Taras, and Erec Koch of Tulane University, New Orleans; Walter Andrews, and Nicholas Heer of the University of Washington. Thank you all for your help, and more so for your lasting friendship.

Many bright students at Berkeley helped me fine-tune my argument by challenging in various ways and formats, in and out of the classroom, my readings of various works discussed in this book. Wherever any of you identifies a trace or hears an echo of a familiar point please revisit it with my thanks. You are simply too many to name.

Anyone familiar with Berkeley knows how continuous the traffic in knowledge is between classrooms and offices on campus and the cozy, adjacent cafes. How often a fresh idea or insight that arises in class towards the end of a session continues to unfold in the short stroll between a classroom and a nearby cafe; and vice versa. Significant parts of this book were in fact written at Cafe Milano, my favorite "secret" haunt. I wish to thank the wonderful team working there: Martin, Silviano, Faviola, Jorge, Nicolas, Tomas, and all the rest. Guys, your mirth, like your coffee, is inspirational!

Eden Orion of the University of Haifa earned my gratitude for his invaluable technical help with the electronic conversion of the manuscript across (often incompatible) word processors.

Special thanks are also due to the editors of the series Curzon Studies in Arabic and Middle Eastern Literatures: James E. Montgomery, University of Cambridge, Roger Allen, University of Pennsylvania, and Philip F. Kennedy, New York University.

Joe Whiting, Natalja Mortensen, and John Clement supervised different stages of the laborious process of publishing the book. I want to thank them all, and the rest of the publishing team, for their patience and unflagging support.

Last but not least, I wish to thank my dear children, Manal and Imran, for occasionally "allowing" me to work at home, though always for the "right" price! It was worth it. Thank you both for your liberating sense of humor.

NOTE ON TRANSLATION AND TRANSLITERATION

Unless otherwise indicated, all translations from the Arabic are mine. This applies equally to hitherto untranslated Arabic texts as it does to texts of which there is a published English translation. Following the guidelines used by IJMES, I give the italicized Arabic title in transliteration first, followed, in parentheses, by the date of publication, and an English translation of the Arabic title. If the English title coincides with that of a published translation, it is also italicized and is followed by the date of publication within the same parentheses. If there is no English translation, the title is not italicized. Occasionally, I give the literal English translation of an Arabic title in the body of the text and reference the published translation, if any such exists, in the footnotes. For the sake of consistency, I use the italicized Arabic titles in the discussion. To the extent that my intention is realized in the text, the transliteration should conform to the IJMES system. The only deliberate exception to this rule is the use of the common English spelling of names familiar to the reader of English, for example, Nasser, instead of Nāṣir, Naguib Mahfouz, instead of Najīb Mḥfūẓ and so on.

1

A GENRE AT WAR

Literary form and historical agency

This introductory chapter aims to map out major areas of intersection and overlap between imaginative and discursive representations of identity in the Egyptian novel. The mapping will identify and examine in some depth instructive instances of the overarching identity discourse against the fluid backdrop of contemporary Egyptian culture, politics, and history. Subsequent chapters will take up and interrogate further the trajectories of the novel and the nation as these interface and intertwine across multiple sites of identity formation.

To launch the investigation, let me begin with a categorical assertion about the state of the Arabic novel. Nearly a hundred years after its halting debut in Arab culture, the novel, in Egypt as elsewhere in the Arab world, remains a highly conflicted and fiercely contested genre.[1] The reasons, grounds, and manifestations of this condition vary, but the phenomenon itself is pervasive and pertains equally to the novel's subject matter and to its formal attributes and theoretical standing. Indeed, until recently the very name of the genre, *Riwāya*, vacillated in both scholarly and popular parlance between play, story, novel, and narrative in general.[2] Occasionally, the tension inherent in the novel's anomalous condition bursts violently onto the social scene to challenge some of the underlying philosophical and epistemological foundations of modern Arab thought and culture. The attempt on the life of Egypt's, and the Arab world's, foremost novelist, Naguib Mahfouz (Najīb Maḥfūẓ) on October 14, 1994, occasioned such a rupture.

But Mahfouz is by no means alone in this regard. Other writers, scholars, and intellectuals have been subjected to equally horrid forms of harassment on account of their non-conformist thinking and writing. Some, like the Azharite shaykh Dhahabī and Faraj Fūda have paid with their lives for expressing unorthodox or unpopular views. Others, like Naṣr Ḥāmid Abū Zayd, Sayyid al-Qimnī, 'Alā' Ḥāmid, Makram Muḥammad Aḥmad, and Ḥasan Ḥanafī have so far endured threats against their lives, loss of livelihood, religious renunciation, exile, and imprisonment.[3] Recently the reprinting in Egypt of a novel by the Syrian writer Ḥaydar Ḥaydar unleashed massive demonstrations by students of al-Azhar that rocked the Egyptian capital for several weeks and caused a minor crisis in the country's political establishment. This controversy followed fast on the heels of yet another that had erupted in the Egyptian press nearly two years earlier over the "propriety" of assigning the celebrated fictional autobiography of the Moroccan writer, Mohamed Choukri (Muḥammad Shukrī), in a class of modern Arabic literature at the American University in Cairo. In the wake of that controversy, Choukri's work, and a spate of others, were summarily banned by the government. In addition to the perennially contraband text of *The Thousand And One Nights*, the list included 'Abdullāh al-Nadīm's *al-Masāmīr* (1898; The Nails) and Khalil Gibran's masterpiece *The Prophet*.[4] The banning of the last two works in particular bristles with irony because al-Nadīm was the spokesman of the first genuine patriotic revolt against foreign rule in the history of modern Egypt, the 1881 'Urābī uprising, and Gibran's masterpiece had been translated into exquisitely elegant Arabic in the 1960s by none other than Tharwat 'Ukāshah, who was twice minister of culture in Egypt.[5]

These inopportune events raise many troubling questions, but one in particular demands urgent attention here. It concerns the inordinate convergence of rival political, social, religious, and cultural forces at the site of the novel in Egypt. This convergence inevitably turns the space of the novel into an arena for lively debates over the critical issues confronting modern Arab culture and identity, even as that space continues in the main to house imagined characters engaged in contrived fictional actions and plots. The double take evident here occludes forthwith any option of viewing Arabic fiction exclusively in aesthetic or literary terms. By the same token, it necessarily implicates the novel (and the novelist) in extra-literary issues and conflicts. How this extensive overlap between novelistic and cultural domains impacts the poetics of the Arabic novel in Egypt is one overarching concern of this study.

It is possible to state this dilemma in slightly more metaphorical terms as the interlocking of trajectories of novel and nation in contemporary Egypt. Ominously, perhaps, the wave of attacks on nonconformist writers, unorthodox scholars, and unconventional books that characterized the last decade of the twentieth century also ushered in the first decade of the new century and the new millennium. What is especially remarkable about this fact is that the books in question had been written or published much earlier and had been available in Egypt for decades. This is as true of Mahfouz's *Awlād Ḥāratinā* (1959; *Children of Gebelawi*, 1981; *Children of Our Alley*, 1996)[6] and the Arabic translation of Gibran's *The Prophet* (1966) as it is of Mohamed Choukri's *al-Khubz al-Ḥāfī* (1982; *For Bread Alone*, 1982) and Ḥaydar Ḥaydar's *Walīmah li-A'shāb al-Baḥr* (1983; A Banquet for the SeaWeeds). Al-Nadīm's work, of course, has been in existence for over a century, and *The Arabian Nights* for nearly a millennium.

As a cultural phenomenon, this compulsive return to earlier, presumably outgrown, phases and sites of contestation may bespeak the presence in the culture of elements it can neither fully assimilate nor decisively reject. From all appearances the phenomenon strongly suggests a return of the culturally repressed in fictional disguise. Examples of this recurrent pattern in modern Arab culture can be traced back at least to the end of the nineteenth century. If the radical vacillation that characterized the past century is at all indicative of the future,

Arab novelists and writers in decades to come may well find themselves grappling with the same fundamental questions of identity that bedevilled successive generations of their predecessors all the way back to the onset of modern Arab history. A gloomy prospect, no doubt, but one not easily wished away or negotiated.

To pursue this line of investigation further is to raise still more troubling questions about the general predicament of modern Arab culture and the vast scholarship of it. One such broad and fundamental question is whether Arab culture has reached a historical impasse, of which the recurrent pattern described earlier is only a symptom. By impasse I do not mean to suggest lack of movement, only the absence of a clear direction or a cumulative, irreversible progress towards a discernible telos or horizon. From this perspective, the crisis of the novel may betray a projection and a displacement of real cultural tensions onto the virtual realm of fiction. Whether this displacement is spontaneous and fortuitous, as often appears from the angry public response to (largely unread) literary texts, or strategic and manipulated for political gain by the powers that be, is yet another question that deserves bearing in mind while assessing the role of the novel in Egypt. Finally, if Arab culture is indeed at a historic impasse, have Arab scholars and intellectuals who studied this predicament extensively under the rubric of "crisis" mistaken a permanent condition for a transient one? For few keywords figure in as many titles of scholarly works on modern Arab culture and identity as does the word *azma* (crisis). "There is a strong feeling in our Arab world that culture is in crisis," begins an article by the prominent Egyptian intellectual Fu'ād Zakariyyā. Instructively enough, the article is entitled: "How to consider the cultural crisis?"[7] Even if not quite an oxymoron, the compund "chronic crisis" is hardly more meaningful, especially if the "crisis" lasts a century or two.[8]

With these preliminary observations in mind, let me return briefly to the list of writers mentioned earlier, which, incidentally, comprises writers of fiction and non-fiction. What these writers share across boundaries of disparate genres, disciplines, and discourses is less evident than the uniformly hostile response their writing has elicited from certain quarters of Egypt's religious and political establishments. [The list of "indicted" writers could be multiplied at will by expanding the geographic scope to encompass other Arab countries, or by extending the temporal span to cover earlier periods of Arab/Islamic history.] One remarkable by-product of the general predicament of writers and intellectuals in the contemporary Arab world has been the emigration of many of them to Western countries and the emergence there of a new form of writing on exile, homeland, and identity. Even outside the Arab world, these writers continue to write on Arab concerns in both Arabic and European languages, primarily in English and French.[9]

Perhaps I should hasten to interject here that there is nothing peculiar to Arab history or culture in all of this. The sorry record of censorship, book burning, and maligning of unorthodox thinkers and writers throughout human history shows that the phenomenon is too universal to dismiss by laying it at the door step of a single culture. To put matters in some historical perspective, it may help to remember that not too long ago James Joyce's masterpiece *Ulysses* was banned in the United States of America and that, still more recently, many prominent American writers were regular guests on the White House's blacklist.[10] But my immediate interest here is in the role of the novel in modern Arab culture, as that role unfolds in the Egyptian national setting.

In many fundamental respects the Arabic novel in Egypt encapsulates and epitomizes the characteristic formal traits, thematic interests, and cultural and structural constraints of the Arabic novel in general. In large measure this coincidence flows from a rare combination of historical and cultural circumstances that render the experience of modern Egypt typical not only of other Arab countries but perhaps also of other Islamic and Third World former colonies that became independent "nation-states" in the course of the twentieth century. Like Egypt, the novel in such conflicted "nation-states" as India, Nigeria, Brazil, and Ireland, for example, cannot be fully comprehended apart from the evolving wider quest for a viable sense of collective identity.[11]

In the last three decades or so this problematic has come under increasing theoretical and critical scrutiny, both within the novel and in culture-oriented novel criticism. To suggest the range of views on this matter it may suffice to juxtapose the egregiously satirical treatment of the national question in Salman Rushdie's *Midnight's Children* and Fredric Jameson's valorization of the Third World novel, primarily in its doubling as a "national allegory."[12] Benedict Anderson's seminal concept of "imagined communities" bridges the ontological gap between the novel's simultaneous dual roles: its participation in defining the norms under which a motley human mass becomes a cohesive "national" community, and its assumption of such an entity as a discursive backdrop for contrived fictional characters and events.[13] This may be another way of restating the perennial tension between the constitutive–performative and the mimetic–descriptive deportments of literary texts, albeit in the case of the novel a tangible shift in emphasis from moral to epistemological concerns is often discernible. Whether the novel procedurally describes or mimics pre-existing types of personality and modes of behavior, or enacts into being such types and modes through the act of narration, is still a moot question.[14] In either capacity, however, the novel's intrusive and all-encompassing reach inevitably pits it against competing visions, representations, and epistemologies within the shared space of national culture. Paramount among these for the Arabic novel, though by no means the only one, is the Islamic epistemological paradigm. In the case of Egypt, the presence of al-Azhar, the Islamic world's oldest and most prestigious center of Islamic learning, in the heart of Islamic Cairo, "city of a thousand minarets," perforce privileges the religious discourse in Egyptian cultural life. What tensions and strains inhere in this situation for the novel will become clear, I hope, as this study progresses. But first, an additional differentiation is in order here.

Other genres of modern Arabic literature share with the novel aspects of the general predicament postulated earlier, but none as extensively or as intensely. The highly charged question of provenance, for example, and the host of related issues concerning the politics of cultural borrowing and the anxiety of consignment to derivative status that attend to it, bedevil in varying degrees modern Arabic poetry, Arabic drama, and the Arabic short story—which comprise, with the novel, the four recognized genres of modern Arabic literature. By way of controversy what these have in common is a dubious pedigree, namely, their putative common descent from Western origins.[15] The key to the singularity of the novel lies in its unique ability to (re)present a convincing illusion of total reality and lived experience. In large measure, what makes this infinitely repeatable feat possible in widely different languages and cultures is the constitutive commitment of the novel to the principle and rhetorical strategies of verisimilitude, without which the novel, as it has evolved in modern history, is hardly conceivable.[16]

An insufficiently studied, though important by-product of this generic peculiarity of the novel has already been intimated earlier. I mean the novel's uncanny ability to manipulate its formal structure and verisimilar effects to challenge prevalent social and cultural norms in the process of "rendering" reality into fiction. Under restrictive conditions, where the exercise of political and cultural authority rests more on coercion than on consent and persuasion, and where freedom of thought and expression are severely curtailed, this aptitude of the novel acquires transgressive and, potentially, subversive power.[17] The very enactment of the real and the quotidian in the structure of the novel tends to legitimate them and, by extension and implication, to question discourses that would deny them representation. A considerable part of the appeal and power of the Arabic novel issues precisely from its sustained effort to reinstate in the Arab public domain "uncomfortable" subjects and discourses long banished from it, such as genuine philosophical investigation, oppositional politics, religious and cultural diversity, the human body, sexuality in all its forms and orientations, overt eroticism, folklore, and popular literature composed in the vernacular, among other tabooed or disparaged concerns.

It is hard to imagine this largely remedial sociocultural work on a large scale without a prerequisite condition, namely, the private nature of the reading experience. As Benedict Anderson argues in *Imagined Communities*, this option is itself a function of a happy coincidence between the novel genre, on the one hand, and mass printing, circulation, and common literacy, on the other. In the case of the Arabic novel, this empowerment has been double-edged. It has made possible the readmission of tabooed subjects into the public realm, albeit in fictional disguise, and has thereby incurred the wrath of one segment of Arab authority or another. Simultaneously, the high level of illiteracy in the Arab world has severely restricted the dissemination of novelistic discourse and ideational import beyond the narrow confines of the small, occasionally vocal, but always vulnerable literate, or, more precisely, *literary* elite. Against the avowed populist and public disposition of the genre, the Arabic novel has thus far impacted modern Arab history primarily through its private influence on remarkable Arab individuals. By far the most outstanding example of the novel's role as a catalyst of direct historical change is the formative effect certain novels are said to have had on the political consciousness of President Nasser in his youth.[18] I shall return to this seminal instance shortly. Here let me hasten to note that, no matter how discreet, the intimate liaison of the novel with arbitrary political power is seldom without a price. The extraordinary circumstances of Mahfouz' most controversial novel, *Children of Our Alley*, and the writer's ambiguous attitude towards the Nasserist experiment, amply illustrate the complex dynamics of this relationship.

However, it is precisely through the intimate but highly problematic relation to reality that the novel alone among the genres of modern Arabic literature has been able to mount a sustained and credible resistance to authoritarian practices and discourses that claim exclusive right to represent modern Arab culture and identity—invariably, it seems, in uniform, monolithic, and completely homogenized narratives. Over against discourses that claim such a prerogative in the name of one supreme imperative or another—whether that be religious, moral, political, or ideological—Arabic novels have, in practice, consistently defended the right to the dialogic, the hybrid, and the heterogeneous. In this fundamental respect, the battle over the identity, status, and legitimacy of the Arabic novel metonymically reenacts the larger battle that rages on contiguous grounds over modern Arab consciousness, culture, and ultimately identity. Indeed, few major concerns have exercised Arab intellectual and artistic energies more than the question of identity and its attendant, janus-faced affinity to the modern world, on the one hand, and to hallowed tradition, on the other. This has been the case, in any event, since the onset of the Arab *nahḍa* (awakening)—itself another fiercely contested concept that is variably located between the French expedition to Egypt (1798–1801) and the end of the nineteenth century.[19] How pervasive and enduring this preoccupation with the subject of identity has been in Arab and Egyptian culture may be gathered from the fact that a hundred years after the extravagant Khedive, Ismāʿīl (1863–1879) declared Egypt an integral part of Europe by a Khideval fiat, President Sadat, the self-proclaimed last Pharaoh of Egypt, was still pondering the issue in his aptly titled, but highly questionable autobiography, *In Search of Identity*.[20]

Admittedly, preoccupation with identity is peculiar neither to Arabic nor to modern literature. In fact, as Northrop Frye puts it, "the story of the loss and regaining of identity is, I think, the framework of all literature."[21] Although Frye is referring to individual identity here, the logic of his statement presupposes a larger, more generalized sense of identity against which the loss and recovery of personal identity is mounted. More recently, just before his death in 1993, Madan Sarup updated this preoccupation with identity in the opening paragraph of his last book. "Wherever I go," he wrote, "I come across people meeting together to hear, read and discuss questions about identity: personal identity, social identity, national identity, ethnic identity, feminist identity, and so on. In Raymond Williams' *Keywords* (1976; second edition, 1983), there is idealism, ideology, image, but no reference to identity. Now it has become a key word; there are conferences, lectures, books and articles on every aspect of identity that one can think of."[22]

In the novel, concern with identity figures in at least two primary senses. The first pertains to the constitutive interest of the novel in individuality per se, the second primarily to species of the genre produced in self-consciously national settings.[23] To reiterate what by now amounts to a truism, the novel, as a distinct literary genre, is literally inconceivable without the grounding concept of individual identity. And although the philosophical and ontological status of fictional individuals is far more problematic than appears on the surface,[24] this notion of the individual still informs our sense perception of fictional representations. As such, it constitutes an identifying characteristic of this most protean of all literary genres. In cultures where the search for a collective identity is still unfolding, including modern Arab culture, individual characters often assume symbolic dimensions that gesture past the individual towards broader horizons of religious, communal, or national identity. Such symbolic transactions are enacted with solemn regularity in a considerable number of Arabic novels.

Recognizing Egypt

So far I have been using the terms Egyptian and Arab interchangeably when speaking of the novel. In the process of so doing I have also been granting these broad and highly essentialized entities a provisional warrant to appear homogeneous.[25] The two entities are not entirely coextensive, even though the overlap between them far exceeds what usually binds a part to a whole, or a subliterary tradition to the main tradition. It may be more accurate to think of the Egyptian novel as the matrix from which, or in relation to which, other novelistic traditions developed and, in time, became relatively autonomous in various parts of the Arab world. In terms of output, historical continuity, scope of novelistic interest, and diversity of experimentation with narrative techniques, the Egyptian novel can be said to encapsulate a microcosmic version of the macrocosm that is the Arabic novel at large. This is particularly true of the novel's treatment of the problematic of identity in a national context where a roughly similar configuration of forces is often at work in most of the contemporary Arab "nation-states."

Arguably, Egypt has experienced the full range of identity discourse perhaps more intensely than most countries in the world. If anything, Egypt seems to have always enjoyed what can be described as a surplus of identity discourse, both in its own narratives of self and in others' narratives of it. The latter, especially in European accounts, often imbue Egypt with an aura and a mystique that resonate with mythopoeic transmutations, always, I may add, to the country's decided detriment, as the chain of enchanted foreign conquerors from Pompey to Napoleon attests.[26] The dismal record of foreign occupation notwithstanding, the "indigenous" identity narratives of modern Egypt seldom escape the effects of the outsiders' gaze. In modern history, Europe, metonymically represented by France and England, occupies that space of the privileged outsider in Egyptian narratives of identity. Within this variation on the colonial situation, reflection on the self invariably evinces a heightened awareness of the view of the cultural "Other."

The Egyptian novel retains a compelling account of the unsettling effects of these refractions and the bifurcated vision of the self that they induce. Although Arabic novels that dramatize the cultural encounter with the European "Other" manifest this thematic most vividly, they by no means have a monopoly on the subject. The disorienting encounter with Western concepts and forms of knowledge in works of Mahfouz, such as *Khān al-Khalīlī* (1946), *Zuqāq al-Midaqq* (1947; *Midaq Alley*, 1966), and *al-Thulāthiyya* (1956/7; *The Cairene Trilogy*) are no less poignant or dramatic than those induced by the simulated, physical encounter with the European "Other" on European soil in such novels as Yaḥyā Ḥaqqī's *Qindīl Umm Hāshim* (1944; *The Saint's Lamp*, 1973) or al-Ṭayyib Ṣāliḥ's *Mawsim al-Hijra ilā al-Shamāl* (1966; *Season of Migration to the North*, 1969).

For the sake of historical accuracy it is important to note, if only parenthetically, that the Arabic novel may capture more fully and analyze more objectively this complex interplay between the attraction to the culture of the "Other" and the concomitant alienation from indigenous culture, but it by no means engenders it. The pull and push of this tangle, and the steady diminution of confidence in the ability of traditional sensibility and forms of learning to withstand the seductive appeal of intrusive European learning can be measured palpably by the difference in the treatment of the subject in two works, neither of which is a novel. In fact, they both belong to quintessentially Arabic narrative forms. The first is a short but exquisite *Maqāma* (assembly) by the distinguished Azharite shaykh, Ḥasan al-'Aṭṭār, on the French (*fil Firinsīs*);[27] the second is Bayram al-Tūnisī's *al-Rajul wa-Imra'atuh fī Pārīs* (1927; The Man and His Wife in Paris). Precociously insightful, the shaykh of al-Azhar already discerned in 1800, in the very midst of the brief but fateful French occupation of Egypt (1798–1801) the irresistible appeal of European learning to the susceptible mind of the colonial subject. In a playful, tantalizingly suggestive style, he marshals the rich rhetorical resources of literary Arabic to cast this widely uneven relationship in more propitious erotic terms. Under the circumstances, the experience is unmistakably homoerotic in nature. The young French scholars who possess and flaunt their superior knowledge, as they do their physical charms and bewitching glances, are depicted as invitingly effeminate.[28]

Contrary to what one might gather from contemporary puritanical and fastidious representations of Islam, this audacious venture of a prominent religious authority into explicit, albeit imaginary eroticism, is neither new nor foreign to Islamic scholarship. In *Rashf al-Zalāl* the eminent fifteenth-century Muslim scholar Jalāl al-Dīn al-Ṣuyūṭī treats sexual intercourse, including the physical attributes of the private parts of the conjugal partners and the most rewarding copulating positions, with a cheerful frankness that would make many a modern author blush. What is more, he does so using the specialized terminology of the recognized disciplines of Islamic studies.[29] As we shall see later, the novel's recourse to this trope realigns it intimately with a venerable tradition in the classical Arab/Islamic heritage.

The novelty in al-ʻAṭṭār's case resides in the foreign identity of the object of erotic desire, namely, the French scholars who accompanied Napoleon in the expedition to Egypt. His treatment of this new reality in traditional literary terms and tropes takes the sting out of the miasmic atmosphere of the colonial encounter and shifts the interest to the erotic motif and the mock infatuation in which it is embedded. In this inverted symbolic economy the surrender and loss of the Egyptian subject in the cultural/political realm is simultaneously his triumph and gain in the amorous exchange. Surely conquest and submission among lovers signify at a different register from military occupation and colonial domination. In this precocious work lie the distant roots of the vast subsequent tradition of Arabic fiction that treats the theme of cultural encounter in sexual or erotic terms.[30]

By contrast, al-Tūnisī's text feigns no such elaborate stratagems. The work is written in the vernacular in the form of a dialogue between an Egyptian couple recently arrived in Paris. Didactic in intent and scathingly self-critical in content and tone, this satirical work *assumes* the superiority of Western culture in all respects, and proceeds to "substantiate" its merits through anecdotal comparisons between French and Egyptian habits and personality traits. Not surprisingly, the hapless wife is the immediate target of the rigorous, programmatic reacculturation, on which the work pins all hopes of reforming the Egyptian character.[31]

To close this parenthetical digression, let me note a relevant biographical fact: Al-Tūnisī wrote this work in the late 1920s in Paris where he had been exiled by King Fuʻād of Egypt for patriotic and anticolonialist agitation. On this score, his "nationalist" and patriotic[32] credentials, like those of ʻAbdullah al-Nadīm before him, are beyond doubt. It is also important to remember that both al-Tūnisī and al-ʻAṭṭār recognized the imperative need for drastic cultural change and expressed this sentiment in traditional forms that owe nothing to Western literary influence. This qualification anticipates an issue to which I shall return later, namely, the inclination to ascribe to the Arabic novel causal agency in generating the very desire for cultural change, not only the ways and means of representing that change.

Hybridity at the core

During the nineteenth century, and for complex reasons that cannot be adequately addressed here, Egypt became a center of gravity in the Arab region. On the whole, it has retained this paramount position for much of the twentieth century as well.[33] Due in large measure to its considerable political autonomy from the Ottoman state, its relative social stability and economic prosperity, and the propitious climate for change and innovation in literary and cultural expression prevalent in it at the time, Egypt became a safe haven for Arab writers, journalists, and intellectuals from other parts of the Arab world that were more repressed under Ottoman rule.[34] This is especially true of Syria and Lebanon in the middle decades of the nineteenth century. The steady stream of remarkable Arab intellectuals and literati into Egypt left an indelible mark on various facets of Egyptian cultural life, especially in the areas of journalism, theatre, and social thought.

Of their many significant contributions, three appear to have had a lasting effect not only on the future of the Arabic novel but on Arab culture in general. These are: the systematic recourse to a simplified form of Arabic for daily purposes of written communication, in place of the traditional, highly ornate, but often turgid and impractical forms used by more conservative writers; the popularization of European "scientific" discoveries in the natural and social sciences, especially the writings of Darwin, Marx, Nietzsche, and Freud; and finally, the significant strengthening of the Arab dimension of Egyptian cultural identity.[35] Let me illustrate the confluence of these factors by a telling example from the work of Mahfouz, who, more than any other Arab writer, has established the parameters and set the canonical standards of the Arabic novel.

At a critical phase in his intellectual development Kamāl 'Abd al-Jawād,[36] the autobiographical protagonist of Mahfouz' *Cairene Trilogy*, takes a keen interest in Darwin's theory of evolution and writes a series of articles for an obscure magazine on the subject. The matter somehow comes to the attention of his father's boon companions who seize the occasion to taunt him on account of his son's views, especially the purported descent of man from ape. Do not worry, says one of them, when Kamāl grows up and leaves home he will realize that (other) human beings hail from Adam and Eve. To which the incomparably witty Sayyid Aḥmad rejoins: "Unless I bring him here, in which case he will realize that some men hail from dogs."[37]

The autobiographical connection between Kamāl and Mahfouz is compelling here. But it is doubtful that it would have been able to carry the avowedly secular import of this episode to successive generations of Arab and Muslim readers without the enabling aid of fictional disguise. Either way, it is probably safe to surmise that more Arab readers learned about Darwin's theory of evolution from Mahfouz' *Trilogy* than any other Arabic source. Nor can the role of humor as an easing lubricant in this connection be overestimated.

Readers familiar with the cultural ferment in Egypt during the first decades of the twentieth century, that is, during Mahfouz' youth (he was born in 1911), will readily recognize the imprint of the Syrian intellectual emigrés in the ideational import of the above fictional situation. By contrast, Mahfouz' proverbial wit,[38] of which Sayyid Aḥmad and his close circle of friends partake freely in the *Trilogy*, may mislead some into ascribing the humor of the scene to Mahfouz himself. In point of fact, except for minor circumstantial modifications, the literary rendition reinscribes almost verbatim an actual event involving two such prominent emigrés, Shiblī Shumayyil and Mayy Ziyāda. Here is how 'Abbās Maḥmūd al-'Aqqād relates that original anecdote in an article published in 1924. "Dr. Shumayyil used to say [to writers]: 'when will you stop meddling (in social thought), you scribbling S.O.Bs!' [When she heard this] Miss Mayy (Ziāda) said 'Writers should have answered him thus: your pen says that we hail from the ape, but your voice says that we hail from the canine. Prey tell us: Who is our true progenitor?' "[39] Most readers will find even more astounding the claim that Mahfouz fashioned the most memorable character of his fiction, the awesome Sayyid Aḥmad of the *Trilogy*, after a "Shāmī," that is, Syrian neighbor by the name of Bashīr. But the source of this claim—highly problematic in other respects, as we shall see in Chapter 3—is none other than Mahfouz himself.[40]

What these ostensibly recondite examples suggest is the subtle, imperceptible ways in which inter-Arab cultural and linguistic hybridity often informs the literary discourse of what appears on the surface as quintessentially, or even parochially, local in nature. The predominant recourse to formal standard Arabic, the *fuṣḥā*, as against the regional vernaculars, in modern Arabic literature bespeaks a similar commitment to irreducible hybridity. Particular, local, and regional experience is systematically committed to an Arabic literary idiom that coincides with none of the spoken dialects in the Arab world but is generally comprehensible to all literate Arabs. For obvious reasons, this issue is particularly germane to the novel, where the language or speech of a character routinely serves a double function: to convey content that advances the plot, and to express, color, or nuance the particularity of that character. Here, too, the example of Egyptian novelists, and of Mahfouz in particular, is fairly representative of the experience of Arab novelists elsewhere. Like all Arab novelists, Mahfouz made a conscious decision early on in his writing career to address not only the Egyptian but also the wider Arab reading public and calibrated the language and style of his fiction to that end. He methodically refrained from using the Egyptian vernacular in his fiction, even in the speech of illiterate or semiliterate characters who are in no position to know the correct rules of Arabic syntax and grammar.[41] It is not uncommon among Arab readers of Egyptian fiction, most of whom are familiar with the Egyptian dialect as a matter of course (thanks to the ubiquitous presence of Egyptian cinema, radio, and television), to mentally "translate" back into the Egyptian vernacular, in the act of reading, jokes and humorous scenes that can be enjoyed fully only in their native dialectal milieu. By casting particular, local, and regional experience in the common idiom of literary Arabic, the novel routinely effects an interdialectal exchange among readers in various parts of the Arab world.

In turn, the linguistic preference of the *fuṣḥā*, or formal Arabic, attests to a tacit ideological position that can perhaps be deduced negatively. It is impossible to explain it fully in terms of literary or artistic necessity. To the contrary, some critics have argued with some plausibility that it seriously compromises the realistic effects of modern Arabic fiction, including that of Mahfouz.[42] But the gesture towards the unifying role of literary Arabic in modern Arab culture is unmistakable. Mahfouz himself has said as much, though less directly: "The vernacular, *'āmmiyya*, is a reactionary movement, the *fuṣḥā*, by contrast, is progressive. The *'āmmiyya* is restrictive, confining, and conduces to isolationist introversion, all of which run counter to the disposition of the modern age toward human expansion, inclusiveness, and diffusion."[43] Moreover, this unifying function of the *fuṣḥā* seems to obtain independently of the writer's conscious political view of the pan-Arab ideology of Arab nationalism, or any specific variety thereof.[44]

Whichever way one chooses to interpret the implications of this linguistic choice, its intrinsic relevance to the thematics of identity in the novel is self-evident.

For here lie the roots of two major and abiding binary opposites in modern Arab identity: local/regional vs. Pan-Arab, and colloquial, spoken dialects vs. the written *fuṣḥā*, that is, formal or standard Arabic. As the *fuṣḥā* branched farther and farther out of the specialized religious discourses and traditional contexts and spread among wider sectors of the reading public through newspapers, translated and Arabized European literary works, and original historical romances, it gradually became more pliable, and consequently more responsive, to the needs of modern imaginative fiction. For the reasons specified earlier, the role of the Syrian emigrés in this historical development cannot be overestimated.[45]

But there is also a vitiating dark aspect to the otherwise touchingly brave undertaking of these spirited Syrian pioneers of "progress." As most of them were Christians whose intellectual formation owed much to modern secular European thought and culture, their enterprise was fraught with a crippling internal contradiction from the outset: The predominantly Islamic society in whose midst they were laboring to disseminate their acquired modern European views was at that very time chafing under direct and often brutal European colonial domination. What is more, that colonial occupation, and the incessant European meddling in the affairs of Islamic societies that preceded and followed it, were often carried out under the pretext of protecting religious and ethnic minorities, especially Christians, in Islamic lands. In Egypt, the Copts were not always immune to this sinister doctrine of divide and conquer. Much of the sectarian strife that has been gnawing at the Egyptian national unity in recent years harks back to these colonialist policies and practices. It is not surprising therefore to find Egyptian writers, from Mahfouz in the 1950s to Bahaa Ṭaher (Bahā' Ṭāhir) in the 1980s and 1990s, devoting considerable space and creative energy to this question of ethno-religious strife. So do, of course, many Coptic writers, such as Edwar Al-Kharrat, Ṣabrī Mūsā, and Ghālī Shukrī, among others. The interrogation of this issue, in direct political discourse as in imaginative literary texts, inevitably foregrounds the latent tension between conflicting definitions of homeland, nation, and the nation-state. The corollary slippage between these designations often consigns non-Muslims in the predominantly Muslim Arab nation-states to a precarious, interstitial position. There is a discernible note of anxiety in the treatment of this issue in the Egyptian novel which may measure the actual uncertainty about the compatibility of modern notions of individuality and citizenship with the historically available modalities of collective, communal, or national experience.

Though fraught with ambiguities, a dogged faith in the redeeming value of the encounter with the West stubbornly persists among significant segments of Arab elites. It so happens, for instance, that one of the early contenders for the title of first Arabic novel, Maḥmūd Ṭāhir Ḥaqqī's *'Adhrā' Dinshawāy* (1906; The Virgin of Dinshaway) commemorates the horrific summary execution of Egyptian peasants by the British colonial army in the village of Dinshawāy in 1906. The presiding judge of the tribunal assembled by the British to try the Muslim suspects was a prominent Christian Copt, Buṭrus Ghālī (grandfather of Buṭrus

Buṭrus Ghālī, who later became secretary-general of the United Nations). During that same fateful year, however, another important narrative work, written in the traditional style of the *Maqāma* appeared. This was *Layālī Saṭīḥ* (The Nights of Saṭīḥ) by Ḥāfiẓ Ibrāhīm, commonly known as "Poet of the Nile" for his impassioned love poems about Egypt. In this work the author pins his ardent hope for the liberation of "Eastern women" on none other than their "Western sisters."[46] The following year, 1907, when Lord Cromer was recalled to London in the wake of the "Dinshaway affair," Ḥāfiẓ Ibrāhīm composed a wistful farewell panegyric in his honor. The dissociation of sensibilities evident in this anecdote baffles comprehension: "The poet of the Nile" wistfully salutes the colonialist ruler who governed Egypt autocratically and magisterially for a quarter of a century.[47]

The bane of this standing contradiction between the emotive appeal of progressive and humane Western ideas in the abstract, and the unspeakable historical record of Western brutalization of much of the non-Western world, continues to haunt the quest for a coherent Arab discourse of identity in the modern world.[48] The uncanny coincidence of the emergence of the novel as a critical genre in the bosom of colonial rule injects yet another note of ambivalence at the heart of the novelistic enterprise, not only in the Arab world, but perhaps in all former colonial societies and cultures as well. The staying power of this congenital stigma shows no signs of abating. In the following section I will pursue some instructive permutations of this coincidence at another juncture where the strands of cultural and historical contingency posited in the above discussion interact forcefully with the trajectory of the novel. Having already mentioned the case of Naguib Mahfouz, I will use for this purpose the very novel on account of which he almost lost his life.

Imagining the unthinkable

Children of Our Alley thematizes in allegorical fashion the common narrative of monotheistic religion as it unfolded progressively in human history, but with a dramatic final twist that highlights the subversive potential of the novelistic imagination. Mahfouz' novel concludes with the death of Jabalāwi, the figurehead "representing" God, and the passing of the scepter of authority from the line of characters "representing" the familiar chain of monotheistic prophets to a line of scientist-cum-charlatan magicians who literally put the old order to rest before they usher in the modern age. The novel was initially serialized in the semi-official Egyptian daily *al-Ahrām* during the last months of 1959.[49] Not surprisingly, the religious authorities in Egypt took exception to Mahfouz' treatment of this tabooed subject and, at one point, intervened directly with President Nasser to halt the publication. A clever, procedural maneuver by the editor of *al-Ahrām*, Nasser's personal confidant, Muḥammad Ḥasanayn Haykal, thwarted this wish and allowed the serialization of the novel to continue to the end. In response to the complaint, Haykal recommended to President Nasser to appoint a committee of members of al-Azhar to examine the matter. By the time the committee delivered its oral report to the President, unanimously recommending to halt the serialization, only a small portion of the novel had remained; Haykal expedited the publication by making the installments appear daily instead of weekly.[50] In a concession to the religious establishment, however, the novel was unofficially, but effectively, banned from publication in book form in Egypt. This ban has remained in effect, even though the novel was subsequently published in Lebanon, where it has since appeared in several printings.[51]

As it happened, this informal "compromise" between the government and al-Azhar solved neither the problem of this specific novel nor the general issue concerning artistic freedom in imaginative literature. In what seems to be a typical *modus operandi* of modern Arab political culture, the crisis was momentarily contained and an open confrontation between the government and al-Azhar, that is, the temporal and the religious authorities, was averted by eliding the fundamental issue at hand. In essence, the confected tactical "solution" merely postponed the conflict until the next conflagration which, when it eventually came during the Sadat era, was exceptionally ruthless and sweeping in its revenge against nonconformist scholars, thinkers, and writers—Mahfouz himself being one of its main targets. The dynamics of this instructive situation bear further interrogation.

To begin with, there is no denying the fact that the master narrative of monotheistic religion underpins the allegorical tenor of the novel and serves as a textual referent to its fictional account. Nothing can be gained, and much can be lost by trying to tamper with this incontrovertible aspect of the novel.[52] The zealot clerics who recognized the familiar religious narrative in allegorical guise, and accused Mahfouz of heresy on account of it, were not poor readers of texts, whatever one thinks of their competence as scholars and interpreters of Islam.[53] To show how the novel invokes the monotheistic narrative, it may suffice to note the thinly veiled allusion to the names of the major figures in that narrative—the veiling or allegorizing veneer consisting primarily of minor linguistic alterations or metaphoric substitutions. Thus, Adam becomes Adham, Iblīs (Satan) becomes Idrīs, Moses (by metonymic substitution with the mountain where he received the tablets) becomes Jabal (mountain), Jesus (by a similar substitution with his sublime quality and his elevation to the presence of God) becomes Rifā'ah (loftiness), and Muḥammad, by substitution with the name of his firstborn son, becomes Qāsim. The names of many secondary characters and a considerable amount of circumstantial evidence conspire to confirm beyond doubt the allegorical relation between the two narratives.

Why then, we may ask, if that is indeed the case, did Mahfouz risk such a hazardous undertaking? The question pertains equally to the broaching of the explosive subject and the specific treatment of it in the novel. Several powerful considerations converge here, and in all of them the personal and the general imperceptibly blend beyond recall. Foremost among the personal considerations is Mahfouz' well-known penchant for philosophy, which may have been innate to his disposition before he undertook its systematic cultivation as a student of philosophy at Cairo University. For several years after his graduation from the university in 1934 Mahfouz agonized over the choice between two callings: imaginative writing and philosophy.[54] Although he ultimately chose creative writing, he did not thereby disavow his passionate interest in philosophy. Rather, it may be more accurate to say that Mahfouz wedded these two abiding interests of his to each other in his writing and remained faithfully in love with both. No serious reader of Mahfouz can miss the philosophical force that animates his rigorous interrogation of all phenomena: social, political, religious, and psychological. Nor is it an accident that his literary talent found its fullest realization in the novel, perhaps the most quintessentially secular and, therefore, most hospitable to philosophical interests and pursuits of all literary genres. It is precisely in this capacity of the Arab novelist as a cryptophilosopher that he inherits the mantle of the Arab/Islamic reformer of the late nineteenth and early twentieth century. By the same logic does the Arabic novel often appear to carry on the cultural work left unfinished by the Arab Awakening (*nahḍa*).

In fact, there is a discreet but compelling affinity between the theme and trajectory of Mahfouz's controversial novel and the general secularizing drift of the *nahḍa*, even though Mahfouz' bold postulation of the symbolic death of *Jabalāwī*/"God" (or the *idea* of God, as he confided to Philip Stewart)[55] in this novel crosses a formidable epistemological and psychological barrier in Arab-Islamic culture. For the first time in this culture a writer dares to imagine the unthinkable on this cardinal tenet of Islam and monotheism in general. What is more, it does so precipitously. Nothing in the fictional plot requires such a drastic break with customary practice. For all intents and purposes, retiring *Jabalāwī* into indifferent oblivion, as Dostoyevsky's Grand Inquisitor does with the figure of Christ in *The Brothers Karamazov* would have served the artistic and aesthetic interests of the novel equally well. Alternatively, Mahfouz could have "disappeared" *Jabalāwī* permanently, as does Beckett in his play *Waiting for Godot*—which is precisely what Mahfouz does in later works, such as *Za'balāwī*, instead of "killing" him off. Furthermore, such an alternative scenario would have aligned the fictional plot more intimately with history, where science and religion continue to coexist—not always harmoniously, perhaps, but coexist they nonetheless do—in the most scientifically advanced cultures and societies in the modern world: witness the United States of America, France, and Japan, for example. In short, more than it answers a question, this drastic measure raises one. What dictated this recourse to a thematic overture whose formal necessity is highly questionable and whose artistic value to the novel is utterly incommensurate with the personal risk and the cultural repercussions it was bound to unleash?

The direct influence of European philosophy cannot be discarded out of hand, given the forceful echo of Nietzsche's announcement of "the death of God" at the close of the nineteenth century.[56] (Allusions to Nietzsche in various novels confirm Mahfouz' familiarity with the work of the German philosopher, if any such were needed.)[57] More importantly, this fictional choice points to the meeting place of a powerful desire and a deep anxiety. The desire is for the (re)inscription of the paradigm of the European Enlightenment in Arab culture; the anxiety is over the dim prospects of such an eventuality. It would appear that Mahfouz reads modern European history as a unilinear and incremental narrative in which subsequent stages supersede and supplant earlier ones. Thus, the crowning of Cartesian reason as supreme arbiter of all matters by the Enlightenment necessitated demoting "God" from that position and replacing faith in religion with faith in science, reason, and progress. By all measures, a redundant "God" is as good as a dead one.

To recapitulate: what Mahfouz does in this novel is to historicize the narrative of revealed scriptures and by so doing to relativize it. This recontextualization of the narrative of monotheism strips it of the metalinguistic and metaphysical elements within which resides its claim to a priori, absolute, universal, and eternal validity. Hence also the decision to draw the arch of the novel so widely as to encompass the entire record of monotheism, a feature that wreaks havoc on the artistic unity of the plot and renders it at once unbearably repetitive and hopelessly flabby.

Herein lies perhaps the most fatal blind spot in the discourse of the reform-minded Arab *nahḍa*, including the literary interventions in that discourse. It is the desperate belief that a sufficient number of desirable features of European modernity can be successfully grafted onto a carefully edited and updated core of Islamic curriculum to catapult Arab and Islamic societies, after centuries of decline and stagnation, directly into modernity.[58] What this discourse overlooks, among other grave matters, is the fact that while single ideas or philosophical concepts can be yanked from their context and ferried across cultural boundaries for transplantation elsewhere, the historically specific cultural context which molds such disparate ideas into a coherent world view that informs both individual consciousness and public conduct is far less amenable to wholesale transmigration. Moreover, whereas in Europe vast advances in scientific and philosophical knowledge—not to mention the Protestant Reformation and the subsequent separation of the religious and temporal domains—preceded Nietzsche's dictum and rendered it more descriptive than prescriptive,[59] in Arab/Islamic culture no such antecedent developments prepared the ground for such a monumental leap. In fact, under the thin veneer of government-sponsored and enforced "modernization" a diametrically opposed undercurrent appears to have been at work in Arab culture during much of the nineteenth and twentieth centuries. As the systematic European colonization of vast regions of the Arab world unfolded throughout the nineteenth century, it set in motion a religious revival that mobilized and coordinated both the spiritual/cultural and the political/military resistance to colonial domination. There is perhaps no clearer symbolic manifestation of this reaction than the instinctive retreat of the leaders of Egypt's various nationalist and patriotic revolutions, whatever their view of institutionalized religion, to the doorsteps of al-Azhar at times of foreign invasions or siege. Nasser did that in 1956, during the Suez crisis; so did Sa'd Zaghlūl in 1919, Aḥmad 'Urābī in 1882, and the Mamlūks in 1798.[60] Napoleon seems to have grasped the adverse implications of this symbolic retrenchment for his control of Egypt when he ordered his army to bombard al-Azhar and his cavalry to desecrate its sacred confines in October 1798.[61]

In any event, one certain outcome of these historical developments has been an exacerbated polarization within Arab culture itself. Instead of the desired synthesis envisioned by the *nahḍa*, this intractable polarization seems to have consigned modern Arab culture to perennial nomadic shuttling back and forth between two ostensibly antithetical frames of reference: one indigenous, religious, and traditional, the other foreign, secular, and modern.[62] Thus far, the differences between the two have eluded synthesis and defied reconciliation, not only in history, but also in imaginative writing, as many Arabic novels concerned with the theme of cultural encounter demonstrate.

Mahfouz' proffered solution of segmenting the linear chronological narrative of monotheism into sharply demarcated phases in *Awlād Ḥāratinā* reveals his impatience with the failed syncretic efforts of his reform-minded predecessors. From this wider perspective what appeared superfluous on the thematic level of the contrived fictional action appears central to the narrative of modern Arab culture. The symbolic death of "God" in the novel renders irreversible the linear narrative that leads inevitably (in the novel as in the European Enlightenment) from a religious to a secular outlook on life and imparts finality and closure to its antecedent religious phases. But because Arab reality marches to a different historical rhythm from the novelistic imagination, it was only a matter of time before it reasserted its own course and order. In the process of bracketing the Mahfouzian intervention it also exposed the limited power of developments in the intellectual and literary spheres to influence the shape of traditional and religious beliefs on the ground. The backlash that almost claimed Mahfouz' life thirty-six years after the writing of *Awlād Ḥāratinā* assimilates the novel's defiant gesture into the aforementioned recurrent pattern that has bedevilled Arab culture with exacting regularity for at least two centuries. Periods of relative freedom of expression and creativity are routinely followed by draconian restrictions on thought and the imagination, all, it often seems, in accordance with the imperatives of political expediency. As a result, the trajectory of the course of modern Arabic literature in general, and the Arabic novel in particular, often appears cyclical and episodic, not incremental and linear. Successive generations of writers set out from the same starting point and face roughly the same set of obstacles encountered by their predecessors. The circumstances surrounding the writing and publication of Mahfouz' most controversial novel bear directly on this recurrent pattern.

Intertwining boundaries: fiction *and* politics?

Paramount among these circumstances is the remarkable confluence of the time and place of writing. By the place of writing I do not mean Egypt in the abstract but specifically the establishment of *al-Ahrām*, which, in 1959, embodied more faithfully than any other site in Egypt the ideology of the Nasserist regime. That ideology, we recall, espoused Arab nationalism as the unifying political and cultural framework for Arabs in the modern world. To the extent that it was based on national rather than religious or traditional tribal affiliation, the union between Egypt and Syria (1958–1961), under the banner of Arab nationalism, marks the high point of conscious political endeavor in Arab history to found an avowedly nationalist Arab state. Mahfouz may not have shared this vision fully; in fact, as we shall see, his attitude towards the Nasserist experiment is profoundly ambivalent. Nonetheless, he sufficiently embraced the common interest in the secular project to publish his most explicitly antitheocratic work in the regime's semiofficial newspaper: *al-Ahrām*.

A similar combination of personal and political motives seems to have informed Nasser's decision to stand by Mahfouz and the novel, even at the risk of alienating further the already hostile religious establishment in Egypt. The personal element pertains to Nasser's touted indebtedness to Tawfīq al-Ḥakīm's famous work, *'Awdat al-Rūḥ* (1933; Return of the Spirit). Empowered in part by that fictional text, Nasser will go on to lead the Revolution that abolishes the monarchy in 1952, expels the occupying British and French forces in 1956, and secures Egypt's national independence after centuries of domination by foreign dynasties and rulers. But, as I intimated earlier, this vicarious agency of fiction is not gratuitous; it exacts a price in different ways, not least in willful misreading and biting irony: For the call to "national (re)awakening" that struck such a responsive chord in Nasser's impressionable consciousness is enunciated in al-Ḥakīim's novel by a French archeologist who, in a conversation with a British irrigation engineer working in Egypt, predicts the inevitable return of the glorious spirit of ancient Egypt to liberate and uplift modern Egyptians from their debilitating stupor and malaise. The irony becomes only too caustic when one remembers that much of the decried malaise, at least as far as Nasser and his fellow free-officer-revolutionaries were concerned, originated precisely in the foreign domination of Egypt, in turn, by France and Great Britain. (Incidentally, al-Ḥakīim's entrusting of the edifying "oracular" utterance about Egypt's past and future to the French archeologist is an example of the privileged position of the European observer/voyeur within Egyptian narratives of identity mentioned earlier. The combination of presumed innate soundness of French cultural sensibility and disciplinary training invests the archeologist's prediction with objective "scientific" validity. He, alone, in al-Ḥakīm's view, is qualified to read and decipher the mysterious writ of Egypt's fate.)

There are other good reasons to suspect that the ideological subtexts of the respective positions of Nasser and al-Ḥakīm operated at cross-purposes in this case, and that the leader's interpretation may in fact have run counter to the writer's intention. For example, the textual allusion to the promised leader who would arise to unite all Egyptians in his person, which Nasser seems to have (mis)appropriated to himself, is not a floating but a marked signifier in the text. The identity of the leader for whom it is earmarked is all but spelled out explicitly. He is unmistakably Sa'd Zaghlūl, the widely popular leader of the Wafd party and the 1919 Revolution, both so fondly immortalized here, as in Mahfouz' *Trilogy* and other works.[63] Nasser's effective reappropriation of the role necessitated decoupling the identity of Egypt's promised (deified) leader (*ma'būd*) from the spirit of ancient Egypt and the Osiris myth that animates it. Having little taste or use for Pharaonic mythopoeia, Nasser's reading simply discarded that part and supplanted it with his fledgling version of Arab nationalism. That this substitution betrays a flagrant misreading of authorial intention is amply evident in the text. In chapter four of volume two of *'Awdat al-Rūḥ*, the quintessential Egyptian *fallāḥ* (peasant), whose eternal "Egyptian" characteristics are said to materialize in, and inform, the character of the awaited modern savior, represents the exact antithesis of "Arab" identity, as this identity finds exclusive and singularly unflattering expression in the image of the seminomadic "Arabs" and bedouins of upper Egypt. Elsewhere al-Ḥakīm expounds on this putative ethnocultural contrast and insists that the Arab veneer that had been forcibly (super)imposed on the Egyptian character has virtually suffocated and stifled it. To this incongruent mix al-Ḥakīm ascribes much of what ails modern Egypt. Accordingly, his proposed solution demands a thorough and complete separation of Egyptian from Arab character.[64]

This, in any event, was his view in the 1930s and 1940s, when the "Pharaonic" ideology of Egyptian separateness was in vogue. It was during this very time that Mahfouz wrote his "historical" Trilogy on ancient Egypt and, according to his own testimony, had prepared material for fifty or more such novels. Nor was this view of the "Pharaonic" identity of Egypt limited to writers. Practically, most of the leading intellectuals in Egypt, from Aḥmad Luṭfī al-Sayyid and Ṭāhā Ḥusayn to Ḥasan al-Zayyāt and Aḥmad Amīn, subscribed to it in one form or another at the time.

A little later, however, in the wake of the 1952 Revolution and Egypt's official embrace of Arab nationalism, al-Ḥakīm discovered more positive aspects in Arab culture and revised his views on Egyptian identity to accommodate that "discovery." For the duration of Nasser's rule (1952–1970), of which al-Ḥakīm was perhaps the most conspicuous beneficiary among Egypt's writers, the Arab and Egyptian components of identity appear to have coexisted rather harmoniously. They will come apart again in 1974, with the publication of al-Ḥakīm's scathing, wholesale attack on Nasser, his regime, and his policies in *'Awdat al-Wa'y* (1974; *The Return of Consciousness*, 1985),[65] the title of which directly invokes and problematizes the celebrated earlier text. Before that, however, al-Ḥakīm would make yet another highly ambiguous interpretive gesture towards *'Awdat al-Rūḥ*.

A day after Nasser's sudden death on September 28, 1970, al-Ḥakīm eulogized him in *al-Ahrām* in terms strongly reminiscent of the unique attributes and virtues he assigned the deified leader/savior in *'Awdat al-Rūḥ*. Whether he did this out of opportunistic motives, as many critics have argued,[66] or out of genuine, but erroneous conviction, as he later claimed in *'Awdat al-Wa'y*, it is hard to say. The sincerity of the sentiment al-Ḥakīm expressed on September 29, 1970 cannot be ascertained because the direction of the political change that was to overtake

Egypt soon thereafter, under the leadership of Sadat, had not yet crystallized. This is not the case in his later renunciation of his lengthy liaison with the Nasserist regime, during which al-Ḥakīm was presumably "unconscious." For, by the time al-Ḥakīm "recovered" his long-lost consciousness in 1974, Sadat's systematic dismantling of Nasser's legacy was in full swing. Although the relation of the fictional signifier *'Awdat al-Rūḥ* to its historical referent is the main casualty of these endless fluctuations of the author, it is by no means the only one. By any account, this is a highly overdetermined case that says as much about al-Ḥakīm's personal integrity as it does about the precarious relation of fiction to politics and, beyond that, perhaps, the ultimate indeterminacy of meaning in all literary texts.

One final point is worth noting in this multilayered collocation. The invocation of the spirit of ancient Egypt as the source of inspiration for curing Egypt's modern ills deliberately elides crucial epochs of Egypt's long history. Not altogether surprisingly, these are the intervening Arab/Islamic centuries. Only a willful misreading of the massive evidence could have allowed the nascent consciousness of an Arab nationalist to translate al-Ḥakīm's Francophile and Pharaonic sympathies into anti-Western, Arab nationalist ideological terms. To add further that al-Ḥakīm's influential work was apparently written in French originally, and was rendered into Arabic by the author after his return from France to Egypt in 1928, is to compound beyond recall the intersecting lines of originality, genealogy, intention, interpretation, and agency.

* * *

It is equally unclear whether Nasser saw the "theological" implications of Mahfouz' *Children of Our Alley*, any more than he was aware of the irony implicit in his (mis)reading of al-Ḥakīm's *Return of the Spirit*. His stand in support of Mahfouz against the religious establishment may have had more to do with the dynamics of internal Egyptian politics than with any firm, or abiding, commitment to the principle of freedom of expression, although, as Mahfouz asserts on the basis of firsthand experience, Nasser always sided with the writers against their numerous, would-be censors in his government.[67] Be that as it may, to check the power of the religious establishment was always a high priority of temporal authority in Arab/Islamic, as indeed in all states. In Egypt this desideratum assumed structural prominence and was exercised consistently in the name of the nation-state since the reign of Muḥammad 'Alī (1805–1849). The constitution of 1923, by far the most liberal in the history of Egypt and the Arab world, went farthest in curtailing the role of the religious establishment, and barely fell short of effecting a total separation between religious and temporal authority.[68] This constitution, like the 1919 revolution that swept the Wafd party of Sa'd Zaghlūl to power in 1922, and the personality of Sa'd Zaghlūl himself, left indelible marks on the consciousness of the young Mahfouz. Eventually these marks would metamorphose into permanent features of Mahfouz' fiction and furnish it with firm moral and ethical standards in political life. In time, they would also become a fecund source of nostalgia, to which several of Mahfouz' largely autobiographical characters return for personal solace during national crises.

Nor did Nasser's intervention in the conflict between the temporal and the religious domains in the nation-state of Egypt stop at these indirect measures. In 1961 his government carried out the most far-reaching reforms ever undertaken in al-Azhar. These reforms introduced the secular sciences into al-Azhar, thereby transforming it from an institution of exclusive religious learning to a full-fledged university.[69]

All that notwithstanding, the personal manner in which President Nasser sought to solve the problem of the publication of *Awlād Ḥāratinā* reaffirmed the traditional dependence of the writer on the ruler in Arab political culture. One wonders, for example, whether the absence in Mahfouz' fiction of any significant attention to the role of the military establishment in public life, especially to its notorious secret services and their ruthless torture of political prisoners under Nasser, has anything to do with this vulnerable state of tacit dependence. This absence is all the more remarkable in light of the fact that Mahfouz showed precocious awareness of the issue and addressed it in one of his early, pre-1952 novels, namely, *Bidāya wa-Nihāya* (1949; A Beginning and an End).

This novel, too, offers a telling anecdote about the vagaries of modern Arab politics, and illustrates further the curious relation of imaginative writing to political power. The novel dramatizes the plight of a lower middle-class family whose life and hopes revolve around the single-minded ambition of a son to graduate from the police academy and become an officer. Just when the dream of upward social mobility appears within reach, everything goes awry; the novel ends with the officer, Ḥasanayn (and his stray sister, Nafīsa) committing suicide. It is reported that Sadat took offense at this thematic turn of events and lectured Mahfouz on account of it after he and the rest of the Free Officers seized power in Egypt in 1952. "How could he (Mahfouz) allow Ḥasanayn to commit suicide? Does he not realize that Ḥasanayn is us (the Free Officers)?" he is reported to have said.[70] A still more prominent member of the Free Officers who was also Nasser's second in command, 'Abd al-Ḥakīm 'Āmir, is said to have voiced similar criticism of Mahfouz on account of *Tharthara fawq al-Nīl* (1966; *Adrift on the Nile*, 1993).[71]

In a similar vein, when Mahfouz' novel *al-Qāhira al-Jadīda* (1945; New Cairo) was reprinted under the auspices of the government-sponsored series of al-Kitāb al-Dhahabī of Nādī al-Qiṣṣa, the title was deliberately changed to *Faḍīḥa fil-Qāhira* (Scandal in Cairo) to smear further the deposed regime. The film version of the novel was titled "Cairo 30" in an obvious attempt by the government of the Free Officers to distance them still further in the public perception from the fictional events and characters of the novel.[72] Subsequent editions of the novel display an added caption on the front cover bearing the same words: "Cairo 30."

In light of all this a troubling question arises. Could the proverbial "sensitivity" of the Free Officers to personal criticism have conspired with Mahfouz' native prudence to dull the great writer's discernment and blunt his concern with the question of torture?[73] It is well known that Mahfouz' first substantive treatment of the subject of torture appeared in his novel *al-Karnak*, which was published four years after Nasser's death, although Mahfouz claims to have written it several years earlier.[74] Be that as it may, this is clearly a case of too little too late, which is all the more striking for at least two additional reasons. The first is Mahfouz' professed abiding interest in politics and his claim that this preoccupation permeates all his novels.[75] The second is the fact that *al-Karnak*'s treatment of the question of political torture practically pales in comparison with works written by younger Egyptian writers, some of whom experienced torture directly, which were published in the late sixties and early seventies, that is, several years before the publication of *al-Karnak*. Sonallah Ibrahim's (Ṣun'allāh Ibrāhīm) remarkable novella *Tilk al-Rā'iḥa* (1966; *The Smell of It*, 1971) is a case in point. As we shall see, during the reign of President Sadat (1970–1981), and as a direct result of his policies towards writers and intellectuals, the very landscape of the Egyptian novel changes and fictional space acquires added symbolic significance. It was also during the fateful decade of the seventies that the religious establishment, re-empowered by Sadat, recovered much of the power it had lost under Nasser and re-embarked upon a systematic reshaping of public consciousness in Egypt. How the novel responded to these historical challenges will concern us later. Here let me turn briefly to the vexing question of origins and the theoretical terms and rhetorical strategies in which it is often expressed.

Historical beginnings and their discursive ends

Two key and seminal terms ground the perennial debate over the origins of the Arabic novel and modern Arabic literature in general. These are: *aṣāla* (authenticity, originality) and *ḥadātha* (novelty, innovation, modernism). A host of cognate and ancillary terms cluster around each to support the respective arguments in the controversy. Binary opposites such as *qadīm* (ancient, classical) vs. *jadīd* (new) and *mu'āṣir* (modern, contemporary); *taqlīd* (imitation) vs. *tajdīd* (renewal) and *ibdā'* (innovation, creativity), invariably figure in the polemics of the opponents. The terms signify differently in different contexts and are susceptible to fluctuation along a wide semantic and interpretive spectrum. Thus, in the lexicon of the opponents of the modern, *aṣāla* appears synonymous with imitation and reenactment of the traditional as it is deemed indigenous. Whatever deviates from the venerated poetic and aesthetic norms of the traditional canon is ipso facto suspect and, consequently, inadmissible on account of its novelty, *ḥadātha*. A "blacklist" of such offenders was compiled by a Sa'ūdī cleric, 'Āwaḍ b. Muḥammad al-Qarnī, in a book titled *al-ḥadātha fī mīzān al-Islam* (1988; Modernity on the Scales of Islam).[76] It includes, among other luminaries of Arabic literature, the eighth century poet Bashshār ibn Burd, the tenth century poet–philosopher al-Ma'arrī, the Palestinian novelist Ghassān Kanafānī and his fellow-Palestinian poet Maḥmūd Darwīsh, the Iraqi poet Badr Shākir al-Sayyāb, the Syrian poet Adūnīs, and, of course, Egypt's Naguib Mahfouz. Admittedly, this is an especially execrable example of Sa'ūdī propaganda masquerading as scholarship, but, as we shall see, it is neither untypical of the general drift of Egyptian culture since the 1970s, nor is it irrelevant to our critical concerns.

In contrast, *ḥadātha*, and its correlate, *tajdīd* (innovation, renewal), are emphatic terms of approbation in the vocabulary of Arab "modernists," not least because they entail departure from the overwrought forms and obsolete modes of traditional expression. In the writings of Adūnīs ('Ālī Aḥmad Sa'īd, b. 1929), perhaps the quintessential Arab modernist poet, these two terms are wedded to a conception of *aṣāla* that equates it with the originality of individual effort. In Adūnīs' view the quest for originality is paramount, but it is applied strictly to a mode of composition that is unprecedented *lā 'alā mithāl*, that is, *sui generis*.

Space does not allow here for a substantive discussion that alone can do justice to Adūnīs' intricate views.[77] Two crucial points, however, demand attention, before returning to our main interest in the novel. The first is Adūnīs' ingenuous conflation of the two categories *aṣāla* and *ḥadātha* into a single trope, and the location of this synthetic entity in the poet's revolutionary stance vis-à-vis tradition—an act that can be repeated ad infinitum by succeeding generations of poets without ever contracting the anxiety of influence because, presumably, what is being imitated is the poet's gesture and stance, not his or her actual poetic composition. In this reformulation the question of borrowing and indebtedness to foreign influence is completely occluded, at least on the theoretical and conceptual, if not always on the practical level. The second point is the charge of obscurantism that is often leveled against Adūnīs in particular, and modern Arabic poetry in general. One apparently lasting consequence of the recourse of modernist Arabic poetry to unfamiliar poetic techniques has been the permanent alienation of the average Arab reader from the whole enterprise of modern Arabic poetry. The novel, and to a lesser extent, the short story, appear to have been the immediate beneficiaries of this demotion of poetry from its traditional supremacy as the privileged genre in Arab culture. As already noted, with this mantle the Arabic novel appears to have also inherited the secularizing legacy of the *nahḍa* (Arab Awakening), and the mortal dangers abiding therein.

It is not difficult to detect in the wholesale rejection of *ḥadātha* a strong trace of the Islamic interdiction against innovation in religious matters.[78] The charge of "innovation" leveled against modern Arabic literature becomes still more compounded when it is coupled with *taghrīb* and *ightirāb* (estrangement, alienation, Westernization). Subsumed under *taghrīb* and contingent upon it, *ḥadātha* thus becomes doubly culpable in the view of its detractors. It forfeits indigenous authenticity for borrowed, that is, sham, innovation.

In the discourse of contemporary opponents of *ḥadātha*, however, the invocation of religious criteria and terminology in the treatment of literary and aesthetic issues often appears cynical and spurious. Following the wave of "Islamist revival" that swept Egypt in the seventies, the renewed attack on literary modernism has been intimately tied to the ideological positions and political interests of what came to be known as petro-Islam, specifically to Saudi Arabia. The scores of religious exiles from Nasserist Egypt who returned from Saudi Arabia and the other Gulf states in the seventies and eighties spearheaded this covert proxy campaign on behalf of their erstwhile hosts and benefactors.[79] Shaykh Muḥammad Mutawallī al-Sha'rāwī, Muḥammad Kishk, and 'Umar 'Abd al-Raḥmān are perhaps the best known among these repatriated exiles who collectively orchestrated and presided over the campaign of religious intolerance that culminated in the attack on Naguib Mahfouz in 1994. But the Saudi regime itself is also directly implicated in this war on *ḥadātha*. The above-mentioned book by Al-Qarnī, for example, was introduced by none other than the late 'Abd al-'Azīz b. Bāz, the highest ranking official of the religious establishment in Saudi Arabia. Moreover, the book was recorded on audio-tapes and distributed widely throughout the world, free of charge. A spate of books in a similar vein were published in the last two decades of the twentieth century, and they all supplement the ritual condemnation of *ḥadātha* with a flimsy mélange purporting to be a theory of Islamic literature.[80]

Interestingly, until the erratic seventies, the paradigm of "authenticity" was more literary and cultural than religious in nature. Thus, in the first half of the twentieth century, prominent writers like 'Abbās Maḥmūd al-'Aqqād and Muṣṭafā Ṣādiq al-Rāfi'ī could and did berate the novel as inferior, not only to poetry, but also to literary criticism and expository writing. Al-'Aqqād locates this purported ontological inferiority in the disproportionately inverse ratio of the novel's *maḥṣūl* (yield, output) to its *adāt* (technique or, more generally, means). "It takes more than fifty pages in a story to express the content (*maḥṣūl*) of one (good) line of poetry." And al-'Aqqād has his favorite examples of such lines, though not of their implied "deficient" fictional counterparts. What Al-'Aqqād's vague terminology and paltry reasoning seem to decry here is the novel's constitutive recourse to the circumstantial representation of reality which, though often bulky and cumbersome, is rarely without artistic merit, especially in the works of such writers as al-'Aqqād mentions, namely, Dickens, Tolstoy, Dostoyevsky, and Proust, among others.[81] Nor does the novel's perceived pandering to the taste and interests of the masses, whom al-'Aqqād invariably describes by the pejorative term *al-dahmā* (the rabble), particularly endear the genre to the peremptory 'Aqqād.[82] It is presumably for this innate inferiority of the genre that al-'Aqqād, who championed innovation and novelty in poetry, shunned the novel, violating his sworn aversion to it only once in his lifetime to write *Sāra* (1938), which seems to have done more to prove than to disprove the charge of "sour grapes" leveled against him on this score.

A similar disdain for the novel's inherent interest in the quotidian experience of common people and in the life of the instincts informs Muṣṭafā Ṣādiq al-Rāfi'ī's view of the genre. In his case, however, this antipathy is consistent with his general aversion to literary innovation and experimentation. The novel's "foreign" origins and its occasional recourse to the vernacular compound its already grave faults because they distance it still further from the highbrow, religiously resonant "authentic" forms of Arabic literary expression.[83] On all accounts, the novel's departure from canonical themes and linguistic, rhetorical, and literary norms dooms it, in this view, as an alien and constitutionally inauthentic genre in Arab culture. And yet, it is precisely the novel's brave departure from these norms that 'Ādil Kāmil celebrates in a scathingly satirical introduction to his novel *Millīm al-Akbar* (1944), perhaps the most elaborate and cogent defense of the novel in modern Arabic literary criticism.[84] Mahfouz himself dramatizes the crippling effects of captivity to the traditional literary canon on the stunted personality of several characters in his early works, notably Aḥmad 'Ākif, the protagonist of *Khān al-Khalīlī* (1946).

* * *

Proponents of the Arabic novel are split over the question of its origins. One view traces the evolution of the genre to indigenous forms, especially that of the *Maqāma* (assembly, session). The subtitle of a book on the tenth-century founder of the *maqāma* genre, Badī' al-Zamān al-Hamadhānī, describes him as "the pioneer of the Arabic story and journalistic essay,"[85] while the title of another book spells out "The Influence of the Maqāma on the Rise of the Modern Egyptian Story".[86] This line of argument found its fullest expression in Fārūq Khurshīd's book *fīl-Riwāya al-'Arabiyya: 'Aṣr al-Tajmī'* (On the Arabic Novel: The Formative Phase), which came out in 1959. In a sequence of patently specious logical moves Khurshīd hypothesizes the necessity of the existence of a body of lost literary prose works in pre-Islamic times. Since ordinary Arabs must have communicated with each other and related stories in less ornate prose than is suggested by the few extant examples of *saj'* (rhymed prose) that made it to the canon, it follows, according to Khurshīd, that literary historians must have discarded an enormous body of fictional works that failed to meet their aesthetic criteria, specifically that of *saj'*. Hence, according to Khurshīd, the gaping lacuna in the genealogy of the modern Arabic novel which, in turn, has necessitated the insertion of the Western novelistic tradition between the modern and the ancient phases of Arabic fiction.

Empowered by this specious genealogy, Khurshīd proceeds to set the record straight by applying the term fiction to practically all modes of prose narrative, from religious homilies in mosques to historical accounts of battles, biographies, folk sagas, as well as genuinely imaginative works such as *The Thousand and One Nights*.[87] From his subsequent creative rewriting in fictional form of several folk epics, such as *'Alī al-Zi'baq*, *Fi Bilād al-Sindbād*, and *Sayf ibn Dhī Yazan*, popular literature, especially that written in the vernacular, emerges as the mainstay of his views on the subject.

More recently, a similar argument in support of this "theory" of evolution and continuity between the novel and antecedent Arabic prose narratives was made separately by the writer Gamal al-Ghitani (Jamāl al-Ghīṭānī) and the literary critic

Sabry Hafez. In addition to the *Maqāma* both adduce the stories of *The Thousand and One Nights*, the folk epics, especially the *Hilāliyya*, the *khabar* (historical anecdote) and the famous *Sīra* genre (biography), among others, as early precursors of the modern novel.[88] In all fundamental respects, this view is similar if not identical to Khurshīd's. Either way, on purely literary grounds this reversion is rather curious because Khurshīd's views had been thoroughly challenged by numerous literary scholars in the intervening years.[89]

But, like everything else concerning the Arabic novel, literary considerations alone cannot account for the entire story. Let me elaborate briefly. While the existence of intrinsic affinities among the various modes and varieties of prose narrative within the vast tradition of Arabic literary prose cannot be denied, blurring the equally crucial distinctions between the modern novel, on the one hand, and all the earlier forms, on the other, buys a simulacrum of literary continuity and literary self-sufficiency at the expense of historical accuracy and conceptual precision.

To begin with, as we shall see shortly, this claim runs counter to the scholarly consensus of historians and critics of the Arabic novel and, more importantly perhaps, to the emphatic testimony of pioneering Arab novelists. Second, this collapsing of constitutive differences between the novel and its putative "ancestors" in the Arab narrative tradition elides the very novelty and uniqueness wherein lies the novel's claim to literary, aesthetic, philosophical, epistemological, and even political agency in modern Arab culture. Given the increasingly more vocal insistence of the "indigenous" discourse since the seventies on cultural differentiation and singularity, and the concomitant equation of authenticity with tradition and inauthenticity with innovation in this economy of representation, it is perfectly understandable why political expediency, apart from intellectual and personal conviction, requires a counterstrategy of "rehabilitating" the novel by insisting on its "pure" Arab lineage. Whatever the accuracy of my reading of the situation, the thought of recourse to intellectual dissembling or rhetorical subterfuge to—literally—save both novel and novelists is itself indicative of the dire predicament of the Arabic novel and contemporary Arab culture in general.

Egyptian writers on their craft

Writing under less adverse historical circumstances, both Ḥusayn Fawzī, in *Sindbād fī Riḥlat al-Ḥayāt* (1968; Sindbad in the Journey of Life), and Yaḥyā Ḥaqqī in *Fajr al-Qiṣṣa al-Miṣriyya* (1960; The Dawn of Egyptian Fiction)[90] come closer to the truth on the vexing question of the origins of the Arabic novel. Here is how Fawzī describes the critical decade following the First World War in the life of his pioneering literary generation.

> That period deserves a separate chapter. Here I only wish to register the phases through which I, and the rest of my generation, went. That period shaped our thoughts and furnished the sources of our intellectual growth.

> It also impelled us onto a new and pioneering path in contemporary Egyptian literature. During that phase most of us were descendents of Maupassant, Balzac, Dostoyevsky, Turgeniev, Chekhov, and Tolstoy. The saying of one of the great Russians, Dostoyevsky perhaps, that "we all hailed from '*The Overcoat*' of Gogol" applies to us as well.
>
> I wish to note this fact: we hailed neither from the garment of "*Zaynab*" nor from that of "*Ḥadīth 'Īsā ibn Hishām*," but rather from the translations of Muḥammad al-Sibā'ī, al-Manfalūṭī, Aḥmad Ḥasan al-Zayyāt, Anṭon al-Jumayyil, al-Māzinī's (*Sanine*?), and the sources from which these, and others, translated.
>
> Nor should I neglect to mention the translators of plays: Faraḥ Anṭon, Ilyās Fayyāḍ, and Khalīl Muṭrān.
>
> We memorized the noble Qur'ān in childhood, so it righted our speech patterns and refined our taste for the awesome beauty of Arabic. We also had, in our youth and early adulthood, a sound introduction to Arabic literature. But our spiritual and intellectual makeup took form and reached its full potential through exposure to the world of European literature, to the extent allowed by the languages we knew.[91]

Partly because of Fawzī's well-known ideological "Pharaonic" and Europhile sentiments, and Ḥaqqī's immeasurably more important contribution to modern Arabic fiction and literary criticism, the latter's views merit greater attention. As it turns out, however, on this crucial issue the respective views of the two writers are hardly distinguishable. An accomplished writer and critic in his own right, Ḥaqqī was also intimately involved with the circle of his relative Maḥmūd Ṭāhir Ḥaqqī, a pioneer of innovation and a founding member of the "New School" of Arabic writing, of which the younger Ḥaqqī in time also became a member. Ḥaqqī thus grew up in the midst of writers and advocates of the new, and himself went on to become a consummate practitioner and stalwart champion of innovation and experimentation in Arabic fiction for over half a century. He is, therefore, uniquely qualified to represent this trend, a task he undertakes with unrestrained relish in *Fajr al-Qiṣṣa la-Miṣriyya*, and elsewhere.

But Ḥaqqī also served for many years as editor of the influential weekly *al-Majalla al-Jadīda* and, in that capacity, cultivated younger writers by opening the pages of his magazine to their innovative and experimental work. Younger writers, especially of the so-called generation of the sixties, readily admit their indebtedness to him more than to any other writer of the generation of the founding fathers.[92] By the same token, however, Ḥaqqī's circumscription points up the very limit of cultural tolerance for artistic freedom of expression. It is thus instructive that he was deeply offended by the explicit nature of certain passages in Sonalla Ibrahim's novella *Tilk al-Rā'iḥa*, and berated him severely in print for it.

Ḥaqqī's imaginative account of the emergence of modern Egyptian fiction admits both aesthetic and cultural considerations. He describes the influence of the European literary models on the nascent artistic sensibility of the first generation of Egyptian fiction writers by means of a naturalistic metaphor: "The winds blowing from Europe carried into Arab society an unfamiliar seed, that of the story."[93] In comparison with this "newcomer" the available forms of indigenous narrative, namely, biographies, tales from *The Arabian Nights*, and specimens of the *Maqāma* were found woefully deficient in some fundamental respects. Foremost among these are the excessive recourse to rhetorical embellishments, the lack of artistic unity, and the inadequacy of the traditional means of expression for the needs of the new society.[94] What made Egyptian society new and, as a result, rendered these traditional modes of literary expression simultaneously obsolete and anachronistic is precisely the incorporation of "aspects of modern civilization that transformed the conditions and customs of society and weakened its links with the past."[95]

Ḥaqqī cites the treatment of the theme of love in the new writing as an example of the cultural change without which this tabooed subject would have remained buried in the recondite allusions and abstract formulations of (classical) Arabic poetry. Not only Arab tradition but also "Arab mentality" favors treating such delicate matters in the abstract, as the latter "would rather talk about the idea of the person than the person himself." Ḥaqqī ascribes this ontological bent of "Arab mentality" to the nature of the desert, the unfathomable vastness of which dwarfs the individual and his personal or private concerns.[96]

Putting aside momentarily Ḥaqqī's amateurish and patently derivative dabbling in ethnographic speculation about "Arab mentality," his account makes two important critical observations about the enterprise of the Arabic novel. The first is the question of compatibility between literary form and certain subject matter. Modern experience, whatever its source and however culturally incongruent it may be, eludes the traditional, intrinsically rhetorical means of Arabic literary expression. Only the new, imported form could render adequately the emergent social reality. But Ḥaqqī goes much farther on this point and insists that only a thorough reacculturation of Arab sensibility can guarantee satisfactory artistic results. The passage in which Ḥaqqī expresses this highly provocative view deserves quoting at length.

> The form (of the story) crystallized in the newly arrived seed and a contemporary style was readied for it. But there remained above and beyond both a mysterious thing which I call the intuitive feel for the soul of narrative art, its rhythm, and its temperament. These were available exclusively to writers intimate with Western culture. Stories written by others, despite fulfilling all the (formal) requirements, still lacked that secret scent which makes story (writing) an art. This phenomenon persists to this day (i.e. 1960). There is no harm, therefore, in admitting that the story came to us from the West and that its foundations here were laid by pioneering individuals who had been influenced by European, especially French literature. For, even though some English

> masterpieces had been translated into Arabic, the origins of the story in our culture are rooted in French literature. The Egyptian temperament at that time felt no alienation from France as it did from England—perhaps because of the cultural similarity among the peoples of the Mediterranean basin. Another factor may have also contributed to that, namely, the fact that some French writers had played important political roles in the history of their country. The names of these writers became widely known as symbols of liberation movements. (Victor) Hugo, whose *Les Miserables* Ḥāfiẓ (Ibrāhīm) translated, was such a writer; al-Manfalūṭī followed suit and rendered in Arabic only texts of French literature.
> (Fajr, pp. 23–24)

This sweeping statement raises with relentless clarity a number of pressing issues. To begin with, it valorizes Western literary models above all others. Only there do the "spirit" and "form" of the "story" blend so perfectly into an artistic whole as to yield a singular aesthetic quality. As such, these models enjoy a monopoly over artistic value. To partake of this exclusive Western legacy, non-Westerners must first undergo thorough reacculturation, since access is denied to all others. Moreover, in the absence of any attempt to situate this artistic value in a historical context, the Western models appear both self-generating and absolute. It is also relevant to note that Ḥaqqī makes only a veiled and elliptical allusion to the central reality of colonial domination. The allusion is carefully buried in the shy distinction between English and French and the vague suggestion about the liberationist dimension of French letters.

On one level, Ḥaqqī's view is profoundly disturbing because it reeks of the inferiority complex and the attendant infatuation that members of the colonized intelligentsia are prone to show towards the culture of the colonizer. If nothing else, Frantz Fanon has taught us this much. From this perspective, the feeble attempt to distinguish between Western cultural hegemony and military domination on the one hand, and French and British colonization on the other, appears as a psychologically elaborate but grotesquely abject retrofitting of the colonialist principle "divide and conquer" to the warped condition of the colonized intelligentsia. It now reads: "divide and be conquered." Likewise, the affected affinity between the two Mediterranean peoples, the French and the Egyptians, is hardly innocent.

This foregrounding of Egypt's geographic proximity to Europe comes at the expense of both its historical and geographic affiliation with the Arab/Islamic world and the African continent. The ideological force of this reorientation is fairly transparent: To embrace the European neighbor on the other side of the Mediterranean basin Egypt must turn its back on the "desert," with all the historical, religious, cultural, and literary associations that cluster around the trope. Particularly significant in this regard is the total absence from Ḥaqqī's statement of any reference to the role of the Arabic language in which the new "European" form of the story will ultimately materialize in Egypt. Since language inevitably and forcefully reasserts that suppressed historical continuity with the Arab/Islamic past, it perforce had to be absented, consciously or otherwise.

Finally, the passage clearly shows that the renewed call for the reorientation of Egypt, and the rest of the Arab littoral, towards Europe, via the Mediterranean, in the current ideological discourse of globalization had been anticipated by practitioners and theoreticians of the Arabic novel, and Arab culture in general, in the early part of the twentieth century. That, too, as Muḥsin Jāsim al-Mūsawī shows in *al-Istishrāq fil-Fikr al-'Arabī* (1993; Orientalism in Arab Thought), was done in imitation of, and under careful coaching by, European Orientalists.[97]

Disconcerting as these assessments may be, they cannot be discarded out of hand. Nor, in fairness, can the phenomenon be laid exclusively at the doorsteps of the naive generation of pioneering writers whom Ḥaqqī so affectionately recalls in *Fajr al-Qiṣṣa*. Third World writers in other cultures and other parts of the world seem to have been just as susceptible to the seductive appeal of colonial literary forms and conventions. Here is how Jose Carlos Mariategui describes the effects of this phenomenon on Peruvian literature.

> In Peru, literature did not grow out of an indigenous tradition, history, and people. It was created by the importation of Spanish literature and sustained by imitation of that literature. ... Peruvian writers never felt any ties with common people. Only the Inca empire and the colony were clearly defined, and the writers chose the colony.[98]

Equally relevant is the fact that younger generations of Egyptian writers, whose anticolonialist views and sentiments are above suspicion, also availed themselves, and just as enthusiastically, of Western literary innovations and practices. Sonalla Ibrahim candidly admits the formative influence of Western writers and literary schools on him and his politically conscious comrades. In an aptly titled testimony, "The Experience of a Generation" Ibrahim relates how the writings of Ernest Hemingway and the French Nouveau Roman school, together with the experimental verse of Soviet poets, "infiltrated" into the remote desert prison—where he and his leftist comrades were serving long sentences for political "crimes" in the early sixties—and left an indelible impression on their literary sensibilities. Thematic, stylistic, and structural evidence of this influence, especially of Hemingway, abounds in Ibrahim's work and is literally flaunted in his first novella *Tilk al-Rā'iḥa*. As if to compound matters still further, Ibrahim affixes to the novella a telling epigraph from James Joyce's *A Portrait of the Artist As a Young Man*. It reads: "This race and this country and this life produced me... and I shall express myself as I am." (Admittedly, out of context, the general tenor of Stephen Dedalus' credo enhances its universal applicability. Otherwise, it is difficult to see how the distinctly Irish context of the cunningly autobiographical aesthete of *A Portrait* at the beginning of the twentieth century applies to the condition of a politically active Egyptian writer in the 1960s.)

Writing in the same vein, but more recently, Ihab Hassan addresses this same question, only more directly and more unequivocally. In "Globalism and Its Discontents: Notes of a Wandering Scholar," he writes

> Somehow, some way, I became cathected then on both the language and the literature of England, and detestation for the English colonizer—technically, Egypt was only a "protectorate"—could not vitiate my elective affinities. How many writers, I wonder, from Morocco and Tunisia to India and Indonesia, have been drawn to foreign tongues? Is affinity the hidden face of imperialism, as power is its open face?[99]

On this issue, then, Ḥaqqī's fairly representative view occasions a stubborn anomaly. By refusing to collapse the literary into the political it also refuses to allow a direct correlation between the attitude of the colonized towards the literature and culture of the colonizer, on the one hand, and towards the colonizer's military power and political hegemony, on the other. For, according to Ḥaqqī, not only did the pioneers of Egyptian fiction simultaneously admire the former and abhor the latter, they in fact drew strength from the one to resist the other. There is no more convincing evidence to the contrary at the beginning of the twenty-first century than there was at the beginning of the twentieth. This being the case, it may be worthwhile to pursue a little further the other tangent present in Ḥaqqī's "thesis," namely, the causal linkage between the advent of the new literary forms and the emergence of new social and cultural attitudes and practices in modern Egypt.

We may recall that Ḥaqqī uses the journey metaphor to describe the arrival of the "seed of the story" in Egypt long before the trope became fashionable in postcolonial studies. To answer to more rigorous criteria, however, the metaphor demands drastic modification for greater specificity. When the novel crosses a national boundary, it does so not as an itinerant traveler or a casual tourist but rather as a permanent immigrant. Unlike other genres, such as the theatre, once the novel strikes roots in a specific cultural setting it tends to make itself indispensable to the discourse of identity in that culture. What this suggests is that the culture in question was itself in the process of migrating from its traditional modes of self-identification and self-expression. It is only when a critical mass of social forces in a culture can no longer recognize themselves in the traditional modes of representation that the culture, as a whole, becomes receptive to imported forms, so to speak. In other words, if it can be said to travel at all, the novel does so on a wide, two-way street, where it meets its future cultural habitat midway. To take only a couple of outstanding examples that may suggest the wider social spectrum, neither the village-born, kuttāb and Azhar-educated Ṭāhā Ḥusayn, nor the son of a lower middle class Egyptian clerk like Nasser, could find a viable sense of selfhood in the traditional modes and forms of literary expression available to Egyptian writers at the turn of the twentieth century. The formative quest for identity in both cases coincided fully with the quest for a new form of literary expression, and both found it in modern narrative forms at the threshold of the novel proper: Nasser in Tawīq al-Ḥakīm's *'Awdat al-Rūḥ* (1933) and Ṭāhā Ḥusayn in his fictional autobiography, *al-Ayyām* (the first and crucial volume of which was published in 1929).

Mahfouz' important novel *Zuqāq al-Midaqq* (1947) graphically captures the tenor of this process in a poignant scene. When the need for modern forms of entertainment outstrips the appeal of traditional forms, the proprietor of the Alley's only cafe swiftly and ruthlessly replaces the blind bard of traditional Arab narratives with a radio set. Coincidentally, as we shall see later in greater detail, with this telling symbolic exchange the novel also tries to capture the spirit of the changing times. It depicts in compelling realistic detail tabooed social and sexual experiences that elude the traditional modes of representation.

* * *

By way of concluding this general mapping of the parameters of the Egyptian novel within the cultural setting of the nation-state, let me recapitulate some salient points and sketch in broad strokes the lines of investigation I intend to pursue in the following chapters. The Arabic novel in Egypt is thoroughly implicated in cultural and philosophical concerns that, strictly speaking, cannot always be subsumed under literary or aesthetic categories. Paramount among these is the novel's preoccupation with the question of identity in its multiple registers: individual, national, religious, communal, and so forth. This quest, perhaps more than any other, has exercised Arab intellectual and creative energies for at least two centuries. Because the interest of the novel in such questions is not exclusively literary or aesthetic, their "fictional" treatment in specific novels often amounts to a direct intervention in other discursive realms. Predictably, just as often does this intervention evoke drastic responses that would be completely out of proportion if the offense were merely aesthetic or literary. What goes for the novel in Egypt goes for the Arabic novel in general, and perhaps for the novel in other ex-colonial countries of the Third World as well.

What makes Egypt highly representative of modern Arab and Islamic countries,[100] and ultimately justifies extrapolating general conclusions from its particular experience, is the convergence in it of three major forces whose interlocking in varying configurations often furnishes the site of identity formation and investigation. These are: (1) the existence of an indigenous, historically tested narrative tradition and culture—in this case Arab/Islamic culture as embodied, for example, in the religious curriculum of al-Azhar, the world's major locus of continuous Islamic learning since its founding by the Fātimids in the tenth century to the present; (2) the cataclysmic encounter with a foreign, technologically superior culture—in this case that of the modern secular West; and (3) the existence of a historical agent possessed of the will and the power to reshape the former culture in the image of the latter. If Muḥammad 'Alī's single-minded drive to "modernize" Egypt furnished the will to change, the idea of the nation-state furnished both the means and the end of that desired change. How the novel partakes of the ongoing dynamic interaction among these dimensions of identity in modern and contemporary Egyptian experience will become progressively clearer, I hope, as this study unfolds.

* * *

Each of the following three chapters canvasses a major area of contestation in the Egyptian novel, and jointly they explore further the main concerns adumbrated in the foregoing preliminary mapping. Thus Chapter 2: "Tangents of Identity: The Poetics of Space in the Egyptian Novel," explores the function of fictional space in the discourse of identity. How different configurations of the same bounded space assume telling symbolic significance and discursive agency is a major concern of this chapter. What particular spaces in Egypt figure in the fictional atlas of the Egyptian novel? By what means of representation does a fragment of space purport to represent a totalized whole? Does the conception of national space and the techniques of representing it change across generations of writers? These are but a few of the theoretical and practical questions I will address in Chapter 2.

Chapter 3: "Divining Identities: Religion and the Egyptian Novel" examines some theoretical and practical implications of engaging religious themes and motifs in the novel. Given the irreducibly secular nature of the novel, the representation of religion in it is bound to raise intriguing questions. What versions or manifestations of Islam obtain in the Egyptian novel and why? What discursive or ideological purposes does the representation of religious themes serve in the novel. Assuming the novel's abiding interest in *national* identity, how do non-Muslims figure in its vision of a religiously sensitive national polity? This question grows steadily more urgent as the discourse of political Islam grows more assertive and more strident in Egypt since the early 1970s.

Chapter 4: "Questionable Subjects: Individuality, Representation, and the Egyptian Novel" explores the problematics of individuality in the novel. Of particular interest to Chapter 4 is the formative relationship between fictional realism and the emergence of the oxymoronic individual who is at once unique and typical or representative. What strategies of characterization attend on these contending demands of representing individuals? I argue in this chapter that the "invention" of the autonomous individual in the Arabic realist novel generates in its wake a reconsideration of the moral, political, and literary representation of selfhood in Arab culture. Manifestations of personal desires, drives, and dispositions, all of which are intrinsic to the autonomous individual as a free moral agent, come up directly against expressions of institutionalized religion, social conventions, and tradition. What norms or moral codes inform the conduct of individuals in this philosophically minded secular genre? And how does the body, long absented from serious or frank representation in modern Arab culture, fare in this context? These and similar concerns will inform the examination of individuality in the concluding chapter.

2

TANGENTS OF IDENTITY

The poetics of space in the Egyptian novel

> The novel functions as the symbolic form of the nation-state... [A]nd it's a form that (unlike an anthem, or a monument) not only does not conceal the nation's internal divisions, *but manages to turn them into a story.*
>
> The novel and the nation-state. So be it. But Lesage's "Mediterranean" interpolations show that their meeting was far from inevitable. The novel didn't simply find the nation as an obvious, pre-formed fictional space: it had to wrest it from other geographical matrixes that were just as capable of generating narrative.
>
> (Franco Moretti, *Atlas of the European Novel: 1800–1900*, pp. 20, 53)

From Ṭābā to Fashuda and back: of borders and the homeland

Like all major features of Egyptian fiction, the deployment of space often resonates with reflections on, and of, identity. Specific configurations and mappings of carefully demarcated areas of the shared national space occasion different readings of the collective and communal identity residing therein. The physical, geographic backdrop to these recurrent imaginative renditions of national space in the Egyptian novel is perforce the nation-state itself, presently known as the Arab Republic of Egypt, though it has at different times in recent history gone by different names.[1] The strident rhetoric of the modern nation-state, and the attendant emphasis on the inviolability of its territorial integrity, enshrined in the often touted, and just as often violated UN Charter that guarantees the right of each nation-state to live safely within its internationally recognized and secure borders, have in recent years all but reduced the complex phenomenon of nationalism to its territorial embodiment in the nation-state.[2] This was not always the case. In fact, the zealous consecration of "national" boundaries, so solemnly enforced in most former colonies in Africa and Asia, but especially so perhaps between and among Arab "nation"-states, may on closer examination be shown to mask the artificiality of the very constructs these borders enclose.[3] Such an examination is also likely to reveal the large extent to which the territorial dimension of national identity regularly intertwines with, and competes against, other dimensions of identity, such as religious, cultural, and linguistic affiliation.

An instructive case in point from modern Egyptian history is the border dispute over Ṭābā, a small sea resort at the western tip of the gulf of ʻAqaba, between the occupying British military administration of Egypt and the Ottoman state in 1906. At that time, as we know, Egypt was still nominally a province of the Ottoman state which, in turn, represented the mainstay of the abode of Islam to the rest of the world, as it did to most Muslims, including most Egyptians. This special relationship was enshrined in the title of Khedive proffered on the rulers of Egypt by the Ottoman sultan since the reign of Ismāʻīl (1863–1879). To sever this formal relationship the British changed the title to sultan in 1915, and to king soon thereafter. It was abolished altogether when Egypt became a republic in 1952.

The conclusion of the dispute over Ṭābā determined Egypt's permanent "international" frontier in that region. Coincidentally, it also established a recurrent pattern whereby the political borders of the rest of the Arab "nation"-states were drawn, often in flagrantly arbitrary manner, by the dominant European powers, especially Britain and France, acting sometimes in concert, more often in rivalry.[4] In the specific case of Ṭābā, however, the familiar catalog of vagaries and distortions generated by such projections of colonial power acquires an added twist. Muṣṭafā Kāmil, perhaps the quintessential Egyptian nationalist, staunch advocate of "territorial patriotism," and founder of a fiercely anti-British and pro-independence party, *al-ḥizb al-waṭanī* (The National/Patriotic Party) sided fully with the Ottoman position against "his own country" on this issue.[5] In his view, the imperative of religious solidarity between Egyptians and Turks, the bond of what Hamilton Gibb called "Islamic patriotism" that unites both Islamic peoples against the foreign enemy, outweighed the imperative of territorial patriotism. As it happened, the British prevailed and Ṭābā was incorporated into Egypt. Three quarters of a century later, Ṭābā was to rivet the Egyptian and Arab public opinion for several years as the embattled symbol of patriotic and nationalist sentiment; the title of one book going so far as to call it "the question of the century."[6] When a dispute over this spectacularly scenic but remote spot threatened to derail the Israeli–Egyptian peace negotiations within the framework of the Camp David accords in the early eighties the Egyptian government of President Mubārak, who also doubles as chair of a party bearing the same name as that founded by Muṣṭafā Kāmil, turned to this very precedent in asserting Egypt's claim to Ṭābā against Israeli counter claims which, ironically, revived and invoked the Ottoman position of 1906. The two states finally submitted the matter to arbitration by a special international tribunal which ruled in favor of Egypt on September 30, 1988.[7]

Muṣṭafā Kāmil died at the young age of thirty four in 1908, but his fiery personality, ardent Egyptian patriotism, and proverbial eloquence continued to inspire both novelists and fictional models for generations to come. In *Fajr al-Qiṣṣa al-Miṣriyya* Yaḥyā Ḥaqqī dates back the very beginning of modern Arabic fiction to the day of Kāmil's funeral, February 10, 1908. We will see later how Ḥaqqī thematizes an aspect of Kāmil's personality in *Qindīl Umm Hāshim* (1944). Here I will discuss briefly a particularly problematic example of this influence on the "founder" of the modern Arabic novel.

Notwithstanding all claims to the contrary, Muḥammad Ḥusayn Haykal, author of the "first" Arabic novel *Zaynab* (1914), was in fact imitating a familiar practice of Muṣṭafā Kāmil when he substituted the sobriquet *miṣrī fallāḥ* (an Egyptian peasant) for his real name on the cover of the first edition of *Zaynab*. Muṣṭafā Kāmil used to sign his patriotic articles in *al-Ahrām* by similar terms, for example, *miṣrī amīn* (a faithful Egyptian), *miṣrī ṣādiq* (a true, or truthful Egyptian) or simply *miṣrī* (an Egyptian).[8] According to his own testimony, Haykal wrote the work piecemeal in Paris, London, and Geneva, between 1910 and 1911, while studying law in Paris, primarily to contain his welling nostalgia for Egypt. But Haykal also mentions two additional, more general motives. The first is to dramatize the plight of the Egyptian *fallāḥīn* (peasants) whom the foreign rulers of the (home)land routinely abused and denigrated, and in whom Haykal, like al-Ḥakīm and others later, locates the quintessential characteristics of Egyptian identity. The second motive is only implicitly stated: to imitate in Arabic the superior stylistic felicity of contemporary French writing.[9]

Reconstructing the scene of writing retrospectively in 1953, Haykal's "testimony" is as notable for what it suppresses as for what it reveals. What it reveals about the intersection of the historical and the fictional, the personal and the general, at yet another critical juncture of Egypt's turbulent modern history is fairly typical of many Egyptian novels. What it suppresses may not be as tractable, especially its unconscious struggle with the "ghost" of Muṣṭafā Kāmil. Curiously, Haykal not only fails to acknowledge his indebtedness to Kāmil on the question of the sobriquet discussed above, but also advances an explanation that sounds somewhat disingenuous. He claims that he refrained from acknowledging authorship of the novel (even though it was, at best, only a poorly kept secret) lest the disrepute in which the public held fiction writers should compromise his prospects as an aspiring lawyer.[10] Muṣṭafā Kāmil also wrote and published literary works under his own name before Haykal, and this fact seems to have hindered neither his career as a lawyer nor his popularity as a political leader and spokesman for Egypt in the court of world public opinion.

Further circumstantial evidence of the workings of what appears to be an oedipal desire to absent the father may be gleaned from yet another surprising elision in Haykal's account. He links his decision to acknowledge authorship of *Zaynab* in the aftermath of the First World War to the "rise" of the nationalist movement, the crystallization of the "Egyptian idea," and its gaining respectability, on the one hand, and his own decision to eschew the legal profession for what turned out to be a brilliant career in writing and journalism, on the other. Since few individuals can be said to have contributed more to clarifying and advancing the "Egyptian idea," or of furnishing a more remarkable example of effective public speaking, than Muṣṭafā Kāmil, his conspicuous absence from Haykal's "testimony" attests to this deep anxiety.

It would take us too far afield here to pursue the question of whether the oedipal connection, if at all valid, suffices to disentangle this knot, or whether Kāmil's idiosyncratic brand of nationalism, which advanced the option of considering Japan an alternative model for Egypt's future in *al-Mas'ala al-Sharqiyya* (1898; The Eastern Question), is also at work here. The relevance of the whole issue to the discussion of the nation, the homeland, and their representation in Egyptian fiction can hardly be exaggerated, given Haykal's centrality to the canon of the Arabic novel. Interestingly, however, the disparate strands of identity, which seem to have coexisted harmoniously in the personality and outlook of the historical Muṣṭafā Kāmil, have since drifted worlds apart, and often occasion fierce strife in his successors, actual and fictional alike.

Though relevant and instructive, the example of Muṣṭafā Kāmil on Ṭābā is not altogether typical of the attitude toward "national" borders and the territorial expanse of the "homeland" they encompass. Consider, in this regard, the case of the eminent historian 'Abd al-Raḥmān al-Rāfi'ī.

Writing in the 1930s and 1940s, al-Rāfi'ī extols the imperial conquests of the Khedive Ismā'īl in the Sudān and central Africa which "stretched the borders of the Egyptian state to the sources of the Nile and the shores of the Indian ocean, that is, to its '*natural frontiers*'."[11] Al-Rāfi'ī speaks with enviable composure about "the origins {and development} of the *national* movement (*al-ḥaraka al-qawmiyya*) in the modern history of Egypt…the emergence of the modern Egyptian state (*al-dawla al-Miṣriyya*), the realization of its independence (*istiqlāl*), and the forging of its national unity (*waḥdatuhā al-qawmiyya*) through the conquest (*fatḥ*) of the Sudān and its annexation (*ḍamm*) to the fold of the homeland (*al-waṭan*)."[12] As late as 1948 (when the second edition of his book on the reign of Khedive Ismā'īl came out), al-Rāfi'ī was still urging fellow-Egyptians to "always remember the name of *Fashūda*, as a historical landmark that records Egypt's *eternal right* in the Sudān against the occupier's denial."[13] (What al-Rāfi'ī is referring to here is the conflict between Britain and France over the small town of Fashūda in the south of the Sudan which brought the two colonial powers to the brink of war in 1898. At the time, Britain claimed that Fashūda, being part of the Sudan, belonged to Egypt. But no sooner did France accede to this demand and withdraw its army from the region, than Britain, in a volte-face, renamed the town Kuduk and took it out of Egyptian control.)[14]

The novel's treatment of "Egyptian" space perforce has had to contend, if only implicitly and indirectly, with this terminological and conceptual ambiguity about the definition of the homeland, the nation, and the state. This is so, in part, because politics is intrinsic and paramount, not incidental to Egyptian fiction. True, the novel is less concerned with borders than it is with horizons, less with actual territory and physical geography than with topography, the human landscapes of "imagined communities," and the virtual contours of "enframed closures."[15]

Still, the cogency of fictional space, especially its symbolic "representative" agency, derives largely from its feigned referentiality. The principle of verisimilitude, in other words, is as central to the novel's treatment of space in the Egyptian novel as it is to that of characters and events.

Historically, this treatment undergoes a categorical change with the emergence of the "mature"[16] realistic novel in the 1940s. Before the Second World War, fictional space served a limited, largely rhetorical, and primarily functional purpose. It was strictly subordinated to formal needs of the plot, the theme, or the discursive intent of the work, and only rarely interacted meaningfully, that is artistically or aesthetically, with these needs. Fictional space, like other coordinates, such as time, structure, and characterization, remained rudimentary until they were cultivated systematically in the realistic works of Naguib Mahfouz, Yaḥyā Ḥaqqī, ʻĀdil Kāmil, and others during the middle decades of the twentieth century. In one pioneering case in particular the traditional conventions of Arabic prose style, especially the predominance of *saj'* (rhymed prose), seem to have constrained the nascent artistic attention to the poetics of space before this period.

At the threshold: a defamiliarized space

Muḥammad al-Muwailiḥī's epochal work *Ḥadīth 'Īsā ibn Hishām* (The Discourse of 'Isā ibn Hishām) is transitional in every respect.[17] Written at the close of the nineteenth century and initially published serially in a newspaper before it appeared in book form in 1907, *Ḥadīth*, perhaps more than any other work of modern Arabic literature, owes much of its lasting appeal to its interstitial state. The subtitle of the work *fatra min al-zaman* (A Period of Time) announces its temporal positionality between two epochs, that is, between the old and the new. Generically, it is interposed between the traditional genre of the *maqāma* and the new genre of the novel. Thus, while the name of its narrator *Īsā ibn Hishām*—which it borrows from the *Maqāmāt* of the tenth century founder of the genre Badī' al-Zamān al-Ḥamadhānī—links it directly to this tradition, its language and style constantly alternate between poetry and prose, archaic and modern diction, ornate *saj'* (rhymed prose) of the *Maqāma* and fluid, functional prose of the newspaper and, eventually, the novel. In like manner, its intent and tone often alternate between serious cultural critique and playful linguistic and rhetorical virtuosity, didactic self-laceration and merry curiosity. The exquisite balance in which al-Muwayliḥī holds these antithetical pressures on the text is at once the source of its arcane charm and stiff immobility.

What is remarkable, as far as the treatment of space is concerned, is the way in which al-Muwayliḥī utilizes the episodic form of the picaresque *maqāma* to canvass the landscape and the social scene of Cairo at the turn of the century. An implausible contrivance sets the fictional action, and with it the "cartographic" surveying, on course. While visiting a cemetery, the narrator dreams that a Pasha from the time of Muḥammad 'Alī rose from the grave and clung tenaciously to him. The two embark upon a journey that begins at the cemetery in Cairo and ends abruptly at the World Exhibit in Paris, where the two remain stranded at the end of the book, though poised to return posthaste to the homeland(s), *Awṭān*.

Ostensibly, the purpose of the journey is to reacquaint the "resurrected" Pasha with the momentous changes that had taken place in Egypt, especially in Cairo, in his "absence." But no sooner do the two set out than the eccentric, rash Pasha runs afoul of the law in a minor infraction that has a domino effect. A series of further complications bring him face-to-face with the new, byzantine legal system and necessitate frequent "visits" to, and discourses about, the different courts and numerous other state and social institutions that define the new social order. This "compulsory" itinerary quickly turns the Pasha's walk down memory lane into a veritable nightmare. Unable to recognize his fellow-Egyptians among the dissolute types he encounters everywhere, he ponders the cause of this general malaise and is helped by the narrator to consider the effects of Western culture on people who can neither assimilate it properly nor shun it effectively. In abject servility, the narrator's contemporaries merely ape the ways of their European colonizers, and al-Muwayliḥī spares the phenomenon none of his lucid critique and scathing satire, half a century before Franz Fanon made it the center of his psychological investigation. The didactic force of this anticolonialist message undoubtedly figured in Jamāl al-Dīn al-Afghānī's enthusiasm for the work; he graced it with an encomium.[18]

While all this is fairly self-evident, the nascent awareness of the role of space in shaping and illuminating character traits and behavior may not always be so. At crucial junctures in the text this awareness appears to be checked by the traditional interest in general types rather than "unique" individuals. A serious attempt to bridge this gap will be undertaken only in the realistic novel of the post–Second World War. With what success, we shall see later. Here it may suffice to note that the list of social types slated for satire is distributed spatially to occasion visits to many important sites and landmarks of both the old and the new sections of Cairo. The loose, episodic "plot" of the picaresque is exceptionally suited for this taxonomical mapping and allows for a broad representation of the physical and human landscapes. In this respect, *Ḥadīth* also mediates between the traditional Arabic *khiṭaṭ* (city planning) genre and modern imaginative fiction, a mode of writing destined to be revived in the 1970s, especially in the works of Gamal Al-Ghitani.[19] Inadvertently, the paramount interest in types occasionally yields stereotypes. Thus, the tortuous search for the deed of an endowment left by the Pasha upon his death ultimately leads to a dark underground labyrinth where the archives of the "Islamic" court are stored. While the Pasha and the narrator stumble upon invisible human bodies and objects in that pitch-darkness, the dim-sighted clerk, bat-like, finds his way around with evident ease. In the old part of Islamic Cairo, we are meant to understand, dark spaces breed obscurantist types and obscure laws, and vice versa.

By contrast, the new "European" sections of Cairo elicit a mixed response from the Pasha. He is at once awed by the architectural splendor of the new quarters of Ismā'īliyya and Azbakiyya, with their wide, clean, and well-lit streets, beautiful opera house, theater, and lavish mansions, as he is appalled by the corrupting influence of things European on the shallow Cairene. While the Pasha laments the historical fact that foreigners, not Egyptians, live in these sumptuous mansions, the narrator bewails the corrosive debasement of cultural monuments such as the opera house and the theater, which on the way from Europe to Egypt seem to have undergone a complete metamorphosis to become crass parodies of their former self. The pronounced dissonance between the elegant material veneer of European city planning and architectural design on the one hand, and the hackneyed imitation of European ways by uncouth Egyptians, on the other, ultimately leads to Alexandria, to Paris, and to the World Exhibit where it all started. For it was during Ismāʻīl's visit to the 1867 *Exhibition Universelle* that he became enamored with Haussmann's redesign of Paris, "conceived" the idea of transforming Cairo into a "Paris on the Nile," and contracted the services of Barillet–Deschamps to implement that ambitious plan.[20]

As it mocks the social and cultural effects of this historical transformation of Cairo, *Ḥadīth* also delineates with remarkable perspicacity the spatial perimeters for treating in fiction the subsequent cultural conflict between East and West, Islam and Europe, and all the other binary opposites that attend on the discourses of modern Arab identity. The three way-stations traversed by the protagonists of *Ḥadīth* on the way from the cemetery to Paris are: the new sections of Cairo, Alexandria, and finally Paris (or alternately London). Often these spaces serve as metonymic representations of the West in subsequent Egyptian novels that thematize the fateful encounter with the cultural "Other."

How deeply implicated the Western "Other" already is in the production of the "self-image," we learn from the last section of *Ḥadīth*, which, admittedly, was added to the original text in 1927.[21] The Egyptian parlor at the *World Exhibit* in Paris, it turns out, parades nothing but a grotesque Orientalist version of what an Egyptian "street" looks like—with its donkeys, loud vendors, lewd belly dancers, and all the rest. To their chagrin, the Pasha and the narrator learn upon inquiry that a fellow Arab, of Syrian origin, rather than a *bona fide* European, is responsible for this travesty, by means of which he sought to cater to the popular European view of the East. Though an addendum, the intent of this section is to show that already by the end of the nineteenth century the sham Orientalist image of a debauched East appears to have become so thoroughly commodified and widespread that trading in it was no longer a direct function of hostile ideology. Both the diagnosis and the critique of this "Orientalist" conceit can be said to have begun in modern Arabic fiction with *Ḥadīth*, albeit liminally. The process of disentangling the "authentic" from the "spurious" strands of identity across multiple layers of discourse and overlapping national and cultural spaces initiated here has continued to preoccupy serious Arab writers ever since. The trajectory of the quest, however, has not always been straight. Between *Ḥadīth* and the realistic novels of the 1940s, attention to the poetics of space seems to diminish significantly in the Egyptian novel. Let me illustrate this "relapse" with an example from the work of Tawfīq al-Ḥakīm.

The opening scene of al-Ḥakīm's major novel, *'Awdat al-Rūḥ*, (1933; The Return of the Spirit) shows a doctor making a home visit to a flu-stricken family whose five male members lie next to each other in a single room. The sight makes the doctor wonder whether he is in a house, a military barrack, or a hospital. He eventually solves this quandary by reminding himself that he had "entered a house with a number." Otherwise, we are left to surmise, it would have been impossible to distinguish the interior of a house from that of a military barrack or a hospital. The conclusion the physician himself draws registers a class differential which, of course, is the very cause of depicting space in this manner in the first place. After patronizing the patients—"you must be from the countryside"—he muses to himself: "Only the peasant can live like this. Only he, no matter how spacious his house may be, has to sleep with his children, his wife, his calf, and his ass in one and the same room."[22]

Internal partitions: an overview

Irrespective of all literary, stylistic, political, and ideological differences among them, Egyptian writers work within a national space that has already been divided and compartmentalized according to several anterior general schemes. One such division is that between "the country and the city," to borrow Raymond Williams' terms.[23] Here the *rīf* (or its more common plural form *aryāf*),[24] that is, rural Egypt, or the Egyptian countryside, stand in opposition to the *bandar*, and its plural: *banādir*, that is, towns and urban centers around which the villages and rural communities cluster, and from which they are usually administered.[25] This opposition was given vogue in Tawfīq al-Ḥalīm's famous work *Yawmiyyāt Nā'ib fil-aryāf* (1937; *Maze of Justice: Diary of a Country Prosecutor*, 1947, 1989) Another division, one more seminal and more versatile in folk culture, is that between *al-Ṣa'īd* (upper Egypt) and all the rest. This contrast seems to be deeply rooted in the Egyptian national psyche and is still capable of generating biting humor and heated controversy, as its recent dramatization in the feature film "*Ṣa'īdī fil-Jāmi'a al-Amrikiyya*—A Ṣa'īdī at AUC"—showed.[26]

Far more significant, however, is the division between the capital, Cairo, and the rest of Egypt. In many fundamental respects, this division amounts to a binary opposition between a center and a periphery, with the center, Cairo, completely predominating the national landscape in the vital economic, political, and cultural domains. In fact, for the rest of Egypt, Cairo is literally synonymous with Egypt, and is better known in the vernacular by the country's name *maṣr (miṣr*, Egypt) than by its official name, *al-Qāhira*. The heavy concentration of the publishing, printing, and entertainment industries, as well as the various governmental departments dealing with culture, literature, cinema, theater and the arts in the capital city explains and reinforces this supreme position of Cairo. Hence also the city's irresistible appeal to successive generations of writers. At present, all Egypt's major writers live in Cairo. This includes not only writers who hail from the *aryāf* (countryside) and migrate and settle in Cairo to launch their literary careers, but also those born in Alexandria, such as Edwar Al-Kharrat and Ibrahim Abdel Meguid. Particularly telling in this regard is Al-Kharrat's almost obsessive preoccupation with Alexandria, his claim that it "stands for Egypt as a whole," and his touching panegyrics for it, all of which are expressed from his permanent residence in Cairo.[27] To stem this tide and contain the negative consequences of the concentration of the national creative talent in the capital, the Egyptian government has for years been experimenting with different ideas to wean *kuttāb al-aqālīm* (writers of the provinces) away from Cairo and to keep them permanently in the provinces. How successful has this policy been is hard to tell. What is certain, though, is that, like Edwar Al-Kharrat, the birthplace of many of these "writers of the provinces" continues to exert an emotional pressure that often induces a return to native surroundings in fictional guises. As we shall see, nostalgia often mixes with ideology in such works, as the desire motivating this fictional trope of return to the sites of childhood simultaneously demarcates the sites of alienation within the national space from which the adult writer wishes to flee. The first step in disentangling this complex issue is to evaluate the deployment of space in the realistic novel.

The identity of a chronotope

Poised to return to Egypt at the conclusion of his medical studies in England, Ismā'īl, the protagonist of Yaḥyā Ḥaqqī's exquisite novella *Qindīl Umm Hāshim* ponders the prospects of how best to serve the homeland which his English professors summarily dub "land of the blind." Although trained as an eye specialist, he momentarily toys with the idea of changing careers and becoming a public figure who would, through public speaking and journalistic writing, awaken Egypt from her deep stupor. In all important respects, for example, the time of the novel's action, the ardent love of, and devotion to, Egypt, and the unselfconscious faith in the efficacy of political education, Ismā'īl appears to echo the historical figure of Muṣṭafā Kāmil here. During the reverie, his hyperactive imagination mythopoeically transforms Egypt from an amorphous mass of land to a veritable sleeping beauty.[28] (This symbolic transmutation of country into beloved woman is more or less a standard trope in the patriotic discourse of modern Arabic literature.) A little earlier, however, while space still retained its immanent physical characteristics, Ismā'īl wondered whether in all of Europe there is a space like the *maydān* (square) of Sayyida Zaynab in the heart of Islamic Cairo, where he, like both Ḥaqqī and Muṣṭafā Kāmil, grew up. The question, of course, is rhetorical and aims to highlight the radically different effect of the contrasting conceptions of space on individual consciousness and identity.

But what exactly is the nature and identity of the homeland to which Ismā'īl is returning? The name "Egypt" recurs several times in the text, but, as a whole, the space the name designates is not outlined, delineated, described, or even suggested anywhere in the text. Rather, an imaginary construct comprising a small, hermetically sealed off, autonomous, and self-sufficient space stands in the novel for the square of al-Sayyida in which Ismā'īl spends his entire life before he goes to England. The complete self-sufficiency of this spatial closure is systematically cultivated in the novel: All the financial, religious, spiritual, and social needs of Ismā'īl and his family are satisfied within the square and, the narrative keeps reminding us, largely as a result of al-Sayyida's blessing. Ismā'īl's father, Shaykh Rajab, we learn from the outset, had migrated to Cairo from the countryside before our protagonist was born, and had settled in the Square precisely to be near his favorite Muslim Saint, al-Sayyida Zaynab.

So emphatic is the text in asserting the Square's spatial autonomy that even Ismā'īl's illicit sexual urges during adolescence find vicarious satisfaction inside it. He takes to sneaking into the mosque to rub himself against women supplicants, including prostitutes, who come to the mosque to seek al-Sayyida's intercession with God on their behalf. (In parenthesis I may note that the detailed depiction of such irreverent conduct in the sanctum sanctorum of a major mosque in Islamic Cairo would have been unimaginable without the enabling recourse to the imperatives, strategies, and techniques of verisimilitude so innate to realistic fiction.) The deployment of time, the strategy of naming, and a considerable part of characterization combine with this organization of space to emphasize the Islamic identity of this chronotope. Within the novel's economy of symbolic representation the square presents a microcosmic version of the world of Islam, albeit in a pronounced Egyptian setting. As the fate of Ismā'īl will eventually demonstrate, movement across the boundaries separating this space from other spaces is fraught with grave consequences to the Islamic identity of its inhabitants.

This metaphorical treatment of space evinces what appears to be a congenital peculiarity of the Arabic novel. No sooner is actual referential space recognized than it is thoroughly compromised by other, often competing demands. Invariably, the deployment of space is assigned a dual mandate: to present a convincing impression of localized, particular space while, simultaneously, investing that selfsame space with symbolic import that evokes broader, more general and more abstract ideas of space. In the present novel, for example, the depiction of space is meant to suggest both the actual square of al-Sayyida Zaynab in Cairo and a microcosmic representation of the world of Islam at large, encapsulated, so to speak, into the space of the Square. This, in any event, is how the spatial closure of a single "Islamic" square is contrasted in the novel with the open-ended spaces of England and Scotland which, in turn, stand for the non-Islamic chronotope of modern Europe and the West in general.

In Europe Ismā'īl flouts his traditional "Islamic" values, renounces religion as "a superstition invented to rule the masses," and embraces science as an alternative religion. Thus the meticulous synchronization of thematic and spatial characteristics in the respective spaces, such as open spaces and a liberal attitude to sex in Europe, and its inverse correlate in Egypt, is meant to emphasize that the metamorphosis in Ismā'īl's belief system and personality could not have materialized fully outside the "alien" European space.[29] In general, this interpretation is valid and confirms Franco Moretti's conclusion that certain plots can happen only in certain spaces.[30] The exquisite quality of the novella, however, resides in its subtle undermining of this schematic division of cultural space by suggesting that fissures and ruptures had begun to appear in the microcosmic "Islamic" chronotope long before Ismā'īl set foot on European soil. The reference in the first paragraph of the novel to the destruction of historical landmarks in Islamic Cairo—in order to make room for modern means of transportation—is but one example of this subversive strategy. Similarly, the description of Ismā'īl's furtive habit of sneaking into the mosque on visitation days to rub himself against female supplicants blurs all boundaries between the sacred and the profane within this strictly "Islamic" closure. One could plausibly argue that what these proleptic signs indicate is that European influences had already penetrated "Islamic" space and were imperceptibly transforming it from within. To extrapolate further from such examples that no space is hermetically sealed off is equally valid and, on one level of textual and ideological analysis, perhaps even necessary. On the aesthetic level, however, its discursive probe threatens to ravage the fine illusion of reality and the delicate symbolic structure that sustain the dramatic conflict of the novel. At the very least, such a scrutiny would reduce the novel's imaginative interest in the poetic symbolism of cultural space to the historical and geopolitical dimensions of the conflict between Islam and the West.

At a crucial juncture in the development of the plot the dual functions of space come into full play. Imbued with secular European knowledge and social and cultural views, Ismā'īl returns home to the Square, only to discover that he had in the meantime completely outgrown its built-in limitations. There he finds his mother pouring hot oil in the trachomic eyes of his cousin, and future wife, in the belief that oil drawn from al-Sayyida's lamp has a healing power. The spectacle sends him into a wild rage against his mother, her "superstitious" belief in the efficacy of the oil, and against the very symbol of Islam in the novel: al-Sayyida Zaynab herself. He dashes to the mosque, smashes the lamp to pieces, and is almost lynched by the incensed crowd of supplicants. This violent turn of events forecloses all prospects of secular European and Islamic worldviews cohabiting the same space in the novel. Coincidently, it also sends Ismā'īl's identity crisis spinning out of control. Who is he, and where does he belong? In the aftermath of his unspeakable act he can neither stay in the Saint's square nor bring himself to return to Europe, an option he considers seriously when he sells the medical equipment he had brought back with him from Europe. Whither Ismā'īl?

A way out of this thematic impasse eventually emerges from the partitioning of space in Cairo and its redrawing along lines of the novel's symbolic patterns. Ismā'īl temporarily leaves the autonomous Square to reside in a *pension* outside it owned by a Greek woman named Iphtalia. The exact location of the *pension* is not specified, but, through metonymic extension, it borrows spatial definition from the ethnic identity of its proprietor: It represents Greece, and Greece, being *in* Europe, willy-nilly, represents Europe. This temporary reconfiguration makes possible a symbolic reintroduction of "European" space into Egyptian national space, while keeping it outside the spaces designating Islam and Europe, the Square and Great Britain, respectively. By the same metonymic device the summary characterization of Iphtalia as a niggardly and grasping woman helps identify the *pension* as an anomalous space, neither quite European nor Egyptian or Islamic in any positive sense. "Indeed," reflects Ismāʿīl, "the Europeans in Egypt have little in common with the Europeans [he] met in Europe." Gradually, the recognition of this anomaly extends to Ismāʿīl's acquired cultural views and this, in turn, makes possible a reconciliation (of sorts) between the various pairs of binary opposites that animate the novel's plot, especially the paramount conflict between faith and science, or its geo-mythological correlate, East and West. The realignment of the antagonistic components of Ismāʿīl's personality along a more transcendental, vaguely mystical vision of existence, makes possible his readmission into "Islamic" space, the successful treatment of Fāṭima's trachomic eyes, and a "happy" ending to the story.

While arguably satisfactory on the aesthetic and symbolic levels, this formal reconciliation never quite yields a convincing synthesis between cultural opposites. Thus, it is significant that in its wake Ismāʿīl leaves the Square permanently and settles in a less Islamically specific space, where he leads a happy and productive, but perhaps not altogether Islamic, way of life. Whatever its value to other concerns of modern Arab culture, the thematic solution to the cultural conflict advanced here is largely a measure of the adroit deployment of fictional space in the novel. For it is precisely through the movement of characters across the imaginary boundaries of discrete spaces that the plot maintains a coherent structure and a compelling verisimilar effect. Ultimately, it is this methodical mapping, partitioning, and redrawing of familiar space into signifying symbolic patterns that enables the novel, at least for the duration of the act of reading, to superimpose its contrived illusion of space onto the reader's experience of actual, fluid, and generally amorphous referential space.

In this connection it is important to note the meticulous orchestration of the temporal and spatial dimensions to effect the thematic reconciliation between the novel's multiple binary opposites. This reconciliation takes place during *laylat al-qadr*, on which the Qur'ānic revelation began (Qur'ān, 97,1) and which is, according to Islamic tradition, the holiest night of the holy month of Ramaḍān. The power of that night obliterates all spatial boundaries between the local, regional, universal, and cosmic spheres as the gates of heaven open up to receive the prayers of sincere supplicants on earth. For the duration of that night the whole universe turns figuratively into an Islamic chronotope. In its subtle allusion to the spatial passage between the terrestrial and the heavenly, the novel also invokes associations with the Qur'ānic narrative about the Prophet's ascent to heaven, dramatized centuries later in al-Maʿarrī's celebrated work *Risālat al-Ghufrān* (Epistle of Forgiveness) which, in turn, is said to have influenced Dante's conception of space in his *Divine Comedy*.[31]

Enter Mahfouz: the outsider within

It is perhaps one of the great mysteries of the Arabic novel that the writer who popularized it most at home and abroad is the least traveled of all Arab writers. Unlike his two famous contemporaries, Yaḥyā Ḥaqqī and Tawfīq al-Ḥakīm, both of whom were seasoned travelers, the first as an occasional diplomat, the second as a student-cum-dilettante artist, Mahfouz left Egypt only twice in his entire life: once to Yemen and once to the former Yugoslavia. Both trips were brief and semiofficial in nature: to represent Egypt at writers' conferences and colloquia. His travels within Egypt have been hardly more extensive. With the exception of the fairly regular visits to Alexandria during his summer vacations, Mahfouz rarely left his beloved Cairo. He is said to have traveled to upper Egypt only once, and to have seen the Egyptian countryside only through the window of a moving train.[32]

And yet, when he was asked which of his many novels he thought stood a chance of surviving the vicissitudes of time and literary taste, Mahfouz singled out only two: *Midaq Alley* and *The Cairene Trilogy*. "These two works may survive," Mahfouz opined "perhaps not as great works of literature but as memorable faces of beloved Egypt."[33] The visual dimension invoked by Mahfouz' facial metaphor speaks directly to the poetics of space in the novel, especially in his own realistic fiction. I will, therefore, use the emblematic text of *Midaq Alley* to explore this dynamic in some detail.

Though less global in embrace than, say, Ḥaqqī's *Qindīl* or Tayeb Saleh's *Season of Migration to the North*, *Midaq Alley* is no less ambitious or adept at the deployment of symbolic space. It shares with most of Mahfouz' realistic novels of the 1940s and early fifties a penchant for using the names of actual streets and neighborhoods in Cairo as sites of the contrived fictional events. Moreover, with the exception of *al-Qāhira al-Jadīda* (1945; New Cairo/Heliopolis), these neighborhoods lie primarily in Islamic Cairo.[34] But to grope, in light of this device, for compelling similarities between the fictional representation of space in these novels and its referential counterparts on the ground is akin to confusing an optical illusion of reality with reality itself. With or without this feature, Mahfouz' fiction is eminently urban in nature. Not unlike him, his fictional characters seldom leave Cairo. And when they do so, as happens in several of his novels of the 1960s, notably *al-Summān wal-Kharīf* (1962; Autumn Quail, 1985) and *Miramār* (1967; *Miramar*, 1978), it is primarily to Alexandria, which, as we shall see, figures in both novels as a place of exile from the seat of power, Cairo. By contrast, Upper Egypt, the Egyptian countryside, and the other remote parts of the country, like the rest of the world outside of Egypt, with the single exception of the holy places of Islam in the Arab Peninsula, seem to lie permanently outside the scope of Mahfouz' fictional interests. The pronounced attention these "neglected" spaces receive in the fiction of younger Egyptian writers may attest to a generational gap and to an undercurrent of resistance to the Mahfouzian literary paradigm, perhaps even to Mahfouz' preeminence in the realm of Egyptian fiction.

Much like *Qindīl Umm Hāshim*, the dominant strategy in the symbolic patterning of space in *Midaq Alley* involves a contrast between an interior and an exterior. The interior space is described at the outset in graphic, but highly ambivalent terms that suggest both its relative autonomy and representative status. Both of the following passages occur on the first page of the novel.

> Though the Alley lives in semi isolation from the surrounding world, it nonetheless throbs with its own life, which connects with the deep roots of life everywhere, even as it preserves a modicum of the mystery of a vanished world.
>
> As the sun began to set, *Midaq Alley* wrapped itself in a tenebrous brown veil of twilight made darker by the alley's enclosure within three walls like a trap. It opens onto Ṣanādiqiyya Street, then winds upwards in no apparent order; hemmed in on one side by a shop, a cafe, and a bakery, and on the other by a shop and a retail store. It ends abruptly, as did its bygone glory, with two adjacent houses, each consisting of three stories.
>
> (p. 5)

If the first passage evokes memories of the naive theory of "a slice of life" that informed so much of the realistic fiction written in Europe during the nineteenth century, it is because the Arabic novel had to encapsulate, primarily at the hands of Mahfouz and his generation, in a matter of two or three decades, nearly two centuries of European novel writing. In that vein, the cast of human characters inhabiting the Alley is meant to furnish, collectively, a representative sample, or a cross section, of Egyptian society. In fact, a far more sophisticated view of realism informs the meticulous selection, inclusion, and exclusion of the human array and material objects that crowd the alley. The hierarchical order of representing both correlates directly with the key figure in the "description" of space in the second passage, namely, the "trap" simile. All the associations the simile triggers point in one semantic direction: the interior space of the Alley spells mortal danger. Momentarily, the forces of nature, that is, the encroaching darkness of twilight, and urban architecture: the enveloping walls, conspire to give the threat an eerie immediacy. Subsequent thematic developments in the novel will actualize this threat, but only as regards a segment of the Alley's population, namely, the socio-economically disadvantaged.

A closer examination of the order of presentation reveals this socioeconomic corollary to spatial entrapment. Consistently, real estate: houses, apartments, shops, and other material possessions receive prominent mention and are often introduced before the human characters who live or work in them. Not so, however, the better-off characters who own property in the Alley. And since "wealth," and the concomitant social standing it bequeaths, consist primarily of real estate in the Alley, upward socioeconomic mobility for those living off their labor is virtually excluded. In this sense, and for this group of characters, especially Ḥamīda, 'Abbās, and Ḥusayn Kirsha, the trap simile invites literal, not metaphorical reading.

All this is part of the deployment of space along the horizontal, inside–outside grid. A more comprehensive view of both space and cast of characters shows a tripartite division of characters who are distributed along a vertical as well as a horizontal spatial expanse. In this scheme, the first group comprises well-off characters, primarily landlords such as Raḍwān al-Ḥusaynī and Saniyya ʻAfīfī, both of whom lease apartments and shops to tenant-characters, and the other proprietors of income-generating spaces in the Alley, Salīm ʻAlwān, the owner of the thriving retail warehouse, and Kirsha, the proprietor of the only cafe in the Alley. Inasmuch as these characters live in the Alley, they invariably inhabit higher floors. By contrast, the poorer characters, for example, "Dr" Bouchy, the quack dentist, ʻAmm Kāmil, the pastry vendor, and ʻAbbās al-Ḥulw, the barber, inhabit the ground floors. Somewhat below them still, in a subterranean space, live three additional characters: the baker Ḥusniyya, her subservient husband Jaʻda, and the enigmatic cripple maker, Zeiṭa. In Zeiṭa's case the socioeconomic and spatial criteria of differentiation are indexed further by a color distinction that places him at the ghoulish black end of a color spectrum. At the other end of the spectrum stands the radiant, saintly figure, Raḍwān al-Ḥusaynī.

Characters on both ends of the vertical grid appear sufficiently content with their life in the Alley. Zeiṭa in particular manages to turn his compounded predicament into a distinct advantage. Through his renowned skill as a cripple maker he reigns over a veritable underground realm of beggars who owe him undivided allegiance. In this regard it is instructive that he is arrested at the end of the novel while disinterring a body from a grave to extricate a set of gold teeth from its skull. Up to that point, the police, as representative of the political and civil authority, remains totally absent from the landscape of the novel, even though it teams with illegal and immoral activities that include bootlegging, black market, hashish smoking, overt homosexuality, bribery, pimping, and prostitution. The unexpected appearance of the police in the manner of a *deus-ex-machina* to arrest Zeiṭa and Dr Bouchy at the end of the novel thus raises more questions than it answers. The event betokens an elaborate network of presences and absences that demands further attention here.

As noted earlier, the distribution of space along the horizontal grid supports an overall division of space into a binary opposition between interior and exterior, inside and outside, in short, between the Alley and the world around it. Each of these two paramount spaces is subdivided further along similar, but far less conspicuous lines. Thus, the space of the alley is divided into an inner, relatively private space (the interior of buildings, flats, and houses) and an outer, emphatically public space (the street, the shops, and especially the Cafe). Similarly, outer space is divided into two main domains: the rest of Egypt outside the Alley, and the Islamic holy places in Mecca and Madīna. Like the arrest of Zeiṭa, these religious spaces loom on the horizon of the novel suddenly at the end, as if to extricate the plot from an intractable moral impasse. Concomitantly, they draw attention to the strategy of inclusion and exclusion that determines what institutions are accorded, or denied, representation in the Alley. Major thematic developments in the novel would be literally inconceivable without the projection of this elaborate cartographic pattern onto the general landscape of the novel. A number of examples may suffice to illustrate this intricate relationship.

The desire for upward socioeconomic mobility is stimulated by, and in turn aggravates, the mordant awareness of the disparity between what exists inside and outside the Alley. Ḥamīda, the poor, orphan, vain, and truculent beauty of the Alley grows livid with envy when she sees, during her daily walks outside the Alley, Jewish and working girls wearing smart new clothes. Once this difference registers in her consciousness, and it does instantly, clothes—like Desdemona's lost kerchief—become a powerful symbol for larger, but less tangible issues; in this case Ḥamīda's total revolt against her lowly station in the social hierarchy of the Alley. Work, for a traditional Muslim girl, does not appear to be an option; only marriage is. The only eligible bachelor in the Alley is 'Abbās al-Ḥulw, the Alley's barber, who loves Ḥamīda but falls far short of her material expectations from a spouse. To meet these expectations, 'Abbās is forced to leave the Alley to work in the British military camps at Tal al-Kabīr, the very site on which the British defeated the Egyptian army of Aḥmad 'Urābī at the outset of their occupation of Egypt in 1882. Instructively, 'Abbās describes this move as a "*hijra*," that is, migration, as if to another country altogether. No sooner does he leave the Alley, however, than Ḥamīda, now formally betrothed to him, resumes her flirtation with the idea of finding a more financially rewarding alternative. Using her ample physical charms as a bait, she succeeds in bewitching Salīm 'Alwān, the owner of the retail store in the Alley to ask for her hand, which she and her foster mother readily accept, even though he is married and has three married and well-established sons of his own. The putative engagement to 'Abbās is brushed aside with token remorse. This alluring prospect proves a mirage, however; for, no sooner is it entertained than the hoary 'Alwān suffers an incapacitating heart attack that puts him permanently out of commission.

Thematically, this abortive attempt demonstrates the futility of trying to circumvent the structural division of space into inside/outside, and the financial correlate of this division that places all the sources of cash income outside and the desire for it inside the Alley. Since the British occupying army looms large as the only source of financial betterment, this episode underlines the impossibility, under colonial occupation, of wedding local capital to native need, no matter how ill-begotten that capital is ('Alwān engages in black market activities with Jewish racketeers, lives in an affluent suburb outside the Alley, and owns a thriving retail store inside it).

In the wake of this episode, another critical absence becomes pressingly conspicuous: that of institutionalized religion. We note, in this regard, the absence of all landmarks, sites, and emblems of religion, notably that of a mosque, from the Alley. This "absenting" is particularly incongruent on two accounts. First, the Alley is situated squarely in Islamic Cairo, a veritable landscape of minarets. Second, the omniscient narrator had from the outset claimed for the Alley a representative status that makes it a microcosmic version of the surrounding world.

For the present, it may suffice to reiterate the view that the selection of fictional space aims to simulate, invoke, or mimic, but not necessarily to describe or reproduce actual referential space.

While the episode of Salīm 'Alwān unfolds, Ḥamīda's foster mother actively seeks some religious sanction for her daughter's enterprising, though morally repugnant, about-face. In the absence of official religious authority, she visits Raḍwān al-Ḥusaynī at home to solicit his *pro forma* approval of the new, more lucrative marriage proposal. Now Raḍwān, though cast in the glowing light of a veritable Job by the narrator, and widely acknowledged in the Alley as a resident saint, is in reality a dropout from al-Azhar who had failed to obtain official authorization as a religious scholar after numerous attempts in as many years. His role as a symbol of piety and custodian of Islamic values in the Alley is thus highly anomalous and profoundly problematic. Implicitly but effectively, it decouples institutionalized religion from piety, and religious scholarship from morality. That he ultimately wields no real power in the Alley is amply evident from his failure to influence the course of events in any of the cases that are brought before him, notably that of Ḥamīda's rescinding of her vows to 'Abbās and Kirsha's open homosexuality. Since the only other "representative" of religious sensibility in the Alley is the Quixotic, half mystic, half unhinged Shaykh Darwīsh, religious authority, and its ancillary moral and ethical attributes, appear sorely absent from the Alley.

Equally conspicuous by its absence is the law. There is no police station, law enforcement agency, or any other governmental office in the Alley. In the absence of all civil and political authority, lawlessness appears to be checked only by the supreme regulative power of money, which, as we have seen, is largely a function of property ownership and illicit dealings in the Alley. Otherwise, in this state of change and flux, the able characters tailor their code of conduct to fit their personal interests and desires, however extravagant and unorthodox these may be.

Politics does enter the Alley at one point, however. And, like Kirsha's homosexual partners, Salīm 'Alwān's fellow-bootleggers, and Zeiṭa's would-be-cripples, politics enters the Alley from the outside, in the form of an election campaign. Kirsha's cafe, being the only available public space, serves as a gathering place for the rally. And it is there that the candidate for political office openly bribes the cafe proprietor in exchange for his support in the "elections."

Far more sinister than this public display of political corruption, however, is the arrival of the pimp Faraj Ibrāhīm in the Alley under the cover of the political campaign. As if to underscore the reality of sham elections as virtual prostitution under colonial occupation, Mahfouz neatly orchestrates their joint debut into the space of the Alley. Thus, while the political campaign unfolds in the background, Faraj spots Ḥamīda and instantly recognizes her susceptibility to seduction and potential recruitment into prostitution. Characteristically, beside his provocative gaze, which teases her "natural" disposition to combat, it is his elegant suit that impresses Ḥamīda most and instantly lures her to his snare.

While inside the Alley, the encounter between the two remains confined to probing gazes, which they exchange across the fluid space between Ḥamīda's apartment and the cafe. It is only when Ḥamīda ventures outside the Alley and crosses the imaginary divide that separates it from the outside world that the seduction plan gets under way in earnest. Not unexpectedly, Faraj systematically plays up the contrast between the inside and the outside, and between Ḥamīda's shabby, traditional clothes and the smart, modern clothes that the Jewish and the working girls wear. Ultimately, a strategic drive in a taxi through the fashionable sections of modern Cairo bedazzles her senses and seals her fate.

In another, exceptionally sardonic reenactment of the correlation of the spatial dichotomy inside/ outside with the pattern of presences and absences, Faraj takes Ḥamīda to his "dance and language school" before he delivers her to American and British officers to be deflowered for a premium rate. This twist simultaneously highlights the absence of a school (or any other educational or cultural institution) in the Alley and, like elections, the prostitution of education under occupation. What Ḥamīda, now renamed Titi, "learns" in this school is how to ape the relevant lewd English words necessary to accentuate the "artistic" display of her flesh before her British and American patrons. It is during one such "educational" session that her former fiance, 'Abbās, finds his death at the hands of British and American soldiers. The sight of these soldiers fondling Ḥamīda's willing body in a bar enrages him, and he throws a bottle that hits her in the face. The soldiers lynch him on the spot. Ironically, he had returned to the Alley from the British camp a few days earlier with an expensive engagement ring in his pocket for Ḥamīda.

It is this tragic turn of events, compounded by the arrest of Zeiṭa and Dr Bouchy in the graveyard, that moves Raḍwān al-Ḥusaynī to make the pilgrimage to Mecca. Though a mandatory religious duty on all mature and able Muslims, Raḍwān performs this commandment on behalf of the community as a whole. He thereby aims to expiate the recent past, heal the wounded spirit of the Alley, and mend the atrophied lines of communion between it and the sources of holiness that lie so far away. Equally mindful of the laws of the genre, however, Mahfouz makes the return of the distinguished pilgrim coincide with the advent into the Alley of a new family "consisting of a butcher, his wife, seven sons, and an extremely beautiful daughter" (p. 245). If this ending suggests a repetition, or a continuation, of the story we have just finished reading, it is because realistic fiction often keeps too close to the pulse of life to allow for final closures. As if to underline the arbitrariness of textual closures altogether, Mahfouz assigns this awkward task to the confused Shaykh Darwīsh, who is rumored to receive "revelations" in both Arabic and English. On several occasions in the text this bilingual competence is called upon to perform an indispensable structural function: By emphatically spelling out the English terms for acts and situations that are unspeakable in Arabic, for example, homosexuality, elopement, tragedy, Shaykh Darwīsh forces recognition of these banished meanings and literally extricates the narrative from tight bottlenecks. Not surprisingly, he has the last word in the novel, END, which, though spelled in capital letters, remains profoundly ambiguous under the circumstances.

One last important consequence of the deployment of space in the novel deserves mention here. Much like the Square of the Saint's mosque, the space of the Alley appears to possess distinct metaphysical qualities, akin to stability and permanence, that cannot be reduced to the sum total of its material and human attributes. Something of the eternal, and yet recognizably personal, seems to attach to both spaces. This is, no doubt, an effect of prosopopoeia, or personification. In *Qindīl Umm Hāshim* this sense of place is cultivated systematically through mystical motifs spun around the holy center, the mosque, and especially the splendid lamp hanging from its dome. In contrast, the interior of *Midaq Alley* is completely vacuous, as we have seen, because the sources of material prosperity, as well as religious and spiritual sanctity, lie largely outside it. Even so, the place appears to possess an innate resilience and a lasting appeal that defy the vicissitudes of time and the upheavals of human history.

Something of this intangible quality inheres in the mise-en-scène and imparts to the social body occupying it an invaluable measure of social cohesion. But this spatial endowment is strictly gender-sensitive: only the men, who enjoy an exclusive and unhindered access to public space, are in a position to partake of it. The hub of that space is Kirsha's cafe, the gathering place for the men's nightly assembly. No sinful, illegal, immoral, or scurrilous act, however egregious, is sufficient to ostracize the perpetrator from this collective body permanently. This is as true of Kirsha's hashish smoking and homosexuality, as it is of Ḥusayn's insufferable arrogance, Zeita's stench, and Shaykh Darwīsh's incoherent and often vituperative outbursts. In the absence of any other religious, social, or public space, the cafe emerges as the exclusive channel for alleviating individual and social pathology within the Alley.[35] It also acts as a catalyst for social cohesion and solidarity, but only for the men in the Alley's segregated society.

In marked contrast, the women inhabit private, interiorized, fragmented, and inexorably discontinuous space. They thus live in double segregation: from the public world of men, and from each other. There is no Mrs Kirsha's cafe in the Alley. This structural segregation of women breeds alienation, which, in turn, breeds secrecy and, at least in the case of Ḥamīda, leads to deviancy. The implicit but poignant contrast between her ultimate fate and that of her foster brother Ḥusayn, in spite of the compelling personal and psychological similarities between them, is largely a function of this division of space. Whereas he can flaunt his miscreant deeds with relative impunity and still return safely to occupy his place in the Alley's public space, she wraps in utter secrecy every step she takes, and thus, every imaginary boundary she crosses becomes a psychological and cultural red line. As a prostitute, her very survival at the end of the novel appears to hinge on the continued separation of the Alley from the outer world she now inhabits. With the possible exception of *The Trilogy*, it is hard to find a similar segregation of the sexes in any other work of Mahfouz. But even there, this analogy holds only as concerns the female members of Sayyid Aḥmad's house, where windows are meant to be barriers, not conduits, between the inside and the outside.

If none of Mahfouz' other realistic novels makes such an extensive symbolic use of fictional space, all of them nonetheless utilize space in varying degrees to enhance the narrative's realistic effect. Thus, for example, all the crucial junctures of *Khān al-Khalīlī's* plot involve relocation from one residential area to another, a structural feature that suggests a causal relation between the two. The primary interest of the novel, however, revolves around the psychological makeup of the protagonist, not the social scene or its spatial lay out. The same holds true for Mahfouz' other works of the 1940s and 1950s, including his masterpiece, *The Trilogy*, where the interest in individual psychology is paramount. It is only in the sixties that space resumes its role as a central player in the fictional dramas of Mahfouz' novels. As we shall see, fundamental changes in the conception and deployment of space are effected to capture Mahfouz' troubled vision of Egypt during that decade. Before we do that however, it may be useful to interrogate briefly the relation of this imaginative rendition of space to its discursive antecedent in the colonialist discourse about Cairo in the late nineteenth and early twentieth century.

One city, two worlds apart?

Implicit in both *Qindīl* and *Zuqāq* is an awareness of the historical process through which the fundamental contrast between the traditional/Islamic and the modern/European sections of Cairo developed. In a sense, the paramount role of space in both novels can be seen as an imaginative attempt to grapple with the abiding political, social, and especially psychological effects of this inherent dichotomy. The mention in the first paragraph of *The Saint's Lamp* of the axe of the Planning Department (*Maṣlaḥat al-Tanẓīm*) that demolished the old "ablution lane" and other "historical landmarks of Cairo" to make room for modern living alludes directly to that process. As mentioned earlier, it was in the wake of his visit to the *Exposition Universelle* in Paris in 1867 that Ismā'īl, soon to become Khedive of Egypt, became infatuated with Haussmann's redesign of modern Paris and wished to replicate that feat in Egypt by transforming Cairo into a "Paris on the Nile." For this purpose, he hired two French architects to design the new sections of Cairo outside the Islamic City. The plan they drew for this purpose was self-consciously European and sought to highlight the contrast between its modernity and the medieval identity of the adjacent Islamic City. Nor was the intended contrast limited to architectural features. As many scholars have shown, it systematically aimed to differentiate the New from the Old, the Medieval from the Modern, and the Islamic from the European along an entire spectrum of identity markers. Here is how Basil Worsfold described the two diametrically opposed entities enveloped by the same metropolitan space in 1899.

> [T]wo Cairos, which, lying side by side without any visible division between them, hold two populations whose lives are absolutely distinct and dissimilar... [A] line drawn diagonally from the railway station on the north to the Citadel on the south... will roughly separate European from medieval Cairo. To the east of this line 500,000 brown-skinned Arabs are living in the quaintest and most delightful, but, at the same time,

> the dirtiest and most dilapidated of streets. Seen from the Citadel, this Cairo presents the appearance of a mass of level roofs, out of which countless minarets and domes rise skyward. To the west of this line are the palaces, public buildings, the wide tree-lined streets, and the gardens of the European quarters. Here, in these infinitely less picturesque, but infinitely more sanitary, streets and squares, the bulk of the 20,000 or 30,000 Europeans live... Seen from the roof of one of the numerous palaces erected on the east bank of the Nile, this Cairo looks like a vast garden intersected with white roads, bordered by lebbek avenues, and variegated by patches of bright-hued flowering shrubs, in the midst of which the white walls and roofs of the houses glitter in the sunshine.[36]

From this and similar descriptions of late nineteenth century Cairo in Western accounts a set of differentiating criteria emerges. The old city is said to be distinguished by its narrow, winding, and mysterious alleys, crammed and disorderly neighborhoods, and exotic but singularly unsanitary bazaars. It is consigned to a timeless medieval eternity in which Western spectators can espy the "rumored" city of Caliphs, harem, intrigue, and romance made popular in Europe by successive translations of *The Arabian Nights* and a strident Orientalist discourse of Otherness. Alternately, the city appears as an amorphous, anemic entity whose inherent chaos, filth, and venality attest to its ontological difference from the European model of order, reason, dynamism, hygiene, and the other amenities of modernity.

The treatment of space in the two novels under consideration problematizes this dichotomy, with mixed results. Drawing on disparate elements from the bipolar paradigm, it gestures towards hybridity and heterogeneity but remains ultimately ambiguous. In part, the heterogeneity flows from the presentation of multiple, often contradictory evaluations of the same space by different characters, and, occasionally, by the same character at different times. Thus, for example, Ismā'īl at one point describes the indigenous spaces of al-Sayyida's mosque and square, and the Egyptian throngs that perennially crowd them in scathingly derogatory terms reminiscent of the worst Orientalist slanders. The *italics* in the following passages attempt to capture the flow of Ismā'īl's thoughts, impressions, and sensations. They also aim to distinguish his "stream of consciousness" from the narrative of the third person narrator

> Ismā'īl entered the square and found it, as usual, teeming with stricken and degraded people. *These cannot possibly be creatures living in an age when even inanimate objects have sprung to life. These multitudes are hallow relics, like the remains of ruined columns, serving no purpose other than to obstruct the access of a passer by. And what is this bestial noise? And that foul food the mouths devour?* He looks at the faces but sees only lingering sleep, as if they are all consumed by opium.... *Those Egyptians! What a frivolous, chattering breed they are! At once hairless*

> *and beardless, naked and barefooted. They urinate blood and excrete worms. A slap on their elongated napes draws an ample submissive smile on their faces. And Egypt! A misshapen piece of rotting mud in a desert. Swarms of buzzing flies and mosquitoes hover over it, and a herd of emaciated buffaloes sinks knee-deep in it... Here is stagnation that defies all progress, nihilism that robs time of all meaning, drug-induced hallucinations, and day-dreaming in broad daylight.*
>
> (pp. 43–44)

And, yet, at other times, these selfsame Egyptians and the square appear in an entirely different, far more benign light.

> (Ismā'īl's) eyes scanned the Square, and rested on the crowds whom he found tolerable now. Gradually, he began to smile at some of the jokes, shouts, and laughs that reached his ears and reminded him of his youth. *No people has preserved its distinctive character like the Egyptians in the face of historical vicissitude and change of rulers.* The natives passing before him now could have jumped directly out of the pages of (the historian) al-Jabarti. He became more calm as he felt the solid ground under his feet. What he saw before him were not hordes of discrete individuals but a cohesive people united by a common bond. It is a kind of faith, the result of long companionship, that matures in its own good time. Now faces began to reveal to him meanings he could not discern heretofore. *Repose, composure, and tranquility prevail here; and the sword is in the sheath. And there: frantic, anxious chase; an executioner in his prime; and the sword is ever drawn. But why compare? A lover neither contrasts nor compares. In comes comparison, out goes love.*
>
> (pp. 46–47)

Still later, at the moment of reconciliation with his estranged culture and surroundings, the indigenous space of the mosque acquires a translucent mystical brilliance that imbues Ismā'īl with an epiphany-like sensation. Significantly, this sensation coincides with a compelling example of prosopopoeia where the Square's "breathing" humanizes it, so to speak, and allows for a "personal" relationship between it and Ismā'īl.

> He was momentarily lost in thought when the sound of heavy breathing in the Square riveted his attention. *This must be Saint al-'Atris.* He raised his eyes and beheld the dome flooded with a shimmering light that engulfed it. Ismā'īl shuddered all over.
>
> (pp. 53–54)

In the novel's elaborate system of predications, the ultimate worth of the indigenous space and its human occupants rests exclusively on Ismā'īl's (and the reader's) willingness to submit to the metaphysical efficacy of the spiritual power residing in the square to erase from consciousness, or at least neutralize, the keen awareness of the historical disparity between East and West.

> *Who could possibly deny the civilization and progress of Europe, or the degradation, ignorance, disease, and abject poverty of the East? History has issued its immutable verdict. There is no gainsaying the fact that our tree blossomed once and bore fruit, but it has since withered away. Would that it could be revived, but that's highly unlikely.*
>
> (pp. 51–52)

Against this acute sense of geo-cultural division and historical dissonance the novel posits the powerful Qur'ānic metaphor of the tree of light that cancels out all space differentiation by being "neither Eastern nor Western." This is on the abstract, metaphysical level. On the more concrete level, against the open, orderly, rational, and hygienic space of the West, as experienced by Ismā'īl in Europe, the novel adduces either a nebulous version of "Eastern" spirituality—in essence a coarse amalgam of maudlin "mysticism" and superstition—or utter formlessness. Ismā'īl's subsequent obesity, and the inarticulate space of his clinic, attest to a spatial inchoateness during the last phase of his life. Instructively, Ismā'īl's "mystical" resignation to his surroundings and his rhetorical inveighing against untoward comparisons provide but a tentative closure to the fictional plot, and a precarious one at that. No sooner is the symbolic reconciliation effected than he leaves the Square permanently and surrenders to a hedonistic life style of excess that ultimately claims his life. The novel thus appears unable to shake loose the terms of the cultural dichotomy altogether. Within this constrained vision, to ward off one set of "negative" terms the novel is forced to embrace another: to "rehumanize" or "rehabilitate" the Egyptians, it ahistoricizes Egypt. In the end, "Eastern" space is reconsigned to its static, timeless, but "spiritual" repose around a pivotal core while the dynamic, material, and eminently historical "Western" space is reconsigned to its traditional place as the space of the "Other."

* * *

Zuqāq al-Midaqq problematizes the relation between the old and the new parts of Cairo more thoroughly. The explicit reference in the opening paragraph to the three historical phases of the Islamic City simultaneously registers the momentary absence of the "other" Cairo.

> Sundry manifestations affirm that *Midaq Alley* was a gem of bygone epochs, and that it once glowed like a brilliant star in the history of al-Mu'izz's Cairo. Which Cairo do I mean? That of the Fatimids, the Mamelukes, the Sultans? Only God and the archeologists know.
>
> (p. 5)

Moreover, the strategy of inclusion and exclusion deployed in the novel suggests a conscious engagement of the historical views about the nature of the City, both Islamic and European. Thus, the absence of official public institutions from the Alley, so crucial to the fictional action as we have seen, is said to be an essential characteristic of the Islamic city in general.[37] It thus enhances rather than diminishes the Alley's symbolic status as a microcosmic representation of Islamic Cairo. Similarly, the identification of the Alley's public space with the male domain echoes another characteristic of the Islamic city.

> Islamic tradition assigns separate roles to men and women and goes to great length to safeguard privacy and female modesty. In principle, public space is considered unsafe and "to be eschewed by women" and even within the home private space is layered to permit further reclusion for individual privacy.[38]

Not all spatial features of the novel yield such direct correspondences with external, discursive, and historical actualities. But some definitely do. Thus, for example, the presence of Faraj's school of prostitution, disguised as a school of languages, in the modern part of the city, appears to mock the fate of its historical antecedent: the school of languages founded by Egypt's, and the Arab world's, pioneering reformer, Rifā'a Rāfi' al-Ṭahṭāwī in 1836. Acting under Muḥammad 'Alī, al-Ṭahṭāwī founded that school soon after his return from France with the ultimate objective of transforming Egypt, through the assimilation of translated European knowledge, into a modern nation-state. The curriculum of the language and dance "school" in which Ḥamīda "enrolls" after she elopes with the pimp, Faraj, also involves "translation," but hardly of the kind envisaged by Ṭahṭāwī. Although the fictional representation of the modern section is a mere parody of the original, still the novel presents a poignant commentary on the wayward turn the idea of progress and modernization had taken in the interval between Ṭahṭāwī's time and that of the novel's action, during the Second World War.

The overall judgment of traditional space, in contrast, appears less severe for two reasons. First, it is textually confined to the rantings of the Alley's main detractors, Ḥamīda and her foster brother Ḥusayn, neither of whom enjoys much credibility or commands much respect. Their invectives are thoroughly offset by the genuine love that other, more sympathetic characters bear for the place they call home. Second, indigenous space is rendered structurally dependent on the surrounding space so that life in it appears naturally susceptible to the disruptive stimuli originating elsewhere. What perhaps slightly alleviates the pressure of this Manichean duality and tempers somewhat the bleak outlook of the novel is the fact that its action unfolds while Egypt is under foreign occupation and the world is at war. The strict mimetic commitment to circumstantiality observed here enables Mahfouz to confine the negative consequences of the novel's action to these immediate causes and thus to effect a momentary separation between the aberrant conditions of occupation and war, on the one hand, and the general condition of Western culture, on the other. In the overall scheme of things, Mahfouz' steadfast resistance to the formulaic casting of the East/West cultural encounter in the stark terms of a Manichean dichotomy may emerge as one of his major contributions to a genuine critique of modern Arab/Islamic, as well as of Western culture. From this perspective his first published novel of the realistic phase, *al-Qāhira al-Jadīda* (New Cairo, 1945) acquires added significance. The novel's action is set in the late twenties and early thirties, arguably the most liberal period in the modern history of Egypt. Already by then, however, political and moral corruption seem to have become rampant in the life of the country's intelligentsia. What is more, the novel allows for no neat separation of internal and external, "indigenous" and "foreign" space. Given the tendency of Arabic fiction, especially that specializing in the theme of cultural encounter, to inventory identity through metaphoric substitution of cultural with spatial categories, Mahfouz resistance to this tendency amounts to an implicit critique of the discourse of "Otherness" in the Arabic novel. This critique will become only more rigorous and more pronounced in his subsequent fiction when it takes a decidedly inward "psychological" turn in the early 1960s.

ALTERNATIVE SPACES, SAME IDENTITY?

The road to Alexandria

Whatever semblance of solidity space had in Mahfouz' realistic novels of the forties and fifties all but vanishes in the so-called psychological or symbolic novels of later decades. Beginning with *The Thief and the Dogs* in 1961, space acquires an ephemeral quality that is at once a reflection and a source of the uncertainty and anxiety besetting the characters of Mahfouz' novels during this decade. There is perhaps more frantic, but always futile movement from one transient place to another in each of the short novels of this period than in any other earlier work of Mahfouz, including the voluminous *Trilogy*. Nor does anything measure the corrosive malaise and profound ambivalence of Mahfouz' fiction towards the Nasserist experiment better than this phenomenon, which is essentially a function of the deployment of fictional space. Break, rupture, alienation, loss, and despair are the dominant motifs in these works, and they invariably trigger a frenzied chase that is partly a flight, partly a quest. Spatial closures and architectural fixity are methodically shunned in favor of indeterminate, unbounded, transient, and semantically ambiguous spaces such as graveyards, deserts, roads, brothels, *pensions*, jails, cars, and boats. The direction of movement in these novels is predominantly centrifugal: away from the familiar sites of stability and permanence in the heart of Cairo to the uncharted space of the periphery. A temporal flight from the unbearable present often sends the characters of these works scurrying for emotional cover in a more benevolent past. This, and a host of other thematic and structural features—for example, the weather, narrative point of view, and mode of narration—combine with the drastic defamiliarization of space to induce an unsettled and unsettling atmosphere in these works. Part of the general malaise evident here undoubtedly carries a negative judgment on the political dispensation brought about by the Revolution. But to read these complex novels exclusively as political allegories is to miss the equally compelling presence of existential and metaphysical concerns they dramatize. In any event, these themes and concerns are interrelated and readily shade into each other.

The reconceptualization of fictional space coincides with, and abets, the altered thematic interests of Mahfouz' fiction during the short but critical period of Egypt's modern history between 1961 and 1967. Let me illustrate this general observation by discussing briefly three important novels from this phase. By happy coincidence, the novels in question fall chronologically at the beginning, middle, and end of this period. In all three, fictional space plays an active role in promoting the metaphysical and political ambiguity that shrouds the fictional action. The first, *al-Liṣṣ wal-Kilāb*, scans the periphery of metropolitan Cairo, the space at the fringes of familiar streets and alleys of the earlier realistic novels. The second, *al-Ṭarīq* (1964) juxtaposes fleeting images of gentle but uninhabitable Alexandria with harsh images of inhospitable Cairo. The third, *Miramār* (1967) renounces Cairo altogether and embraces Alexandria as a permanent asylum. The following remarks, though brief, may suffice to put these general observations in context.

* * *

The release of Sa'īd Mahrān, the protagonist of *al-Liṣṣ wal-Kilāb* from prison at the beginning of the novel sets in motion a quest that grows more elusive at every turn. (Sa'īd entered prison for theft before the 1952 Revolution, that is, under the monarchy, and came out four years later, on the anniversary of the Revolution. This time frame is crucial because it authorizes the implicit comparison between the two periods and the attendant judgment contained therein.) As he gropes for a safe mooring in the familiar places that grounded his identity before he entered prison Sa'īd discovers that these had in the meantime assumed not only unfamiliar but also downright hostile and enigmatic airs. Sa'īd's search proceeds along a carefully calibrated trajectory that correlates three modes of relationship with three discursive realms of identity. These modes are: the personal, the spiritual, and the ideological, which correspond to the family, religion, and politics respectively. Though bitter and bent on revenge from the outset, Sa'īd nonetheless exhausts all options at every stage of his deadly march to reassemble the disparate parts of his conflicted identity.

Initially, Sa'īd pins his ardent hopes for such an eventuality, and for a new beginning, on his little daughter, Sanā'. But she recoils from him in horror, when he tries to take her in his arms at his erstwhile home, now occupied, like his former wife, by his treacherous underling, 'Alaysh, who had betrayed him to the police four years earlier. When the promise of redemption through blood relations goes awry, Sa'īd turns to religion and visits the abode of a Ṣūfī shaykh, whom his father used to revere and would occasionally take him along, as a child, when visiting the Shaykh. Although shaykh Junayd gives him shelter for the night, he is too absent-minded to heed Sa'īd's pressing needs. Disappointed there as well, Sa'īd turns next to politics and seeks out his erstwhile socialist mentor, the journalist Ra'ūf 'Alwān, who used to sanction, on "philosophical" grounds, Sa'īd's professional thieving. This tangent proves no more viable than the other two. Ra'ūf, it turns out, had in the meantime, and in the name of the Revolution, replaced the very rich against whom he used to inveigh and to incite Sa'īd. He now lives in a sumptuous villa overlooking the Nile and works as a "journalist" in one of the regime's publications. Understandably, the last thing he needs now is a ghost from his past to remind him of his old ideals and former self. Sa'īd's disappointment from the renewed contact with Ra'ūf, coming as it does on the heels of the chilling encounter with his estranged daughter and the enigmatic meeting with the Ṣūfī shaykh, practically seals off his chances of adjusting lawfully to the new order under the Revolution. He decides to take the law into his own hands and to exact a full measure of revenge from all his enemies together.

Significantly, it is through toponomy—itself a function of space—that moral responsibility for the social ills is charged to political authority. Thus, the statement that Ra'ūf speaks with the "frankness of the July sun" (p. 48) alludes sarcastically to both the Revolution, which took place in July, 1952, and to the weekly column of Muḥammad Ḥasanayn Haykal in *al-Ahram* "*bi-ṣarāḥa*" (frankly speaking), which for years represented the thinking of the Free Officers' government, especially Nasser. Similarly, scattered reference to *military ramparts* (p. 69), *army street* and (Nasser's residence at) *manshiyyat al-Bakrī* (p. 81), and *evacuation bridge* (p. 140) are barely shy of spelling out Nasser's regime by name. Sa'īd's donning of officers' uniforms to disguise his identity as a would-be murderer, underlines still further the implicit criticism of the Revolution.

Two interrelated consequences flow from Sa'īd's decision to become a law unto himself. He becomes a fugitive, and his movements underground effect a reversal in some basic values and functions, including that of space. As he pursues his tormentors, the thief is transformed into a hero in the public imagination, even though he clumsily mangles the attempt to kill 'Alaysh and to rob Ra'ūf. With the police fast on his heels, Sa'īd finds a momentary shelter in alternative spaces: the dark back-rooms of a cafe, the house of a prostitute on the border line between a graveyard and the desert, and the desert itself. The generally negative associations that inhere in these spaces, as in prostitution, give way to positive ones in the new equation whereby the thief is a hero, the prostitute is a saint, the government agents are lowly dogs, and the graveyard, the desert, and the cover of darkness aid the "noble" fugitive, at least for the duration of the breathtaking chase. The novel thus carefully orchestrates the implied critique of political corruption with the natural sympathy of the public for the underdog and the craving of popular imagination for mythic heroes. It also paves the way, though only tentatively, for charting alternative spaces to Cairo as the exclusive measure of Egyptian identity in Mahfouz' fiction.

* * *

The quest action of *al-Liṣṣ wal-Kilāb* unfolds along two closely parallel but not quite interchangeable lines: one political, the other metaphysical. In addition to the toponomy discussed earlier, the political allegory finds thematic expression through the alienation of the protagonist (and the other positive characters) from the space they consider home(land), that is currently usurped by opportunistic representatives and agents of the Regime. Where the correspondence between the allegorical layer of the narrative and its referential substratum breaks down, a window opens onto metaphysical realms. The mutually incomprehensible exchange between the Ṣūfī shaykh al-Junayd and Sa'īd Mahrān, for example, occasions such an instance in the novel. This dual thematic interest is bifurcated in Mahfouz' two subsequent novels. Thus *al-Summān wal-Kharīf* (1962; *Autumn Quail*, 1985) pursues the theme of political opportunism and its alienating effects under the Revolution, while *al-Ṭarīq* (1964; *The Search*, 1987) dramatizes the elusive metaphysical quest for certainty in a hybrid plot comprising flight, romance, murder, and imprisonment. What is interesting for our immediate purpose is the fact that the actions of both novels foreground the liminal contrast between the two spaces that vie, in fiction as in history, for representing authentic Egyptian identity: Cairo, a hub of intrigue and the seat of arbitrary political power, and Alexandria, a welcoming safe haven and a cosmopolitan asylum.

In contradistinction from Mahfouz' other major characters, the protagonist of *al-Ṭarīq*, Ṣābir Sayyid al-Raḥīmī, is actually a native of Alexandria. He spends the first three decades of his life happily in the immediate, lavish care of his beautiful mother, a *madam* by profession. The novel begins on the last day of her life when, literally on her deathbed, she reveals to him a profound secret about his father, whom he had assumed to have been dead all along. Now she says otherwise and hands him a thirty-year-old wedding photograph showing her in white gown next to his father, who had disappeared soon after the photograph was taken. Although she had not heard from him since, she convinces Ṣābir that his father is still alive and encourages him to look for him in—where else?—Cairo. With these words, she closes her eyes, never to open them again. Immediately after her funeral, Ṣābir sets out for Cairo, the wedding photograph in hand, and little else.

Toponomy, and naming in general, hold the key to a major thematic strand in the novel. I will note here only the most compelling instance of this connection. The house of Basīma 'Imrān, Ṣābir's mother, in which he grows up in Alexandria is (strategically) located in Nabī Dānyāl (Prophet Daniel) street. Although she leads a life of crime and violence there, both she and Ṣābir, like biblical Daniel in the den of lions, escape unharmed. Alexandrine space acquires additional positive charge, here as in *al-Summān*, from references to streets named after Sa'd Zaghlūl, the revered leader of the Wafd party whom Mahfouz adored. Similarly, the significance of affixing the word "freedom" to nothing other than the name of a grocery store in Cairo, is blatantly transparent. Mindful of the mortal dangers that lurk in wait for him in his mother's absence, Ṣābir wastes no time in fleeing Alexandria in panic immediately after her funeral.

Ostensibly, he heads for Cairo to look for his absent father, Sayyid Sayyid al-Raḥīmī. But, as is readily apparent, this name is hardly common. In English it translates roughly as "Lord, Lord, Merciful." This feature combines with his equally abstract and enigmatic attributes—that is, proverbial physical beauty, fabulous fame and wealth, a roving lifestyle that makes him omnipresent, and a reputation for wielding influence that suggests omnipotence. The resultant composite image of al-Raḥīmī is carefully calibrated to the conceptual gap between a personal and a heavenly father. (The mother's family name, 'Imrān, reinforces the implicit association of the absent father with the invisible God. 'Imrān is the family name of Mary, whose *direct* contact with the divine is limited to the act of conceiving and giving birth to Jesus in the Qur'ān.)

Unbeknown to Ṣābir, however, Cairo had in the meantime assumed a sinister quality in the cosmography of Mahfouz' fiction. As the seat of political power, it stands now for intrigue, treachery, and ultimately murder, hardly the place to house a paternal symbol of mercy. On a less metaphysical plane, Ṣābir is said to have never visited Cairo before the onset of the novel's action, which is highly implausible in a thirty-year-old Egyptian born and raised in Alexandria. But Mahfouz seems willing to stretch to a breaking point the laws of plausibility in order to establish the existential, spiritual, and metaphysical alienation from the space symbolizing political power. Ṣābir not only feels and acts like a stranger in Cairo, he says so, only more poignantly. He tells Ilhām, an innocent girl who falls in love with him, "I'm a complete stranger in your *balad*" (p. 40). If we remember that *balad* can mean both town and country, and combine that with the fact that Egypt's Arabic name, *miṣr* stands for both Cairo and Egypt, we will begin to appreciate the central thematic function of space in the novel. Not surprisingly, therefore, no sooner does Ṣābir arrive in Cairo than he is sucked into a labyrinth, in the form of a *pension*, that leads to murder, and ultimately to prison, where we leave him at the end of the novel awaiting execution. For the first time in Mahfouz' fiction, the interior of a building (the *pension*) is mapped carefully, with minute attention to spatial detail, in preparation for the crime. This turn to interior space coincides in the novels of the 1960s with Mahfouz' thematic preoccupation with perturbed individual psychology, especially as this relates to political discourse and practice. All these motifs and tropes will figure in Mahfouz' most complete Alexandrine novel: *Miramār* (1967).

* * *

Published on the eve of the 1967 Israeli-Arab war, *Miramār* carries these tentative attempts at reconceptualization of space a decisive step forward on several fronts.

Thus, the steadily growing alienation from Cairo reaches its logical end in the permanent move of the octogenarian protagonist, 'Āmir Wajdī, to Alexandria. Here, too, personal characteristics, including character names, are carefully coordinated with thematic, structural, and spatial attributes to produce optimal discursive results. 'Āmir's old age, fragile health, unquestionable patriotism, and personal integrity, make him the "conscience" of the novel. The structural prominence he enjoys by virtue of narrating the first and last chapters of the novel reflects his privileged "moral" status. The middle, uniformly troubled narratives of the other characters, are literally embedded in his own, so to speak, and this narrative strategy contains somewhat the negative fallout of these embedded narratives.

The significance of all this to the question of alienation from the space of political power becomes clear when we realize that 'Āmir did not voluntarily opt to leave Cairo. He was literally pushed out of his job as a journalist by ruthless, opportunistic upstarts who had taken over the field on pretensions of modernist credentials and revolutionary zeal. After a lifelong service in the national cause, shoulder to shoulder with the admired leaders of the Wafd party, he is cast out to fend for himself alone, homeless, childless, a lonely old man. Thus estranged from his beloved native Cairo, 'Āmir heads for Alexandria with a single hope in his heart: to find the only person he knows there, Mariana, the Greek proprietress of the *pension* Miramār. When this wish materializes and he joins her in the *pension* as a permanent tenant, he extends this ardent wish a little further: that Mariana survive him, if only by a single day, lest he die homeless, and with no one to see him to his grave.

Alienation is endemic in *Miramār*, and this fact makes space all the more pertinent. With the exception of the "representative" of the regime, an opportunist by the name of Sarḥān al-Buḥayrī, the rest of the tenants are disaffected Egyptians who flock to the *pension* for psychological and ideological shelter. Frequent allusions to the stormy weather of Alexandria in Autumn makes this a literal as well as a figurative quest. Herein lies the grating incongruity. Mariana, the Greek proprietress of Miramār, is a lone remnant of the once thriving foreign community of onetime cosmopolitan Alexandria. She owns the only space in the novel's landscape where the *bona fide* Egyptian characters can enjoy fleeting moments of freedom from surveillance and political harassment. The irony built into the situation is tangibly poignant. In the postcolonial phase of national independence from foreign rule the only safe haven for a "representative" sample of Egyptians is a distinctly foreign space, *Miramār*. This permutation reverses the treatment of the dichotomy of "indigenous" vs. "foreign" space we encountered earlier in Ḥaqqī's *Qindīl Umm Hāshim*. Unlike Ḥaqqī's novella, the expression of authentic Egyptian identity is possible for the Egyptian tenants of *Miramār* only within this "foreign" enclave in the space of the nation-state. In the wake of this gradual, but irreversible, process of alienation, Cairene space will never again evince the kind of solidity it once had in abundance in Mahfouz' realistic novels. In fact, this evanescence of space is forcefully suggested in Mahfouz' earlier novel, *Thartharah Fawq al-Nīl* (1966), the "action" of which takes place mostly on a boat (*'awwāma*) adrift on the Nile, while the characters are in a state of continuous stupor from hashish and alcohol.

* * *

To suggest, in light of the foregoing analysis, that Mahfouz' treatment of space is largely metaphorical is to understate the case by a wide margin. I use the term metaphorical in a slightly idiosyncratic sense. It does not mean that space is represented by other linguistic tropes, which is always the case anyway, given the temporal nature of narrative, but rather that what is represented there has little, if anything, to do with actual, referential space. In this sense, it is not only fictional, but also fictive or fictitious, that is, imaginary space. It would be unthinkable, for example, to entertain seriously the idea of attaching a map of the actual sections and alleys of Cairo as a guide to Mahfouz' description of them, the way a map of Dublin was affixed to the first printing of James Joyce's *Ulysses*. Thematic and discursive needs, rather than fidelity to actual space, often inform the representation of space in Mahfouz' work. To put the matter in yet another way, space is fully "plotted" here, in the sense that material objects forfeit their innate physical characteristics and specificity in order to signify propitiously in the overall structure of the plot. Here is a fairly typical example from *al-Ṭarīq* describing the interior of the room soon to become a scene of murder.

> She led the way to show him the small flat, going through the hall into a large bedroom, with an adjoining door to a smaller dining room. Except for the toilets, nothing else was there. He glanced at the furniture in the bedroom and it seemed to him that the bed, the sofa, and the Turkish divan had eyes and were staring at him coldly, indifferently. He was about to make known his feelings, but held back for shame, and merely said: The room is gloomy.
>
> (p. 102)

The question of political choice for Egypt always boils down to two equally undesirable alternatives in Mahfouz' fiction: The Muslim Brotherhood or the Communists. So it does in *Miramār* during a conversation between 'Āmir Wajdī and a representative of the defunct Egyptian aristocracy: Ṭulba Marzūq. To 'Āmir's shocked disbelief, Ṭulba demurs at the limitation and adds a third choice: to be ruled by America, from a distance, through "reasonable" Egyptians. As for himself, Ṭulba already has other plans. He intends to join his daughter and her husband in Kuwait. This elliptical allusion to distant alternatives to indigenous space will become dramatically more pronounced in the following decade.

An equally portentous remark during a conversation between 'Āmir and Mariana momentarily suspends the metaphorical view of space in favor of its unsavory reality. To Mariana's complaint about the sudden piling up of trash in the streets of Alexandria, after the departure of the foreign communities, 'Āmir retorts wryly: "it [Alexandria] has reverted to its rightful owners." Profoundly disturbing as it may be on cultural grounds, 'Āmir's incisive observation momentarily suspends the convention of "editing" space for literary representation and registers a hurried recognition of the legitimacy of representing space as it may happen to be. That is precisely what some younger Egyptian writers were already doing as a matter of course.

* * *

What general conclusions can be drawn from the strategies of representing space in Mahfouz' fiction? A couple can perhaps be advanced here, however tentatively.

Formally, space is routinely aestheticized for purposes of the plot in Mahfouz' work. It is often a function of thematic developments and makes little coherent sense outside of these. More imagined than described, fictional space points textually towards the logic of the plot more than it does referentially towards external reality. Mahfouz thus consistently "plots" space out of its physical attributes for emotive and perlocutionary effects in his fiction.

This general strategy supports a more abstract, and far less innocent, semantic equation that may ultimately rest on ideological grounds. In the realistic novels of the 1940s and 1950s, as we have seen, the action is invariably set before the Revolution of 1952. While they critique social conditions severely, the criticism in these novels is evenly diffused among sociological, cultural, and political domains. Individual psychology is pitched there against a rich tapestry of intertwining thematic threads that blend imperceptibly into complex semiotic patterns and formations. The extensive interplay among these domains checks the tendency to predicate general thematic effects on single causes. The agency of the political is thus limited and relativized.

In the novels of the 1960s this elaborate artifice is reduced to skeletal bareness. Not only is the political assigned direct causal agency for the general malaise here, it, in fact, becomes the source of a far more corrosive indictment. In these novels the political regime becomes synonymous with the homeland to such an extent that political alienation literally spells death or exile. It is true that the place of exile is physically still within the "homeland"—the desert and cemetery in *al-Liṣṣ wal-Kilāb*, the *pension* in *Miramār*, and the boat in *Tharthara fawq al-Nīl*—but it is no longer an integral part of it in any sense except, perhaps, negation and disclaimer. There is a spiritual and existential finality to the alienation of characters here that makes unthinkable the prospect of their return to the fold. Whether this drastic shift in the perception of space is entirely the function of political alienation, or whether it is, like political alienation itself, a function of more abstract philosophical and spiritual developments in Mahfouz' personal life, cannot be ascertained. But as is often the case in Mahfouz' fiction, advances on one level of meaning are reinforced by ostensibly unrelated developments and arrangements elsewhere in the text. In *Miramār*, for example, the division of characters into two distinct age-groups reinforces the correlation described earlier.

Thus, the three characters representing the "old guard"— 'Āmir Wajdī, Ṭulba Marzūq, and Mariana—whose political education and psychological formation predate the 1952 Revolution, uphold a code of personal conduct that enables them to maintain correct personal relations and a modicum of human empathy, in spite of their numerous and pronounced ideological and political differences. That touch of grace is sorely missing in the younger group of *Miramār*'s tenants, the (male) generation of the Revolution, all of whom are simultaneously agents and victims of senseless violence.

The sources of this drastic, patently schematic contrast between the pre- and post-Revolution generations cannot be explained fully in terms of political disaffection, however. The convergence of other personal and historical motives may have contributed to coloring the overall picture. The fact that Mahfouz' putatively happy childhood, adolescence, and university experience coincided with the political preeminence of the Wafd party under the leadership of his revered political idols, Sa'd Zaghlūl and Muṣṭafā al-Naḥḥās, during the most liberal period in Egypt's modern history, strongly militates against reducing this overdetermined situation to direct political equivalency; unless, that is, one expands the contours of the political to accommodate materials of what Frederic Jameson called "the political unconscious." Such an expansion has the added advantage of explaining an oft-repeated statement of Mahfouz, namely, that no work of his ever escapes the ubiquitous presence of politics.

Even as Mahfouz was "plotting" space out of its physical attributes, other Egyptian writers were hard at work reclaiming for fictional space that very dimension of physicality. The streets of Cairo; the nooks and crannies of Alexandria; the caves of Upper Egypt; the countryside; the far off stretches of land in the Sinai; the Nubian desert; the Red Sea littoral mountains; and beyond these still, Palestine, Lebanon, and the Gulf region, all these spaces come increasingly within the purview of the Egyptian novel during the 1970s and 1980s. The contrast with Mahfouz' treatment of space could not be more pronounced, though it may not always be intentional. Either way, one profound difference stands out: these isolated, "decentered" fragments of Egyptian space betray no sense of dependence on a center in relation to which they are contingent or "peripheral." The elaborate symbolic economy of binary opposites and somewhat schematic metaphorical substitutions we discerned in Mahfouz' and Ḥaqqī's treatment of space give way to greater fluidity and spontaneity in the deployment of space in the works of younger generations of Egyptian writers. In the following sections I will discuss a number of "representative" novels that illustrate the range and quality of this different attitude to fictional space.

The making, unmaking, and remaking of Alexandria

"Only the city is real," writes Laurence Durrell in a prefatory note to his famous work *The Alexandria Quartet* (1957–1960).[39] All the rest is mere invention. The city in question is, of course, Alexandria. Not so, says Alexandria's best known contemporary native writer, Edwar Al-Kharrat, whose lifelong quest it has been to reclaim in literary form the true image of his beloved native city. Durrell, Al-Kharrat contends, saw only the external facade of Alexandria, and even that primarily through the skewed perspective of the thin crust of foreign diplomats, business men, correspondents, and deracinated individuals adrift at the top of the city's social pyramid.[40] The mansions, flats, offices, and retreats of the lead cast in the novel's drama demarcate the insular space in which they live and move. That space lies wholly in the new, European part of the city. Moreover, it is structurally pitched against the older, far less articulate "Arab" part, which lies outside the novel's purview and remains largely off-limits to its non-Arab characters. True, the main actors in Durrell's drama are helped to their daily routine of sex, intrigue, espionage, and other shady activities by a supporting cast of minor "Arab" characters whose grotesque physical deformities and uncanny personal characteristics serve as a constant reminder of their intrinsic Otherness. Al-Kharrat rightly identifies this as a rehearsal in imaginative fiction of familiar Orientalist views and has his list of examples from the novel to substantiate the claim.[41]

On one crucial point, however, Al-Kharrat is in full agreement with Durrell. That is, the causal agency they both assign the city in shaping the course of human destinies, interpersonal relations, and even personalities. "We are the children of our landscape; it dictates behavior and even thought in the measure to which we are responsive to it," muses the narrator of *Justine* (pp. 39–40). But the direction of this magic influence and the attitude towards it are diametrically opposed in the respective works of the two writers. As has already been intimated, this magic quality of the city is essentially negative, often outrightly sinister in Durrell's novel. The space of the city is immanently haunted and its landscape is eternally marked by the ethnic/cultural divides that punctuate and scar it. So intensely felt is this quality of Alexandrine space by Durrell's characters that the simple act of eating a few Italian olives in solitude at the beach suffices to induce a momentary sensation of rapture in the narrator, transported as he is by an ardent longing to be on the "right side" of the Mediterranean (*Justine*, p. 31). This is quite symptomatic of the general feeling that permeates the novel: What makes Alexandria at all bearable for these characters is precisely the reassuring knowledge that Europe lies at the other shore.

Of the numerous divides that Durrell effects in the physical topography and human landscape of the novel, two in particular seem to bear obsessively on the neurotic lifestyle of the protagonists, especially Justine and the narrator. These are: the division between the Arab and the European sections of the city, and the more pervasive division along the color spectrum between black and white. Here is a fairly typical example of the egregious "representations" of the Arab quarter in the novel.

> I found Melissa, washed up like a half-drowned bird, on the dreary littorals of Alexandria, with her sex broken.... Streets that run back from the docks with their tattered rotten supercargo of houses, breathing into each

> others' mouths, keeling over. Shuttered balconies swarming with rats, and old women whose hair is full of the blood of ticks. Peeling walls leaning drunkenly to east and west of their true center of gravity. The black ribbon of flies attaching itself to the lips and eyes of the children—the moist beads of summer flies everywhere; the very weight of their bodies snapping off ancient flypapers hanging in the violet doors of booths and cafes. The smell of the sweat-lathered Berberinis, like that of some decomposing stair-carpet. And then the street noises: shriek and clang of the water-bearing Saidi, dashing his metal cups together as an advertisement, the unheeded shrieks which pierce the hubbub from time to time, as of some small delicately-organized animal being disemboweled. The sores like ponds—the incubation of human misery of such proportions that one is aghast, and all one's feelings overflow into disgust and terror.
>
> (*Justine*, p. 26)

The relentless amassing of sordid details, and the graphic depiction of filth and ugliness we witness here is intended to do the ideological work of the novelist through the novel. If we remember that space plays a constitutive role in shaping the personality and behavior of the human beings residing therein, it will not be difficult to surmise the outcome predicated on such representations of space. Here is a similar piece of unreconstructed ideological "description" that reeks of execrable racial prejudice.

> The Women of the foreign communities here are more beautiful than elsewhere. Fear, insecurity dominates them. They have the illusion of foundering in the ocean of blackness all around. This city has been built like a dyke to hold back the flood of African darkness; but the soft-footed blacks have already started leaking into the European quarters: a sort of racial osmosis is going on. To be happy one would have to be a Moslem, an Egyptian woman—absorbent, soft, lax, overblown; given to veneers; their waxen skins turn citron-yellow or melon-green in the naphtha-flares. Hard bodies like boxes. Breasts apple-green and hard—a reptilian coldness of the outer flesh with its bony outposts of toes and fingers. Their feelings are buried in the pre-conscious. In love they give out nothing of themselves, having no self to give, but enclose themselves around you in an agonized reflection—an agony of unexpressed yearning that is at the opposite pole from tenderness, pleasure. For centuries now they have been shut in a stall with the oxen, naked, circumcised. Fed in darkness on jams and scented fats they have becomes tuns of pleasure, rolling on paper-white blue-veined legs.
>
> (*Justine*, p. 59)

It is against such gross and wanton trafficking in stock images of his native Alexandria that Al-Kharrat often rails in his critical writings and that he seeks to undo in his fictional works. He finds particularly offensive Durrell's representation of Alexandrine women, the Coptic community of Alexandria, and other Egyptian Christians as habitually persecuted and maligned groups. As we shall presently see, the Alexandria of Al-Kharrat's childhood, adolescence, and early youth—which roughly coincide with the time of the novel's action—bears little resemblance to Durrell's grotesquely violent and garishly exotic city.

But Al-Kharrat's view of fictional space also differs categorically from that of other Egyptian writers, notably Naguib Mahfouz and 'Abd al-Raḥmān al-Sharqāwī. He writes:

> No matter how well-disposed a writer like Mahfouz may be to the alleys and streets of al-Jamāliyya, (the quarter in which Mahfouz was born and grew up) or a writer like 'Abd al-Raḥmān al-Sharqāwī and other novelists of rural Egypt to their villages, the city—like the land—serves primarily as a background decor for them. At best, it serves as a subject or a stage for the novel's action.[42]

In marked contrast to all, Alexandria for Al-Kharrat is

> not only a beautiful geographic location, and a place of meeting and confrontation between people who work, love, and die in the course of daily life; nor is it merely a storehouse of deep-seated ancient and modern cultures and civilizations. It is all that, to be sure. But it is also a condition of the soul, a quest adventure to grasp an inner truth, in addition to being a metaphysical encounter with the obscurity of the abstract and death, stretching over a now placid now tumultuous surface of the sea, towards an enigmatic, limitless horizon.[43]

Such hymns to Alexandria reverberate through all the works of Al-Kharrat, but with special resonance and poignancy in the three "novels" that refer or allude to the city in their title. In order of publication, these are: *Turābuhā Za'farān* (1986; *City of Saffron*, 1989), *Yā Banāt Iskandariyya* (1991; *Girls of Alexandria*, 1993), and *Iskandariyyatī* (1994; *My Alexandria*). Though their characters and events are sufficiently interrelated and overlapping to suggest a single *roman fleuve*, the three can also be loosely considered a fictional autobiography. Al-Kharrat himself prefers to identify them, like his other works, by less common nomenclature. Thus, while the cover jacket dubs *Yā Banāt Iskandariyya* a novel (*riwāya*), the subtitle of *Turābuhā Za'farān* is *Nuṣūṣ Iskandarāniyya* (Alexandrine Texts), and that of *Iskandariyyatī* is *kulāj riwā'ī* (a novelistic collage). This concern with formal designation is vitally relevant to the treatment of space in Al-Kharrat's work and to his views on the art of fiction in general. Perhaps more than any other Arab writer he has been systematically cultivating a "theory" of writing that blurs generic distinctions and differentiations by combining in the same text features and tropes from different artistic media, different modes and styles, and different genres.[44] Al Kharrat calls this mode of writing "trans-generic" (*al-kitāba al-'abr naw'iyya*) and ascribes to its practitioners "a new sensibility" (*ḥasāsiyya jadīda*) that distinguishes them from the older, more formally orthodox and genre-bound novelists.[45]

But how, in concrete terms, does this fabulously real Alexandria of Al-Kharrat, if an oxymoron be momentarily allowed, how does it figure in his peculiar brand of poetics of space? And how does it participate, through this aesthetic elaboration, in the ongoing cultural/political debate about identity in Egypt?

To begin with, what marks Al-Kharrat's use of fictional space is the unmistakable quality of lived experience that always animates it. In large measure, this is a direct consequence of the predominantly autobiographical mode that characterizes much of Al-Kharrat's writing. A typical narrative situation thus comprises the following elements: an actual place in Alexandria, a powerful sensation, or rather the kernel thereof, originating in childhood or youth, that remains stored in memory, fluid and inchoate, for eventual transmutation into literary form, and retrieval in different textual versions, much later in the writer's adult life.[46] This intimate association of space with personal experience and memory, especially those of childhood, often imbues it with vivid, pulsating immediacy. But it is first and foremost the availability of remembered, not imagined or contrived, space that makes the retrieval of the Proustian sensation embedded therein possible. Whether the experience itself is actual or virtual is quite immaterial to this narrative dynamic. Far more relevant is the fact that the more intense the desire to recapture that original experience, the more vividly is the space adumbrated.

By far the most intense experiences in the works of Al-Kharrat are those associated with the early stirrings of sexuality in childhood and with political consciousness and activism a little later in youth and early adulthood. Given the perennially charged subject matter of both, it is not surprising that a note of mystery and magic inheres in the depiction of the space in which either germinates or materializes. While Magda al-Nowaihi notes the dominant role of open spaces, especially the sea and the sky, in several of Al-Kharrat's works, and relates these thematically to the quest for love as a means to beguile death and nothingness in such works as *Turābuhā Za'farān*,[47] I discern a different, though not necessarily incompatible key pattern at work. This pattern yokes certain fundamental spatial forms to intensely felt sensations, of distinctly erotic nature, on the one hand, and to memories of social cohesion and harmony within the shared space of a pluralistic, multiethnic, cosmopolitan Alexandria, on the other hand. Let me elaborate.

Statistically, architectural and structural apertures, such as entrances, doors, thresholds, windows, staircases, and balconies, figure perhaps more prominently than any other spatial outline in Al-Kharrat's work. Of these, tenebrous staircases, dim, gaping entrances, and doors slightly ajar, top the list in both frequency of appearance and intensity of the psychological sensation they evoke in the protagonist child, Mikhā'īl.[48] There is compelling evidence to suggest that the psychological import accrues to this spatial feature from its affective association, in Mikhā'īl's febrile imagination, with the erotic cleavage in the female body, both high and low. Whether the implicit association is genuine, that is, authentic to Mikhā'īl's childhood experience, or a learned, retrospective interpolation by the author, cannot be ascertained. Its presence and effects, however, are beyond doubt. The following few examples may suffice to suggest both its ubiquity and potency. The first describes a recurrent experience during Mikhā'īl's elementary school years, and it occurs at the very beginning of *Yā Banāt Iskandariyya*.

> As if I am entering through the narrow door, straight to the dark, stone stair-case, in the house in Jullanār Alley.
>
> And it is as if I sense Mona, brimming with life, there, behind the door, in the ground floor apartment, to the right.
>
> Before the vacation, on my way home from school, her door would always open just as I would reach the foot of the stairs. In that narrow ground-space her face would light up to me, suddenly, in the fleeting moment between the retreat of the afternoon and the tenebrous, slightly dank entrance.
>
> Her dress shies short of her knees as it flows over her rounded thighs, and I sense her small breasts, free, firm, erect. She raises her face to me, at once bashful and daring, and looks at me with her slightly swollen, aslant eyes. My heart would tremble at her gaze, the meaning of which I never knew.
>
> (p. 9)

On the following page, the source of this erotic sensation in Mona's body is pinpointed even more precisely.

> She had changed (her clothes). The top of her summer, home dress, that reveals her slender legs, is wet, and clings to her chest, defining the position of her small breasts as they lie firm under the wet garment. I was unable to turn my eyes from the depth of the desired darkness between her legs, which appeared more limpid and more sumptuous in the enveloping darkness.
>
> (p. 10)

Similar descriptions, marked primarily by poetic and stylistic, not thematic variations, record Mikhā'īl's uniformly erotic response to the various female characters of his childhood and adolescence. Here is how one, Madonna Gabriel, is described.

> Her body is a temple. Her legs two strong, polished pillars, capped by the hidden, treasured crown. A baptismal basin. A fountain of living water whereof I drink, never to thirst again.
>
> (p. 64)

To switch momentarily to *Turābuhā Za'farān*, we will readily note how the same downstairs space, now occupied by an entirely different woman, nonetheless induces an identical erotic sensation in the boy, Mikhā'īl. Thus, the opening scene of that work may sound familiar: "The windows of the lower flat were always shut, while the door, as I often noticed when returning from school, would be slightly ajar, and I would glimpse Ḥusniyya behind it." Like all the rest, Ḥusniyya, the prostitute, will go on to tantalize the imagination of the impressionable Mikhā'īl with the familiar seductive poses, revealing as much as they hide before his craving eyes (p. 13). But beyond this familiar trope, she stands out as one of the most memorable characters in Al-Kharrat's entire work.

Other female characters fulfill a similar function in *Turābuhā Za'farān*, regardless of age, relation to Mikhā'īl, and other such incidentals. Thus, the "dark, smooth, ample breasts" of madam Wahība, the family neighbor and friend of his mother, register in his consciousness as keenly as does the touch of "the heavy, firm, breasts" of his spinster cousin Olga (pp. 16 and 33 respectively). Nor is the pull of this fascination limited to real women. The silhouette of a female figure on the cover of a book (p. 76), or the poster of an actress on the billboard of a theater evoke an identical response in him (*Yā Banāt Iskandariyya*, p. 60).

If this fascination with the cleavage of the female body appears indiscriminate, the reason is not far to seek. It is, in fact, indiscriminate to the point of being emotionally promiscuous. In Mikhā'īl's libidinal forage, one girl of Alexandria is as good as another, and, collectively, they are altogether interchangeable. Al-Kharrat himself is perfectly aware of the dynamics of this obsession and tries to "theorize" it into a general principle. As it happens, the generalization seems to describe the symptoms more than it explains the underlying causes of the phenomenon. Simultaneously singular and multiple, unique and universal, one and many, the girls of Al-Kharrat's Alexandria are at once palpably corporeal and elusively ephemeral, touchingly human in their suffering and unearthly in their beauty and Keatsian agelessness.[49] In such laudatory, though enigmatic terms does Al-Kharrat describe the girls of Alexandria in a prefatory note to the text.

But what is the critic to make of all this, especially if one keeps in mind the companion trope of liminal, tenebrous space within which the erotic motif often unfolds, and the broader interest in the nexus of national space? To view the matter in psychological terms is to raise the possibility of an arrested sexual development. Satisfying, mature sexual relations are conspicuously absent from Mikhā'īl's adult life. "Nothing new has come my way since the onset of youth, nothing save the reassertion of that which is too certain to require reaffirmation," muses the adult narrator of *Yā Banāt Iskandariyya* in evident disillusionment. Al-Kharrat addresses this complex issue directly in *Turābuhā Za'farān*. The occasion of this rare authorial intrusion is the erotic attraction to the neighbor, Madam Wahība, who is roughly the age of Mikhā'īl's mother. The potential explanatory power of this association is deflected by the injection of the religious factor into the equation. Unlike Mikhā'īl and his Coptic family, Madam Wahība and her husband, Ḥusayn Effendi, are Muslims. Here is how the adult narrator meditates on the iterative practice of entering Wahība's house, ostensibly to borrow books from a chest there. The rest of the episode, left untranslated here, strongly suggests that Mikhā'īl's entrance interrupted a scene of lovemaking between the couple, and excited him sexually. As Wahība opens the door for him, still disheveled, he relates, "I would hurry in, embarrassed and aroused" (*mustathār*). He continues

> Sometimes she would let me enter the house alone to search through the chest and take my pick. She would stand behind me in her light night-gown, plump, feminine, full-bosomed; her breasts dark-brown and smooth, as I would espy them through the gap of the gown, above me, swaying staidly, confidently.
>
> Entering their house always struck awe in my heart. It was at once exciting, terrifying, and happy, a sensation akin to illicit pleasure, to be privy to the secret atmosphere of their house.... Moreover, since they were Muslims, an added element of mystery, awe, and alluring secretiveness always hang in the air.... To this day, entering the flats of strangers inspires awe in me, as if I step into a foreign world that warns, invites, and repels me by the danger it harbors.
>
> (p. 16)

Erotically charged foci like the above punctuate Mikhā'īl's childhood memories and proliferate in the narrative. In the text these foci are strategically placed to anchor his movements as he crisscrosses the streets and alleys of Alexandria from one end to the other: going to, and coming home from, school; visiting relatives on holidays; going to the beach with family and friends; and moving with his family from one modest section of the city to a poorer one as the family's economic status steadily declined. In the process of retracing Mikhā'īl's movements, Alexandria itself comes alive in its most intimate physical details, inscrutable charm, and boundless diversity: a city unified yet manifold, cohesive but varied, and as intimate as it is inaccessible. This, at any rate, is the dominant image of Alexandria as it is reconstructed by the adult narrator from Mikhā'īl's earliest memories, sensations, and impressions. But it is not the only Alexandria in Al-Kharrat's narrative. Lurking below the surface of the idyllic image is a far less benign city whose harshness we barely glimpse because it is systematically kept in check in the narrative. The scene described here shows how these emotional and psychological crosscurrents coincide in one and the same narrative situation.

There is a subtle but crucial shift in the temporal scheme of the above scene. The time of the iterative event is Mikhā'īl's childhood, while that of narrating it is the narrator's adulthood, much later in life. The sudden eruption of the awareness of religious difference into Mikhā'īl's private erotic space is identified retrospectively as the cause of a permanent psychological inhibition in the adult narrator. In other words, it is experienced by the adult narrator at a vastly different emotional register, one perhaps more keenly aware of, and pained by, the social and sectarian strife besetting Egyptian society and body politic at the time of writing, in the waning years of the twentieth century. Mikhā'īl the child, by contrast, experiences the social space of Alexandria through his private, interpolated, microcosmic version of it. At the core of that private microcosm, as we have seen, the formative experience and conceptualization of space invariably implicate the erotic, or, more precisely, the libidinal. The qualification may be apt because it is at the libidinal level of erotic or sexual play that the objects of desire are so readily interchangeable. The phenomenon that Al-Kharrat recognizes in Mikhā'īl's voyeuristic, promiscuous imagination, and strives to generalize into a principle—whereby all the girls of Alexandria blend into a single "archetypal" female—can perhaps be adequately broached in psychosexual terms. For it is a mark of the blind libido that its playing field is perfectly even.

From another angle, however, it is possible to read this obsessive craving for "all the girls of Alexandria collectively and for each of them individually" as a political metaphor. In this sense, it would be the equivalent of Tawfīq al-Ḥakīm's ardent longing for the "adored" leader who would unite all Egyptians in his person. In other words, the familiar political slogan "all in one, and one in all" seems to be transposed here into the erotic domain. In "DissemiNation" Homi Bhabha assigns the "languages of literary criticism" a similar political function. He writes: "*Out of many one*: nowhere has this founding dictum of the political society of the modern nation—its spatial expression of a unitary people—found a more intriguing *image* of itself than in those diverse languages of literary criticism that seek to portray the greater power of the idea of the nation in the disclosures of its everyday life; in the telling details that emerge as metaphors for national life."[50] What encourages the political reading of Al-Kharrat's erotic metaphor is precisely the haunted awareness in the texts of the presence of agonistic forces that militate against the representation of both the erotic and the political.

Two instances in these Alexandrine texts of Al-Kharrat gesture towards the other, potentially repugnant Alexandria, against which these texts are consciously set. The first concerns a fleeting but memorable adolescent "love affair" with a Muslim girl whose name Mikhā'īl does not even know, but calls her Susu, though he is certain that that is not her real name. What matters however is not her name, but his. In the midst of an exquisitely tender and romantic scene on the beach she asks for his name. He tells her, and the recognizably Coptic name lands on her like a thunderbolt. She maintains her composure for the rest of the outing, but they part without a single word. Although he "loves" her enough to retain in memory a moving portrait of her until the time of writing, the two never meet again after that beach episode (*Yā Banāt Iskandariyya*, p. 38).

The other episode involves Mikhā'īl's initiation into "revolutionary" politics. He is lured by a fellow Copt named Iskandar 'Awaḍ one day to a dim, underground bar, ostensibly to meet with fellow revolutionaries to plot against the Egyptian monarchy. In point of fact, his "friend," turns out to be a plant of the secret police engaged in laying traps to would-be conspirators and revolutionaries. Mikhā'īl is miraculously saved in the nick of time by a kindhearted prostitute who takes a liking to him, mixed with pity, and forcibly whisks him out of the bar, with a kiss on the cheek, just before the secret police arrive (*Turābuhā Za'farān*, pp. 36–41). Although she remains nameless, this prostitute appears as a reincarnation of Ḥusniyya from Mikhā'īl's childhood. What may be even more instructive about this episode is the narrative value accorded to it. Measured in terms of textual space and fullness of narrative, this failed trap receives far greater attention than does Mikhā'īl's subsequent arrest and imprisonment. The latter is related in a stark, impersonal, matter-of-fact fashion, solely as a marker of chronology: "Before I was arrested on May 15, 1948, I had rented, under an alias, a room on the top floor of a four-story building, on a side street that splits from Muḥarram Bey Street" (*Iskandariyyatī*, p. 208).

A closer scrutiny may reveal a causal relation between Al-Kharrat's disenchantment with, and subsequent repudiation of direct political activism, and his tremendous literary investment in reinscribing the image of the Alexandria of his childhood in fiction. To gauge the full political and ideological significance of Al-Kharrat's seemingly obsessive return to the Alexandrine chronotope in these novels it is necessary to disclose the implicit, agonistic relation between the time of writing—the 1980s and 1990s—on the one hand, and the time of the narrative's action—the 1930s and 1940s—on the other. Such juxtaposition of the diegetic with the historical time schemes might show how the autobiographical subject matter joins forces with the author's lyrical conception of space to do ideological battle against the politics of sectarian and confessional strife into which Egypt was precipitously sliding during the decades of the 1970s and 1980s.

It is against this ominous historical backdrop that Al-Kharrat's imaginative reinscription of an inherently pluralistic, multiethnic, multilingual, and cosmopolitan Alexandria is mounted. The autobiographical thrust inevitably foregrounds the Coptic milieu in which Mikhā'īl grew up. Coptic proper names, holidays, rituals, cuisine, forms of personal address and greeting, terms of endearment and fervent supplication, with recognizably Christian ring, proliferate in the narrative. What is more, these appear perfectly natural in the context. Within that irreducibly hybrid space the Christian "Our Father That Is In Heaven" mingles freely with the Qur'ānic verse of the Throne (*Yā Banāt*, p. 171). Similarly, nationalist and patriotic fervor unites all, Muslims, Christians, and Jews in the love of the homeland and the desire to see it free and independent of British rule (*Yā Banāt*, pp. 162–163). In retrospect, the mere revisiting of that long since vanished Alexandria endows the fictional narrative with political agency. What appears innocently nostalgic within the text is unmistakably utopian in the larger historical context. This is more or less on the level of the political unconscious.

But Al-Kharrat also appears painfully aware of the irrevocable changes wrought by the passage of time on his beloved Alexandria. Interspersed with the sentimental recollection of Mikhā'īl's childhood experiences are haunted reminders of pending loss. The fullness and naturalness of Coptic life that is fondly celebrated on one level is problematized and challenged on another. The episode I cited earlier in which Mikhā'īl's Coptic name stifles a nascent love relationship with a Muslim girl occasions such a moment of agonized soul-searching in the adult narrator. Here is the pertinent part of that scene again.

> She turned to me and, for the first time, asked about my name. I told her, in the roofed balcony of the cabin, where the sound carries an echo. The effect of the characteristically Coptic name was strange, even to my own ears, and unwarranted, as it has always been throughout my life. *Is my very existence likewise unwarranted, in another context?*
>
> (*Yā Banāt*, p. 38) [emphasis added]

A similar note of dissonance issues from the mention of the fact that during Mikhā'īl's youth the Arabic department at the university did not admit Coptic students (*Yā Banāt*, p. 27). For this reason, as well as his father's wish, the gifted, literary-minded Mikhā'īl had to endure training as an engineering student and to spend several years of his early adulthood sidling his real calling as a writer. We glimpse in the slogans raised during mass demonstrations for Egypt's independence from Britain in Mikhā'īl's youth a proleptic manifestation of the abiding tension between the two rival agendas of Egypt's discourse of national liberation. In the same demonstration Mikhā'īl's consciousness would register both inclusive patriotic slogans such as "we are all ready to die so Egypt may live free" and more exclusive, specifically Islamic slogan such as "The Qur'ān is our constitution, and the Prophet our leader" (*Yā Banāt*, p. 96). If slogans of the first variety gesture towards what Eric Hobsbawm and Terence Ranger call "the invention of tradition," slogans of the second variety gesture in the opposite direction. The tradition being invented in this case is that of secular nationalism and all-encompassing patriotism. It posits independent Egypt as the nation-state of all its citizens, regardless of religious affiliation. In contradistinction, slogans of the second variety seek to assert Egypt's Islamic identity and to incorporate (or reincorporate) it into the larger Islamic community, if not geographically, at least politically and culturally.

By way of concluding this section, a composite picture can be drawn to tie together several key strands in the foregoing discussion. To the extent that the identity of the narrator, presumably the adult Mikhā'īl, can be collapsed into that of the author, Edwar Al-Kharrat, a three-fold alienation from the nourishing sources of identity in the Alexandrine milieu of Mikhā'īl's childhood becomes apparent. The first is strictly spatial and involves the writer's permanent move from his native Alexandria to Cairo in the early 1950s. The second is temporal and involves the steady receding of childhood into an ever more distant past. The third is existential/political in nature. It relates the subjective anxieties of the adult narrator/author to the objective disintegration of the delicate mosaic of Egyptian society and its drift towards sectarian and ethnic strife in the postcolonial phase of national independence. The driving psychological force behind the obsessive return of the composite persona of the author/narrator to the sites of childhood and adolescence in Alexandria is the inconclusive rites of passage represented by Mikhā'īl's irresistible attraction to, and fear of, liminal spaces, where crossing a threshold spells trespassing. These enigmatic border spaces appear in the text as synthetic apertures designating now architectural entrances and openings, now erotic zones of feminine cleavage. While Cairo, and the rest of Egypt, remain conspicuous by their complete absence from the narrative, old Alexandria emerges, or rather *re*emerges, simultaneously as the object of gripping nostalgia, a utopian, multiethnic, and multilingual space, a veritable metaphor for an alternative vision of the homeland called Egypt.

* * *

A similar concern for Christian–Muslim relations in the Egyptian body politic informs the view of another novel of Alexandria: *Lā Aḥad Yanām fil-Iskandariyya* (1996; *No One Sleeps In Alexandria*, 1999) by Ibrahim Abdel Meguid (Ibrāhīm 'Abd al-Majīd). Like Edwar Al-Kharrat, Abdel Meguid is a native of Alexandria, and, also like him, he left his native city for permanent residence in Cairo at the outset of his novelistic career. But unlike Al-Kharrat, Abdel Meguid is a Muslim. As it happens, this biographical fact can hardly be deduced from the thoroughly ecumenical thrust of his work. So determined is Abdel Meguid to assert the viability of Egyptian national unity across religious and ethnic divides that the novel occasionally risks lapsing into programmatic tendentiousness. What ultimately saves it from this untoward fate is the structural constraint that prevents all fictional characters, however minimally realized, from turning into outright authorial mouthpieces or disembodied voices.

Central to this nexus of artistic/discursive complications, as we shall see shortly, is the relation of the time of writing, the early 1990s, to that of the novel's action, the first years of the Second World War. At the onset of the war, but quite unrelated to it, a young Muslim couple are forced out of their village as a result of a blood feud that decimates the ranks of both rival families. To put an end to the bloodshed, Shaykh Majd al-Dīn, a devout, learned Muslim of fine personal qualities, takes his wife and infant daughter and moves to Alexandria, leaving his beloved land and village behind. In Alexandria, he joins a younger brother who had been the unwitting source of extraordinary occurrences that border on the occult and the mystical. A halo of light is said to have formed around him at birth and fastens to him for the rest of his life. With this supernatural endowment comes a magic power that casts a spell on every woman who lays eyes on him. Like this brother, Shaykh Majd and his immediate family find shelter in Alexandria with a Christian family who rent out rooms in their flat to make ends meet.

The physical proximity of shared space thus brings these rural Muslims into a sustained, face to face contact with their Christian compatriots for the first time in their life. This motivation of the plot defamiliarizes both groups, but especially the Christians, about whose religious and social practices the rural Muslims appear to have had little prior knowledge. As the raging war draws ever closer to Alexandria, it throws into disarray the already precarious lives of the characters, Muslims and Christians alike, and makes them scurry into each other's embrace for emotional cover. But even this ephemeral solace is available only figuratively. For, in reality, the movement of the plot is centrifugal in direction and continuously hurls the characters farther away from the city in which they had hoped to find a safe haven from their multiple anxieties.

Two major lines of the plot carry the bifurcated action of the novel in two opposite directions away from Alexandria. The first takes Shaykh Majd and his Christian coworker, Dimyān, to the Egyptian–Libyan border in the Western desert, where German and Allied armies were posed to fight some of the fiercest battles in the history of warfare. The two spend the rest of the time in a largely deserted outpost manning a railroad crossing that is seldom used. The second thrust involves a love affair between a Christian girl and a Muslim boy that impels them both to leave Alexandria: the former to a convent in upper Egypt, the latter to nomadic wandering.

This constant movement and relocation of the main characters conspires with the general frenzy of the war to deny space all semblance of solidity and permanence. Spatial diffusion, in turn, rends further the delicate social fabric of the nascent community, which the characters try to build in Alexandria, just as it tests the very limits of human endurance. Practically all the families in the novel are torn asunder, either by the war or by the impossible love affair between (Muslim) Rushdi and (Christian) Camelia. And yet, the movement of the characters, whether in flight or on the march, demarcates the geographic/political boundaries of the homeland and defines the relation of its parts to each other.

From the numerous, deep-seated tensions among various segments of the Egyptian national mosaic, as represented in the novel, the idea of national unity, like that of a cohesive, well-defined homeland, appears remote indeed. I have already mentioned the blood feud that drives Shaykh Majd and his immediate family out of their village and into exile in Alexandria. His younger brother, Bahiyy, who had preceded him along that same path, is finally killed in Alexandria in a feud of a different kind, one between migrant peasants (*fallāḥīn*), and fellow-Egyptians from Upper Egypt (ṣa'āyda), as these two groups vie for turf in Alexandria. References also abound to divisions between *fallāḥīn* and *badw* (bedouins), *qiblī* and *baḥrī* (Southerners and Northerners), *rīf* and *bandar* (rural and urban), and so on.

Into this colorful human array Abdel Meguid drags yet another factor that complicates still further the idea of the Egyptian homeland. Among the many different troops that the British Command ferries to Egypt to defend "the great homeland, stretching from New Zealand to India" (p. 127) are two Sudanese soldiers, one of whom is temporarily stationed with the Egyptians Majd and Dimyān. When this soldier tells his Egyptian interlocutors that "the Sudan must gain its independence from Egypt after the war" (p. 339) the Egyptians assume that he made a mistake and try to correct him. "You mean independence from Britain?," rejoins Majd. "From both, Shaykh Majd," he insists pointedly. (As we remember, at least until 1948, the noted historian 'Abd al-Raḥmān al-Rāfi'ī, like many Egyptians, considered the Sudan "an integral part of the Egyptian homeland.")[51] Allusions to Jewish platoons in the British army receiving warm welcome from the Jewish community of Alexandria as they pass through the city on their way to, or from, the front, hint at the unfolding Zionist designs on Palestine, and at the potential alienation of Alexandria's Jewish community from their city (and country) on account of their sympathy with Zionist plans and aspirations.

By far the most corrosive division in the novel, however, is that between Muslims and Copts. And it is to this deep wound in the national body and psyche that the novel devotes greatest attention and narrative space. As noted earlier, this antagonism (re)surfaced during the reign of President Sadat (1970–1981), largely as a result of his devious sectarian policies. By the time of writing in the early 1990s, these policies had taken on a life of their own and were engulfing Egypt in a cataclysmic spiral of sectarian violence quite unprecedented in scope and intensity in the country's modern history. Only at the time of the French expedition to Egypt (1798–1801), and largely as a result of deliberate colonial policies, does one find a similar eruption of sectarian violence on such a scale.[52]

The novel addresses this grave issue on two simultaneous levels: individual human consciousness, and scriptural intertextuality. Because it carries the latter far beyond the usual invocation and incorporation of religious themes and motifs in the narrative, I will discuss it more fully in Chapter 3. Here let me only note that recognition of the legitimacy of religious difference entails further logical consequences that, if allowed to run their course, are apt to bring fictional choices in the text into collision with the law of the (home)land outside it. The specific context in which this potential conflict arises in the novel is that of mixed marriage between Muslims and non-Muslims in Egypt. Since, in such cases, Islamic law permits conversion only from other religions to Islam, the implicit inequality carries profound doctrinal and theological implications for followers of other religions. As we shall see, the novel's originality on this score lies in the drastic measure it proposes to extricate the image of the homeland, represented by the image of a multiethnic, pluralistic Alexandria, from this impasse.

Meantime, the thorough fragmentation of space we noted earlier, and the attendant disintegration of human communities brought about by the combined force of traditional local antagonisms and world war, necessitate a shift of emphasis from the spatial/geographic to the human element in the compound nation-state. Intimate personal friendships and tender love relations emerge as the only viable substitutes for the atrophied civil, political, and geographic motives of unity. In other words, the novel predicates the prospects of national unity and cohesiveness in Alexandria (as Egypt) on intrinsic personal rectitude and individual decision. In this register, the nation does indeed become an ongoing "daily plebiscite," in

Renan's terms—only here the plebiscite goes exclusively through the prism of interpersonal relations. Until the realization of this utopian project, however,

> the streets of Alexandria (which uniformly bear the names of flowers) are worn out, debilitated, and crowded with tired, homeless people. No one realizes that these people belong to the big city, where everything is in (constant) motion, except this place. Those who live in this place do not belong to Alexandria at all. White, cheerful, excited Alexandria is completely oblivious to them. They are refuse cast in it by distant towns and villages. And who ever pauses to take note of refuse?
>
> (p. 256)

Beyond Cairo and Alexandria: can the periphery speak?

"Every year [at Muslim and Christian feasts] before the war," muses the narrator of *Lā Aḥad Yanām fil-Iskandariyya*, "the lights would go as far as Raghib and the Rail Way Station, that is, the Kawm al-Dikkah Station, which the Alexanderines renamed 'Maṣr Station' because they cannot imagine the existence of other cities outside Alexandria, save Cairo, which is Maṣr" (p. 265). For the city folks of *Lā Aḥad Yanām* the two cities, Cairo and Alexandria, not only dominate but practically exhaust the Egyptian landscape. Whatever lies off, or beyond, this axis perforce lies outside the realms of meaning and significance in this imagining of the national homeland. On the face of it, this intimation runs counter to a widespread view about the centrality of rural Egypt, represented by the potent trope of the land, and the peasantry (*fallāḥīn*) living on and cultivating that land in the symbolic economy of representing Egypt. During the first four decades of the twentieth century the *fallāḥ* was valorized in the Egyptian political, ideological, and imaginative narratives of nationhood as the carrier and custodian of quintessential Egyptianness. In his biography of Sa'd Zaghlūl, for example, Al-'Aqqād singles out the leader's descent from peasant stock as the major source of his strength of character, personal virtues, and popular appeal.[53] Somehow, though, neither the chronological primacy of Haykal's *Zaynab* (1914), with its lavish romanticization of the countryside, nor the blatantly ideological valorization of the *fallāḥ* in such hugely influential works as al-Ḥakīm's *'Awdat al-Rūḥ* (1933; Return of the Spirit), proved sufficient to sustain novelistic interest in rural Egypt and peasant life as representatives of Egyptian identity. The onset of the realistic phase in Egyptian fiction in the immediate aftermath of the Second World War also occasioned a drastic spatial and thematic shift from rural to urban space and modes of experience. Nowhere is this shift more evident than in the works of Mahfouz: It is only when peasants migrate to the city that he takes note of them, as is the case with *Zohra* in *Miramar*, and even then, only provisionally. Until she is duly civilized (read:urbanized), *Zohra* is to be seen (and perhaps also molested), but not heard. Because of this intrinsic bias it is always hazardous to view things

Egyptian, including space, primarily through Mahfouz' representations, tempting as that may be, given his towering presence.

Similarly, to call the rest of Egypt outside of Cairo and Alexandria periphery is to acknowledge the novel's complicity with the prevalent discursive bias in favor of metropolitan space. As we have seen, factors of autobiography and personal taste figure in this valuation, but its onus lies primarily with the novel's generic predisposition to complex social structures and to the kinds of intricate, unpredictable, interpersonal experiences that they engender. The theoretical assumption behind this generalization is that only in such urban settings can a modicum of privacy, secrecy, and anonymity obtain to enable fictional characters in the process of formation to improvise their individual selves in uncharted moral and social terrains.[54] For better or for worse, it is the city, as the space of moral and ethical wilderness, that has given modern Arabic literature its most memorable fictional characters to date.[55]

To return briefly to the question raised by the simple folks of Alexandria about the relation of the Egyptian countryside to the dominant axis Cairo–Alexandria, we may note a curious coincidence between *Lā Aḥad Yanām* and an earlier novel that is centrally, though not exclusively linked to Alexandria. The novel in question is *al-'Awda ilā al-Manfā* (1968; Back to Exile) by Abū al-Ma'āṭī Abū al-Najā. As if by design, the events of this novel, set over half a century before those of *Lā Aḥad Yanām*, nevertheless anticipate them to an astonishing degree. Thematically, *al-'Awda ilā al-Manfā* recasts in fictional form the dramatic life of 'Abdullāh al-Nadīm, the native prodigy of Alexandria who rose by sheer wit and personal tenacity from downtrodden existence to national prominence during the 'Urābī uprising of 1881–1882. The son of a destitute baker, the gifted Nadīm honed his survival skills in the streets and cafes of Alexandria and the neighboring towns before he moved to Cairo in the early 1870s. Once there, he instantly joined the small circle of the legendary Jamāl al-Dīn al-Afghānī, under whose coaching the restless creative energy of al-Nadīm was channelled in a revolutionary direction. What is particularly striking about this turn of events is the manner in which al-Nadīm "translated" al-Afghānī's revolutionary teaching into programmatic action. In a rare reversal of what becomes the dominant paradigm, al-Nadīm leaves Cairo and returns to Alexandria. From his native city, and with little more than his visionary zeal and infinite resourcefulness, he goes about setting up makeshift schools and cooperatives, which also double as theaters and hubs of political agitation, all over Alexandria and the surrounding towns of the countryside. Through his frantic, incessant physical movement among these different loci in the service of a nationalist idea, and a patriotic project, al-Nadīm connects the disparate parts of the national homeland into a recognizable whole, perhaps for the first time in the history of modern Egypt.

This dynamic process of unification is further aided by al-Nadīm's equally original journalistic activity. Through a succession of newspapers that he single-handedly edits and launches, using a rare mixture of vernacular and literary Arabic, and writing in a simple, straightforward style, he manages to disseminate in ever wider circles of readers the idea of patriotism for an enlightened, multi-religious homeland governed by a constitutional government. Rarely, it seems, did the paramount role Benedict Anderson assigns print journalism and the vernacular in abetting the will of an imagined community to modern nationhood been more strikingly evident than it is here. Admittedly, al-Nadīm's frequent speaking tours in the provinces, his proverbial eloquence, and personal charm, did much to bolster the views he was expressing in print. For this rare combination of gifts al-Nadīm will go on to become the official "speaker of the ('Urābī) Revolt," and, for posterity, also "the champion of patriotism," and "the orator of the East." It is in this multiple capacity that he becomes the mentor of Muṣṭafā Kāmil and future generations of Egyptian patriots. The pronounced streak of religious tolerance, especially the Muslim–Coptic solidarity in the common struggle for the independence of Egypt we observed earlier in the works of both Al-Kharrat and Abdel Meguid owes much to the example of their celebrated Alexandrine fellow patriot. Antipathy to the dominant Turkish and Circassian aristocracy within Egyptian society, as well as aversion to Ottoman despotism, permeate al-Nadīm's thought and writing. Within his nationalist economy, hostility to these opponents counterbalances and reinforces his emphasis on Muslim–Coptic national unity. He was so committed to the principle of an egalitarian, multi-religious homeland that he gave his own son a Christian name, Ilyās.

While *al-'Awda ilā al-Manfā* culls much of the factual evidence about al-Nadīm's life from historical sources, the fictional account alone provides an imaginative correlative of al-Nadīm's lived experience, with all the rich and complex emotional and psychological tonalities of such an extraordinary life. The mapping of the homeland through the naming of its constituent parts, which al-Nadīm visits frequently, however, is eminently realistic. This activity reaches a frenzy in the months following the 'Urābī Revolt, during which al-Nadīm crisscrosses the length and breadth of Egypt to gather support for the Revolt. In the process his travels literally etch the body and contours of the homeland.

At the collapse of the Revolt and the onset of the British occupation in 1882 all the top leaders are either incarcerated or banished; all, that is, except al-Nadīm. He goes underground where he lives incognito for nine years. During these long years the mapping activity goes on unabated, as the celebrated fugitive and his servant scurry about the villages and towns of the Nile Delta. With a high prize on his head, and numerous government agents, under direct British supervision, fast on his heels, al-Nadīm manages to elude his would-be captors by disguising himself now as a sufi shaykh, now as a learned scholar from the ḥijāz or Morocco, and now again as a Yamanī merchant. For the duration of the suspenseful chase, the towns and villages of rural Egypt become one in their protective embrace of the patriotic fugitive. Nowhere in modern Arabic fiction does mere physical geography imbue national space with such affective force.

It so happens that the end of al-Nadīm's dramatic life also anticipates more recent developments in contemporary Egyptian fiction. For no sooner does al-Nadīm surface from underground than he is banished from Egypt to Palestine, where he spends several months in the port city of Jaffa. A Khideval pardon in 1892 enables him to return to Egypt and to resume his journalistic activity for a couple of years. But when his agitation against the British occupation becomes too strident, the British send him packing again. This time to Istanbul, where he dies a few years later, a lonely exile, but not before he writes *al-Masāmīr*, destined to be banned in his homeland a century later.

Primarily because of its historical underpinnings, *al-'Awda ilā al-Manfā* stands out among Egyptian novels in its effective treatment of national space as a cohesive, harmonious whole. For the duration of 'Urābī's brief hold on power, and largely through al-Nadīm's tireless traversing of all regions of the land, the countryside and the periphery are momentarily integrated in the all-encompassing spatial frame of the homeland. If the popularity of 'Urābī's patriotic position lent legitimacy to his authority, his peasant background effected a rare reconciliation of rural Egypt to the seat of power in the capital. Momentarily, Alexandria becomes a sister city, not an implacable rival of Cairo. That sense of spatial unity survives the collapse of the 'Urābī revolt in the novel, but goes with al-Nadīm underground, so to speak, never to surface again with such compelling authenticity in Egyptian fiction. For, as a rule, whenever they obtain at all, totalized images of the homeland are recalled nostalgically as fleeting childhood sensations or as haunted memories of unfulfilled political desire.

* * *

Rarely, in modern Arabic fiction, has borrowed narrative technique been so unabashedly flaunted and yet so effectively wedded to indigenous subject matter as it is in Sonalla Ibrahim's *Tilk al-Rā'iḥa*. The technique in question is a self-conscious amalgam of Hemingway's lean, telegraphic style, and the equally sparse, experimental style of the French Nouveau Roman.[56] The experience this technique seeks to capture, however, is unmistakably Egyptian in content and color. In a nutshell, it consists of a skeletal description, in shorthand, of a few uneventful days in the life of a former political prisoner who spends his days walking the streets of Cairo, or visiting friends and relatives, and his nights under house arrest in his desolate apartment. The novella's pioneering treatment of space can be gauged best perhaps against the dominant aesthetic model, on the one hand, and the more general "theory" concerning the relation of literary representation to extratextual, referential reality, on the other hand.

Structurally, the treatment of space, like everything else in the novella, is strictly contingent on the first person narrative point of view. That, in turn, is largely limited to recording the surface impressions of objects and events as these tangentially brush against the consciousness of the narrator, only to be refracted thence without leaving a trace or hint of more substantive meaning. Absent the illusion of metaphoric depth and the suturing effect of interpretive mediation, the places the narrator visits and enumerates paratactically assume paramount thematic significance. Somewhat paradoxically, the sheer physicality of a prison cell, an apartment, a metro station or, above all, a street of Cairo, acquires a metaphysical, but inscrutably eerie, quality in the absence of emotive mediation. What is more, these places harbor an unspeakable melange of cruelty, violence, hypocrisy, banality, and outright filth—all described in minute clinical detail, but none condemned or adjudged. And this is precisely where the departure from formal realism leads directly to unseemly reality. Moreover, contrary to common sense, which in interpretive practice often amounts to a learned response, the neutral, matter-of-fact description of the successive rape of a minor in a squalid prison cell—the walls of which are bloodstained from bug bites—is no less shocking for the lack of mediating authorial commentary on such a ghastly scene (p. 27). An equally shocking effect accrues from the mere description of the breakdown of the sewage system and the flooding of the fashionable streets of modern Cairo, hardly a rare phenomenon in itself, but until now inadmissible in fiction for reasons of propriety and aesthetics. It is in breaking these taboos that *Tilk al-Rā'iḥa* makes its strongest intervention against the dominant paradigm of representing space and against the dominant theory about the relation of literary representation to referential reality. This last question comes up explicitly in the text in connection with a statement attributed to Maupassant concerning the aesthetic mandate of literature, namely, to beautify and uplift, not to replicate or reproduce unsavory reality. *Tilk al-Rā'iḥa* confounds this principle, and not only through the detached, object-oriented narrative technique described earlier. In other fundamental respects as well—such as "plot," characterization, and, especially, the treatment of space—the text appears purposely poised to mock another important Egyptian novel that exemplifies the debunked dictum attributed to Maupassant. The novel in question is none other than Mahfouz' *al-Liṣṣ wal-Kilāb*.

Much like the protagonist of Mahfouz' novel, the narrator of *Tilk al-Rā'iḥa* is also released from prison at the beginning of the novel, having spent roughly an equal length of time in prison. And, also like him, once released, he has nowhere to go. But, unlike Sa'īd Mahrān, the thief-turned-hero, the nameless narrator of *Tilk al-Rā'iḥa* is decidedly an anti-hero. Therefore, no sooner is he released than he is brought back to prison because he fails to furnish an address where he can be kept under police surveillance to verify compliance with the terms of house arrest. It is this temporary detention in a crowded cell at the police station that occasions the shocking description of the repeated rape scene in the squalid interior of the cell and sets the tone for the narrator's impassive attitude to his surroundings. Neither the rape nor any of the other cruel acts of senseless violence and degradation that chance in the cell elicit any response from him.

Notwithstanding this profound textual ambivalence, neither the writer nor the police had any doubt about the novella's relevance to the discourse of national politics and the image of the homeland. In the introduction to the 1986 complete edition, Ibrahim admits to having entertained serious reservations about the initial publication of the novella in 1966, lest the event prove "detrimental to the interest of the homeland at a particularly critical stage of its ongoing struggle against American imperialism, Zionism, and reactionary Arab regimes" (p. 13). The secret service deemed the threat so imminent that the minister for interior affairs, 'Abd al-Qādir Ḥātim, personally hand-carried a copy of the confiscated text to President Nasser (p. 14). Though the rest of the copies were swiftly collected from the market and the book was banned, the dreaded reincarceration of the author did not materialize.

(Re)claiming a patrimony

Ibrāhīm Aṣlān's remarkable novel, *Mālik al-Ḥazīn* (1983; The Heron) loosens further the grip of the symbolic and metaphorical representation of space in Egyptian fiction, but in a completely unexpected direction. The space in question is Imbāba, a sprawling popular suburb on the outskirts of metropolitan Cairo, where the historic Kit Kāt square is located. An old building at the center of the square used to house the Kit Kāt cabaret, historically renowned as a haunt of king Fārūq and of Allied officers during the Second World War. At the time of the novel's action, this building, the streets of Imbāba, and, ultimately, during the anti-Sadat "bread riots" of 1977, the streets of downtown Cairo become hotly contested spaces. More than anything else, therefore, this novel tells the story of an embattled place: the Kit Kāt and its environs. It is important to note from the outset, however, that the depiction of space brooks no aesthetic embellishments or romantic affectation here. This is a place where people urinate against a wall in the open and where the unsavory spectacle of killing a chicken, plucking it, and throwing its rancid entrails to funky street cats unfolds in full public view. On the whole, this is a shabby place in the process of dismemberment and decay, and nothing is done to hide this indecorous reality. And yet, for all that, the identity of the inhabitants, both individually and collectively, appears inextricably bound up with that of the place. Much of the struggle in the novel revolves around the attempt to beguile, or at least delay, for the longest time possible the ineluctable fate to which the place appears doomed. All that impending gloom notwithstanding, this is by far one of the most humorous, though also eminently serious, novels ever written in Arabic. The secret magic resides in the fact that it recounts a story of hardship through, not against, the characteristic *joie de vivre* of common Egyptians.

On several occasions, characters in the novel reflect on the centrality of the Kit Kāt to their own sense of identity and wonder what would become of them without it. For the entire community, but especially for members of the younger generation who were born and raised in the Kit Kāt, the 'Awaḍallāh Cafe, much like Kirsha's Cafe in *Zuqāq al-Midaqq* serves as an exclusive hub of social life. Some of the older residents, like 'Amm 'Imrān, witnessed the construction of the Kit Kāt and the adjacent houses from the beginning, and retain in memory a vivid record of the entire history of the place and its people. 'Amm 'Imrān inadvertently recapitulates this oral history in public one day through the microphone of a loudspeaker whose switch was left on after a Qur'ānic recitation at a memorial had ended and the mourners had turned to social gossip. The "inadvertent" public exposure extends to everything happening in the square, which is, of course, the subject matter of the novel, but rehearsed here with a special penchant for the scandalous. Incidentally, this highly creative and effective recourse to oral modes of narrative distinguishes Aṣlān from all his contemporaries, and contrasts sharply with Sonalla Ibrahim's recourse to borrowed narrative technique in *Tilk al-Rā'iḥa*, as we have seen.

Thematically, the identity of the place is entangled with the question of legal ownership, on the one hand, and, on the other, with the far more elusive reality on the ground. A state of rife lawlessness separates the two realms and requires considerable negotiation to translate the inhabitants' physical affiliation with, and emotional attachment to, the place into commercial assets for local and foreign profiteers. It transpires from the account of 'Amm 'Imrān, for example, that the Kit Kāt is being sold piecemeal and that grubby haggling among prospective local buyers and middlemen over the booty is what stands in the way of concluding the deal. Of particular interest in this connection is the story of shaykh Ḥusnī, whose father is said to have helped himself to enough of the fine wood imported from abroad for the construction of the Kit Kāt to build a fine house of his own. Shaykh Ḥusnī, it transpires, had already sold that selfsame house to a local drug dealer for a certain amount of ḥashīsh, delivered in daily doses over a limited period of time. The dealer, in turn, sold the house to a local nouveau riche, who sold it to another, to be demolished, with other landmarks of the Kit Kāt, to make room for a high-rise apartment building. The events of the novel unfold literally against the backdrop of these Gordian negotiations. This clever ploy permits a final glance at a vanishing world that envelops a historical piece of Egyptian real estate and supports a unique mode of social interaction and experience. In a poignant scene on the eve of the demolition of the cafe that his own father built, one of the characters reminisces on the interlocking trajectory of his life with that of the place. As he scans the intimate space, his forlorn gaze lands on the historic stone gate to the square, on the high arch of which is written: "The battle of the Pyramids ended here on July 21, 1798." The reference, of course, is to the last battle between the French army and the Mamelukes, before Napoleon's triumphal stroll into Cairo.

Given the centrality of this event to the subsequent history of the region, it is hard to miss the poignancy of the gesture toward which the inscription points: The long and fateful history of the colonial encounter is literally engraved in stone here. By the same token, it is hard to predict whether the drift of events in the novel threatens to obliterate or to reenact that bitter history. For, while local parvenus are busy dividing up the pie, an old–new threat to the identity of the place looms on the horizon. An Italian tourist, newspapers report, has launched a law suit in the Egyptian courts claiming legal ownership of Imbāba, which he claims to have purchased in 1944, with the help of Egyptianized Europeans, and has in his possession all the deeds and legal documents to prove his case. Although this issue, like all the rest, remains pending at the end of the novel—shortly after the "bread riots" of January 1977—the juxtaposition of the two European motifs in the text occasions an ironic contrast. Napoleon, as we know, conquered but could not possess Egypt. Neither his military might nor his elaborate histrionics in courting Egyptian public opinion ever made him feel welcome in Egypt. In due course, his imperial claim to the land whittled down to a lone inscription of precarious standing at the sight of his perhaps greatest single battle: that of the Pyramids. The Italian tourist, by contrast, wields an Egyptian, not a foreign weapon in his fight for Imbāba. Outlandish as it may seem, his claim borrows credibility from the formal legalism and profusion of unfeasible laws through which President Sadat sought to peddle his touted "state of law" (*dawlat al-qānūn*). The surrealistic lawsuit patently caricatures this ersatz legalism, which the common criminals of Imbāba, with intuitive perspicacity and finesse, readily appropriate to their buoyant miscreant.

It must be clear from the foregoing remarks that the novel is neither oblivious nor indifferent to the politics of national identity, a subject that perforce summons images of the space of the nation. How then, we may ask, does the novel broach this all-consuming topic and still refrain from investing space with symbolic significance? In other words, how does the space of the nation manifest itself if the action is completely localized, and local space is denied representative symbolic agency? Aṣlān accomplishes this feat, I think, by crafting a multilayered text in which different significations and levels of consciousness resonate contrapuntally, but do not interact directly in the text. Several structural and stylistic features combine to sustain this functional compartmentalization while, at the same time, imparting to the whole an unmistakable air of national allegory. Foremost among these is the absence of a central, overarching plot, by means of which space traditionally serves as a unifying factor in the novel. It also allows the disparate strands of anecdotal narrative to coexist paratactically, in a simulacrum of random spontaneity akin to lived experience. The unfettered use of the colloquial (*'āmmiyya*), the extensive use of the native talent for storytelling, and the irrepressible sense of humor that permeates the narrative, contribute significantly to this impression of artless fluidity.

Nowhere is the combined effect of these features more transparent than it is in the case of the aforementioned shaykh Ḥusnī. Ingeniously, Aṣlān makes this vagrant, blind, ḥashīsh-crazed "shaykh" the unwitting agent of a major underlying intention: to demonstrate the natives' indisputable, de facto possession of local space. Though completely blind, shaykh Ḥusnī pretends otherwise and, through his intimate knowledge of his surroundings, convinces not only others, but also himself, of his ability to see. With the occasional help of an accomplice who lures blind stragglers into the Kit Kāt in his direction, shaykh Ḥusnī swindles a considerable number of them by acting as guide and escorting them around the streets of Imbāba. He feels so much at home in these streets and alleys that he occasionally drives a motorcycle and takes a fellow blind shaykh for a felucca sail on the Nile.

Shaykh Ḥusnī's blindness obviously accentuates this unmediated, unselfconscious oneness with the place; but the other characters experience it no less intensely. Not so the narrator, however, especially when he doubles as an implied author and reflects, from an extra-diegetic position in the text, on his inconsequential life and his limping attempt at writing a novel (within the novel). This wistful voice betrays a haunted political consciousness bedevilled by tender love for the place and an impotent rage at his inability to prevent its demise. To the sensibility associated with this voice belongs, in part, the task of relating local space and developments to the broader national space and context.

The close coincidence between the time of writing the novel (December 1972–April 1981), and the reign of President Sadat (October 1970–October 1981), serves a similar function. This temporal correspondence permits a reading of the illicit dealings in Imbāba as a mock translation of the IMF-inspired policies of economic reform and liberalization into the vernacular of native practice. Finally, the general conflagration that erupted all over Egypt, "from Aswān to Alexandria," in January 1977, when the government tried to comply with the demands of the IMF by lifting of the standing subsidies on basic commodities, such as fine flour, some sugar, rice, and oil, forcefully reintroduced the national agenda into the contested local space of Imbāba.[57] But even at that crucial intersection of the fictional and the historical, the local and the national, the novel upholds a fine separation of realms, especially between the personal and the political. This paramount imperative is illustrated in a minor, but telling, anecdote toward the end of the novel. As battles rage, shaykh Ḥusnī straggles into an area of confrontation and sustains a head wound. He is momentarily helped to the interior of a house where his wound is hastily bandaged, but, with his wound still bleeding and bullets still flying everywhere, he returns to the streets alone to retrieve his lost walking cane. Another character braves the same blazing streets to collect a complete set of serially numbered, American made, tear gas canisters. Through it all, shaykh Ḥusnī, like the rest of the characters, remains unmindful of the symbolic potential of his personal story to the unfolding national narrative. Likewise, the text steadfastly refuses to make the connection directly, even as it presents compelling circumstantial evidence to that effect. The net result, as far as fictional space is concerned, is an added measure of autonomy from the disfiguring clutches of direct symbolic manipulation.

All that notwithstanding, the novel does intervene in the enduring debate over Egypt's identity and orientation, by analogy. The force of this analogy stems from the structural coincidence of the novel's temporal and spatial dimensions, or chronotope, with the political and historical conditions of Egypt at the time of writing. In this respect, the decision to end the novel's action during the mass bread riots of January 1977 is highly strategic: It leaves the contested space—locally in Imbāba and nationally at the heart of Cairo and the rest of Egypt—open to two contending possibilities, both of which enlist strong thematic support within the text as well as powerful historical precedents outside it. And they both authorize extrapolation by analogy. The first caps the disparate allusions to Western encroachments on Egyptian space to highlight the unfolding piecemeal mortgaging of Egypt's sovereignty to Western interests. Thus, the legal claim of the Italian tourist to Imbāba acquires added urgency from the seemingly fortuitous reference to Napoleon's association with the place. Although the text remains silent on this crucial point, we know that the legal pretext Napoleon used to justify his occupation of Egypt was the Mamelukes' supposed ill-treatment of the French merchants residing in Egypt, who numbered no more than fifty or sixty at the time.[58] The second, and still more compelling analogy arises from the noted similarity between the general conditions of Egypt under President Sadat and the Khedive Ismā'īl (1863–1879). To be sure, the analogy originates neither with Aṣlān nor in fiction, but was fairly widespread in Egypt. Here is how John Waterbury puts the matter in the context of discussing Egypt's posture vis-à-vis the IMF and other would-be debtors in 1977: "Morgan Stanley International of New York was retained by the GODE and Egypt to manage repayment of the short-term debt, owed almost exclusively to Western banks. It did not escape the notice of many Egyptians that there was a disquieting similarity between the GODE's grip upon Egypt's foreign exchange position and the *Caisse de la Dette Publique* set up a century earlier (under Ismā'īl) by Egypt's European creditors to manage the country's finances."[59] The disastrous consequences of Ismā'īl's reckless policies are a matter of the historical record. Suffice it here to note that they ultimately brought about the prolonged British occupation of Egypt from 1882 to 1956. Whether the shot heard at the end of the novel, proleptically anticipating the end of the Sadat regime, and the actual assassination of the President a few years later, has spared Egypt a (re)visitation of its earlier predicament is a matter of interpretation. That, however, lies well beyond the scope of the novel.

To recapitulate, fictional space is organized around three overlapping circles in the novel, namely, the Kit Kāt, Imbāba, and the center of Cairo. For much of the novel, the relation between the first two and the third remains implicit and indirect. Although, structurally, it is the pressure emanating from the open door policies at the center that infects the local scene in Imbāba, where enterprising profiteers compete furiously for possession of the square's prized real estate, this tacit causal connection eludes the participants in the rat race. Consequently, developments at the local level appear to have an inner dynamic and a pace all their own. The novel's irrepressible humor thrives on the incongruence between the presumed objectives of Sadat's national economic policies (themselves originating farther away in the offices of the World Bank and the IMF in Washington) and the concrete, invariably warped realization of these policies on the ground. Only when the scene shifts to the streets of downtown Cairo during the "bread riots" of 1977, do the local developments in Imbāba and developments on the national level converge to foreground the implicit causal links connecting them.

The widespread riots also help reintegrate, momentarily, the disparate spaces of Imbāba, downtown Cairo, and the rest of Egypt into a single spatial frame. The decision to end the novel in the middle of these riots bespeaks a desire to consecrate the promise of a new chronotope in which the time and space of the nation-state of Egypt are more intimately harnessed to a different nationalist ethos and agenda. (It helps to remember in this regard that the novel was finished in 1981—that is, long after the promise of change in 1977 had dissipated and the government of President Sadat had reasserted its hold on power for another four years.) For, it is only at that moment of thematic and spatial convergence that the imminent threat to the identity of the historic Kit Kāt, its environs, and inhabitants is momentarily stayed. Rather than refute or gloss over the traditional identification of the center (Cairo) with political power and the antagonism between it and the periphery, the proffered reintegration confirms both. It is only when the regime's grip on power loosens in the capital and elsewhere that these spaces loom on the horizon of the novel. The novel thus implicitly predicates the integration of the disparate parts of the homeland into a unified space on the promise of drastic change at the center. The source of that change, the novel strongly suggests, lies squarely within Egypt itself, in its very streets and alleys. In this inward turn, *Mālik al-Ḥazīn* is somewhat unique among Egyptian novels of the Sadat era and its immediate aftermath. Many of these novels exploit the shift in space occasioned by forced exile and physical dislocation from Egypt to reflect on the identity of the homeland, even though their main emphasis tends to be on the plight and fate of the individual characters involved. Among such novels it may suffice to mention here Sonalla Ibrahim's *Najmat Ūghusṭus* (1974; The August Star) and *Beirut, Beirut* (1984), Ibrahim Abdel Meguid's *al-Balda al-Ukhrā* (1991; The Other Village), and Bahaa Taher's *al-Hubb fil-Manfā* (1995; Love in Exile, 2001).

The view from the (country)side

Given the fundamentally political nature of the idea of the nation and its structural incarnation in the nation-state, it should come as no surprise that Egyptian writers often imagine national space in political terms. Hence also the persistent metaphoric conflation/substitution of national space with the space of the capital and the identification of that space with the political authority that emanates from the center and projects its coercive power outwardly. Two significant consequences flow from this frequent visualization of the spatial through political lenses. The first is the injection of a note of ambiguity and conflict at the site of imagining and representing national space. The second is the endowment of sheer distance from the center with redemptive values and regenerative potentialities. To one degree or another, these general principles inform the treatment of space in most of the novels we have discussed so far. But they are especially evident in novels of rural Egypt; that is, novels that dramatize events in the far-flung provinces and rural areas, away from the two metropolitan centers of Cairo and Alexandria.

Much of the preliminary critical and historical ground work on this subject, especially as it pertains to the earlier phases of the Egyptian novel, has been covered by other scholars, notably the late ʻAbd al-Muḥsin Ṭāhā Badr.[60] Of particular interest to the relationship of fictional imaginings of space to the nation-state is the following observation by Badr. At a critical phase of its historical development, the nascent Egyptian bourgeoisie, represented by such writers as Muḥammad Ḥusayn Haykal, floated the idea of the common land, Egypt, as an alternative instrument of bonding among Egyptians to the Turkish aristocracy's insistence on common religion, Islam, through which it dominated and exploited Egypt.[61] The kaleidoscopic, and much abused slogan "Egypt for the Egyptians," coined by pioneering advocates of Egyptian nationalism, aimed, according to Badr, to delegitimate and ultimately dislodge the supercilious Turkish aristocracy from Egypt and to replace it with a homegrown class of wealthy, landowning Egyptians, whom Badr lumps collectively as the Egyptian bourgeoisie.[62]

Turning his attention to Haykal's pioneering novel *Zaynab*, Badr notices a further permutation in the idea of the homeland, through which the novel performs an ideological task on behalf of the class of its author. Haykal, according to Badr, effects a division between the land of Egypt and Egyptian society; more specifically, between the topography of the countryside and the *fallāḥīn* (peasants) who cultivate the land and live on it. Badr detects this division already in the subtitle of the novel "rural scenes and manners."[63] The significance of this division is that it enables Haykal, and other like-minded writers after him, to celebrate the idyllic beauty of the landscape while remaining largely oblivious to the socioeconomic plight of the peasants who till the land.

Whether or not Haykal's separation of the human from the physical landscape is as schematic as Badr makes it out to be, there is no doubt that the representation of space in *Zaynab* is inalterably static. Little changes here, beside the seasons—unless it be the weather, to reflect changing moods of the main characters. Social relations, especially class stratification, appear as immutable as the natural order they mirror. This fundamental structural correspondence precludes politics from the equation, and with it the idea of significant change. Moreover, in the process of consecrating the status quo and the class division inscribed therein it occludes class conflict altogether. No matter how dire their condition, or how arduous their work, the peasants in Haykal's novel are always content with their lot. They are said to derive ample recompense from the serene beauty of the landscape, which, it so happens, they cultivate for the benefit of avaricious landowners.

The traditional antagonism between center and periphery, city and countryside, is likewise elided here. What is dramatized instead is the failed attempt of the romantic heroine, Zaynab, to bend social conventions in favor of personal happiness. Her love for Ibrāhīm notwithstanding, her family prefers Ḥasan because he comes from a slightly better-off family. Too docile to disobey, she marries Ḥasan, only to die of consumption, in the good old tradition of romantic heroines, a few months later. On her deathbed she admonishes her mother for forcing her to marry against her will and enjoins the practice as evil.

Given its limited artistic claim, *Zaynab* would not have warranted all the critical attention it has received if it were not for its pioneering status, on the one hand, and, on the other, Haykal's emphatic, extradiegetic assertions that he intended the depiction of rural space to symbolize Egypt as a whole. Writing parts of the novel alternately in three major European metropolises, Paris, London, and Geneva, between 1910 and 1911, Haykal seems to have been impelled as much by a psychological need to combat a nagging sense of "Otherness" in these imposing cities, compounded by a longing for the homeland, as by the political expediency of promoting a vision of the national landscape consonant with both his romantic disposition and class interest. The structural configuration underpinning thematic developments in the novel can best be understood perhaps in terms of the dual purpose it serves: It satisfies Haykal's subjective desire to advocate women's rights exclusively in affairs of the heart, while safeguarding the interests of his class from untoward consequences of any meaningful social change in other realms.

It is this disabling combination of unbridled subjectivity and stringent ideological bent that prevents the novel from realizing the innate potentialities and constitutive need of the genre for a credible simulacrum of autonomy from referential contexts. The same holds true for other major prose works, written between the two world wars, that dramatize the plight of the *fallāḥīn* in terms of the cultural and social, but not political antagonism between the city and the countryside. The primary force of these works lies elsewhere, not in their generic affiliation with the novel. Tawfiq al-Ḥakīm's *'Awdat al-Rūḥ* and *Yawmiyyāt Nā'ib fil-Aryāf* (1937), and Ṭāhā Ḥusayn's *Du'ā' al-Karawān* (1934; The Call of the Curlew, 1980), exemplify this type.

Like other aspects of the novel, the treatment of rural space undergoes a drastic change in the immediate aftermath of the Second World War. The publication of 'Abd al-Raḥmān al-Sharqāwī's *al-Arḍ* (1954; Egyptian Earth, 1990) marks a milestone in this development, its evident numerous artistic shortcomings notwithstanding. In a rare intertextual gesture the autobiographical narrator of *al-Arḍ* makes a direct reference to a number of earlier works against which the narrative of *al-Arḍ* is pitched. Beside Haykal's *Zaynab*, the list includes Ṭāhā Ḥusayn's *al-Ayyām*, and Ibrāhīm al-Māzinī's *Ibrāhīm al-Kātib* (1931; Ibrāhīm the Writer). But it is specifically with *Zaynab* that the intertextual gesture is concerned. For *al-Arḍ* consciously sets out to debunk *Zaynab*'s romantic depiction of rural life in Egypt and to demystify the whole tradition that *Zaynab* at once embodies and fosters. The polar contrast between the two works is already evident in the typological shift in the title: from the human individual in *Zaynab* to the contested land in *al-Arḍ*. More than a difference of ideological perspective and worldview inhere in this shift. It also involves what Raymond Williams calls a different "structure of feeling."[64] As in pastoral poetry, the aesthetic appreciation of the picturesque landscape in *Zaynab* entails a systematic suppression of the human suffering and misery involved in its upkeep. By focusing attention on the unseemly side of rural life *al-Arḍ* indexes the aesthetic to the factual, thus reversing the order established by *Zaynab*, and, in effect, inaugurating the realistic tradition in the treatment of rural life and space in modern Egyptian fiction. Here is how the autobiographical narrator reflects, extradiegetically, on this altered perspective.

> I would often reflect on *al-Ayyām*, *Ibrāhīm al-Kātib*, and *Zaynab*. In my village I had seen many a child whose eyes had fell prey to flies, just as in the village of the author of *al-Ayyām*.

> I had often wished also that my village were trouble-free, like the village in which Zaynab lived, where the *fallāḥīn* did not fight for, nor did the government deprive them of, irrigation water, expropriate their land, or dispatch men in khaki uniforms to flog them with whips, where children did not eat mud, nor did flies drop on their beautiful eyes.
>
> I wished that my village were like that of Zaynab, where men and women did not pass blood and pus with their urine. Would that sudden illness did not afflict the inhabitants of my village to make them writhe in pain as they emit harrowing, desperate screams.... And then fall silent, forever!
>
> To be sure, my village was as beautiful as that of Zaynab. The cycamore and mulberry trees lined along its back cast a filigree shadow on the surface of the river's water.
>
> (p. 342)

In light of this abject poverty and dire socioeconomic reality, it is no wonder that land ownership, as such, irrespective of size, becomes the standard and measure of all things in the village. It is the single, nonnegotiable attribute at the core of the village's value system. The heroine, Waṣīfa, articulates this principle at one point in the novel, to her own subsequent detriment. "He who has no land, has nothing, not even honor," she says. In the small world of the village, this seems to be a universal rule. Only those women whose families have land to sustain them can afford to be choosy in conjugal affairs. For the rest, like the vagrant Khaḍra, selling their body is often the only available means of survival (p. 39). Waṣīfa's father still had his half *dunam* of land when she enunciates this principle. But no sooner does he loose that land than she, too, begins to taste the cruel workings of the principle she so approvingly invoked a little earlier. As the workers carve up her father's small plot to pave a road to the governor's mansion, they openly start making lewd remarks about her shapely body and what it would fetch in ears of corn daily in exchange for sexual favors, if she were only to join the scores of hired girls working in fields.

It may be one of the more pronounced artistic shortcomings of the novel that it upholds this abstract principle rather schematically. Thus, until the reversal in her father's fortunes, Waṣīfa was the center of attention and competition among the eligible bachelors in the village. Towards the end of the novel she appears destined to marry an elderly man, twice her age; the other suitors having nonchalantly withdrawn from the scene. Parenthetically, we may note the similarity between this indexing of personal value to land possession and Mahfouz' predication of personal worth on ownership of real estate in *Zuqāq al-Midaqq* as we saw earlier. In both instances personal merit and social standing are decidedly subordinated to material possessions. Whatever one thinks of it, this conceptual revolution in the traditional anthropocentric value system is undoubtedly a function of the novel's realism, although in al-Sharqāwī's case the entire transaction seems too mechanical to command much credit.

Interestingly, the famed village of *al-Arḍ* remains anonymous in the novel, and is identified only by the narrator as "my village." The novel compensates for this nominal lack of specificity by distributing space among three concrete, fairly distinct spatial zones: the space of the village as a whole, the internal divisions of that space, and, finally, the relation of the village to the surrounding space. The spatial unity of the village obtains not only through emphatic assertions about "the indivisible oneness of its land" (p. 313), but also through the collective, largely public nature of the novel's action. Whatever divides them internally, the inhabitants of the village often act in unison against the outside world, and this thematic feature often infects space with a similar sense of totality. As we shall presently see, this is particularly true as concerns the relation of the village to the urban centers from which it is administered and the spatial symbols of political power, internal and external alike. These spatial delineations and configurations combine to validate the intended representative standing of the village as a microcosm of rural Egypt.

Given this emphasis on spatial unity, it may be more accurate to read the demarcations of internal divisions within the village as shades of a spatial continuum rather than enforceable border lines. This holds true for the vague division between the houses and the fields, as it does between one field and another. For, no matter how sacrosanct these boundaries appear as registers of private property, at moments of crisis they instantly melt away. This view of peasant consciousness and solidarity obviously betrays a political and ideological desire that seeks to influence, not merely to describe, historical developments.

A similar leveling effect, however, seems to wreak havoc on the principle of mandatory separation of sacred from profane space in the village. Specifically, the issue concerns the space designated for public prayer, the *muṣallā*—a makeshift structure at the edge of the fields, though not quite a full-fledged mosque. On two different occasions in early adolescence, Waṣīfa and the narrator use this very space for illicit sexual trysts. Though no sex is consummated on either occasion, the two events leave an indelible mark on the consciousness of the narrator and are recounted numerous times in various forms in the narrative. The ultimate objective of this procedure in al-Sharqāwī's novel appears to be the following: To destabilize the notion of the sacred, by decoupling it from its traditional signified, the religious, in order to reassign it to a different, political alternative. This narrative intention crystallizes at a later point in the novel when the political struggle over the land is in full swing. In that adjusted perspective, wherever the oppressed peasants and farm laborers struggle for economic and social justice, there shall a mosque be, regardless of formal or official designations (p. 258). Other aspects and ramifications of the novel's treatment of religious subjects will concern us elsewhere. Here it may suffice to note that the diminution in the status of formal symbols of sanctity, spatial as well as thematic, paves the way for an alternative organization of national space around the idea of the homeland: *waṭan*.

That is where the relation of the village to the outside world unfolds. The symbolic economy of binary opposition between inside and outside grounds develop along this axis. In connection with this division, we note that physical residence in the village, no matter how prolonged, does not confer *bona fide* affiliation. Origin, lineage, and, above all, land possession, are mandatory requirements for that privilege. Failure to meet these requirements dooms individuals like 'Alwānī and Khaḍra to permanent outsider status. Nor is the force of this stigma limited to life: upon her mysterious death the outcast Khaḍra is denied burial in the cemetery of the village. While other considerations figure in this extraordinary harshness, there is no doubt about the validity of the general phenomenon it records, namely, the peasants' innate suspicion of outsiders. Examples of this peasant xenophobia abound in Arabic fiction, from Egypt and elsewhere.[65]

In *al-Arḍ*, as in many other novels of rural Egypt, the quintessential adversary is the central government in Cairo and, by association, its representatives in the provinces. Thus, the mere rumor that the government intends to establish a permanent police post in the village strikes unprecedented terror in the hearts of the residents. While this generalized suspicion of political authority provides the historical context of the antagonism between the village and the capital, the reign of terror unleashed by the brutal government of Ismā'īl Ṣidqī in the early 1930s, the time of the novel's action, furnishes the specific focus and address of the immediate animus. To these political determinants must be added the inherent cultural tension between rural and urban traditions and mores that perennially lurks below the surface of rural consciousness, ready to mutate at the slightest provocation into outright hostility. *Al-Arḍ* dramatizes the unsettling effects of the convergence of these forces in the space of the village and the life of its inhabitants.

From the parochial perspective of the village, Cairo—"city of the government" (p. 50) and "center of the universe" (p. 151)—is at once irresistibly enticing and willfully menacing. Routinely mystified, the city appears as a fabulous place of mythic proportions and potentialities (p. 15). As such, it confers mystique and magical powers on those who can negotiate its mysterious ways and spaces. Thus, for residing in Cairo and attending school there, the twelve-year-old narrator enjoys exclusive privileges in the village. Not least among these is the free access he has to Waṣīfa's body. But even residence in lesser urban centers, such as a provincial town (*bandar*), is apt to confer extraordinary amenities. Waṣīfa's own licentious ways, quite extraordinary for a village girl, are vaguely ascribed to her five-year-residence in such a town (p. 38).[66] Conversely, Cairo, and cities in general, also induce corrupt, effeminate mannerisms that the villagers find utterly repugnant (pp. 304–305). Even for a semi educated character like Muḥammad Effendi, the thought of going to Cairo for a few days to deliver a petition on behalf of the village occasions a vague but poignant sensation of uprootedness (p. 124). On this deep-seated cultural antagonism is grafted the primary layer of political/ideological antagonism that motivates the plot.

The immediate conflict between the village and the central government in Cairo involves the fate of arable lands slated for expropriation by the government, ostensibly to pave an agricultural road connecting the village to the provincial capital, but actually to punish the village for its patriotic stand against the party in power. The local *ma'mūr*, district commissioner, latches onto the idea with a scheme of his own: To seize more lands from the village in order to extend the road to his outlying mansion. The half *dunam* that Waṣīfa's father owns appears to be a primary target of this vindictive-cum-expedient scheme. How to avert this impending calamity becomes the overriding concern of the village and the source of considerable internal maneuvering and jostling for public attention and recognition. More importantly, al-Sharqāwī uses the occasion to revisit the idea of the homeland and the conditions necessary for its reinvigoration. Initially, the villagers try to plead with (and to bribe) "officials" they believe to be influential with the government in distant Cairo. When this fails, they turn to more direct action and cast the material slated for the project in the Nile. The government lashes back with vengeance and proceeds to implement the project with full force and speed. At the end of the novel, the village appears resigned to the inevitable outcome and prepares to act accordingly. The sudden reversal in Waṣīfa's marriage prospects adequately measures the depth of this resignation.

Dismembering the village thus and deepening its hatred of the government in the capital hardly augur well for the idea of the nation and the homeland. The novel restricts the potential damage to both by effecting a dual narrative strategy. It delegitimates the unpatriotic government of Ismā'īl Ṣidqī, on the one hand, and, on the other, it recalls an alternative patriotic past to instruct the present and thus set the national homeland on a different trajectory. The first task is accomplished through the systematic personalization of the government as a villainous, lawless strong arm. The dramatic effect this personalization achieves comes at a price. The excessive particularity it evinces deprives the conflict over the land of the potential for broader significance. As an erratic act of a brutal government, the agricultural road that so mercilessly mangles the lands of the village and rends the lives and dreams of its inhabitants, connects with no larger historical or economic processes, such as the inevitable mechanization of farming and the consolidation of small farms into profit-generating agricultural capitalism.

A similar strain vitiates the central motif in the plot, namely, the design on the land of Muḥammad Abū Suwaylim, Waṣīfa's father. More specifically, the issue concerns the size of the parcel. By any standards, half a *dunam* is hardly enough to sustain a family, even in the poor Egyptian countryside. Yet, the land has to be small enough so it can be devoured whole by the proposed agricultural road. The central development in the plot, namely, the reversal in the fortunes of the heroine, is predicated entirely on that prospect. The novel as a whole, not only the treatment of space, suffers from these unconvincing concatenations.

A different, immeasurably more benign Cairo emerges from the retrospective narration of the events of the 1919 Revolution under the leadership of Sa'd Zaghlūl and the Wafd party. An Azharite native of the village, who was an active participant in the demonstrations for Egypt's independence in those days, mediates the temporal rupture between the present and the past and the spatial distance between rural Egypt and Cairo. After many years of absence, he returns to his native village at the critical juncture to reignite the spirit of opposition to the collaborator government of Ismā'īl Ṣidqī and to revive Sa'd Zaghlūl's and the Wafd's vision of a free, independent, united, and pluralistic Egypt. It is through this discursive rehearsal of the local and national narrative that the past and the future of the village are reconnected so as to enable it regain a place on the virtual map of a fairer Egypt in a more enlightened world.

Obviously enough, this vision is no closer to realization at the end of the novel than at any other time. Even so, it is worth noting the interplay between its postulation in the text and the actual time of writing. Al-Arḍ was written in the immediate aftermath of the 1952 revolution of the Free Officers, led by Nasser, and was serialized in "*al-Miṣrī*" during 1953, before it was published in book form in 1954.[67] These biographical facts are instructive. For, it is hard to imagine a period in the history of modern Egypt that involved as much or as intense political soul-searching. Under the circumstances, valorizing the memory of the Wafd and its leader, even if only in fictional form, must be seen as a direct and courageous political intervention in the discourse of the nation and the homeland. All the more so, perhaps, because the populist Wafd was an anathema to the mind-set of the Free Officers. Be that as it may, after *al-Arḍ* the fictional representation and interpretation of rural Egypt became practically impossible without a political lexicon.

The spell of *The Mountain*

Abiding suspicion toward the resident government in Cairo also informs the view and treatment of space in Fatḥī Ghānim's novel *al-Jabal* (1959; The Mountain).[68] But unlike al-Sharqāwī's novel, this hostility carries no specific political or ideological markings in *al-Jabal*, beyond the vague suggestion that its "events happened more than seven years ago," that is, from the time of narration. Since that time is not specified, however, and the novel was published in 1959, we can conclude with certainty only that the action takes place before the 1952 Revolution. Textual reference to the exploits of the king's sister, a certain princess, during the span of the action corroborates this general time scheme but does little to specify the time of action any more precisely. To grasp the full significance of the interplay between these different time schemes, it is imperative to bear in mind the historical circumstances of Egypt, especially at the time of writing in the late 1950s. For the novel mounts a scathing, but also prophetic, critique of the theory of development and forced "modernization" that informed much of the political, economic, and social policies in Egypt, as in many newly independent nation-states in Asia and Africa, in the post– Second World War era. Decontextualized from these historical circumstances, the critique loses much of its force and relevance. *Al-Jabal* sustains this critique through a careful demarcation and orchestration of spatial boundaries and enclosures. Ingeniously, Ghānim dresses these abstract theoretical concerns and historical exigencies in the garb of detective fiction.

The formal action of *al-Jabal* revolves around a strange complaint involving, in one swoop, theft, larceny, and the government. The narrator, explicitly identified in the text with the actual author, is an overseer of investigations in the department of education in Cairo. He is summarily dispatched to upper Egypt one day to investigate a complaint against the government sent to Cairo on behalf of a small mountainous village near Luxor, in the vicinity of ancient Thebes. No sooner does he arrive in Luxor, however, than he is enmeshed in an ever-widening web of entanglements and mysterious revelations. A Cairene by birth and upbringing, the narrator admits from the outset that little in his urban background prepares him to venture into "the strange, distant world" of rural Egypt, and even less, "to investigate a conflict between a village and the government" (p. 24).

> The minute my eyes fell on the first lines (of the complaint) I felt that I was being transported into a strange world, far removed from reality, wherein dreams and fantasy abide. For this is how we, city folks, habitually view a milieu with which we are unfamiliar. We instantly transform it in our minds into an illusion, a fable, a flick, or a myth.
>
> And this is how we imagine these distant regions in the heart of the countryside. Those who live in the city soon forget their relatives in the rural areas and the terra incognita of the countryside. Or rather, they ignore their existence altogether. A total rift thus divides kin and sunders the bonds between parents and children, sending each to their separate fate: one group to the rural trap, the other to the city trap.
>
> (p. 8)

Equipped with little else beside urban myths about the countryside, the narrator sets out to upper Egypt, determined to botch in typical bureaucratic manner this highly irregular and exceptionally unwelcome assignment. In the event, however, his short trip to the mountainous village turns out to be life-transforming. He emerges from the experience a changed person, no longer capable of the dissembling and deceit required for the official mediation of knowledge about the countryside and the administration of justice there. Although this outcome seems a little far-fetched, given the short duration of the trip, it is meant to measure the unfathomable chasm that separates the village from the capital.

Spatially, the journey into the unknown begins as soon as the narrator alights from the train in Luxor. The official in charge there apprises him of the political geography of the area, especially as concerns the west bank of the Nile, in which the village in question is located.

> In any event, the west bank lies outside our bounds, beyond the reach of the law, the city, and all security and police concerns. Not even a single police officer, or a foreigner, is to be found there at this hour of the night. Neither tourists, nor we, nor even the inhabitants of Luxor dare stay on the west bank at night. We may venture out there in the morning, as tourists or archeologists, but as soon as the sun sets, everyone leaves.

> Only the mountain people stay, alone with their mountain. Neither the state nor any other creature is allowed to share it with them.
>
> (p. 18)

To negotiate his way into the forbidden terrain, the narrator has first to divest himself of all signs of official affiliation with the government in Cairo. For that purpose he is made to undergo frightening ritual trials highly reminiscent of the rites of passage and the birth of the individual, all properly orchestrated against the enveloping darkness of the night. Only after these elaborate measures is he allowed access to the source of knowledge concerning his mission: the real grounds of the complaint he came to investigate.

Space, it turns out, is itself the issue, not just the frame thereof. Specifically, the crux of the conflict between the village and the government is the interior space of the mountain the village straddles. The government, like the villagers, believes that untold Pharaonic treasures lie buried deep inside the caves of the mountain. In an attempt to dislodge the villagers from their traditional habitat, the government builds for them a new town, furnished with all the amenities of modern comfort. Ostensibly, the government's objective is to lure, but if necessary forcibly catapult, the villagers into the modern age of the nation-state. An equally pressing objective of the government is to safeguard from pillage the said Pharaonic treasures. Both of these objectives, that is, forced modernization and the preservation of the putative national heritage, inhere in the ethos of Third World nation-states during the second half of the twentieth century. The villagers view the first objective with disdain, the second with mistrust. To renounce their traditional way of life by abandoning the mountain and moving into the model village strikes them as the epitome of lowliness and self-effacement. Moreover, to do so is not only to betray the legacy of their ancestors and to compromise their identity, but also to abandon the precious dream of fabulous wealth in pursuit of which generations perished trying to dig their way in the hard rock of the mountain to the treasures believed to be buried there. Neither the recurrent disappointment of discovering that each new site they reach, always after much toil and tragic suffering, had already been visited by their forefathers, nor the relentless pressure of the government, appear likely to sway the villagers. Although a symbolic gesture in the direction of reconciliation between the government of President Nasser and the village is made at the end of the novel—the government is also reported to have abandoned its plan to forcibly relocate the inhabitants in the new village—(and turned the new structures into tourists' accommodations), the larger, historical conflict between the center and the periphery remains unmistakably open-ended. Here the machinery of nation building comes up against stubborn local resistance. The claim of the state to the contents of the Pharaonic tombs in the name of the supreme national interest is challenged by the claim of the locals to their historic patrimony. Faced with these irreconcilable claims, the narrator simply withdraws from public life; but the problems persist, all the same.

For some unclear reason, interest in rural space subsides in Egyptian fiction during the decade of the 1960s. Any conjecture about this phenomenon must take into account the high political drama unfolding in the capital Cairo during much of this decade, at the center of which, for better or for worse, was always the towering image of president Nasser. Egypt's posture in the world, as a leading member of the movement of non-aligned states, combined with Nasser's charisma and popularity in Egypt and the rest of the Arab world, did much to rivet attention to Cairo as a hub of frantic national, regional, and international bustle. Huge, state-sponsored projects originating at the center, such as the high dam in Aswān, the agrarian reforms of 1961, land distribution and reclamation, rapid industrialization and urbanization, contributed much to the fascination with Cairo's magnetism during this period. By the same token, the abrogation of political rights and the stifling of all dissent that accompanied these dramatic measures seems to have stimulated the search for an alternative space to represent the nation in Egyptian fiction. As we saw earlier, Alexandria emerges during this decade as a political rival to, and a space of refuge from, Cairo, at least in the stupendous imagination of Naguib Mahfouz.

Two additional factors may have contributed to the phenomenon under consideration. The first is the fact that many of the younger generation of Egyptian writers were in prison for political offenses for at least half of that decade. 'Abd al-Ḥakīm Qāsim, writer of one of the finest novels of rural Egypt, *Ayyām al-Insān al-Sab'a* (1969; The Seven Days of Man)[69] was among these. So was Sonalla Ibrahim, Ilhām Sayf al-Naṣr, Ra'ūf Mus'ad, and many others. The second factor is that they all were, whether in or out of prison, still experimenting with narrative forms, primarily through short stories and short novels, to discover their own distinctive style and collective literary portrait, away from the limelight still occupied by the generation of giants: Mahfouz, Ḥaqqī, al-Ḥakīm, al-Sharqāwī, and others. But, whatever the causes, the fact remains that fictional interest in rural space during the decade of the 1960s pales in comparison with the two decades preceding and following it. By contrast, the 1970s witnessed an unprecedented resurgence of interest in the countryside, the periphery, and beyond, that practically transformed the fictional landscape of the Egyptian novel. As fictional space is integral to all other aspects of the novel, I will discuss in the next Chapter novels that belong as much here as they do there. I have in mind particularly Ibrahim Abdel Meguid's Alexandria novels and Bahaa Taher's *Khālatī Ṣafiyya wal-Dayr* (1991; *Aunt Safiyya and the Monastery*, 1996).

3

DIVINING IDENTITIES

Religion and the Egyptian novel

> I have never read a good novel about Heaven.
>
> E. L. Doctorow

> When one reflects on the modern history of Egypt, from its inception to the present moment (1982), one discovers a strange fact, namely, that modern Egypt was formed, fashioned, stimulated intellectually, prompted to action, and launched on the course of *nahḍa* (awakening, renaissance) by turbaned shaykhs who did not shed off their traditional garb in the process. On the contrary, they held on steadfastly to the norms of traditional life, in private as in public. They ate, drank, and socialized the way their fathers and forefathers had done. And yet, jealous as they were in guarding tradition and precedent, these shaykhs were also leaders of modernizing movements, pioneers of liberation drives, sowers of revolutionary seeds, and vanguards of a new age. They revolted and took up arms against mightier powers. But as they did so, they did not tremble, abandon their mission, succumb to fear, or entertain inferiority complexes.
>
> Fatḥī Raḍwān[1]

By now, I hope, the centrality of religious concerns to the enterprise of the Egyptian novel has become too self-evident to require further affirmation. The thematic preponderance of issues of recognizably religious nature in so many novels, and the direct bearing of these issues on the social and personal crises these novels field, are too compelling to be accidental or inconsequential. The phenomenon is particularly persistent in realistic novels, beginning with such works as Yaḥyā Ḥaqqī's *Qindīl Umm Hāshim* and Naguib Mahfouz' *Zuqāq al-Midaqq* and lasting well into the present. It thus appears as an attendant by-product of the novel's realism, broadly defined. Whether in this respect the novel merely depicts what already exists, patently or only in latent form, in the complex web of social life, or actively promotes confrontation with institutionalized religion for purposes that lie beyond mimetic veracity, remains to be seen. Some aspects of this general problematic have already surfaced in the previous chapters and were discussed there, albeit tangentially. In this chapter I examine in greater detail and depth instructive modes of wrestling with religious content in Egyptian imaginative fiction.

Before launching that investigation proper, however, it is necessary to speculate, if only briefly, on another theoretical question of some relevance. The issue warrants stating in categorical terms because it, too, is symptomatic of discursive practices in other realms of modern Arab culture. To date, and contrary to a spate of recent, highly dubious allegations, no recognizably Islamic novel of unequivocal artistic merit has emerged in Egypt or anywhere else in the Arab world.[2] This sweeping generalization obviously excludes on generic grounds the largely didactic romances of writers like Jurjī Zaydān, 'Abd al-Ḥamīd Jawdat al-Saḥḥār, and others who dramatized, often in tenuous fictional guise, themes, events, and personalities from Islamic history. It also excludes the well-known *Abqariyyāt*, biographical narratives or psycho-histories of prominent Muslims, by 'Abbās Maḥmūd al-'Aqqād, Ṭāhā Ḥusayn, and 'Abd al-Raḥmān al-Sharqāwī, among others. The following working definition of our basic terms will have to do, inadequate and tentative as it may be. By "Islamic novel" I simply mean a serious work of imaginative fiction, of defensible artistic and aesthetic quality, whose outlook and value system are consonant with the fundamental tenets of Islamic faith and practice. To simplify matters still further, one could just as readily stipulate that such a work be written by a believing and devout Muslim author.

As it happens, the historical record seems to militate against the admixture, not only in Arabic, but perhaps in other novelistic traditions in other national cultures as well. With the possible exception of a handful of writers, such as Graham Greene and C. S. Lewis, for example, it is difficult to think of many novels or novelists in the stupendous tradition of fiction written in English that answer to the specification. The aforesaid definition *prima facie* excludes such masterpieces of world literature as Dostoyevsky's *The Brothers Karamazov*, James Joyce's *A Portrait of the Artist as a Young Man*, and Nikos Kazantzakis' *The Last Temptation of Christ*. For, although preoccupied with religious concerns, these works are not religious in our sense of the term. Rather than confirm or reinforce religious belief, such novels tend to problematize it beyond recall. A similar fate besets religious subject matter in most serious Arabic novels, in Egypt as elsewhere in the contemporary Arab world. It is perhaps no accident that the first serious attempt to write a work of fiction in the spirit of Islam that comes close to meeting the criteria stipulated earlier is also the last. I mean, of course, that precocious, but inalterably transitional work of Muḥammad al-Muwayliḥī, *Ḥadīth 'Īsā ibn Hishām* (1899, 1907).[3]

If the aforesaid observations have any bearing beyond the confines of Arabic fiction, it would suggest that radical skepticism toward religious dogma may be intrinsic to the novel as a literary genre (with only rare exceptions). Broadly speaking, such a formative disposition would place the novel squarely in the camp of philosophy rather than theology, at least vis-à-vis institutionalized interpretations of religion. That would also explain some of the fierce contestation at the site of the Arabic novel we have often encountered in this study. (Parenthetically, it may be worthwhile to bear in mind that neither philosophy proper nor literary texts with recognizable philosophical import ever fared well in Islamic history, any more than they did in other religious traditions, for that matter.) One notable upshot of this situation is also paradoxical: The treatment of religious concerns in the Egyptian novel is largely a secular affair.

Closely related to this observation is a patently curious phenomenon. Several of the most prominent Egyptian writers of the twentieth century who began their careers as creative writers of fiction uniformly abandoned this calling later on in life and reverted to a traditional mode of discursive writing on common Islamic subjects. Muḥammad Ḥusayn Haykal exemplifies this type perhaps better than anyone else. He began his literary career by writing *Zaynab* (1914), arguably the first full-fledged Arabic novel, and ended up writing biographies of the Prophet and his companions, for example, *Ḥayāt Muḥammad* (1935; The Life of Muḥammad, 1976), *al-Ṣiddīq Abū Bakr* (fifth edition, 1964; The Righteous Abu Bakr) and *al-Farūq 'Umar* (1945; Omar the Just). Ṭāhā Ḥusayn, 'Abbās Maḥmūd al-'Aqqād, and 'Abd al-Raḥmān al-Sharqāwī did likewise, although, as we shall see shortly, the case of al-Sharqāwī is particularly egregious. In any event, to the extent that the phenomenon constitutes a recanting, serious doubt has been raised about the sincerity of the gesture, especially in regard to Ṭāhā Ḥusayn.[4]

Be that as it may, the phenomenon itself was not limited to members of that generation of pioneering writers. The case of Sayyid Quṭb (1906–1966) possibly the most colorful Muslim personality in the entire Arab world during the second half of the twentieth century, is particularly instructive. Sayyid Quṭb began his intellectual career as a literary critic and prose writer of exquisite style and considerable promise. In the preface to his delightful fictional autobiography *Ṭifl min al-Qarya* (1945; A Village Boy) he openly acknowledges indebtedness to the first volume of Ṭāhā Ḥusayn's epoch-making work *al-Ayyām* (1929; An Egyptian Childhood, 1932) which he consciously sought to emulate. Soon after his return to Egypt from a two-year sojourn in the United States (1948–1950),[5] however, Quṭb disavowed all interest in literary criticism and imaginative fiction and devoted himself entirely to political activism within the ranks of the Muslim Brotherhood, or on the margins thereof. After serving prolonged prison terms for alleged subversive activity, he was finally executed in 1966. I will return to the case of Sayyid Quṭb shortly.

Though far inferior in caliber and originality, the examples of the Marxist-turned preacher Muṣṭafā Maḥmūd, and the former theater critic Ṣafīnāz Kāẓim reinforce the Sayyid Quṭb model. Like Quṭb, Kāẓim spent several years at American universities studying literature, mainly theater. According to her own account, she fell madly in love with New York, savored T. S. Elliot's poetry, and identified with the Argentinian Marxist revolutionary, Che Guevara.[6] Subsequently she would renounce all this after performing the pilgrimage in 1972, put on the veil, and, after a brief marriage to the well-known poet of the vernacular, Aḥmad Fu'ād Najm, devote herself entirely to Islamic activism.[7] With the onset of what came to be known as the "Islamic awakening,"[8] in the climate of President Sadat's "counter-revolution,"[9] the phenomenon of "recanting" intensified and reached the ranks of Egypt's top artists, singers, and performers. It may suffice to mention here the cases of several celebrated performers like the singer and actress Shādiya, the highly gifted stage and screen actresses Suhayr al-Bābilī, Shahīra, Shams al-Bārūdī, and 'Afāf Shu'ayb, all of whom abandoned brilliant artistic careers, donned the veil, and more or less disappeared from public life in the 1970s and 1980s.

As we saw earlier, these developments in Egypt cannot be isolated from the more general ascendancy of Saudi-manufactured and financed "petro-Islam" throughout the world. The 1973 oil embargo, and the sharp rise in the price of oil that followed, propelled Saudi Arabia to regional and international prominence. As a result, strict Wahhābī versions of Islam, Saudi style, became readily available for export and transplantation anywhere in the world, from northern Nigeria to the Philippines.[10] For complex historical, economic, and geopolitical reasons, Egypt appears to have been especially susceptible to this doctrinaire Saudi encroachment.

Its particular circumstances aside, the "recanting" phenomenon under consideration is uncannily consistent with—perhaps even constitutive of—the recurrent pattern of false starts and discontinuous modernity projects postulated in Chapter 1. Followed to their logical ends, both the phenomenon and the historical precedents animating it may suggest that Islam and imaginative literature are irreconcilable binary opposites, bound together by a negative dialectic of either/or. Though tempting, it would be singularly futile to attempt to address this intractable question here. In principle, though, the question lends itself to theoretical as well as historical considerations. So far, only the latter have received some serious attention in a work of Arabic fiction. Perhaps not altogether surprisingly, the text in question is none other than al-Muwayliḥī's pioneering work *Ḥadīth Īsā ibn Hishām*, in which a scathing critique is mounted against the austere, presumably spurious prohibition on music, dance, and poetry in Islam. In opposition to this restriction, propagated by grim, reactionary Azharite shaykhs, al-Muwayliḥī introduces an "enlightened" shaykh who proffers a sustained, sophisticated defense of these modes of artistic creation and expression. In the positivist, *fin-de-siecle* spirit of late-nineteenth century, the shaykh's discourse appeals to "scientific" biological "evidence" as well as historical precedent in support of his utilitarian view of the arts. The impressive range of the shaykh's erudition and command of comparative noetic knowledge from both East and West does not escape the notice of his interlocutors; it remains unsurpassed in modern Arabic fiction to this day.

What matters still more for the question of the novel's general agency in modern Arab history and culture are the operative theoretical premises and analytical procedures involved in the production of the shaykh's discourse on the arts. On the one hand, we note the disarming, unself-conscious ease with which he draws on non-Islamic, specifically Western sources of knowledge. This fictional postulate is, at least in part, descriptive. It rehearses a type of religious scholar that found its fullest historical incarnation in a chain of unique individuals beginning with Ḥasan al-'Aṭṭār (d. 1834?) and running through Rifā'a Rāfi' al-Ṭahṭāwī (d. 1871), Jamāl al-Dīn al-Afghānī (d. 1897), Muḥammad 'Abdu (d. 1905) and the circle of prominent disciples of the last two, who, collectively, left an indelible mark on the course of modern Egyptian and Arab thought and culture. It may suffice to note that, in one way or another, the following luminaries were among these disciples: Adīb Isḥāq, 'Abdullāh al-Nadīm, Sa'd Zaghlūl, Qāsim Amīn, 'Alī and Muṣṭafā 'Abd al-Rāziq, and Amīn al-Khūlī. For the brand of Islamic reform associated with this "school," the appropriation of beneficial knowledge by Muslim individuals and societies is not only permissible but also obligatory.[11] On the other hand, and notwithstanding this enabling abstract principle, a determined effort is nonetheless always made, in fiction as in other domains, to furnish a legitimating textual genealogy from within the corpus of Islamic sources for this act of desired appropriation. In *Ḥdīth 'Īsā ibn Hishām* this practice eventuates in the compelling array of historical anecdotes of the shaykh marshals to show that the Prophet, his immediate companions, and a host of other prominent Muslims of earlier times, had far greater appreciation and tolerance of literary and artistic talent than the benighted, later-day shaykhs of al-Muwayliḥī's time.

But the fictional model is also prescriptive in at least two important respects, both of which tend to privilege the fictional at the expense of the historical. The first has already been adumbrated in the foregoing remarks, namely, the total absence of any awareness on the part of the shaykh of the problematic nature of the act of cultural borrowing, even in the realm of scientific knowledge. The shaykh appears as blissfully oblivious to the immense cultural difference between the European context in which the desired knowledge was produced, and the Egyptian context, as he is to the cultural influence that inevitably attends on such an eminently one-sided traffic in cultural goods. The second aspect is directly related to this and involves an active suppression of highly relevant historical facts from the fictional purview. For, to the extent that the fictional model reenacts historical precedents such as al-Afghānī and 'Abdu, surely the grave charge of "innovation" and "heresy" that was frequently leveled against both by more orthodox religious scholars, deserves attention in the narrative. What necessitated this neat editing of the historical record is the felt need to valorize an alternative model of religious scholar, one who would embrace the idea of reform and the project of the *nahḍa* without expressly infringing or abandoning the Islamic epistemological paradigm.

Ḥadīth 'Īsā ibn Hishām is also silent on another crucial matter. How, why, and when in Arab/Islamic history did the spurious views on artistic creativity replace the "authentic" and enabling precedent bequeathed by the Prophet and his pious companions? Particularly poignant is the text's silence on the role of the institutions of religious learning in the matter at the time of writing. We note, for instance, that the trafficking in unorthodox "illicit" knowledge on such "secular" subjects as politics, literature, and the arts takes place entirely outside the corridors of al-Azhar—at a wedding in *Ḥadith*, in cafes and private homes in actual history.

This was the case with al-Afghānī and his circle of intimate associates and disciples in the 1870s as with al-Marṣifī and his intimate students, especially Ṭāhā Ḥusayn, a few decades later. Eventually, as we learn from Ṭāhā Ḥusayn's *al-Ayyām* the University of Cairo (founded in 1908), will become the natural abode of this kind of "forbidden" knowledge.

As if by an ironic twist that confirms the recurrent pattern we have often encountered in this study, the twentieth century ends on a less sanguine note than it began on this score. The veritable expulsion of Naṣr Ḥāmid Abū Zayd from the University of Cairo has been hailed by such prominent Islamists as 'Abd al-Ṣabūr Shāhīn as a sign of the general retreat of secularism at the University.[12] The compartmentalization of knowledge evident in this situation is at once a cause and an effect of the abiding split between "secular" and "religious" orientations in modern Arab culture.

In the overall historical scheme, the kind of religious scholar the text valorizes becomes a public figure in its own right only during the last quarter of the nineteenth century and the first quarter of the twentieth. He thus appears bracketed between two nearly identical versions of his antithesis: that of al-Jabartī's time (end of the eighteenth century, beginning of the nineteenth), so amply documented in the historian's chronicles, and that of more recent times (end of the twentieth century, and, from all appearances, beginning of the twenty-first) so oppressively prevalent among "religious" movements and circles that would sanction violence even against the paragon of Arab novelists, Naguib Mahfouz.[13]

Where al-Muwayliḥī's *Ḥadīth* leaves off, Ṭāhā Ḥusayn's *Al-Ayyām*, and its direct descendent, Sayyid Quṭb's *Ṭifl min al-Qarya*, pick up. It is safe to say that all subsequent representations of forms and varieties of institutionalized Islam in Egyptian fiction owe something to these two autobiographical accounts, especially to *al-Ayyām*. What is particularly noteworthy about *al-Ayyām's* depiction of religious subjects is the tightly knit relation the text weaves between, on the one hand, Islamic schooling and curriculum, and, on the other hand, the unsavory type of religious cleric the system routinely spews out in the grotesque form of the *kuttāb's* head master, the nameless *sayyidunā* (our master). Operating in virtual autonomy, the village *kuttāb* presents a miniature version of the Islamic educational system under laboratory conditions. Its raison d'etre, to teach the Qur'ān, is routinely frustrated by its "pedagogy" of teaching exclusively by rote, through mechanical repetition. With unfailing predictability, the boy, young Ṭāhā Ḥusayn, manages to forget the Qur'ān, or large portions of it, as soon as he "officially" completes memorizing it and, thereby, acquiring the ostentatious, but, under the circumstances utterly meaningless epithet of *shaykh*. What is far worse is the total absence of any internal or external incentive, or mechanism, for reforming the system. Having mastered the techniques of prevarication and manipulation, the headmaster manages to weasel his way out of every personal predicament his dereliction brings about. No vain oath is in vain if it helps preserve the status quo in his *kuttāb* and the material benefits that accrue therefrom. Equally without fail, he passes on his chicanery to his subordinates and pupils, who, in turn, pass it on to theirs in an infinite, closed, and self-perpetuating system of corruption and deceit.

Though incomparably odious and rampant in the *kuttāb*, dissembling and dishonesty are by no means confined to it. They appear as pervasive in all walks of life in the village, though perhaps in a slightly less egregious form. Thus, for example, the boy's father, his grandfather, Azharite brother, and the Ṣūfī shaykhs who frequent the family home, all partake, in one degree or another in the headmaster's lax standards of veracity. So much so in fact that the boy himself, though eventually destined to achieve personal and intellectual integrity, appears to have become, already at that tender age, totally immune to the psychological ravages of habitual mendacity and hypocrisy. Particularly instructive and chilling in this respect is his nonchalant indifference to the headmaster's flagrant and often gratuitous lying under oath. In due course, the boy will go on to perpetrate his share of fibs and subterfuges in a manner that confirms the self-regulating and self-perpetuating "efficiency" of the corrupt system.

Ṭāhā Ḥusayn's "clinical" diagnosis of the ills of the Qur'ānic school system, and those of Egyptian rural life in general, is fully corroborated by the experience of Sayyid Quṭb at another *kuttāb*, in another village, at another time. Although, as already noted, Quṭb's *Ṭifl min al-Qarya* was directly inspired and influenced by Ḥusayn's earlier work, this literary affinity is no sufficient cause to question the factual veracity and accuracy of the autobiographical account in either text. Moreover, whatever one thinks of Sayyid Quṭb's politics, his personal integrity was never in doubt at any point in his turbulent life. In any event, though compelling in its own right, the account of his travails at the village *kuttāb* adds only sordid details of unspeakable physical filth to the repugnant picture sketched in *al-Ayyām*.

But the impact of Sayyid Quṭb on the course of the Egyptian novel is by no means limited to this specific matter, even though in most instances it is indirect and circumstantial. This proposition finds a graphic illustration in the following anomaly: Quṭb was the first prominent literary critic to recognize the nascent talent of Naguib Mahfouz in the mid-1940s, and the Muslim thinker and activist who, more than anyone else, "theorized" and legitimated the Islamic backlash that almost claimed Mahfouz' life half a century later.[14] Such extreme polarities marked every stage of Quṭb's tragic life.[15] During his "secular" phase, prior to 1951, he not only wrote criticism, fictional autobiography, and poetry, but also tried his hand at actual fiction, ominously titling one of the two novels he wrote *Ashwāk* (1947; Thorns). Moreover, during this phase he was apparently so infatuated with Western culture that, at one point, he went so far as to advocate public nudity in Egypt.[16] He was equally frank about his atheism, which is said to have lasted eleven years.[17] Of particular relevance is his insistence on the need to keep religion and imaginative literature apart, and the evident pride he took in the artistic achievement of Naguib Mahfouz as a novelist. When Mahfouz' *Khān al-Khalīlī* appeared in 1946 Sayyid Quṭb praised it as

> a milestone on our way toward a distinct national literature, quintessentially Egyptian in spirit, unadulterated by foreign influences—though benefiting

> from them; a novel of evident national identity we can present before the world without fear that it might be readily co-opted and lose its distinctive characteristics.[18]

All this changed to its diametrical opposite in 1951, the year of Sayyid Quṭb's proclaimed rebirth. Politically, his touted close relations with the Free Officers (some of whom, including Nasser, are said to have met occasionally in Quṭb's backyard in Cairo's Ḥilwān suburb to plot the Revolution),[19] went sour soon after the Free Officers took over in July, 1952. From 1954 on, his hostility to all secular matters, including imaginative literature and the rest of the humanistic disciplines, which he so fervently championed before, steadily took on a more extreme form. As it turned out, his senseless execution by Nasser's government in 1966 added the mystique of martyrdom to the appeal of his message; the force of both is yet to dissipate fully. Meantime, the gaping polarity and apparent irreconcilability of secular values and religious belief at the center of modern Arab culture continue to plague the quest for identity, in Egypt as elsewhere in the Arab and Islamic world.[20] This abysmal polarity finds a vivid fictional incarnation in the grim ending of Mahfouz' masterpiece, *The Cairene Trilogy* (1956–1957) where the two politicized grandsons of Sayyid Aḥmad are led to prison, one as a communist, the other as a Muslim Brother.

By all accounts, Mahfouz' *Cairene Trilogy* marks the zenith of the realistic phase in Arabic fiction and we will return to its treatment of religion later. Here it may be useful to recapitulate two major propositions implicit in the crucial intervention of *al-Ayyām* and *Ṭifl min al-Qarya* in the critique of institutionalized Islam. The first concerns the total bankruptcy of the Islamic educational system when measured in terms of propitious learning and genuine knowledge. Both texts make this point emphatically about the village *kuttāb*; the second and third parts of *al-Ayyām* extend the harsh judgment to al-Azhar as well. The second proposition concerns the total divorce of religious learning in these institutions, flimsy as that may be, from genuine piety and personal morality. Nowhere is this divorce more evident, or more troubling, than it is in the official and nominal custodians and representatives of religious knowledge and practice: the headmasters of the village *kuttābs*, the shaykhs of al-Azhar, the Ṣūfī masters, the theologians, and the patriarchal figures in the community. Since both propositions become axiomatic in much of the subsequent treatment of aspects of institutionalized religion in the novel, it is necessary to interrogate them a little further here.

To begin with, there is no doubt that the autobiographical experience in both texts lends referential validity to the representation. Against that, however, one must weigh in the historical circumstances surrounding the writing of both works. In the case of Ṭāhā Ḥusayn, the first part of *al-Ayyām* was written in the acrimonious atmosphere following the publication of his most controversial work, *Fil-Shi'r al-Jāhilī* (1926; On Pre-Islamic Arabic Poetry).[21] In that book Ṭāhā Ḥusayn, following a number of Orientalists, notably D. S. Margoliouth, openly questioned the historical validity of certain narratives of the Qur'ān, especially the account of building the Ka'ba by Ibrāhīm (Abraham) and his son Ismā'īl (Ishmael).

The publication of the book generated a heated debate in Egypt and the rest of the Arab world, in the wake of which legal charges were brought against the author. The first volume of *al-Ayyām* was written, or rather dictated, in the heat of that controversy (1929), which did not subside even after the case was shelved by the eminent judge, Muḥammad Wajdī, in 1932.[22] Similarly, Sayyid Quṭb's work was written at the zenith of the atheist phase of his life and, therefore, could not have remained immune to its ideological fervor, in color and tone, if not in substance.

Against the foregoing critique of institutionalized Islamic practices stand two equally cogent arguments. The first is that, deficient as it may have been, the Islamic school system nonetheless withstood the historical challenge of foreign occupation and colonial domination, and thus preserved, more or less intact, the Arab/Islamic identity of Egypt. Second, as the epigraph to this chapter shows, some scholars, such as Fatḥī Raḍwān, credit the same system and the same shaykhs so mercilessly lampooned by Ḥusayn, Quṭb, and others, with the Promethean task of spearheading the movement for reform and modernization in Egypt, without thereby abdicating their Islamic identity and worldview. With equal plausibility one could ascribe at least part of the responsibility for the deterioration of religious education to the fierce competition it faced from the more secular, public school system founded by Muḥammad Alī (d. 1849) to train prospective recruits for the army and the nascent state bureaucracy. The mendicant state of the headmaster of Ṭāhā Ḥusayn's and Sayyid Quṭb's *kuttābs*, and the public jeering at religious figures in *Qindīl Umm Hāshim* attest to the low esteem in which religious figures and institutions were held during the early decades of the twentieth century. That dual educational system, as we know, was introduced into Egypt in the wake of the French expedition to Egypt (1798–1801) and under the relentless pressure of the European nation-state model.

Whether all this warrants assigning *exclusive* blame for the shortcomings of the Islamic school system in Egypt to direct or indirect European machinations, as some scholars have tended to do, is a moot question.[23] Similarly, Fatḥī Raḍwān's sweeping valorization of the role of the turbaned shaykhs in the history of modern Egypt, especially in promoting progress and sowing the seeds of enlightenment and revolution, while presumably remaining faithful to their traditional way of life, is outlandish, to say the least. It completely elides the fact that the very shaykhs, whose dural role of religious scholar and enlightenment thinker, he celebrates, for example, Muḥammad 'Abdu, were often ostracized by their own peers and institutions. If anything, these remarkable—and remarkably few—shaykhs stand out precisely because they were *atypical*. Nor does their alleged contribution to the reconciliation of the Islamic and non-Islamic facets of identity pass historical muster. After all, it was Muḥammad 'Abdu himself who made this point emphatically when he said that he spent twelve years at al-Azhar and the rest of his life trying to rid himself of what he memorized there.[24] The Egyptian novel is perhaps closer to reality when it shows that a satisfactory solution to this chronic problem and the realization of a viable cultural synthesis between Islamic and secular (or Western) values, continue to be as elusive and as pressing as ever.

It may not be entirely accidental that the Egyptian novel's "coming of age" in the 1940s also witnessed an extensive investigation of this conflicted legacy. In the following section I will examine permutations of this troubled legacy in a number of realistic novels that, collectively, delineate the general contours of the treatment of religion in Egyptian fiction.

* * *

> As a boy, my grandfather, shaykh Rajab 'Abdullāh, used to come to Cairo with the men and women of the family to visit and seek the blessings of the (saintly) descendants of the Prophet. No sooner would they approach the doorsteps of Sayyida Zaynab's mosque than his father would push him down on his knees, like the rest of the family, to kiss its doorsteps. In time, the habit of imitation made the push unnecessary, as the boy learned to fall down on his own and to flood the marble threshold with his kisses—the feet of those entering or exiting the mosque barely missing his head. Whenever a bookish man of religion happened to witness this spectacle he would avert his gaze, inveigh against the times, and invoke God's protection from such (evil) innovations, idolatry, and ignorance. The rest of the people would smile benignly at the simplicity of these rural folks—their clothes reeking of the smell of milk, mud, and fenugreek—and would understand the ardent passion and longing of their hearts, which they could express adequately only in their actions. *After all, it is the intention that counts* [emphasis added].

This memorable opening paragraph of Yaḥyā Ḥaqqī's novella *Qindīl Umm Hāshim* illustrates the direct intervention of fiction in religious concerns. The vivid descriptive quality notwithstanding, the dramatic episode is entirely fictional and the crux of the matter is unmistakably theological in nature. In a nutshell, it concerns the problematic status of saints and saint "worship" in Islam, represented here by the symbolic act of prostration before and kissing the doorsteps of the mosque of (Saint) Zaynab—Umm Hāshim—the granddaughter of the Prophet. The larger issue ultimately involves the question of the legitimacy of popular or folk religion in Islam, including, as in the present case, supplication for the intercession of "saints"—*awliyā'*. How the text presents the issue on the diegetic level is, of course, part of its strategy of intervention on the extradiegetic and extratextual, that is, discursive/historical levels. Here, for example, the characterization of the "man of religion" as a *muta'ālim* rather than a *'ālim*—that is, a pretentious, rather than a genuine scholar—casts doubt on his judgment from the outset. Several other factors in the paragraph combine to reinforce this negative characterization. In the immediate context, the haughty religious scholar is presented as a lone voice, the austere one against the tolerant many. This is a fairly obvious invocation of the democratic principle of majority vs. minority; better still, an overwhelming majority vs. a distinct minority of one.

But Ḥaqqī is too fine an artist to predicate the outcome of an essentially theological issue on the extraneous criteria of numerical equations. He therefore encloses the whole controversy between two unmistakably Islamic motifs: The first is the very name of the subject of the controversy, the little boy who will eventually grow up to become the narrator's grandfather and the protagonist's (Ismāʻīl's) father. The name consists of the Islamic epithet, *shaykh*, the first name, *rajab*, which is also the name of one of the months of the Islamic calendar, and the surname, *'Abdullāh*, which means "servant of God" and was, of course, the name of the Prophet's father. This heavy investment in Islamic toponomy appears intended to fend off, proleptically, the very accusation of idolatry and heresy subsequently levelled against the boy-shaykh by the severe "man of religion." But, like the democratic principle of majority rule, this rhetorical ploy provides no adequate refutation or counterweight to the grave charge of idolatry. Hence the ultimate recourse to the second Islamic motif, namely, the invocation of the sound Prophetic tradition that predicates the judgment of deeds on the intentions underlying them: *innamā al-aʻmāl bil-niyyāt*. As we can see, the principle of authenticating all knowledge concerning every crucial aspect of life by means of, and in reference to, Islamic sources that we encountered in al-Muwayliḥī's *Ḥadīth* is in full force here as well.

In addition to the eponymous names of the protagonist, Ismāʻīl (Abraham's firstborn son and putative "father of the Arabs"), and his cousin and future wife, Fāṭima al-Nabawiyya (Fāṭima of the Prophet) the workings of this validating principle are also evident in the proffered solution to the conflict between faith and science the novella dramatizes. After testing in three successive phases the available, but insufficient modalities of identity for Ismāʻīl/Egypt: indigenous/Islamic, acquired/European, and a (failed) synthesis of the two, the novella ultimately opts for a mystical way out of the historical/discursive impasse. In fact, however, the trumpeted formula of "science fortified by faith" by means of which Ismāʻīl cures Fāṭima's trachomic eyes—which also encapsulates the novella's discursive contribution to the ongoing debate on identity—readily collapses under any rigorous interrogation.[25] Not so the underlying mystical yearning and resonance that animate the pervasive allusions to the Qur'ān, especially to verse 35 of the chapter of Light (XXIV) and to *Laylat al-Qadr*, during which the Qur'ān was revealed.[26] Equally important in this respect is the implied rehabilitation of the prostitute Naʻīma, whose supplications seem to have been answered through the intercession of al-Sayyida Zaynab, Umm Hāshim. It is ultimately this wedding of popular belief to mystical allusion that anchors the religious significance of the novella.

To sum up, Ḥaqqī's approach to religious matters is essentially cultural and unmistakably liberal. The solution he envisions to intra-religious, as well as inter-religious and inter-cultural difference is tolerant, compassionate pluralism.

Hence the categorical renunciation in the novella of the principle of comparing cultures in terms of value, and the equally resolute suspension of moral judgment on the characters, even when their conduct appears patently reprehensible. Joseph Conrad's supreme moral imperative for the novel: "to make (the reader) see," has rarely, if ever, found a more palpable expression than in this charming novella.

* * *

By marked contrast, 'Abd al-Raḥmān al-Sharqāwī's treatment of religious questions appears shrill and blatantly ideological. We have already seen how his most important novel *al-Arḍ* (1954; *Egyptian Earth*, 1990), treats religious subjects, especially religious space, with evident impertinence, made all the more egregious by the lack of any pretense to artistic justification. Thus, the *muṣallā*, or prayer space, at the edge of the village, is not quite a mosque, *jāmi'*, but rather a makeshift place of prayer. Even so, it is associated more with sexual desire and illicit intent than with piety and worship in the novel. Although no sexual acts are consummated on the premises, it is not for lack of trying. The repeated attempts to desecrate the space of the *muṣallā* in this fashion presents an instructive example of the interplay between the artistic and the ideological dimensions of the text.

Given the implausibility of much of the amorous import in the novel, the motif of "sex" in the sacred place appears blatantly contrived. Indeed al-Sharqāwī must have been aware of the permutations of the motif in Yaḥyā Ḥaqqī's *Qindīl Umm Hāshim*. It is just as likely that both writers were aware of the mythic origins of the motif in the story of *'Isāf* and *Nā'ilah* who had a tryst in the *Ka'ba*, according to ancient Arab folklore, and were turned into stone for defiling the sacred place.[27] But in contrast to Ḥaqqī's tight, causal integration of the motif in the larger schemes of characterization and plot, al-Sharqāwī merely floats it, for no clear artistic purpose or structural design. What is more, the narrative keeps reverting to this motif, almost compulsively. Now, since no sharp distinction is drawn between the voice of the grown up, largely authorial third person narrator, and that of the adolescent first person narrator who experiences these amorous adventures in the *muṣallā*, the obsessive reiteration of the motif appears to be a function of ideological rather than psychological or literary considerations. In other words, the gratuitous incident forms part of a deliberate strategy by al-Sharqāwī the "socialist" (at the time of writing) to debunk religion by debasing the space that represents it metonymically in the novel.

Other examples of the treatment of religion in the novel bear out this interpretation and reveal other components of the strategy. Progressively, as the conflict between the government and the village over the land intensifies, so does the debate over religion. When the paramount conflict over the land occupies center stage it becomes the measure of all things, including all things religious. Eventually, the imperative to defend the land of the village interlocks with that of defending Egypt as a whole, and everything in the novel becomes subject to reevaluation in terms of its congruence, or lack thereof, with this dual supreme imperative.

Traditional religion fairs poorly in this new dispensation, which renders it contingent, not primary. Nor is its case helped by the opportunistic shaykh who represents religion in the village: a man of little knowledge, and even less common sense and discretion. His frequent malapropisms and mechanical invocation of the doctrine of retribution often backfire and embolden the villagers to question openly the efficacy of performing the mandatory religious duties, such as public prayers, and the relevance of the doctrine of retribution altogether to their predicament. This systematic erosion in the status of traditional religion culminates in its permanent subordination to the dual imperative of social justice and national liberation. A succinct dictum toward the end of the novel indexes the very idea of the sacred to political commitment: where there is struggle for liberation, there shall a mosque be, and there shall prayer be held (p. 258).

It goes without saying that al-Sharqāwī's ideological strictures severely hindered his artistic insight and caused him to misread—by a wide margin, it turned out—the profoundly religious disposition of his fellow-Egyptians. The subsequent zealot backlash against all manifestations of socialist and secular ideology in Egypt, though exacerbated by external factors and often instructed by superstition and outright ignorance, nonetheless substantiates this generalization. What is perhaps less comprehensible, and far more problematic for the enterprise of the novel and modern Arab culture in general, is al-Sharqāwī's perceived decoupling of Islam from current politics in such a way as to merit him official Saudi approval. He was awarded the hefty King Fayṣal prize shortly before his death in 1987.

* * *

As in other areas, Mahfouz' treatment of religion is more extensive and more problematic than either of his two compatriots. More philosophical than both, it seldom sinks to the level of al-Sharqāwī's ideological rant or rises to the level of Ḥaqqī's soothing lyrical mysticism. A profound alienation from all forms of conventional and institutionalized religion nonetheless seems to lie at the core of Mahfouz' outlook that renders all manifestations of organized religion in his works at best irrelevant and at worst outrightly pernicious. What is more, this alienation seems to be abiding as it informs the treatment of religion in works written at great intervals in the novelist's long writing career. Worst of all fares al-Azhar for its alleged dogmatic rigidity, especially in matters of thought and conscience.

There is no doubt that *Awlād Ḥāratinā* (1959) is Mahfouz' most controversial novel as far as the treatment of religious subject matter is concerned. Since I have already discussed this novel at some length in Chapter 1, I will leave it largely out of this discussion. Instead, it may be useful to retrace here the trajectory of Mahfouz' preoccupation with religion from the formative stage at the outset of the realistic phase in the 1940s and follow its permutations in subsequent works, especially those he wrote during the troubled decade of the 1960s, where religious and existential anxieties intersect with, and are further compounded by, a corrosive sense of national malaise in Mahfouz' fiction.

In every other respect, Mahfouz' first two novels in the realistic vein, *al-Qāhira al-Jadīda* (1945; New Cairo) and *Khān al-Khalīlī* (1946) present little more than projects for novels of ideas.[28] Both serve primarily as grounds for testing the interplay of certain "philosophical" theses and personality types against the fluid social reality of contemporary Egypt. *Al-Qāhira al-Jadīda* in particular appears as a veritable debate among four university students, each of whom represents a specific discursive position or orientation. I use the term "represent" in the dual sense of embodying innately, as if by natural predisposition, and consciously espousing and championing, as an ideology or a lifestyle. Reduced to skeletal bareness, the division of ideational labor among the four characters runs as follows: Maḥjūb 'Abd al-Dāyim, nihilist–opportunist; 'Alī Ṭāhā, secular–materialist–socialist; Ma'mūn Raḍwān, idealist–Islamist; and Aḥmad Budayr, uncommitted (journalist). Of the four, only Maḥjūb's nihilism is explored in some depth. He accedes to a sham marriage with Iḥsān, the neighborhood beauty and one time sweetheart of his friend, 'Alī Ṭāha, as a cover for her ongoing liaison with a wealthy politician who literally buys her off from her debauched parents. The marriage comes unraveled in a public scandal soon enough, and this outcome explicitly discredits nihilism and opportunism on the thematic or ideational level of the narrative.

But this is hardly the only signifying level. The personal quality of the characters obviously bears on the respective positions they espouse. And although Mahfouz accords each character sufficient social background to explain, if not always to justify, their outlook and conduct, there is no doubt that Ma'mūn Raḍwān's personal integrity—readily available in his positive, meaningful Islamic name—is valorized above and beyond this call of duty. This, in turn, lends greater credibility to the Islamic option he champions.

The credit accruing thereof, however, is significantly diminished by several counter thrusts in the novel. Foremost among these is the structural leveling of the narrative perspective that places the Islamic option on equal footing with all the others. From the viewpoint of its advocates, who maintain that Islam is inclusive, all-encompassing, and holds the key to curing the ills of Egypt and all other Arab and Muslim societies, this structural arrangement amounts to a veritable demotion. The religious option is confined here to the realm of personal choice and no longer enjoys an a priori universal sanction. It has to vie for that ascendancy against contending world views and ideologies that clamor for equal representation, that is, equal narrative space, in the text. And since there is no discernible substantive difference between the textual and the extratextual formulation of the Islamic option, its performance in the text is not indifferent to its actual or desirable standing in the real world. In the text, the religious option is severely curtailed by the considerable polemical force vested in the representation of nihilist, materialist, and forthright atheist views. This thrust is further abetted by uninhibited, often direct verbal attacks on religion, including equating it with myths, valorizing Satan for his insubordination, and calling for the outright banishment of God and religion from the confines of the University (of Cairo). All this antireligious import, we may note, is authorized by the implicit appeal to the double-edged principle of verisimilitude and its uncanny ability to promote and promulgate even as it appears only to describe and relate. For instance, the repeated reference to the fashionable public confession of *ilḥād* (atheism) in Egypt at the time of the novel's action, (the early thirties), is fully corroborated by the well-known examples of Ismāʻīl Adham and Sayyid Quṭb, whatever other ideological purposes or agendas it may concurrently serve.[29]

Somewhat less readily apparent, but perhaps no less detrimental to the religious position, is the rhetorical strategy of appropriating religious tropes and terminology for nonreligious or even antireligious purposes in the novel. The insistence on performing the marriage rites in accordance with Islamic norms when the whole sordid affair is a thin cover for adultery is a good example of this strategy. It is not hard to imagine the erosion in the moral standing of religion that flows from such categorical divorce of "religious" practice from religious intent, the material uses of religious agency from the spiritual ends of religion. This susceptibility of the religious discourse to manipulation for unethical and immoral ends is methodically explored in Mahfouz' realistic novels—long before swindlers conned millions of poor Egyptians of their lifetime savings in the name of "Islamic" banking, financing, and other shady schemes during the 1970s and 1980s.[30] But even as it enables him to debunk the sham, the insight into the actual workings of religious agency also prompts Mahfouz to search for alternative sources of spirituality and genuine piety outside the purview of institutionalized and traditional religion.

* * *

Khān al-Khalīlī, which Sayyid Quṭb praised lavishly as a fine specimen of national literature has in fact little to show for it in artistic merit. The novel is only slightly less a symposium of abstract ideas than the earlier one. Its treatment of individual psychology and religious themes, however, stands out. The novel offers another example of the skewed manipulation of religion, although the motive here remains largely unconscious. An ostensibly religious motif triggers the main action of the novel.

A single, middle-aged, unmistakably oedipal protagonist, Aḥmad ʻĀkif, moves into Khān al-Khalīlī with his decrepit father and youthful mother to escape the German air raids on Cairo during the Second World War. The operative assumption behind the hasty move originates in a popular belief that the Germans, for a variety of reasons, would not attack this quarter at the heart of Islamic Cairo because of its proximity to the mosque of al-Ḥusayn, the grandson of the Prophet, and to the famous mosque of al-Azhar (p. 10). The odd reasons range from the superstitious to the outrightly bizarre; from faith in the supernatural powers of the saintly al-Ḥusayn to avert harm from those who seek his protection, to the belief that Nazi Germany, being a friend of Muslims, would not attack such a highly visible symbol of Islam. This fantastic line of reasoning culminates in the absurd claim that Hitler had, in fact, converted to Islam, though, for obvious reasons, he had kept the matter a guarded secret (p. 67).

That none of these "safeguards" ultimately avails, as the quarter comes under repeated attacks, is of little consequence. More important is to note how the novel's contrived action occasions a thorough critique of "religious" superstition, and the glaring difference in the treatment of this issue between Mahfouz and Ḥaqqī. We recall how Ḥaqqī finagled a solution to the conflict between science and superstition by projecting the whole matter onto a more metaphysical plain of symbolism reinforced by vague mystical intimations and resonance.

That willed solution is ultimately rhetorical, not analytical, in that it fabricates a simulacrum of synthesis not so much between faith and science as between an even less compatible binary pair: reason and superstition. Mahfouz' unflinching commitment to the novel's rational–philosophical mandate shuns such rhetorically elegant but intellectually fraudulent contraptions. Even as the novel debunks through action the feeble reasoning that breeds superstition, it leaves unresolved the conflict between traditional Arab/Islamic culture and its counterpart in the modern secular West. On this point the novel simply reenacts the continuing historical impasse.

The aforesaid observations address only the manifest discursive–polemical layer of the narrative; they hardly exhaust its meaning. A closer scrutiny may adduce a more comprehensive interpretation, one that brings into a single frame disparate strands and clusters of narrative that would otherwise remain diffused and disconnected. For instance, interpretation must ultimately address the question of whether or not the move to the vicinity of al-Ḥusayn is causally related to the stillborn romantic "relationship" between the middle-aged protagonist and a sixteen-year-old neighbor who takes a liking to him, implausible and unconvincing as that may be. Since the move literally sets these thematic complications in motion, to assume that the connection is purely incidental is to indict the novel, not only for artistic shallowness but also for intellectual dishonesty. At the very least its invocation of the religious associations and mystique of al-Ḥusayn would have been in vain—these having served no tangible purpose beyond the polemic against superstitious belief.

As I intimated earlier, a causal connection does seem to exist and to operate at the unconscious level, and not necessarily of the characters alone. The key to this connection must be sought in the tabooed, patently oedipal relationship between the protagonist, Aḥmad 'Ākif, and his mother. There is ample evidence to substantiate such a reading. Merely to illustrate the point, the following examples may suffice: the repeated references to his arrested development, morbid recoiling from meaningful relations with women, and habitual regression to infantile dependence on the mother for protection from the real world; the mother's coquettish manner with him is more apt for a romantic than a filial relationship; the extraordinary efforts she makes to conceal her true age, in order to narrow the age difference between the two of them, foreground the man–woman aspect of the relationship, at the expense of the mother–son aspect; the putative, though not entirely convincing frailty of the father, serves to neutralize him as a *bona fide* husband without removing him from the picture as a father figure; and finally, the prolonged absence of the younger, more extroverted brother from home and his eventual death soon after he returns.

It is against this heavily stacked potential for a "family romance" that we must read the implausible attraction of a sixteen-year-old girl to the balding, bashful, and preternaturally timid bachelor of forty. If the presence of the mother checks the oedipal son's gravitation towards other women, the presence of the father figure checks the inverse gravitation towards the mother. It is here that the proximity to al-Ḥusayn and to the source of religious authority emanating from his mosque makes its most crucial contribution to the structure of meaning in the novel. The frequent reference to the veritable thicket of minarets, domes, mosque tops and walls, and especially to the towering minaret of the Ḥusayn mosque, which is visible from the balcony of the family's apartment, keeps the symbols of religion in full view and places the family literally in the shadow of religious edifices and monuments (p. 12 ff.). This ubiquitous presence of emblems of religion serves to reinforce the taboo regime against the oedipal drive in the absence of coercive paternal authority.

It is instructive to note the telling contrast with *Zuqāq* on this point. Like *Khān al-Khalīlī*, *Midaq Alley* also lies at the heart of Islamic Cairo. The fictional space of that novel, however, is marked by nothing more than the conspicuous absence of any physical reminders of institutionalized religion. As we saw earlier, the Alley in fact has no mosque. Nor, for that matter, does it have any children. It may not be entirely accidental that the narrative is completely devoid of any reference or allusion to the oedipal entanglement as well.

A similar commingling of religious and oedipal motifs obtains in Mahfouz' major work, *The Cairene Trilogy* (1956–1957). There, in a childish but symbolically telling act of defiance, the largely autobiographical Kamāl attempts to usurp the place of the father in his mother's life, and almost causes her ruin in the process. During a momentary absence of the despotic father, Aḥmad 'Abd al-Jawād, from Cairo, the ten-year-old Kamāl accompanies his mother—a virtual prisoner in her husband's house until then—to the very mosque of al-Ḥusayn to pray and seek his blessings. Little Kamāl, however, has other designs on her, now that she is out with him alone, in stark violation of the strict rules of the father. At his insistence, she agrees to deviate from the main route for a little outing in the side streets of Cairo, whereupon she is hit by a car and sustains an injury. For this act of disobedience she is banished from her husband's house, and is allowed to return only after sustained intercession on her behalf. Again, what matters here is the uncanny, though hardly surprising coupling of religious motifs and associations with demonstrably oedipal situations and dynamics. This highly original side of Mahfouz' work has yet to receive the critical attention it deserves.

* * *

Zuqāq al-Midaqq (1947) marks a drastic leap in every respect in Mahfouz' fiction, including its treatment of religion. The structural feature noted earlier, namely, the absence of a mosque from the symbolic space of the Alley, signals Mahfouz' lasting attitude towards institutionalized religion, embodied in the Azhar itself. This attitude finds thematic expression in two important developments. The first has already been intimated. It is the complete decoupling of genuine piety, ethics, and spirituality from official, institutionally sanctioned religious scholarship and status. In the total absence of material and symbolic representation of formal religion in the space of the Alley, Raḍwān al-Ḥusaynī, a failed student of the Azhar, steps forth to fill the void. Notwithstanding his proverbial piety, kindness, and patience, and the compelling linguistic–thematic associations that link him to al-Ḥusayn, on the one hand, and to Job, on the other,[31] Ḥusaynī has no official religious standing whatsoever, having failed numerous times, in so many years, the *'ālimiyya* (certification) test of the Azhar. This investment of the positive values of religion and personal integrity in a failed student of the religious educational system is a pointed commentary on the latter. It also offers a good example of the novel's contribution to the debate on the need to reform the Azhar's curriculum, a matter that finally materialized in the sweeping reforms of 1961 that transformed the Azhar from an institution of exclusive religious learning to a full-fledged university.[32]

The roots of this alienation from the Azhar, however, seem to be more deeply embedded in Mahfouz' creative imagination. We can perhaps gauge this depth from the fact that Mahfouz returns to the question of the Azhar's rigidity, with only minor variations, twenty years later, in *Miramār* (1967), that is, six years after the drastic reforms of 1961. But since the novel's action takes place around that time, revisiting the issue of al-Azhar's obscurantism in *Miramār* may be read as a tacit endorsement of the reforms, without necessarily commenting on, or relating to them directly. Either way, we surmise from the narrative that 'Āmir Wajdī, the octogenarian narrator of the frame chapters of the novel, was expelled from the Azhar as a young man, for expressing unorthodox views. The act, however, causes the breakup of his engagement to his beloved and dooms him to lasting (and painful) bachelorhood. Like his predecessor, Raḍwān al-Ḥusaynī, 'Āmir acts as the veritable conscience of the novel, at a time of rampant moral degeneracy and rife corruption. Moreover, 'Āmir's habit of reciting passages of the Qur'ān, privately, and by heart, especially the chapter of *The Merciful* (55), *al-Raḥmān*, serves to confute the charge of heresy levelled against him, and to indict the inordinate harshness of the Azhar's sentence on him.

These examples illustrate the first of the two developments in Mahfouz' attitude toward institutionalized religion that crystallize for the first time in *Zuqāq al-Midaqq*. The second is the introduction of the figure of the eccentric "shaykh" who mediates the distance between holiness and madness, partaking of both in equal measure as he drifts across spatial and social boundaries and states of consciousness. Shaykh Darwīsh plays this vital role in *Zuqāq al-Midaqq*, as does shaykh Mutawallī 'Abd al-Ṣamad in *The Cairene Trilogy*. Situated midway between the saintly and the unhinged, the savant and the licensed fool, this peripatetic figure serves a variety of purposes in Mahfouz' fiction. For one thing, his affiliation with religion, though only numinous, still fills some of the structural void left vacant by the absence of formal religion. A relic of folk religion, this figure shows enough resilience to withstand the ravages of modern times better than its counterpart in the secular realm, the bard of traditional tales and sagas, who is summarily replaced by a radio at Kirsha's cafe at the beginning of *Zuqāq al-Midaqq*. From his perennial position on the fringe of normative sanity, the "shaykh" is empowered to name things that philistine respectability would rather disown and, by disowning, annul. As I noted earlier, shaykh Darwīsh's enunciation of the English words *elopement*, *homosexuality*, and *tragedy*, among others, punctuates the Arabic text and "confirms" his putative bilingual aptitude to receive "revelation" in both Arabic and English. Similarly, shaykh Mutawallī's blunt exhortations to al-Sayyid Aḥmad 'Abd al-Jawād in *The Cairene Trilogy* mark him out for his audacity against the haughty despot and keep in periodic view the religious imperatives which the profligate Sayyid habitually flouts. To be sure, neither this token intervention, nor that of shaykh Darwīsh and Raḍwān al-Ḥusaynī, ever achieves any tangible results, but that is itself a measure of the diminished status of religious authority in personal and public conduct in Mahfouz' fiction. Dissolute characters like Kirsha in *Zuqāq al-Midaqq* go so far as to claim an implicit religious sanction for deviancy: He brazenly tells those who admonish him that he would repent of his homosexuality when God wills it, but not before. This perverse logic also informs the use of religious terminology for decidedly antireligious actions and intentions, such as drinking and illicit sex.

If the very existence of this eccentric figure attests to the failure of conventional religion to keep abreast of wayward reality, it is no less a standing testimony to the failure of the Ṣūfī alternative to institutionalized religion. As we saw earlier in the discussion of *al-Liṣṣ wal-Kilāb* (1961) the reclusive Ṣūfī shaykh to whom the troubled protagonist, Sa'īd Mahrān, turns for shelter and instruction in his distress, has little to offer beside dry, impersonal formulas of ritual and trite exhortations for self-control. It is little wonder, then, that the search for religious and metaphysical certainty remains an open-ended quest in Mahfouz' work to this day. Sufism fares slightly better in such works as 'Abd al-Ḥakīm Qāsim's *Ayyām al-Insān al-Sab'a* (1969; The Seven Days of Man) primarily because the narrative reenacts an autobiographical childhood experience. But even there it is an apt subject for nostalgic reflection, not a viable option, or endowment, for modern living.

The Cairene Trilogy and the search for a secular theology

As intimated earlier, flouting religious edicts and norms is practically a way of life in Mahfouz' masterpiece, *The Cairene Trilogy* (1956–1957). The conceit takes different forms and spans a wide range of practices, from drinking, adultery, and homosexuality to philosophical skepticism, apotheosis, and outright atheism. In all instances, the marks of the pleasure principle are as visible as they are ubiquitous. Nowhere in modern Arabic literature, perhaps in all of Arabic literature, are sensuality and erotic desire given such a free reign and their workings such a thorough venting. The unique contribution of *The Trilogy* to the enduring debate on the role of religion in modern Arab experience, culture, and identity, stems, in large measure, from the unflagging rigor and unflinching intellectual honesty with which it faces the consequences of this unabashed celebration of desire.

Unavoidably, the forceful conjoining of such opposites as religion and hedonism recalls Freud's lasting preoccupation with the dyad. The nature and extent of *The Trilogy's* appropriation of psychoanalytic theory, especially as it bears on religion, will claim our attention shortly. Here let me anticipate a couple of mildly theoretical questions that flow directly from this line of investigation. The first concerns the primary fidelity of the critical performance: Is it to the text, with the historical cognitions and literary/aesthetic norms that inform it, or to the changing paradigms, interests, and tastes of the discipline and/or the critic? In the case of *The Trilogy*, for example, the preponderance of textual evidence points directly to oedipal themes and complications along classic psychoanalytic lines. If this is indeed the case, what is one to make of the massive assault on the foundations of psychoanalysis from various corners and the drastic revisions and modifications that have significantly transformed the field in the last fifty years or so?[33]

As it happens, the problem is perhaps less acute in the case of Arabic than other national literatures because there is no tradition of psychoanalytic criticism of Arabic literature to begin with. To date, for example, only one book dealing explicitly with the Oedipus complex in Arabic fiction has appeared; and, remarkably enough, it has nothing to say about *The Trilogy*.[34] Arguably, this dearth may itself be indicative of the force of cultural constraints against which the Arabic novel wages continuous war over "forbidden knowledge." It would follow, I suppose, that every cogent psychoanalytic interpretation is, *ipso facto*, a significant intervention in this ongoing contestation. Irrespective of that, however, a psychoanalytic interpretation that can explain what has remained enigmatic in *The Trilogy* after so many decades and such copious criticism, needs no further justification. "The validation of a psychoanalytically oriented criticism," writes Frederick Crews, "rests on whether at its best, it can make fuller sense of literary texts than could the most impressive instances of a rival criticism."[35] To go one step further, in the absence of an alternative theory, Islamic or otherwise, to account for the proliferation of the oedipal theme in the novel one is compelled to grant it, however provisionally, a measure of universal applicability. The familiar question of (Western) cultural influence such a recognition inevitably raises in its wake, especially given the "origins" of psychoanalysis, must ultimately be interrogated against the gripping power and pulsating immediacy of the strong passions and emotions rendered in *The Trilogy*. Whence do these come? To target Mahfouz and his "infatuation" with Western models on this score may be ideologically soothing to some, but it hardly brings us any closer to understanding the phenomenon in question, namely, the preponderance of oedipal complications in this quintessentially Arab/Egyptian novel.[36]

A related theoretical question concerns the relationship of the author to the fictional creation in the psychoanalytic framework. In *The Trilogy* this matter draws added weight and urgency from Kamāl's evident autobiographical affinities with Mahfouz.[37] Though fascinating, this tangent cannot be pursued any further here without taking us too far afield. I will bracket it therefore by recalling the immensely complex, roundabout ways in which repressed libidinal drives and impulses in creative individuals may manifest themselves in displaced and sublimated forms of artistic expression. Almost a century ago Otto Rank warned emphatically against a direct, mechanical transposition of the manifestations of oedipal themes in a literary creation onto the author's biography. "Therefore," he wrote, "as we have suggested extensively above, it is psychologically misguided to look for actual experiences in the author's life as parallels to his literary themes, because the themes are the products of fantasy activity, for which actual experiences are only raw material subject to the most extreme modifications."[38]

But if a detailed examination of the intricate relationship between Mahfouz and Kamāl can be bracketed out of this discussion, Kamāl's own severe psychological problems cannot. These are identified as such in the text, not least by Kamāl himself. In the third volume of *The Trilogy*, for example, we often find him engaged in "self-analysis," consciously trying to uncover the source of what he variously calls his "chronic illness"—*maraḍ muzmin* (S. 271) "secret or abiding illness" *maraḍ kāmin* (S. 243) or "pernicious illness" *dā' wabīl* (S. 129). Others around him are no less mindful of the presence or the severity of his problem, but its precise etiology eludes their necessarily limited view of his interior psychic life. Instructively, the recurrent speculation on the matter is often triggered by the subject of marriage, which grows steadily more pressing as Kamāl approaches middle age in the second half of *al-Sukkariyya*. At one point his only remaining intimate friend, Riyāḍ Qaldas, comes close to identifying the nature of the problem when he advises Kamāl to seek out the help of a psychoanalyst *muḥallil nafsāni* (S. 236, 273). He further avers that Kamāl is a sick person who "refuses to get well" (S. 278). It so happens, Kamāl tells him, that the title of his latest, pending article is: "How to Psychoanalyze Yourself." Directly related to this question is Kamāl's inclusion of "Freud's works" among the major sources necessary for a decent modern education (S. 91) and the frequent recourse of the narrative to recognizable psychoanalytic terminology, especially the unconscious, for example (S. 236, 242 ff.).

Such overt references to Kamāl's persistent psychological problems, his curious "intellectual" dabbling in psychoanalysis, and his repeated attempts at self-analysis, all but invite a psychoanalytic reading of the novel. Even so, they neither exhaust the reasons for such a reading nor do they, in themselves, amount to a psychoanalytic interpretation. Before attempting such a reading, however, let me mention briefly a number of the outstanding issues still awaiting satisfactory explanation in *The Trilogy*. Foremost among these, of course, is the enigmatic personality of al-Sayyid Aḥmad 'Abd al-Jawād. To read him exclusively, or even primarily, as a projection of male fantasy of limitless patriarchal supremacy and sexual prowess is to dwell on the surface level of the narrative. A more comprehensive reading must seek to relate these obvious traits causally to the profound effects they leave on al-Sayyid's children, especially on his youngest son, Kamāl, the autobiographical center through whose consciousness much of the narrative is filtered. Equally baffling is the twisted sexuality of both of al-Sayyid's surviving sons: Yāsin and Kamāl. Finally, such an interpretation must account for the calamity that befalls 'Ā'isha, al-Sayyid's younger daughter, and sends her back to her parent's house to spend the rest of her life with her younger bachelor brother Kamāl and their aging parents.[39] These major, powerfully charged currents cannot be deemed accidental in a novel whose plot revolves around a nuclear family headed by a modern incarnation of the mythological primal father. The underlying premise at work here bears stating a little more categorically: Much of the force animating the novel's psychosexual drama, including the attitudes toward religion, seems to originate in the use (and abuse) of the coercive paternal regime in charge of enforcing the sexual taboos against incest.

Like every great novel, however, *The Trilogy* weaves the various themes of its narrative into a single tapestry whereby discrete strands frequently intersect and intertwine. Even so, there are discernible patterns of organization in the overall panoramic structure of the novel. At that level, for instance, the treatment of religious issues and motifs seems to proceed along lines that pair general conceptual categories with generational markers. In the experience of the three generations of al-Sayyid's family with which the narrative is concerned, that treatment is predominantly theological in the case of al-Sayyid, philosophical/aesthetic in the case of his son Kamāl, and political/ideological in the case of his grandchildren: Raḍwān, 'Abd al-Mun'im, and Aḥmad. The transposition of the religious subject along these thematic and generational lines roughly coincides with the spatial shift from *Bayn al-Qaṣrayn*, of volume one, to *Qaṣr al-Shawq*, of volume two, and finally to *al-Sukkariyya*, of volume three.

The major "theological" question with which *The Trilogy* grapples directly revolves around the personality and lifestyle of al-Sayyid Aḥmad 'Abd al-Jawād, specifically his touted womanizing and drinking. In a nutshell, it can be stated as follows: What is the status of a believing Muslim who professes sincere devotion yet indulges his illicit desires liberally? Permutations of this question echo throughout the text, but it first surfaces as a discursive issue in chapter seven of volume one of *The Trilogy*, during a memorable encounter between al-Sayyid and the vagabond shaykh Mutawallī ʻAbd al-Ṣamad, in al-Sayyid's provisions store.

To the pointed question of the shaykh: "how do you, pious believer that you are, explain your lust for women?" Al-Sayyid responds obliquely: "What harm is in that? Does not the Messenger of God, peace be upon him, speak of his love of perfume and women?" We cannot fail to recognize in this retort the familiar practice in modern Arabic fiction of trying to enlist Islamic sanction for profane experience. Understandably, the shaykh refuses to oblige and chides al-Sayyid for the disingenuous attempt to blur the crucial distinction between licit and illicit sex, marriage and adultery. Shifting his defense strategy from religious precedent to personal ethics, al-Sayyid asserts that his amorous adventures do not infringe the rights, or stain the honor, of anyone, as he conscientiously refrains from courting married or unavailable women. The shaykh rightly reads this as another stratagem to deflect the real issue by subordinating absolute religious imperative to relative human expediency. From a religious point of view, adultery is no less unlawful when it is not compounded by aggravating circumstances. Accordingly, he remonstrates with al-Sayyid to eschew such "lame logic" and to follow in the footsteps of his own venerable (late) father who is said to have married "twenty times." Against this challenge al-Sayyid musters a socioeconomic rejoinder. His father's numerous marriages were prompted by the unfulfilled desire to beget another child beside him, an irrelevant consideration in his case, as he already has three sons and two daughters. If anything, he insists, his paternal responsibility towards his children militates against additional marriages, lest he squander *their* patrimony, as his father had done with his. Moreover, he argues, "today's courtesans are yesterday's maids, the possession of whom God has permitted, and God is eternally forgiving, merciful." Casuistic as it is, this argument nevertheless provides a formal closure to the discussion of adultery, at least as far as al-Sayyid is concerned. It does so, we may note, by reinstating the objectionable practice of adultery within a recognizably Islamic ethos and frame of reference. Whatever one may think of the disingenuous analogy between the lawful "possession" of *jawārī* (maids) and the unlawful intercourse with *ghawānī* (courtesans), the appeal to God's ultimate mercy cuts through and supersedes all this casuistic squabbling.

The prohibition against alcohol occasions further probing into the aforesaid problematic. How can al-Sayyid reconcile his partaking of it with his fear of God and submission to Him, muses the shaykh aloud. Does not the wedding of these incompatible positions spell a contradiction between words and deeds in al-Sayyid's attitude? Al-Sayyid appears as genuinely baffled by this line of reasoning as he is oppressed by the chilling force of its impeccable logic. While he agonizes over the quandary, the narrative point of view shifts to an extradiegetic level whence the omniscient narrator recasts the whole issue onto the ontological plane of al-Sayyid's psychological constitution. At that formative level of cognition, the narrator avers, al-Sayyid grasps religion naturally, not intellectually or theologically. He *lives* it spontaneously and *knows* it intuitively, not logically, or discursively. In that undifferentiated, natural state, he appears incapable of imagining an angry, much less a vengeful God, who would punish believers for such harmless infractions of the law as drinking and fornication. He therefore brushes aside the shaykh's rebuke and passionately reaffirms the sincerity and integrity of his piety, drinking and adultery notwithstanding.

Whatever logical cogency this lay theology may have is amply reinforced by the unique blend of character traits in al-Sayyid's extraordinary personality. He is at once a strict disciplinarian despot who imposes a reign of terror on his wife and children at home, and a cheerful, kind, generous, and eminently convivial epicure outside the home. A considerable amount of narrative space and energy is devoted precisely to establishing (and maintaining) the plausibility of this highly improbable composite psychological amalgam. It is significant to note in this regard that when we meet him, at the beginning of *The Trilogy*, al-Sayyid is already at the prime of his manhood at the age of forty five, fully developed and firmly set in his ways. For all practical purposes, he is a law unto himself, and the sole, indisputable sovereign of his little universe. How he came to be what he is, and what aberrant conditions in his past shaped his dreadfully authoritarian personality, we are never told. The narrative is suspiciously silent about al-Sayyid's childhood, youth, upbringing, and everything else that may hint, however remotely, at a "personal" past. It may be useful to keep this telling omission of characterization in mind because it figures prominently in the psychoanalytic reading of the novel.

To what mysterious force in the imagination or the psyche such an awesome specimen answers, we may never know with any certainty. From the available textual evidence, as I have been intimating, there is reason to suspect an oedipal complication that works its way via the autobiographical protagonist, Kamāl, perhaps all the way back to the author's unconscious. While we ponder this hypothesis, we may note that in the text's symbolic economy al-Sayyid's positive personal traits are readily convertible to assets in other domains, including the religious. Shaykh Mutawallī concedes from the outset that, were it not for his "levity," al-Sayyid "would have been perfect," for his otherwise "impeccable character." Even so, the narrative leaves nothing to chance. Before the "sudden," "unexpected" appearance of shaykh Mutawallī at the entrance of the shop, in chapter seven, the scene is carefully prepared to preempt any potential assault on the sincerity of al-Sayyid's piety. Thus, our attention is immediately drawn to the *basmala*, the formulaic Islamic invocation: "In the Name of God, the Beneficent, the Merciful" emblazoned in gold ink on a calligraphy placard and strategically hung on the wall, right above al-Sayyid's desk. Among the repertoire of daily routine in the shop we also learn of another shaykh whom al-Sayyid is said to have contracted to recite a daily portion of the Qur'ān when the shop opens every morning. From its somewhat garbled syntax and abrupt appearance and disappearance in the text, this background "filler" has all the marks of a staging afterthought, added for good measure, so to speak. Nothing else is said about it in the text; nor is the Qur'ān reciter ever seen or heard from again. Even before the scene is over, he simply recedes into oblivion, leaving no trace behind. While his brief "performance" lasts, however, it proves effective: Both al-Sayyid and his assistant are said to follow the shaykh's recitation with evident fealty (B. 37).

* * *

It must be clear from the foregoing remarks that the "theological debate" between al-Sayyid and shaykh Mutawallī is heavily stacked in favor of the former. This is hardly surprising, given the avowed secular sympathies of the novel in general and this novel in particular. Nor is it surprising that the two men part amicably: the shaykh with his usual gift, a bundle of provisions and foodstuff, and al-Sayyid with the shaykh's blessings and fervent supplications on his behalf. This informal "conclusion" of the exchange amounts to a form of tacit "religious" sanction of al-Sayyid's illicit conduct. Granted, the eccentric "shaykh" Mutawallī is more a caricature of religious authority than a representative of it. Still, there is nothing frivolous or facile about the substance of the discussion itself. From a theological point of view, no Muslim authority, however eminent, can circumscribe, let alone foreclose, the mercy God. This is the bottom line of al-Sayyid's defense, as it has indeed been of a redoubtable chain of professed transgressors in Islamic history going all the way back to the notoriously profligate Abbasid poet, Abū Nuwās, if not much earlier.

But the novel goes further than this general Islamic principle. It seeks to articulate a version of Islam tolerant enough to accommodate not only varying degrees of religiosity but also different, unorthodox, and even heterodox life-styles. Chapter forty-two of the second volume of *The Trilogy* offers a good example of this brand of Islam. There, a group of friends and acquaintances from different religious and social backgrounds gather around the bed of the recuperating al-Sayyid, at his house, to commiserate with him. It transpires from their convivial conversation that they hold such widely divergent views of religion and religiosity that the ardent supplications of shaykh Mutawallī intermingle with the taverner's loud praises of his wines. The shaykh protests, to be sure, but not so vehemently as to disrupt the congenial company. In Mahfouz' work, as indeed in Arabic fiction in general, such ecumenical gatherings and the free expression of difference they evince must be read as functional metaphors for the novel's vision of the national polity and civil society. The metaphor will gather added political significance as the idea of the nation is carried to center stage by the younger generations of al-Sayyid's family, in the third volume of *The Trilogy*. To gauge that progression properly, however, it is necessary to examine first Kamāl's way of wrestling with the twin forces of oedipal attraction and incest taboo.

Religion between psychoanalysis and aesthetics

Nothing would have fazed little Kamāl, the youngest son of al-Sayyid Aḥmad, more than the thought of his ruthless father harboring submissive feelings towards a mightier being, even if that be God. In his strictly enforced separation of realms, the autocratic al-Sayyid allows his family to see only the austere, wrathful side of his dual personality. The veritable thrall in which he keeps his wife and children leaves lasting psychological scars on all of them, but especially on Kamāl and his burgeoning consciousness. Much of what happens in Kamāl's adult life, including his complex attitude to sexuality and religion, seems to be causally linked, at one remove or another, to his childhood experiences under this regime of terror. Particularly relevant in this regard is the traumatic separation from his mother at bedtime, accompanied, as it was, by threats of castration, and instigated, as always, by the father. This traumatic experience was further compounded a little later by the painful separation from his two sisters, especially his beloved 'Ā'isha. Al-Sayyid's inscrutable cruelty and inordinate physical and psychological violence towards Kamāl inscribe the other side of what looks like an oedipal coin. This central point bears further elaboration.

The excessive violence visited on Kamāl, ostensibly for purposes of discipline and education (i.e., for his own good), is often cast in recognizable symbols of castration, for example, the cutting off of hands (B. 46–47) and a second circumcision "to remove what was left" (B. 50). This specific characterization of the threat all but spells out the sexual nature of the suspected offense. From the earliest dramatized scenes of family life in *The Trilogy* we become aware of a fierce, though tacit rivalry between father and son over the attention and affection of the mother. In this triangular relationship the father's freewheeling hostility toward Kamāl acquires a deeper ulterior motive than the "educational" one al-Sayyid assigns to it. Kamāl literally seeks to usurp the place of the father in the mother's life. An instance of this desire is dramatized in chapter four of *Bayn al-Qaṣrayn*. As a rule, the father's stifling presence renders his children virtually immobile at breakfast. No sooner does he leave the house, however, than they regain their spontaneity and indulge their appetites and whims freely. Kamāl uses the occasion to mimic the father's ritual routine of preparing to leave, during which al-Sayyid claims Amīna's undivided attention. When she fails to play her scripted part in full in this telling parody, little Kamāl insists on it until she obliges. As we saw earlier, it is this irresistible urge to replace the father in the mother's affection, if only temporarily during the father's brief absence from Cairo, that motivates the memorable outing to the mosque of al-Ḥusayn, which brings hapless Amīna to the verge of ruin, and earns Kamāl yet another sound beating. The outing is presented in the text as "a collective revolt against the will of the absent father" (B. 159). Eventually, both Kamāl and Yāsīn will come to entertain conscious intimations of revolt against the despotic father, *al-abb al-mustabidd*, and to announce the sentiment in public at least once, though under the "liberating" influence of alcohol (Q. 381). Understandably, the motif has immeasurably greater significance for Kamāl than it does for Yāsīn because the father plays a far greater role in Kamāl's psychological and mental life.

In this intricate psychodrama two simultaneous processes intertwine in Kamāl's psyche. The first has already been adumbrated earlier; it concerns the collapsing of the image of a fearful God onto that of the even more fearful Father.[40]

The psychological explanation of this "heretical" inversion in Kamāl's mind is simple: God's punishment is virtual and protracted, the Father's is real and swift (Q. 345). The second is the internalization and extension of the incest taboo to all future choice objects of erotic desire, notably the love of his life, 'Āida.[41] Eventually Kamāl will outgrow the dread of the Father, but not soon enough to undo its disabling effects on his psyche and life. As his father's health progressively deteriorates with advancing age it becomes possible for him to unpack the complex God/Father lodged in his psyche. He does so by renouncing the first, and with it all forms of religion, and embracing the second in his vulnerable, Lear-like humanity. But even as this "resolution" is effected in conscious, discursive terms, the thematic permutations of the oedipal entanglement continue to proliferate on the structural and symbolic levels to the very end.

Like the explicit references to psychoanalysis mentioned earlier, some manifestations of the oedipal theme are too self-evident to warrant extensive elaboration. Most salient among these is the recurrent pattern of father and son, or both brothers, having sexual relations with the same woman, concurrently or consecutively. Thus, for example, both Yāsīn, al-Sayyid's eldest son from an earlier marriage, and al-Sayyid himself sleep with *Umm* Maryam, Yāsin's future mother-in-law. Her status as a mother figure occurs to Yāsīn before he sleeps with her, but that proves no sufficient deterrent to make him desist (B. 124). Maryam, whom Yāsīn briefly marries thereafter, had also been the sweetheart of his brother Fahmī, who was killed by the British in a peaceful student demonstration during the 1919 nationalist uprising. Similarly, both Yāsin and al-Sayyid take turns with the same mistress, Zannūba, before Yāsin finally marries her. When al-Sayyid discovers the identity of his rival in her life he utters an unmistakably oedipal cry: "If you must have a murderer, let it be your own son" (Q. 315). There are strong incestuous innuendoes in *al-Sukkariyya* that involve Kamāl with Jalīla, formerly a famed mistress of his father (S. 216). Also instructive is the fact that Madam Jalīla invariably calls him "*nephew*," and he calls her *aunt*, at the brothel (S. 91, 109, 212, 214, 215). On at least one occasion, she goes even further and calls herself his *nena*, that is, mother, to his face (S. 111). Finally, both Yāsīn and Kamāl take turns with the prostitute, 'Aṭiyya, at Jalīla's bordello. (There is more to this matter than can be surmised from this bare fact, however.)

Yāsīn's notoriously promiscuous sexuality is practically incomprehensible outside the context of his troubled relationship with his mother. It is instructive that, of his putative sexual exploits only those that carry an incestual charge are dramatized. Two of these are with recognizably surrogate mother figures: the abortive attempt at the family maid *Umm* Ḥanafī, and the consummated affair mentioned earlier with *Umm* Maryam. The mother is also deeply implicated in Yāsīn's compulsive repetitive behavior, on which, incidentally, the narrative of *The Trilogy* dwells just as compulsively. We know that, as a child, Yāsīn used to act as an unwitting go-between messenger to his divorced mother and her local patrons. Vivid impressions of these visitations are all he retains from his tortured childhood, and they return frequently as involuntary memories and flashbacks to haunt him in adult life. These memories also underpin his perverse conviction that all women are thinly masked whores. His active pornographic imagination sustains and nourishes this conviction with the help of a probing voyeuristic gaze that draws streams of lurid images from every chance encounter with a female, irrespective of her dress, or time and place (Q. 124, 132; S. 56).

Also germane in this regard are the numerous allusions to sibling and parental incest that al-Sayyid and his circle of intimate friends bandy about in jest in their boon gatherings (Q. 85). Yāsīn's more rowdy and far less urbane colleagues taunt him with thinly veiled allusions to his "pimping" his mother in their boisterous drinking sessions at the tavern (S. 290). Though only verbal and figurative, these allusions nonetheless reinforce the centrality of the oedipal theme in the novel. So does the relevant statement concerning "the peculiar obsession of the Egyptian people with the subject of maternal (dis)honor" (S. 290). Withal, the incest theme finds its fullest and most unsettling expression in Kamāl's personal experience.

Like other protagonists of the *bildungsroman*, the narrative of Kamāl's life is fairly substantial, and is presented in a linear chronological vein, roughly from the age of ten to the age of forty, with occasional flashbacks into still earlier phases of his childhood. What stands out in the flux of circumstantial details about his early childhood, however, are the twin forceful emotions: attachment to the mother, and fear of the father. It is instructive in this regard that his earliest childhood memory dates back to the traumatic separation from the mother at bedtime, noted earlier. Although she makes every effort to soften the effects of this rupture by valorizing it as a rite of passage, he nonetheless views it as a singular act of perfidy on her part, and vows "never to forgive her" (B. 65–66). Both the concrete measures she takes to mend the "relationship" between them, and the language in which the endeavor is couched, strongly suggest the oedipal rivalry over the mother in the triangular plot of family romance. The whole scene also bears an uncanny resemblance to parallel situations in Proust's *Remembrance of Things Past* and Joyce's *A Portrait of the Artist as a Young Man*.

Equally instructive is the thorough commingling of the oedipal and the religious motifs in this scene. For its uniqueness in Arabic fiction, as well as its centrality to our discussion, the passage may warrants quoting at some length. The context, we may note, is the routine practice of Kamāl rehearsing to his mother the contents of the daily lesson in religion he learns at school—religious narratives being her favorite subjects, and his surest way to her heart and attention. The third person pronoun refers to Kamāl.

> He asked himself: when will I see God? And what will *He* look like?
> Changing the subject again, he suddenly asked his mother:
> Does my father fear God?
> Taken aback by the question, she said, disapprovingly:
> What a strange question! ... Your father is a pious man, son, and a pious man surely fears his Lord.

He shook his head in bewilderment, then said in a low voice:
I can't imagine my father fearing anything.
The woman said, reproachfully:
May God forgive you! ... May God Forgive you! ...
He apologized with a tender smile for what he had said, and invited her to rehearse the new sūra, the verses of which they started to recite and repeat in order. When they finished, the boy rose to go to sleep, and she followed him to tuck him in his small bed. She then put her palm on his forehead, recited the Throne Verse, and, leaning over him, pressed a kiss on his cheek. In response, he flung his arms around her neck and gave her a kiss that welled up from the bottom of his small heart.

She always had difficulty extricating herself from him, when tucking him in, because he would spare no effort to keep her beside him for the longest time possible, if sleeping in her arms should prove impossible. Nothing served this purpose better than his request that she recite over his head, after the Throne Verse, a second sūra, and a third.... Should he espy a parting smile on her lips, he would entreat her to stay longer, citing the fear of staying alone in the room, or the disturbing dreams that visit him, against which only a prolonged recitation of noble sūras avails. He would even go so far as to feign illness, finding no wrong in this stratagem. Rather, he would see it as a minimal realization of a sacred right of his that was grossly violated the day he was unjustly and maliciously separated from his mother, to be brought to this solitary bed in his brothers' room. How he hankers for the recent past, when they slept together, his head on her arm, and her gentle voice pouring in his ears accounts of the prophets and the saints! He would fall asleep before his father had returned from his nightly jaunt, and would wake up after the father had gone to shower. He would thus see no third person with him and his mother, and no one else would share the world with him. And then, in a stroke of blind fate, the wisdom of which he could never fathom, they separated them. He had looked for the effects of his banishment on her, but was surprised to discover her complicity with it instead, for she encouraged, and congratulated, him, saying; "Now you are a man and, therefore, deserve to have your own bed." Who said that it pleased him to become a man, or that he wished to have a bed of his own? And yet, even though he soaked his first pillow with tears, and warned his mother that he would never forgive her, he did not dare sneak back into the old bed because he knew that his father's intractable will lay behind the cruel, treacherous move. So sad was he that the essence of sadness seeped into his *dreams*. And how angry he was with his mother! Not only because he was incapable of mustering the will to be angry with his father, but also because she was the last person he had thought would let him down. But she knew how to win him over anew, and gradually mend the rift. She always made sure to stay beside him in the

> beginning until he fell asleep, and would say to him: "You see, we have not been separated, as you claim; we are together, and will always be together. Only *sleep* will separate us, as it used to do when we were in the same bed."
> (B. 65–66)

At the time of the frame narrative of this passage, Kamāl is ten years old. His age at the time of the embedded action, the "expulsion" from the mother's bed, is not specified, but we assume it cannot be more than three or four. The oedipal fixation is fairly transparent, and becomes only more so if we substitute for *dreams* and *sleep* in the passage their metonymic equivalents: the *unconscious* and *death*, respectively. The note of sadness that seeps into Kamāl's *dreams* is none other than the malady, illness, curse, or whatever else he calls it, that abides in his unconscious and prevents him from marrying or developing normal sexual relations with other women. Similarly, the mother's vow that only *sleep* (read, *death*) will separate them, forcefully suggests a marriage vow.

Equally inseparable in the scene from which the passage is taken are religious texts, themes, and motifs, on the one hand, and Kamāl's furtive intimacy with his mother and two sisters, on the other. This copresence at once continues the motif of rivalry with the father over the female members of the household, and checks it by interpolating the will of the father, now transposed into a religious imperative in Kamāl's nascent superego. The father, we may note, is so protective of his females that the mere mention of their names by another man, even a harmless one like the decrepit shaykh Mutawallī, vexes him immensely. Nothing illustrates better the permanent conjoining of the desire for private intimacy with the mother and the religious dimension than the disastrous outing to the mosque of al-Ḥusayn during the temporary absence of the father from Cairo, discussed earlier. It is important to remember that it was at Kamāl's insistence that the mother agreed to deviate from the straight path to the mosque onto a side street. The accident happens exactly at the intersection of time and place where the outing changes from a religious quest, so to speak, to a pleasurable promenade. It is hard to imagine a more tightlyknit and overdetermined chronotope.

Although at the age of ten Kamāl is said to have forgiven his mother her "infidelity," the textual evidence suggests otherwise. What he seems to have done, rather, is to resign himself to the fact of her inaccessibility, owing to the omnipresence of the omnipotent father. (It is symbolically significant that the last scene in which the three are together, shortly before his death, toward the middle of the third volume of *The Trilogy*, the father, now old and decrepit, literally stands between Amīna and Kamāl as the two help him home from an underground shelter where they had sought cover from attacking German planes.) This conscious act of resignation is abetted by the gradual transference and rechanneling of the incestuous libidinal energy away from the mother toward the sisters, especially 'Ā'isha. It also coincides with the stirring of vague sexual desires in Kamāl at the onset of puberty. During the earliest phase of his sexual awakening Kamāl's attention is riveted by the picture of a scantily dressed woman on a billboard he sees on his way to and from school. As the following description clearly shows, the erotic scene leaves an indelible impression on his imagination and carries strong incestuous overtones.

> As was his daily habit at that hour, he stood under the billboard, raised his small eyes to the colored advertisement depicting a woman lying on a sofa, a cigarette between her crimson lips, from which curling smoke rose. The woman's elbow rested on a window sill, and through the parted drapes appeared a meadow of palm trees and a stream of the Nile. In secret he used to call her "*abla* 'Ā'isha" due to the resemblance between the two, especially their golden hair and blue eyes. Even though he was nearly ten years old, his fondness for the woman in the picture was boundless. How often he imagined her enjoying life in all its splendor! And how often he imagined himself sharing that happy life with her, between a cozy room and a pastoral landscape whose land, palm trees, water, and sky, were hers—theirs! He would swim in the lush stream, or cross the river in a boat that loomed at the edge of the picture, like a mirage, or shake the palm trees and fresh dates would drop from them, or sit between the arms of the beauty and stare deep into her dreamy eyes.
>
> (B. 48)

The image of a primordial Garden of Eden flickers visibly behind the Egyptian topography in this palimpsest; so does the image of 'Ā'isha behind the model in the advertisement poster. It is hardly necessary to spell out the rest of the story in this imagined reenactment of the prelapsarian narrative. What is less self-evident, perhaps, is the ingenious use in this context of the Egyptianized Turkish honorific *abla*, which in the Egyptian dialect can mean both sister and *Miss*.[42] Much of Kamāl's psychosexual paralysis originates in his inability to effect a viable transition from the real object of desire, whether mother or sister, to a more adequate, that is, less transparent substitute. As is often the case whenever his unconscious tries to disguise the incestuous drive by means of gimmicks such as the one here, the religious taboo erupts into the narrative to check the process. The direct allusion to the chapter of Mary in the Qur'ān, through the shaking of the palm tree(s) and the falling of the dates, serves this purpose in the above passage. The invocation of the image of Mary in particular reiterates her proverbial chastity, which, in turn, reinforces the internalized taboo in Kamāl's psyche, not only against incest but also all other forms of normal sexuality. After his one-sided "love affair" with 'Āida ends, Kamāl maintains regular sexual relations only with prostitutes.

Nor are Kamāl's sensual fantasies entirely limited to the theatre of his imagination. An example of a more "physical" expression of this erotic attraction obtains in a strange habit of his. During this phase, whenever thirsty, he would always offer the jug of water to 'Ā'isha first and then put his own lips precisely where hers had been, while the spot was "still wet with her saliva" and drink therefrom (B. 63, 245). In light of this attachment it may not be surprising that 'Ā'isha's marriage, when Kamāl is about twelve, occasions a painful experience. All along before that fateful day he had been pleading with his mother and ardently imploring his favorite saint al-Ḥusayn to avert that horrid eventuality (B. 146, 156, 162 ff.). On the day of the wedding, however, he is torn between two conflicting emotions. On the one hand, he is aghast at the prospect of losing his "favorite sister, after his mother" to a stranger; on the other, he relishes the relative freedom accorded him during the festive occasion, especially "in his smart new clothes, which make him look as if he is the bridegroom" (B. 242). Before the day is over, Kamāl manages to push this loaded motif dangerously close to the edge of social scandal and literary implausibility. He confides to his mother on the way home that, peeping through the keyhole of the bridal chamber door, he saw the bridegroom fondling his sister and kissing her (B. 261–262). On a return visit to 'Ā'isha's new home, a couple of days later, he schemes to have her take him to her bedroom, locks the door behind them, and insists that she sit beside him on the same bed where "the scandalous scene" was performed (B. 280). The sexual connotations of this episode are transparent enough on their own.

Kamāl's infantile attachment to 'Ā'isha persists well into puberty. Even after the marriage of Khadīja, "his second mother," Kamāl never reconciles himself to the fact that the departure of his sisters from home is permanent; nor does he renounce his strong desire to see them return home, especially 'Ā'isha. On one occasion in *al-Sukkariyya* Khadīja brings this matter up, with a poignant twist. During one of the frequent conversations about Kamāl's perplexing aversion to marriage, Khadīja notes wryly: "We used to think that his objection to marriage was on account of his love for *us* (his sisters), not because of an abiding aversion to marriage he has harbored since childhood" (S. 128). Khadīja names all the pieces of the puzzle, but fails to connect them to solve the riddle. In what appears to be a conscious gesture of kinship with the archetypal master/victim of riddles, Oedipus, Kamāl at one point refers to himself as "a riddle between two riddles"—*lughz bayn lughzayn* (S. 38). It is also possible to discern direct echoes of Hamlet in some of Kamāl's reflections on his condition, for example, "... and he still ponders the question: to marry or not to marry?" (S. 281). Most astonishing, however, is the uncanny eruption of reality onto this little drama. While Ḥasan Imām, the director of the film version of *Qaṣr al-Shawq*, was scouring for an actor to play the role of Kamāl, 'Ādil Imām recommended to him a young actor (Nūr al-Sharīf), whom he had seen performing the role of Hamlet on stage.[43]

If the foregoing amassing of textual evidence with clear oedipal and incestual charge appears excessive, it is only to forestall any charge of selectivity when it comes to far-reaching conclusions such as the following: On the underlying psychosexual level of the plot, 'Ā'isha's return to her parents' house, after the summary removal, through death, of her husband and three children, must be seen as a fulfillment of Kamāl's infantile wish at the time of her marriage. At the end of the novel, with the mother literally on her death bed (the father having died a while earlier), the bachelor brother and widowed sister are left alone in the family house. Admittedly, 'Ā'isha, now shrivelled and prematurely aged, is a mere shadow of her former self, and the energy driving the oedipal wish in Kamāl's psyche is all but spent. The prospect of a romantic "reunion," therefore, appears even more grotesquely macabre under the circumstances. But the force of such drives is primarily internal, and it is in Kamāl's psyche that their meaning should be sought. Repugnant as it may be from moral and emotional standpoints, the place of 'Ā'isha's calamity in the structure of the oedipal plot in this family romance seems incontrovertible. Even as this effect of the plot is unfolding on one front, however, other effects continue to proliferate elsewhere and to wreak havoc on Kamāl's psyche and emotional life, as we shall see in the next section.

* * *

Kamāl is nearly thirteen at the end of the first volume of *The Trilogy*, the action of which ends in 1919. The second volume, *Qaṣr al-Shawq*, begins five years later, in 1924. During the interval, Kamāl appears to have been launched on an emotional trajectory that confirms the foregoing analysis of his predicament and compounds still further his oedipal obsessions. His passionate, but hopelessly one-sided love for 'Āida Shaddād, provides the matrix for his psychological mutations, including his profound alienation from religion. 'Āida is at once a glaring example of a failed transference as a choice object, and a successful one as an authority figure. The two, we recall, are bound together in a dialectical relationship: as oedipal desire and religiocultural taboo, in *The Trilogy*.

Few issues in a man's life are as thoroughly negotiated as that of choice object. Roughly what this means in psychoanalytic terms is that the two constitutive components of love, the affectionate and the sensual, must be united in a single, "lawful" object of desire in adulthood for "normal" sexual relations to take hold. Conversely, individuals bedevilled by oedipal complications tend to keep these two components apart. It is typical in such situations to reserve affection and delicate sentiments for an overvalued, desexualized object, that is, a mother or sister surrogate, and to channel sexual energy towards a debased object, usually a prostitute or a person of demonstrably lower standing.[44] Kamāl displays these characteristics vividly, but in successive phases. Love and sex never meet in his experience.

As intimated earlier, 'Āida is the prism through which the various coordinates of Kamāl's personality interface. In some crucial respects, she is a reincarnation of 'Ā'isha, but on a more abstract, celestial plane. The process of her deification in Kamāl's psyche is already well underway at the beginning of *Qaṣr al-Shawq* and persists with increasing intensity until her marriage to someone else and her departure for Paris, midway in the volume. As sole object of worship and adoration, she replaces the composite God/Father in Kamāl's psyche. Her apotheosis also makes decoupling the pair possible. As the father steadily shrinks to human dimensions—eventually to revert to childlike dependence on Kamāl who, at one point, literally carries him in his arms when he is no longer able to walk, shortly before his death—the scepter of absolute authority over Kamāl passes from al-Sayyid to ʿĀida. But with one crucial difference: now his subjection is internally induced, self-propelling, and self-regulating. In a specially lucid moment of introspection, Kamāl causally relates the two modes of despotism, and interrogates the wider nexus of relations between his personal predicament and traditional patterns of parental and cultural authority (Q. 385). The narrative takes the form of a diary entry motivated by the discovery of the hedonistic side of his father, shortly after ʿĀida's marriage. Earlier in the evening, Kamāl runs into his brother, Yāsīn, at the door of a prostitute, whom they both frequent. The two brothers proceed from the brothel to a tavern, where Yāsīn divulges to his incredulous youngster the fabulous secret history of their father. Here is part of what Kamāl confides to his diary on that momentous occasion.

> Father, let me be frank with you. I'm not upset by what I have discovered about your person. What I didn't know about you is far dearer to me than what I did. I'm impressed by that urbane, convivial, profligate, libertine, reckless side of you, so beloved by all those who know you.... But let me ask you: why did you have to confront us with that coarse, dreadful mask of yours? Don't bring up principles of education. You know nothing about that. The evidence is what you see, and don't see, of Yāsīn's conduct, and mine. You did nothing but hurt us and torment us much through ignorance that cannot be mitigated by good intentions. Don't worry. I still love and admire you, and will always do so.... You were never the friend that strangers knew. Rather, we knew you only as a vicious, despotic, tyrannical ruler (عرفناك حاكمامستبدا شرسا طاغية) as if you were the very one meant by the saying: better a wise enemy than an ignorant friend. Therefore I shall hate ignorance more than anything else in life... I still love and admire you, though, even after you lost the divine airs that my bewitched eyes beheld in you. Yes, your might is nothing but a fiction now. Nor are you the only one whose image has changed. God Himself is no longer the God I used to worship of old. I'm bent on weeding out of His attributes might, tyranny, oppression, dictatorship, and all other human caprices... Do you know what was the result of my love for you, in spite of your despotism over me? It was that I worshipped another tyrant who oppressed me readily, in appearance as in reality, and enthralled, but did not love me. Even so, I worshipped (her) from the bottom of my heart, and still do. You are, therefore, responsible for my love and my torment. How accurate is this proposition? I wonder. I'm not entirely comfortable with it. For, no matter how real love is, its roots undoubtedly hark back to deeper origins in the self... Be that as it may, you, father, made oppression palatable to me by your relentless tyranny. And you, mother, do not stir at me disapprovingly and ask: what have I done? Ignorance is your fault, too... My father is

> the embodiment of crude ignorance, and you are the embodiment of tender ignorance. For as long as I live I shall remain the victim of this contrast. It was your ignorance that filled my soul with superstitions. You are the link between me and the cave world. I'm as wretched now trying to free myself from your legacy as I will be tomorrow when I try to free myself from my father's. If only you had spared me this arduous struggle! I therefore recommend—and let the darkness of this room be my witness—that the family be abolished—this room with its brackish waters—and that fatherhood and motherhood be likewise abolished. Only grant me a homeland without history and a life without past.
>
> (Q. 385–386)

It may be instructive to note that this pained confessional confrontation with the internalized image of the father ends with a reference to the prostitute 'Ayyūsha, to whom Kamāl flees directly after 'Āida's wedding. The symbolism of this sequence is not without significance.

As this reshuffling of energies and allegiances continues, God's fortunes decline further in Kamāl's view until he succumbs to total atheism—but not exclusively thanks to 'Āida. True, in his imagination Kamāl projects on her the divine attributes of omnipotence, eminence, and glory, together with the power to bestow, or withhold, heavenly bliss. Like God, for example, she is not only unique, but also inimitable, *sui generis*, and apt for worship: *ma'būdatī 'alā ghayr mithāl* (Q. 46). This description of 'Āida strongly echoes the Qur'ānic description of God: *lays ka-mithlihi shay'*—like Him is naught, in A. J. Arberry's rendition.[45] Elsewhere she is called the holy ghost' *al-rūḥ al-qudus*. (This wording conforms to the Arabic translation of the New Testament; in the Qur'ān the phrase is *rūḥ al-qudus*, II, 253.) Kamāl's fleeting aleatory encounters with her in the alcove of her family's mansion are described as epiphanies, and his visits to her fashionable quarter of *'Abbāsiyya* as a pilgrimage during which he performs the ritual circumambulation around her house, just as a devout Muslim pilgrim does around the house of God in Mecca (makka). When she shuns him he feels banished from paradise (Q. 254). Under her "divine" influence, Kamāl contemplates "writing a book the size and form of the Qur'ān," in which she will figure prominently (Q. 61).

The constitutive connection between 'Āida's deification, taboo, and the suppression of sexual desire comes to the fore immediately after her marriage. Nearly drunk for the first time in his life, Kamāl contemplates sex with a prostitute. "What does he want? One of those women who disgust him while he is sober? And does drink make degradation more palatable? He used to fend off instinctual desire with the help of 'Āida and religion; now desire has a free reign" (Q. 362). As noted earlier, the prostitute he visits on that occasion is named 'Ayyūsha, which is a diminutive of 'Ā'isha.

But before proceeding any further, it is necessary to interrogate briefly here the alleged causal connection between the modes of subjection Kamāl endures at the hands of his father and his beloved. It is instructive that he questions the proposition, even as he advances it. Similarly, the drift of his "reasoning" seems to belie the validity of this mechanical allocation of cause and effect. Particularly relevant to considerations of etiology is the gigantic leap at the end of the passage from personal circumstance to universal principle and the attendant predication of personal happiness on the abolition of parenthood, which is tantamount to the abolition of the nuclear family. Needless to say that such a drastic revolution in the social structure of filiation would also remove all taboos against endogamous sexuality, and, with that, the very foundation of the Oedipus complex. Until then, it seems, the "mysterious" forces that lurk in the "foul waters," *al-mā' al-āsin*, in Kamāl's *dark* room will continue to bedevil his life.

It may also be relevant to note the minor, though potentially telling discrepancy between the formal setting of writing and the content thereof. Kamāl is supposed to be writing the above diary entry in his room; how could he be writing in the dark? The only way out of this incongruity is to assume that Kamāl uses the motif of darkness metaphorically, as he does with that of the foul "waters" which obviously cannot be taken literally. Either way, if we allow for the substitution of *self* for *room* the nagging sense of something "dark" and "rotten" at the core of Kamāl's psyche becomes all the more acute.

Recent approaches to the question of the subject, specially to the dialectic of desire and prohibition, can perhaps shed some light on this aspect of Kamāl's condition. It would take us too far afield here to engage extensively any of the valuable findings of these approaches. One enabling insight, however, bears directly on the question at hand, namely, the possibility that Kamāl's willing subjection to 'Āida is indeed causally but inversely related to the habitual, seemingly gratuitous cruelty he receives at the hands of his father. According to this teleology, the oedipal desire and the prohibition against it appear ontologically coeternal and bound together in an always already order of temporality. To put this slightly abstract formulation in concrete terms we may say the following: not only is the cruelty of the father a function of anterior oedipal desire in Kamāl's psyche, but it is also, and somewhat paradoxically, constitutive of that desire.[46] This remapping of the dialectic of oedipal desire and its prohibition may finally account for the enigmatic personality of al-Sayyid Aḥmad 'Abd al-Jawād, especially as concerns his uninhibited enjoyment of carnal pleasures and his concomitant suppression of Kamāl's libidinal drives. To go one step further, it is the always–already present oedipal desire that stipulates the presence of its structural repressive countermeasure. Only in this reading does the gaping absence of significant biographical details about al-Sayyid's background, before the onset of Kamāl's oedipal attachments, make sense. In his capacity as a projection of the anti-oedipal force the father needs no personal background, only an intractable will to "discipline" and to interdict. In fact, the less particularized the figure of the father is in this symbolic economy, the more available it becomes for appropriation into the son's mythopoeic narrative. Moreover, once internalized in the psyche, the external form of this interdiction, and with it the actual presence of the father, become redundant, which is precisely what happens in Kamāl's case. As his libidinal drives shift from the oedipal objects (mother and sister), to ʻĀida, the grip of the father on him loosens accordingly. Here is how Slavoj Zizek puts this complex dynamic as it is transposed across the Freudian–Lacanian terrain.

> The Oedipus myth is based on the premise that it is the father, as the agent of prohibition, who denies us access to enjoyment (i.e. incest, the sexual relationship with the mother). . . . The myth of the primal father in *Totem and Taboo* complements—or, more precisely, supplements—the Oedipus myth by embodying this impossible enjoyment in the obscene figure of the Father-of-Enjoyment, i.e. in the very figure who assumes the role of the agent of prohibition.[47]

* * *

Pivotal to this reading of *The Trilogy* is the proposition that, in Kamāl's psyche, ʻĀida is a surrogate for ʻĀ'isha. A primary distinction must be immediately drawn, however, between the "real" ʻĀida and Kamāl's mental representation of her. From the few scattered details available in the text about ʻĀida's "objective" personal attributes, Kamāl's deification of her appears so extravagant as to betray thematics of oedipal overvaluation, especially as it often arouses in its wake caustic sensations of self-berating and denigration (Q. 330). Nor is it surprising that ʻĀida's common, albeit highly stylized beauty, is fairly obvious to other characters, though perforce not to Kamāl himself (Q. 272). Eventually, though, he, too, comes to realize the discrepancy and to wonder how a woman of such unremarkable characteristics could have captivated his imagination so fully and for so long (S. 113). His sole wish: "to see her, if only once, while free from her tyranny, *istibdād*, in order to know her as she is, and thereby to know (*his*) *own self*" remains unfulfilled (S. 254). A few years after her marriage, her aristocratic family goes under, her father commits suicide, her own marriage falls apart, she returns to Egypt a broken and neglected woman, marries a widower twice her age, and dies soon thereafter of illness. Unbeknown to him, Kamāl walks in her humble funeral, assuming that she is no more than the wife of the principal of the school where he teaches.

Understandably, then, the similarity between ʻĀida and ʻĀ'isha is to be sought primarily in Kamāl's psyche, particularly in his unconscious. But there are also ancillary circumstantial clues that reinforce the functional resemblance. For example, like ʻĀ'isha, ʻĀida is a few years older than Kamāl (Q. 330). Her name also links her to ʻĀ'isha, both phonologically and semantically. As an active participle, the name means *she who returns*. When transcribed consistently, both names follow the same pattern in formal Arabic and in the Egyptian vernacular. Instructively, though, Mahfouz mixes the forms across the linguistic levels by using the formal spelling for ʻĀ'isha and the colloquial version for ʻĀida. (Hence also my own attempt at "textual fidelity" in the "irregular" transliteration of ʻĀida's name.) In one critical instance, however, Mahfouz deviates from this general principle and aligns the two names fully, as if to reinforce their common identity in Kamāl's mind. On the night of 'Āida's wedding, Kamāl steals a look at the women gathered on the balcony of the Shaddād mansion and wonders whether *'Ā'ida* is among them (Q. 317).

That momentous event occasions other telling associations. Later in the evening, for example, after all the guests leave, Kamāl returns to the site, hides behind the wall of the Shaddād mansion and, shivering in the cold of the 'Abbāsiyya desert, fixes his gaze at the dimly lit bridal chamber in the absurd hope of catching a glimpse of his beloved in a moment of exquisite intimacy "for which (he) would give (his) entire life" (Q. 331–332). This unmistakably neurotic behavior graphically reinscribes what he did on the night of 'Ā'isha's wedding, only now he is a young man of twenty, not a boy of ten or twelve. Likewise, the first ululation he hears at 'Āida's wedding transports him instantly to the scene of 'Ā'isha's wedding and evokes similar sensations in him. Earlier still, the sight of a water jug in the alcove of the Shaddād mansion triggers in him associations that link 'Āida directly to 'Ā'isha and implicate both in his erotic fantasies. The thought that, perchance, 'Āida's lips may have touched the jug induces in him a sensation akin to that he used to experience when drinking from the same jug after 'Ā'isha, in "childhood" (Q. 155).

On several occasions, Kamāl draws a direct comparison between 'Āida and his sisters, but only to highlight the categorical difference. Invariably, as has already been noted, his mental representation of 'Āida disencumbers her of all bodily needs and functions, specially those traditionally assigned to women, for example, domestic chores like cooking and cleaning, and even more so of such unseemly "impediments" of female physiology as menstruation, pregnancy, and child-birth (Q. 46). Kamāl's inability to distinguish between 'Āida's "physical reality," including her sexuality, and his rarefied mental representation of her, brings him dangerously close to self-exposure during her wedding. Near distraction, he asks a friend whether the rumored things about the "wedding night" do indeed take place (Q. 332). Twice in that context he links 'Āida directly with other "inviolable" entities: daughter, mother, and the sacrosanct (Q. 328, 330).

Nothing defines this attitude of Kamāl towards 'Āida better than the psychoanalytic term overvaluation. Now, by its very nature, overvaluation is distinctly subjective. In *The Trilogy*, however, Kamāl's idolization of 'Āida is buttressed by two ostensibly objective considerations. The first is her superior aristocratic standing, which places her socially beyond his reach. On the oedipal level of the plot, this class differential replaces consanguinity as a barrier to sexual relations with tabooed objects of desire. The second is Kamāl's touted physical "deformities," notably his disproportionately large head and big nose. Though he is often taunted by others on account of these "oddities," it is only when 'Āida takes note of them that they become a source of abject self-loathing and anxiety for Kamāl (Q. 330). But if overvaluation of the oedipal choice object is one side of the triad according to psychoanalysis, self-berating and the debasement of sex are its two other sides. Kamāl in effect turns his inferiority complex vis-à-vis 'Āida into a safety valve against unrealistic expectations from his unrequited love for her. He is content to ponder the prospect that "in heaven, where no artificial distinctions exist, no large head or big nose, she will be mine, and mine alone" (Q. 222).

The attendant debasement of sex manifests itself clearly in Kamāl's relegation of it exclusively to the realm of prostitution. No sooner is 'Āida married than he takes to drinking and frequenting prostitutes. Curiously, as I noted earlier, the first prostitute he visits is called 'Ayyūsha, that is, diminutive of 'Ā'isha (Q. 386). It may also be interesting to note that the name of the other prostitute he frequents at the house of his "aunt" Jalīla, 'Aṭiyya, also begins with the first letter of the names of both 'Ā'isha and 'Āida. In the mysterious life of the psyche, as in detective fiction, these subtle clues may not be entirely accidental or fortuitous.

A final boost to this reading of 'Āida as a surrogate oedipal choice object in Kamāl's psyche accrues from the account of the renewed encounter with Budūr Shaddād, 'Āida's younger sister, whom he knew as a child, and whom he now meets as a fellow student at the University of Cairo. In the intervening years, we recall, the Shaddād family had been reduced to poverty, and Budūr appears unmistakably receptive to Kamāl's shy and hesitant "advances." At the critical moment, however, he recoils, and she slips away. The last time he sees her she is wearing an engagement ring and clasping the arm of her fiance. Instructively, this scene unfolds as he is standing before the window of a toy shop, immersed in reflection on his own childhood, and wondering what it would be like to revert to that stage again (S. 283). Since Budūr diverges in name, age, social standing, and attainability, from the oedipal pattern governing Kamāl's choice of erotic object, his inability to move decisively to break out of that pattern only confirms its irresistible hold on his psyche. Outside this context, the whole thematic detour of the encounter with Budūr appears as a superfluous interpolation.

The nation, religiously speaking…

Little of "the idea of God" survives the process of 'Āida's deification as sole object of worship in Kamāl's psyche. That elaborate artifice, we realize, is essentially aesthetic in nature, and comes about largely through skillful manipulation of narrative techniques peculiar to the novel, especially the sustained use of the metaphor of interiority. What does survive that process is readily swept aside by Kamal's concomitant exposure to Western philosophy and direct sense perception. In this two-pronged process, personal observation of the laws of nature and the material world pave the way for the admission of "imported" knowledge. That knowledge, in turn, flows from three simultaneous sources: the secular curriculum of the Teachers Training College (Dār al-Mu'allimīn al-'Ulyā), which Kamāl attends; his private reading of major works of the "Western canon"; and his journalistic apprenticeship at an obscure, avant-garde periodical devoted to disseminating secular ideas of modern European culture. (It is there that he publishes the piece on Darwin's theory of evolution, on account of which al-Sayyid's friends taunt him mercilessly, albeit amicably.) The role of English is paramount in this "education" of Kamāl. Thematically, the influences flowing from these sources are mutually reinforcing, and they all draw added force from 'Āida's purported affinities with Paris, "city of light," though these tenuous affinities appear strictly limited to matters of taste and fashion, both of which she is said to have acquired during the few years she spent there in her childhood.

Kamāl's predisposition to the effects of European philosophy and culture is both anticipated and spurred by his disillusionment with traditional "religious" knowledge. True, whatever textual knowledge he has of Islamic sources is strictly limited to memorized passages of the Qur'ān, and, as we have seen, these invariably come packaged with superstitions about ghosts and spirits he avidly imbibes with his mother's tales, in early childhood. Particularly disconcerting in this connection is the "discovery" that the account of the miraculous journey of al-Ḥusayn's severed head from Iraq to Egypt, to be buried in the mosque that bears his name, near the family home, is a crude fiction of popular imagination. Kamāl is said to have been so pained by that "discovery" that he "soaked his pillow in tears that night," just as he did on the first night of separation from his mother (Q. 73–74). The disillusionment is all the more poignant because it comes on the heels of an experiment he carries out soon after the death of his brother Fahmī. To ascertain the fate of the body after death he buries a dead bird in the back yard, and is shocked to discover when he disinters it a few days later, that it had completely decomposed in the meantime. The combined effect of these disillusionments on his impressionable mind are drastic and lasting: Kamāl grows up to become a professed atheist. What matters even more on the discursive level is that, unlike the historical recanter discussed earlier, he does not "repent" or disavow his philosophical skepticism about religion as time goes by. Toward the end of the novel, however, he begins to entertain some doubts about the viability of skepticism as a permanent way of life.

The confluence of these noetic and emotional forces at the site of the formation of Kamāl's individual consciousness coincides in *The Trilogy* with a similar convergence of historical forces at work on the identity of Egypt during an acutely critical phase of its modern history. We need only remember in this regard that the span of the novel's action, roughly 1916–1945, unfolds entirely against the backdrop of British colonial occupation of Egypt (1882–1956) and the fierce struggle for national liberation and independence. This interfacing of domains inevitably recalls the problematic of binary oppositions between the personal/psychological, on the one hand, and the public/political, on the other. A further subdivision of the personal, in *The Trilogy* as elsewhere in Egyptian fiction, makes possible the embrace of the culture of the (Western) colonizer while resisting his political domination. Thus Kamāl embraces fervently both the literary, intellectual, philosophical, and scientific conventions of the modern West, and Sa'd Zaghlūl's impassioned struggle for the liberation of Egypt from British rule. Chapter four of *al-Sukkariyya* juxtaposes graphically the private affinity Kamāl feels with Bergson, Darwin, and Russell, whose thought he relishes in the privacy of his library at night with the ordinary masses of *Wafd* supporters in whose midst, during the day, he regains a sense of belonging and equilibrium. Both, he holds, are equal makers of history.

This fastidious compartmentalization of allegiance nonetheless elides a couple of urgent questions that inhere in such recurrent postulates within Egyptian and Arabic fiction. The first question concerns the extent to which the seductive appeal of colonial culture to the colonized, especially to its intelligentsia, is itself a form of political indoctrination that, in one way or another, eventuates in subordination. The trajectories of identity formation, *re*formation, and *de*formation, are always so entangled here that it is almost impossible to pry them apart. In *The Trilogy*, for example, Kamāl's attempt to balance the opposite ends of the abstract formula: resisting the occupier politically, while embracing him culturally, leads to identity crisis and chronic paralysis. In this respect, his fate is emblematic of a familiar type of protagonist prevalent in Arabic fiction that dramatizes the cultural encounter with the West. Kamāl's example appears more authentic than his counterparts, however, because it dispenses with the spurious ploy of relocating the protagonist (physically) to the West to set the crisis in motion. Close to the end of the novel a friend describes Kamāl as one "eternally lost between East and West" (S. 191).[48]

What is more, this paralysis at the micro level of the individual protagonist appears symbolic of, or analogous to a more general crisis at the macro level of the nation. For instance, the same vocabulary of "retardation" and "backwardness"—as a result of oppression, irrational beliefs, and "religious" superstitions—is employed to diagnose the ills besetting both the individual and the nation at large (e.g. S. 36, 38, 90, 91 ff.). In this respect, the novel anticipates the subsequent adoption of the vocabulary of "development" and "underdevelopment" to undergird, even as it masks, the ideology of political and military hegemony of the industrialized West over the rest of the world, especially the "developing" or "underdeveloped" countries of what used to be called the Third World.

On a discursive level, the grounding homology between the individual and the nation launches the discourse of national identity into a vicious circle. If individual consciousness is simultaneously a product of the aggregate of social and cultural norms in society and the basic unit, or "building block," in the edifice of national identity, whence will transformative change come? The prevalent paradigm we encountered in Ṭāhā Ḥusayn's *al-Ayyām*, Sayyid Quṭb's *Ṭifl min al-Qarya*, and Yaḥā Ḥaqqī's *Qindīl Umm Hāshim* suggests that this circle is not only vicious but also tightly sealed. *The Trilogy* is unique in this regard because it predicates national "salvation" on individual "*re*formation" and predicates that, in turn, on an unswerving commitment to a regime of personal truth and self-knowledge founded on a customized version of radical Cartesian skepticism (Q. 397–400; S. 284–285).

Still, the opposites that can in the meantime be made to coexist within the confines of a conflicted individual consciousness defy such enticements in the public arena of national identity. Thus Kamāl can strike a tenable, though specious balance between his avowed atheism and his public display of piety (entertained exclusively out of consideration for his parents' feelings), with relative ease. Such "solutions" to the problematic question of religion are not available to the irreducibly political discourse of the nation. How, then, does religion figure in *The Trilogy*'s treatment of the identity of the nation?

Properly speaking, religion emerges as a contested dimension of national identity only in the third volume of *The Trilogy*. It does not thereby cease to figure in other areas of experience, such as the psychosexual, but these now recede into relative marginality. To take just one telling example, it may suffice to mention the all-but-overt homosexuality of Raḍwān, Yāsīn's son from his first marriage. Neither Raḍwān's liaison with the homosexual Pasha, through which he secures all kinds of favors for his family, nor the latter's odious habit of mixing acts of piety—saying the *basmala*, ritual ablution, prayer, thoughts of repentance and pilgrimage—with illicit acts and lewd thoughts—drinking, homosexuality, seduction, and political corruption—occasion more than a factual description in the narrative (S. 73,74, 299, 305 ff.). By contrast, the struggle for power on the national stage, and the fierce competition among the various ideologies vying to represent the nation, become all-consuming. So thoroughly is Raḍwān's homosexuality subsumed by the political power he wields by means of it that the "deviancy" itself goes completely unnoticed by the rest of his family, adept in matters of sex as they are.

But the interest of *al-Sukkariyya* is less in politics, per se, than it is in the ideological framing of politics, particularly in the role of religion and ethnicity in the ideological construction of national identity. It is primarily in that capacity that *The Trilogy*'s intervention in the discourse of the nation is still insistently contemporary. The fundamental issue it raises can perhaps be encapsulated in a single question: What is the status of non-Muslims in a "nation"-state comprising a Muslim majority and a non-Muslim minority? In this case the question primarily concerns the status of Copts in modern Egypt. Although it is situated within the specific chronotope of *al-Sukkariyya* (Egypt 1935–1945), the significance of the discussion is confined neither to fiction nor to Egypt, much less to the limited time of the novel's action. To date, no satisfactory answer to the question has emerged either at the level of Islamic political thought and theory or at that of historical praxis. It may be useful, therefore, to measure the fictional treatment of this issue over against the trajectory of constitutional thought in Egypt, on the one hand, and the sequence of relevant historical facts, on the other.

Not altogether surprisingly, the task of voicing concern over the legal and theoretical status of Copts in modern Egypt is assigned in the novel to an articulate Copt. Riyāḍ Qaldas, Kamāl's friend and intellectual interlocutor, broaches the issue directly in a semi-confessional conversation with Kamāl. The *Wafd* party of the revered leader Sa'd Zaghlūl, he opines, used to be "the proper home of pristine (Egyptian) nationalism." The short passage in which he elaborates this view is worth quoting because it tacitly conceptualizes a prerequisite principle of modern nationhood.

> All Copts are *Wafdists*, because the *Wafd* is the party of pristine nationalism. It is not a religious party, like the (pro-) Turkish *al-Ḥizb al-Waṭanī*

> (The Patriotic Party),[49] but rather the party of a *nationalism* that makes Egypt a free homeland for all Egyptians, regardless of ethnicity or religion. The enemies of the people know this only too well. That's why the Copts were persecuted throughout Ṣidqī's reign, and will continue to suffer persecution henceforth.
>
> (S. 148)

As we shall see, that celebrated moment of grace, in which the *Wafd* was the all-inclusive party of Egyptian nationalism (roughly 1919–1930), is not entirely free of ambiguity. Riyāḍ's comment situates it between two phases diametrically antithetical to it, both marked by sectarian violence in Egypt. If Ṣidqī's "reign of terror" (1930–1935) consecrated, as it exploited, religious discrimination against the Copts during the latter phase, evidence of the virulent anti-Christian rhetoric characteristic of the former phase is not lacking in the novel. An exceptionally violent example obtains in a statement attributed to the prominent leader of *al-Ḥizb al-Waṭanī*, the Azharite, 'Abd al-'Azīz Jāwīsh (S. 150). Subsequent historical developments fully bear out the novel's apocalyptic forecast of interreligious conflict in Egypt. It may suffice to note in this connection that violent clashes between armed Muslim and Christian factions raged throughout Egypt, especially in upper Egypt, during the last two decades of the twentieth century. In a single such confrontation in the town of al-Kushḥ between December 31, 1999–January 3, 2000, twenty-one people were killed and dozens more wounded. Inexplicably, nineteen of the dead were Copts.[50] Fahmī Huwaydī notes the disconcerting fact that at the end of the twentieth century sectarian strife was far worse in Egypt than it had been at its beginning.[51] Mīlād Ḥannā, a prominent Parliamentarian and public figure of Coptic extraction, traces that phenomenon directly to President Sadat's policies of courting Islamic extremism and applying its exclusionary rhetoric to the Egyptian body politic.[52] Although President Sadat himself may have been the most prominent victim of the violence his policies authorized, the scourge of sectarian strife he unleashed was not exorcized by his death on October 6, 1981. On the contrary, it not only escalated steadily, right to the end of the twentieth century, but also ominously ushered in the new century and the new millennium.

Obviously, such complex phenomena as sectarian strife and civil discord cannot be reduced entirely to the idiosyncratic personality of a leader, however capricious that may be. A brief glance at the trajectory of constitutional thinking in Egypt suffices to show that a general drift in the discourse of identity toward the "Islamization" of the nation/state was well under way before the time of Sadat. Egypt's first constitution, that of 1923, already specifies Islam as "the religion of the state." But it does so only in the section of "general principles" (article 149), at the end of the document, as if in an afterthought.[53] All subsequent constitutions adopt the definition but accord it increasingly greater prominence. Without fail, however, they all also "guarantee" equal rights to all citizens regardless of "origin, language, or religion."[54] Thus, the first constitution after the Revolution of 1952, that is, under the Republic, which was adopted in 1956 specifies Islam as "the religion of the state"[55] and goes on to reaffirm the equality of all Egyptians before the law, "irrespective of gender, origin, language, religion, or belief."[56] The constitution of 1964 retains this definition intact.

The prominence this stipulation accords to religion would seem to be out of line with the heavy emphasis the 1956/1964 constitution lays on the social transformation and recasting of Egyptian society along socialist lines. Mīlād Ḥannā, however, considers the drastic socialist measures undertaken by President Nasser, like his personal friendship with the Pope of the Coptic Church, and his general sensitivity to the needs of the Coptic minority (as manifested in his committing of state funds to building the famous Coptic Cathedral in Cairo in 1965), effective practical countervailing measures to the partial language of the constitution. To these and similar measures does Ḥannā ascribe the notable absence of sectarian strife in Egypt under Nasser.[57]

It is not until President Sadat's rise to power and the adoption of the constitution of 1971 that Islam becomes a constitutive, not merely a descriptive, component of the identity of the nation. The change flows directly from the adoption of Islamic law (*sharī'a*) as a source of legislation, an addition that vested with actual power the otherwise symbolic gesture of identifying Islam as the religion of the state. Here is how article 2 of that constitution reads: "Islam is the religion of the state, Arabic is its official language, and the principles of Islamic law are a major source of legislation."[58] In the May 1980 constitution, this same article undergoes yet another crucial change. Now it identifies "the principles of Islamic law as *the* major source of legislation."[59] The drift, as Mīlād Ḥannā points out, is clearly towards making Islamic law not only "the major source of legislation" but, ultimately, "the only one."[60] President Sadat's deliberate cultivation of his "Islamic" image and his divisive rhetoric combined with this incremental constitutional change to alienate the Copts further from the national polity and to sow the seeds of unprecedented sectarian violence in the history of modern Egypt. Barely a month before his assassination, President Sadat had ordered the summary detention of the top echelon of the Coptic Church and the dismissal of the Pope—an unprecedented event in the history of Egypt.

Be the circumstantial similarities or differences among leaders and epochs as they may, the issue of national affiliation, or membership in the nation, is rooted in something far more fundamental. Not to mince words, the religious bond among fellow-Muslims is deemed paramount in the Islamist ideology. As such, it supersedes all other forms of bonding, including, or perhaps especially, that of modern secular nationalism. This is particularly true when the latter is strictly limited to the precarious affiliation with the nation-state in its dawdling Arab variety. That, in practice, the attendant imperative of Islamic solidarity only rarely rose to the level of either theory or historical challenge in Arab/Islamic history has in no way diminished the cogency of the Islamist ideology or its emotive appeal to large numbers of Muslims the world over. The direct reference in Riyāḍ's comment about religion and the (pro) Turkish Egyptian party identifies the two crucial aspects of the issue: the theoretical and the historical.

To begin with the latter, the position of *al-Ḥizb al-Waṭanī* of the firebrand Muṣṭafā Kāmil, and later Muḥammad Farīd and ʻAbd al-ʻAzīz Jāwīsh, in support of retaining and strengthening the bond of Islamic solidarity between Egypt and the Ottoman state comes at the expense of the internal national cohesion and unity between Copts and Muslims in Egypt itself. To uphold the supremacy of the Islamic bond is simultaneously to relegate the Copts to the status of tolerated religious minority within a sovereign, supranational, and extraterritorial Islamic polity. This is another way of defining Islam as a super-nation, or a universal homeland of all Muslims. Not only the implicit ideology of *al-Ḥizb al-Waṭanī*, but also the explicit ideology of the *Muslim Brotherhood*, as it finds expression in the views of shaykh ʻAlī al-Munūfī and his followers in the novel, assert the primacy of Islam in regulating all aspects of the life of Egyptians. Here is how he formulates this fundamental doctrine:

> The teachings and principles of Islam are all-encompassing. They regulate the life of human beings in this world and the hereafter. Those who think that these teachings address only the spiritual and devotional aspects are totally mistaken. Islam is at once creed, worship, homeland, citizenship, religion, state, spirituality, scripture, and sword.
>
> (S. 294–295)

To this totalizing view of Islam, Kamāl's nephew, ʻAbd al-Munʻim, adds

> Let us prepare ourselves for a prolonged struggle. Our mission is not confined to Egypt but is intended for all Muslims on earth. It will succeed only when Egypt and the rest of the Islamic nations (*umam*) collectively embrace these Qur'ānic principles. We will not lay down our arms until the Qur'ān becomes the constitution of all Muslims.
>
> (S. 295: 83–84)

The full force of this blatantly ideological interpretation of Islam, especially in its implacably militant posture, will become transparent only in the last decades of the twentieth century. *The Trilogy*'s prescient anticipation of the phenomenon nearly half a century earlier registers once more the novel's visionary insight into the mysterious workings of history.

No less important, however, is the novel's rigorous pursuit of the theoretical consequences of this ideology to their logical end. If Islam is, or should be, the "homeland" of all Muslims, regardless of such "incidental" attributes of identity as race, language, culture, history, geography or, indeed, variant interpretations of Islam itself, why should not Christianity, or any other religion, for that matter, serve a similar function for its respective followers? I pose as a hypothetical question what is for Riyāḍ Qaldas an acutely felt existential problem. Though rationally an avowed secularist, he nonetheless feels a need to retain the option of retreating into an equally essentialized abstraction of "universal" Christianity, as an alternative homeland to alienation from his native Egypt.[61] The novel leaves no doubt as to Riyāḍ's "quintessential Egyptianness" (S. 148). As he spells out his anxieties and apprehensions before Kamāl, the latter cannot help noticing his strikingly "*Egyptian*" features—*miṣrī ṣamīm*—that remind him of Pharaonic images (S. 148).

To sum up, the crucial conceptual leap the novel makes in the discourse of the nation is to place the decision concerning the question of equality in a bi- or multi-religious society squarely in the hands of the minority. In other words, the question of whether the Copts feel equal and secure in an Egypt governed by Islamic law, or ideology, is for the Coptic minority, *not* the Muslim majority, to decide. The same holds true for other minorities and disenfranchised segments of societies presumed to be so governed. To cite the fact that women cannot vote or drive cars in Saudi Arabia, or attend school in Afghanistan under the Taliban—all in the name of "Islam"—is not to stray too far afield. It is precisely this radical conceptualization of the question that has so far eluded the self-referential reasoning of the proponents of the "Islamic solution"—*al-ḥall al-Islamī*—to the problematic of identity in the era of secular nationalism and the nation-state.[62]

But as I intimated earlier, the "solution" proffered by the novel, in the form of tacit endorsement of the nationalist ideology of the *Wafd* in its heyday, is not without its own problems. If the singular show of Copt–Muslim unity during the anti-British popular uprising of 1919 brought forth that ideology, the constitution of 1923 sought to inscribe it as the exclusive law of the land. Two major reservations somewhat vitiate this otherwise remarkable achievement. The first is that it was drafted, if not exactly under the guns of the British occupation, then definitely under its menacing gaze. In the prolonged negotiations to vacate Egypt, the British always insisted on retaining the right to intervene militarily "to protect religious and foreign minorities in Egypt." The absence of all reference to religion in the body of the constitution and the assertion, there, of total equality of citizens before the law, appear less compelling against this historical backdrop than they would have, had they originated in the collective free will of the Egyptian people.

Related to this matter is the second reservation, namely, the evident foreign provenance of both the spirit and the letter of the constitution. In point of fact, it was self-consciously fashioned after the constitutions of France and Belgium.[63] Moreover, the language of the constitution explicitly foregrounds the paradigm of dependency by predicating Egypt's independence on its eager willingness to cultivate the political and cultural values that will render it fit to join the host of civilized (read Western) nations. In other words, at the time of drafting the constitution the Egyptian nation appears to its own leaders as a work in progress, or a nation on probation. *The Trilogy* shows no interest in reflecting on this problematic rise of the most liberal and most secular constitution in the history of Egypt and the Arab world under direct foreign occupation and influence.

It shows even less interest in the equally problematic historical background against which the Muslim Brotherhood was founded in Ismā'īliyya in the late 1920s. As the prominent Egyptian historian Ṭāriq al-Bishrī shows, the emergence of this organization was preceded by extensive European missionary proselytizing in the Suez Canal region.[64] It was during his sojourn as a public school teacher in Ismā'īliyya that Ḥasan al-Bannā became aware of this missionary activity and sought to confront and curtail it by founding the movement in 1927. The lesson of this dialectical interplay between Western encroachment on Islamic domains, and the counterreaction it inevitably draws, does not seem to have been assimilated by either side yet. In any event, *The Trilogy* wisely shies away from effecting any spurious reconciliation among the rival forces and trends it canvasses. Not surprisingly, it ends in ideological disarray, as the police round up representatives of both the left and the right. In retrospect, one can perhaps read into this ending a sort of momentary quiet before the storm. Although there is no concrete textual evidence to substantiate any claim that *The Trilogy* "predicted" the 1952 military coup d'état of Nasser and the Free Officers, there is also no doubt that the novel maps accurately the political void that the coup came to fill. *The Trilogy*, we should bear in mind, was completed before 1952, even though it was published only 1956–1957.[65]

Back to basics: recontextualizing the nation

There is a notable tendency in Egyptian fiction of the last three decades of the twentieth century to overwork the trope of return. Whether it manifests itself in the thematic revisiting of earlier, formative phases of personal experience, especially childhood, as in most autobiographical and first-person narratives; in the reappropriation of historical accounts, as in Abū al-Ma'āṭī Abū al-Najā's fictional rendition of the life of 'Abdullāh al-Nadīm, spokesman of the 'Urābī uprising of 1881, and Bahaa Ṭaher's salute to Rifā'ah Rāfi' al-Ṭahṭāwī; or in forms and idioms of traditional Arabic narratives, as in the "historical" works of Gamal Al-Ghitani, the ploy invariably occasions a meditation on the present condition of the nation.[66] Structurally, the movement often originates in crisis and rupture that trigger a flight from present to past chronotopes. As I tried to show elsewhere, alienation from the political power at the center often figures as the motivating device behind this type of plot. The spatial trajectory of the flight is uniformly centrifugal: away from Cairo and towards the periphery, whether that be Alexandria, upper Egypt, or the countryside.

In one way or another the question of religion is intimately tied here to the status of non-Muslims in Egypt. These in turn divide roughly into two main categories: indigenous Copts, and Christian communities of "European descent," for example, Italian, Greek, French, and so on. Madam Iphtalia, the Greek proprietress of the *pension* in Yaḥyā Ḥaqqī's *Qindīl Umm Hāshim*, and Mariana, her counterpart in Mahfouz' *Mīramār* (1967), illustrate the anomalous condition of these "foreign" communities in Egypt. In both novels the role of the "foreign" characters is limited to providing a temporary shelter for the "Muslim" protagonists when these become alienated from the collective or communal ethos. In this capacity they, and the space they occupy, appear antithetical to the collective in whose midst they exist. More to the point, they figure as a precarious extension of the cultural "Other." With the exception of works written by Coptic writers, especially Edwar Al-Kharrat, and Mahfouz' *Cairene Trilogy*, credible Coptic characters are conspicuous by their absence from Egyptian fiction written before the 1970s. In a way, this absence appears to be a function of the all-consuming preoccupation with the image of the *European* cultural "Other" that is practically coeval with the history of modern Egypt. The chain of literary representations substantiating this preoccupation extends all the way back to the French occupation of Egypt (1798–1801) and shaykh Ḥasan al-'Aṭṭār's tantalized homoerotic fascination with the French occupier, *qua* effeminate savant.

The treatment of religion in Egyptian fiction during the last third of the twentieth century cannot be assessed properly outside the historical context delineated earlier. Specifically, that treatment must be read against the progressively more exclusionary discourse of political Islam on the identity of the nation and the place of non-Muslims in it. The thematic and structural reinscription of non-Muslims and non-Islamic religious motifs and practices in the narratives of this fiction measures the novel's moral response to that exclusionary ideology. A brief comparison between Mahfouz' novel *Mīramār* (1967) and two subsequent novels by writers of the post-Mahfouz generation may suffice to illustrate this crucial development.

In *Mīramār* we recall, the protagonist, 'Āmir Wajdī, flees to Alexandria from Cairo, alienated, dejected, and literally homeless. The nation and the homeland are reduced in his experience to the tenuous relationship with "foreign" Mariana, on the one hand, and the transient stay at her *pension*, *Mīramār*, on the other. His predicament is compounded. The immediate cause of his alienation and flight from Cairo is the climate of venal political culture cultivated by the regime, which turns the homeland into a veritable hotbed for opportunism. His alienation from institutionalized religion and the religious establishment harks back to a more distant past when the dogmatic rigidity of Azharite shaykhs condemned him to unhappy celibacy for entertaining unorthodox thoughts. The narrative leaves no doubt as to the sincerity of Wajdī's piety, but it does so by making religion a strictly personal and private matter; that is, by divorcing it from ideology and politics, ostensibly, at any rate. Thus, while he regularly recites verses of the Qur'ān, 'Āmir Wajdī does so only discreetly, in the inner recesses of his consciousness, so to speak.

Implicitly, this meticulous division of blame between the political and the religious dispensations gestures in the direction of historical accuracy. For, however numerous and egregious the excesses and transgressions of the Nasserist experiment, catering to political Islam and fostering religious strife cannot be counted among them. These would have been completely out of line with the regime's professed nationalist, socialist, and pan-Arab orientations. After all, the regime was literally in the process of executing Sayyid Quṭb and decimating further the ranks of Islamic activists as the novel was being written in 1966.

On the whole, Mahfouz' treatment of both religion and the status of non-Muslims in Egypt is largely discursive and often polemical in nature. By contrast, Bahaa Ṭaher's novel, *Khālatī Ṣafiyya wal-Dayr* (Aunt Safiyya and the Monastery) thoroughly shuns polemics. Its contribution to the debate on the role of religion in the identity of the nation takes a more primary form. It is, in fact, built into the structure of the physical space that metonymically represents and figuratively houses that identity. The space in question consists of an isolated Muslim village and an adjacent Christian monastery in upper Egypt. The physical proximity of the two places and the corresponding warm neighborly relations between their respective communities are presented matter-of-factly as the natural order of things. A measure of the profound respect with which the Muslim village holds the monastery can perhaps be gathered from the following anecdote: At a crucial juncture of the plot the elders of the village can think of no safer place to shelter a Muslim fugitive from a personal vendetta than the Christian sanctuary. Similarly, the Muslim revenge seeker could find no one but a Christian bounty hunter willing to violate the sanctity of the place.

The relevance of these seemingly atemporal narrative details to the issue at hand becomes clear when we juxtapose the time of writing to the time of the novel's action. At the end of the novel the author specifies the exact time of writing: January 1990–April 1990. From textual evidence we gather that the time of action is roughly the decade of the 1960s. Between the two time schemes lie the fateful decade of President Sadat's reign and its immediate aftermath, with all the horrific sectarian strife that period was to visit on Egypt. It is against that imminent disruption of the timeless repose and harmonious coexistence of the village and the monastery that the novel's indirect but forceful intervention must be read. Proximity to the Pharaonic sites at Luxor and its vicinity act as a backdrop to the novel's chronotope and lend added depth to the historical continuity of amicable interfaith relations.

Nor is the choice of a remote monastery in upper Egypt to reinscribe Christian presence in the contemporary narrative of the nation an accident. These monasteries were built by devout ascetic Christians in inaccessible places precisely to escape the reach of the central authority bent on persecuting them.[67] Their very existence therefore attests to unquestionable faith and endurance. Historically, the status of the places of worship of non-Muslims under Islam has been the litmus test of Islamic tolerance, or lack thereof, towards followers of other religions.[68] It is thus instructive that the wave of sectarian violence that swept Egypt during the past three decades was triggered by the burning of a Christian church at Khānka, in northern Cairo, on November 6, 1972. Similar incidents followed in other parts of Cairo and elsewhere in Egypt during and after the reign of Sadat. The situation was further compounded by recurrent disputes over certain sites to which both Muslims and Christians claimed a right to build a mosque or a church. Uniformly, the ruling party of President Sadat sided with the Muslims and, by blatantly taking sides, aggravated the situation immensely.[69] It is against this troubled, intensely ideological national background that the simple act of narrating accounts of common amity between Muslims and Copts, a Muslim village and a Christian monastery, assumes a countervailing symbolic significance.

Both of Ibrāhīm Abdel Meguid's Alexandria novels *Lā 'Aḥad Yanām fil-Iskandariyyah* (1996; *No One Sleeps in Alexandria*, 1999) and *Ṭuyūr al-'Anbar* (2003; Ambergris Birds) take this "revisionist" process a drastic step forward. True to the paradigm sketched above, the action of both novels takes place in Alexandria: the first during the Second World War, the second during the decade of the 1950s. A primary concern of both novels is to chronicle the devastating effects of external wars and internal strife on the delicate fabric of Alexandria's cosmopolitan, multiethnic, and multireligious society. This is particularly true of the second novel, the action of which unfolds against the 1956 Suez war and its dramatic aftermath. With haunting precision the novel records the number of "foreigners"—Greeks, Jews, Italians, French—involved in each of the successive waves of emigration out of their beloved, but no longer hospitable city. A poignant sense of loss and bereavement inheres in the cold citation of statistical data about the steady depletion of the ranks of these celebrated communities of Alexandria through death, lower birthrate, and steady emigration. The deep pathos of the novel inhabits the gaping void between the inexorable logic of numbers and abstract historical processes, on the one hand, and the baffled incomprehensibility of such abstractions by the hapless victims thereof. The touchingly naive protagonist of the novel wonders: why have the lonely, middle-aged Greek, Italian, and Jewish women he has always known as true Alexanderines suddenly become "foreigners" in the only homeland they recognize? On the discursive and extradiegetic levels of the narrative the question is of course rhetorical. All the same, it points up the incompatibility of religious differentiation with the fundamental principle of equality of all citizens before the law in a properly constituted modern, liberal nation-state.

It is in *Lā 'Aḥad Yanām*, however, that Abdel Meguid makes the most daring leap into uncharted territory. As indicated earlier, the novel's action unfolds against the bloody backdrop of the Second World War and, in a sense, mirrors in miniature the senseless violence that cataclysmic event visited on innumerable victims the world over. In the novel the strife revolves around two traditional monads of Egyptian life: the "tribal" rivalry between two major clans in a remote village in upper Egypt, and Muslim–Christian touchiness. Aversion to violence drives the Muslim protagonist, a young Azharite shaykh, out of his village in upper Egypt into Alexandria, where, for the first time in their life, he and his young wife come into intimate contact with Christian neighbors. Even as this thrust gathers momentum and brings the neighbors closer together, a love story between a Muslim boy and a Christian girl launches a counterthrust that reinforces difference and rupture.

The "forbidden" love story reenacts the familiar tropes of fatal attraction, limitless devotion, and inevitable separation—the Christian girl to a convent in upper Egypt, the Muslim boy to Europe. Conversely, the story of friendship between the Azharite shaykh, Majd al-Dīn, and his Coptic friend Dimyān, takes an unusual turn. It is primarily, but not exclusively, through this relationship that Christians and Christianity are reinstated as integral components of the national narrative. To begin with, we note the use of the Coptic calendar on its own, that is, unaided by either the Muslim or the common calendars.[70] This stark assertion of uncontingent identity is quite common in the works of Coptic writers, especially Edwar Al-Kharrat, but not in the works of their Muslim counterparts. The fact that this calendar is universally comprehensible in Alexandria is, of course, a testimony to the city's irreducible pluralism and diversity.

Other innovations reinforce this trend in the novel. To take just one example, the introduction of a naive Muslim woman from upper Egypt to the cosmopolitan milieu of Alexandria occasions a recounting (through defamiliarization) of daily experiences of ordinary Copts as perfectly normal. Through affectionate personal contact Zahra, Majd al-Dīn's wife, soon takes to the ecumenical habit of native Alexanderines, at least as far as celebrating all religious holidays is concerned. With time, Christian prayers, homilies, and supplications to revered saints of the Coptic Church, elicit from her only awed, not baffled or disapproving response. Thus "naturalized" in the text, Christian beliefs and practices appear different only in form, not substance or value, from their Islamic correlates. The ecumenical parity advanced on all these levels reaches a climax in the occasional convergence of scriptures in the text (p. 390). Ultimately, Dimyān's identity is explicitly inscribed in the very text of the Qur'ān. Distraught by the death of his Coptic friend, Majd al-Dīn cannot get him out of his mind while reciting the Chapter of *al-Raḥmān* (the Merciful), many verses of which rhyme with the name Dimyān. The following passage captures the gist of that unprecedented practice in Egyptian and Arabic fiction; the Qur'ānic verses are in italics.

> Dimyān! Dimyān! Dimyān! *The Most Gracious. He has taught the Qur'ān. He has created man.* Dimyān! Dimyān! *He has taught him speech. The sun and the moon follow their courses punctually. The stars and the trees bow in adoration.* Dimyān! Dimyān! *And the sky He had raised high and He has set the measure.* Dimyān! Dimyān![71]

* * *

To conclude, the treatment of religion in Egyptian fiction is inherently problematic. Many weighty, rival factors converge at the intersection of dogma and genre to create a site of permanent contestation. Foremost among these are the novel's constitutive commitment to plausible varieties of verisimilitude, its equally formative predisposition to "philosophical" skepticism, and consequent secularizing effects. Perhaps it will be more accurate to identify the institutionalized interpretations of religion, not religion itself, as the primary foe of the novelistic imagination. In the Egyptian novel this tension often occasions a distinction between formal, public displays and manifestations of religiosity, and less perceptible, more private modes of piety and spirituality. Whether in so doing the novel merely transcribes, or fashions, reality, is a moot theoretical question in novel criticism.

Either way, the question of religion is inseparable in this fiction from the question of the nation. And that, in turn, is often equally inseparable from the question of non-Muslims in Islamic society. Under the historical circumstances of modern Egypt the status of religious minorities was from the outset entangled with the designs of European occupation, colonization, and hegemony. During the first half of the twentieth century, characters representing these non-Muslim communities stood for the European cultural "Other." While this paradigm reigned, the indigenous Christian Copts were hardly visible in the fictional landscape. The situation changes categorically in the aftermath of the Second World War. From the late 1940s to the present, the treatment of the Copts shows both continuity and progression. The continuity emanates from the felt need to reinscribe the Copts in a viable, all-inclusive narrative of the nation. In this undertaking the novel seems to mount an explicit challenge to exclusionary ideologies that tend to collapse into a single monolith national affiliation and religious identification. The more complete the identification between the religious and the national, the less hospitable is the discourse of identity to religious difference; and vice versa. The "readmission" of the Copts into the symbolic narrative of the nation as *bona fide* Egyptians, thus carries a subversive potential when the nation is essentialized or reified as a religious community of Muslims.

This counterdiscourse of the novel proceeds along different lines. In Mahfouz' *Cairene Trilogy* it takes the form of a discursive assertion by Kamāl about Riyāḍ Qaldas' quintessential Egyptian physiognomy. In the novel's economy of representation, Pharaonic features assign historical precedence and this, in turn, proffers entitlement. It is hard to imagine a greater affiliation with Egypt than that inscribed in the flesh.

In the works of Edwar Al-Kharrat, perhaps Egypt's most prominent Coptic writer, the presence of Copts in the Egyptian landscape, especially in the writer's native Alexandria, is assumed even as it is problematized. The depiction in minute detail of daily experiences of "ordinary" Copts, including their distinctive cuisine, forms of greeting, religious invocations, visits to church, festivities, calendar, and so on, imparts a fullness to the narrative and lends an air of solidity and normality to their presence in the land. But there is also a haunted awareness of the precariousness of that presence in a society where political Islam is growing steadily more strident. Already in joint Christian–Muslim demonstrations for Palestine in Alexandria in 1947–1948 Islamist slogans similar to those voiced in *Sugar Street* are heard in tandem with slogans calling for Egypt's national independence from British rule. That haunted awareness is made all the more poignant by the nostalgic, retrospective pining of the narrative after the effervescent childhood experiences of the largely autobiographical first person narrator.

Bahaa Ṭaher's *Khālatī Ṣafiyya* assigns to space the agency that inheres in physiognomy in Mahfouz' *Trilogy* and in a peculiar sensibility and temporality in much of Al-Kharrat's fiction. Although living in total harmony, the village and the monastery are not exactly coeternal. In order of appearance, first was the monastery, and then came the village. Over against the rampant sectarian strife at the time of writing, the novel posits this tacit anteriority and subsequent harmonious coexistence between the symbolic space of the village and that of the monastery.

4

QUESTIONABLE SUBJECTS

Individuality, representation, and the Egyptian novel

All the ambiguities and complexities that beset the other formative tropes of identity in the Egyptian novel attend with added force to the problematic of the individual. While some of these inhere in the subject itself, others bear the peculiar marks of modern Arab culture. The term's endless semantic shuttling back and forth among its numerous metonymic components—person, self, ego, mind, body, soul, voice, and so on—betrays a degree of slippage and indeterminacy that would seem incommensurate with the foundational role of the concept in human civilization and culture.[1] Historically, too, the concept has been a perennial site of religious, moral, ethical, ideological, and political contestation and agency. However, the individual remains the single, utterly indispensable constitutive unit of the novel. But that is hardly surprising in a genre whose genesis is literally coeternal with the birth of the sovereign individual, at least according to the tradition that traces the genealogy of the novel to Defoe's *Robinson Crusoe* (1719). In so far as this generalization about the genre is valid, the Arabic novel necessarily partakes of it like other novelistic traditions in other languages and national cultures. To note further that *Robinson Crusoe* was one of the first English novels translated into Arabic is to add historical filiation to generic affiliation.[2] We shall see shortly how "translation" of Western fiction informed the dominant idea of the writer at the beginning of the twentieth century. That idea found historical expression in the curious, but highly celebrated, figure of Muṣṭafā Luṭfī al-Manfalūṭī, and was later thematized in Mahfouz' Cairene *Trilogy* (1956–1957).

Another landmark of the "English" novel, James Joyce's *A Portrait of the Artist as a Young Man* (1916), written two centuries after *Robinson Crusoe*, provides yet another crucial point of reference for the trajectory of the individual in fiction. Here the individual is situated not on a remote island, where the sources of the autonomous self can be studied in relative isolation, but squarely in a particular, and highly troubled national setting. As we know, at the end of the novel the largely autobiographical Stephen Dedalus, about to embark on self-imposed exile from his native Ireland, vows, somewhat melodramatically, "to forge in the smithy of (his) soul the uncreated conscience of (his) race." It is precisely this intricate intertwining of the individual and personal with the national that prompts Sonalla Ibrahim, one of Egypt's leading novelists on the subject of troubled identity, to inscribe one of Stephen's musings on the matter as an epigraph to *Tilk al-Rā'iḥa*: "This race and this country and this life produced me . . . and I shall express myself as I am."

Though half a century separates *Tilk al-Rā'iḥa* from *A Portrait of the Artist As A Young Man*, and another half separates Ibrahim's text from our own post-colonial moment, the problematic of the individual continues to reverberate against an unsettled national backdrop, though now in a highly ambivalent climate of globalization and an irreducibly intertextual space. To date, Ibrahim's novella remains one of the most poignant interrogations of contemporary Egyptian identity. It has, in addition, almost single-handedly, inaugurated the tradition of the antihero in modern Egyptian and Arabic fiction. The full significance of this imaginative breakthrough will become apparent only when measured against the dominant tradition of the heroic in Arabic literature, especially the reflexive relationship between the writer and his often highly idealized, "autobiographical" hero.[3] Perhaps no other issue or trope marks as graphically the rupture between the two generations of Egyptian novelists: that of Mahfouz, on the one hand, and that of the so-called generation of the sixties, on the other, as does this emergence of the antihero as a paradigmatic figure. To what extent loose, informal "membership" in such an amorphous, imaginary construct as literary generation grounds individual identity will concern us later. Here it is important to note that interest in the problematic of the individual in fiction logically and epistemologically limits the scope of this investigation of the individual to literary, and specifically narrative representations of individuality. Whether non-representational, or nonnarrative, forms of individuality and selfhood exist at all, is a question that may have metaphysical, but hardly practical relevance to the interests of the novel.

But this narrowing down of the scope of the investigation to narrative forms of individuality only partly alleviates the predicament of the Egyptian novel on this score. For, by a fiat of history, the Egyptian novel came into being in a cultural context already fully mapped out, with clearly demarcated lines and limits of what can and cannot be represented in writing, and equally strict conventions about the sanctioned forms, modes, and styles of rendering literary representations. To the intrinsic cultural constraints prevalent in Egypt during the novel's gestation period, roughly from the last quarter of the nineteenth century to the middle of the twentieth, one must add the immensely complicating factor of foreign—British—occupation (1882–1956). I want to argue in this chapter that, broadly, the identity of the individual in modern Arab culture is intimately bound up with that of the novel and, further, that both bear the disfiguring scars of this double bind. In Chapter 1, I touched briefly on certain manifestations of the throes of the Egyptian novel; here I will examine a little more deeply some crucial implications of these theoretical/polemical debates about the nature and status of the Arabic novel.

These debates, as we shall see shortly, stimulated a reexamination, and a redefinition, of the identity and role of the writer in modern Arab society and culture.

* * *

Whatever disagreements divide critics concerning the provenance of the Arabic novel and other issues of periodization and historical schemata, there is a practical consensus on the fact that by the mid-1940s the novel had established itself as a legitimate contender to special literary status and historical agency in Arab culture. Recourse to realism was the midwife to this (re)birth of the genre in Arabic, and the systematic appropriation and application of its narrative techniques and strategies underpinned the novel's claim to both uniqueness and authenticity, especially as regards the representation of modern Arab reality. Paramount interest in individual experience is pivotal to this claim of entitlement. Sayyid Quṭb, as we saw earlier, was most perceptive when he recognized the originality of the realist novel in rendering modern Egyptian reality artistically and faithfully, as exemplified by Mahfouz' second novel of the realist phase: *Khān al-Khalīlī* (1946). It is equally indisputable, I think, that realism, in its variegated manifestations, has been not only the supreme, but also the exclusive, mode of representation in modern Arabic fiction, in Egypt as elsewhere in the Arab world. Witness, for example, the near total absence from this narrative tradition of less mimetic modes of imaginative grappling with "reality," such as utopia, myth, fantasy, mystery, detective and science fiction. In fact, little remains of the Arabic novel if one excludes from the corpus novels written in the realist and historical modes, the distinction between the two in this regard being the added referential dimension of the latter. To note further that the alternative modes just mentioned are equally rare in contemporary Arab culture is to reaffirm the symbiotic relationship between novel and culture, and to highlight the novel's underlying order of priorities. In a sense, this "servile" mimetic panting after the "real" prevents the novel from getting out of touch or out of step with Arab reality and consciousness, both of which it appears bent on cajoling into self-reflection and self-recognition—these being prerequisite steps on the path to eventual change and progress. It is not hard, I think, to detect the familiar reformist impulse behind this self-regulating restraint of the novelistic imagination.

Herein, however, lies a bottomless source of the Egyptian novel's dilemma. Major areas of the reality the novel seeks to canvass are cordoned off and rendered inaccessible to the novelistic probe. The full range of modern individuality is one of these. Numerous religious, political, and social constraints converge to enforce this stricture against a thorough, comprehensive mapping of modern individualism. By that I mean simply the representation of actual things that ordinary men and women do, feel, think, imagine, or desire. We have already encountered examples of such restrictions in previous chapters. The veritable taboo against imagining the religious subject, for instance, and the grave peril its violation brooks, were graphically demonstrated by the attempt on Mahfouz' life, the hounding of Naṣr Ḥāmid Abū Zayd out of Egypt, the constant harassment of nonconformist writers, and the periodic appeal to haphazard censorship regulations to ban one book or another. The travails of the famous film director Youssef Chahine (Yūsuf Shāhīn), with the religious authorities in Egypt over his attempt to recast the story of Joseph in modern cinematic idiom shows that the restriction on representation is not media (nor historically) specific and applies equally to the visual arts, be these sculpture, painting, or film.[4] Similarly, the sensitivity of the military/political power to its public image, as attested by Sadat's reported ire over Mahfouz' fictional representation of a suicidal officer in *Bidāya wa Nihāya* (1949),[5] may explain the rarity in Egyptian fiction of characters representing military or political authority. Given the centrality of the religious, the military, and the political in Egyptian public life and culture, it is not hard to surmise the extent of the (realist) novel's difficulty in maintaining the illusion of presenting a credible panoramic, comprehensive view of society. The taboos against the representation of all forms of sexuality and explicit eroticism, including all references to genitalia, intimate body parts, scatology, and bodily functions in general, are perhaps even more strict and narrow further the range of representable individual experience.

But even as it severely circumscribes the novel, the taboo against the representation of carnality reaches much farther than the horizons of imaginative fiction. Tendentious contemporary "interpretations" of Islam often betray an acute discomfort with the human body, and sexuality in general. This unease is patently at odds with the disarming openness with which Qur'ānic narrative occasionally relates episodes and motifs of sexual desire. To take only a mild, but telling example, the manner in which most English renditions of the Qur'ān "translate" the verse describing the attempted seduction of Joseph (12: 24) by Zulaykha, may suffice to suggest this anxiety. I enclose "translation" in quotation marks because the rendition in effect edits the text of the Qur'ān, expressly against the grain of the narrative and the explicit linguistic evidence.

The verse in question uses the exact same verb to describe both Zulaykha's desire for Joseph and his reciprocal desire for her: ولقد همت به وهم بها، لولا ان رأى برهان ربه. Accordingly, the most widely used authoritative Arabic commentary on the Qur'ān, that of *al-Jalālayn*, minces no words in stating the obvious: It interprets ولقد همت به simply as "she desired intercourse with him"—قصدت منه الجماع—; and, وهم بها, as "and he (too) desired that"—وقصد ذلك—. The rest of the verse following the conditional لولا is equally clear and registers the timely, though highly moot,[6] divine intervention, in the nick of time, so to speak, to avert the impending (illicit) coitus, and spare Joseph the odium of adultery. Here is how A. J. Arberry renders the relevant part of that verse into English: "For she desired him; and he would have taken her but that he saw the proof of his Lord."[7]

By contrast, Abdullah Yusuf Ali, Marmaduke Pickthall, Muhammad Muhsin Khan, and others drastically change the meaning by forcing the syntax. In the process of doing so, they also dispel the powerful dramatic tension built into the original.

Here is how the verse now reads in Yusuf Ali's "translation"—the versions of Pickthall and Khan differing from it only in minor stylistic details: "And (with passion) did she desire him, and he *would have* desired her, but that he saw the evidence of his Lord"[8] (emphasis added).

What this "variation" on the original seeks to accomplish is fairly transparent: to exempt Joseph from susceptibility to temptation by making him immune to (illicit) sexual desire. Joseph, according to this reading, is not only incapable of committing an actual sin or transgression; he is, like all prophets, incapable of *wishing* or *feeling* a desire to do so. This rhetorical maneuver relocates the barrier against wrongdoing to an anterior, or inner, layer of the prophet's ontology. By doing so, it also sets him, *qua* prophet, apart from the rest of mankind. In this new dispensation, the prophet appears innately immune to temptation in the realm of emotions, drives, and desires, as he is infallible in matters of creed and dogma. What we witness here is the collapsing of the principle of creedal *'iṣma* (infallibility or inerrancy) onto the sensual domain of the body. If it does not quite deify prophets, this turn obviously raises them above other mortals as regards weakness of the flesh. Consequently, it places them in an intermediary station, somewhere between the divine and the human. Needless to say that such overtures, irrespective of the intention behind them, run directly counter to the emphatic assertion of the Qur'ān concerning the strictly human nature of the prophets, notwithstanding their superior (human) character.[9]

The phenomenon I am describing seems to be a product of the twentieth century. Moreover, it seems to obtain primarily in English translations of the Qur'ān made by Muslim "translators." These two observations, if accurate, may not be entirely unrelated. What's more, their confluence may betray a vitiating defensiveness vis-à-vis the hegemonic West and an abject pandering to its dominant image of Christ as man-God.

The relevance of all this to our immediate interest in individuality lies in an equally incongruent proposition. For even as the prototype of the prophet was being thus abstracted in one corner of modern Islamic consciousness, its paradigmatic standing as an exemplary model of, and for, *the* Islamic personality was being reinvented and reintroduced in other parts. The often quoted Qur'ānic verse: "لقد كان لكم في رسول الله اسوة حسنة...", you have a good model (to emulate) in the messenger of Allah . . . ,[10] and two less frequently cited verses of similar content,[11] anchor this idea in Islamic textuality. In this respect, the renewed historical/literary interest in the biography of the Prophet and his immediate companions in Egypt since the 1920s, like the emergence of the Muslim Brotherhood in 1927 as a political/educational movement whose primary objective was to "rehabilitate" Muslims into greater conformity with the Islamic ideal,[12] and the subsequent, steadily more visible reversion to an Islamic dress code and personal demeanor, appear intimately related phenomena. In the semiotic scheme of things, they all form part of the Islamic response to the political and cultural hegemony of the modern West, particularly, perhaps, to the cult of overindulgent individualism abiding therein. (In a sense, what makes the signature image of Osama Ben Laden and his right-hand man, Ayman al-Ẓawāhirī, as they brave the treacherous terrain of eastern Afghanistan, in plain, traditional "Islamic" garb, so potent is the direct appeal the image makes to the rugged, stoic, irreducibly simple, and ultimately *atemporal* paradigm of individuality represented in Islamic lore by the first Muslims, especially, the Prophet and his immediate companions and followers. It is precisely this resonant image in the popular imagination that President Sadat sought to muster by the carefully cultivated public persona of a pious ruler he projected during his carefully staged and fully televised visits to the local mosque of his native village of Mit Abu Elkoum in lower Egypt. Perhaps because his insincerity showed through the sham, he was ultimately less successful in his quest than other, less feigning contenders to the mantle of Islamic "authenticity." Belief, however, may measure the sincerity of the believer, not the validity of the object of belief—and in this case, the availability of what purports to be a paradigmatic model of "the Islamic personality," *al-shakhṣiyya al-Islāmiyya*).[13]

Although it is most highly visible in the political domain, the versatile paradigm is by no means limited to it. At a slight remove from the political realm, one can readily discern its workings at other sites of identity formation. The veritable explosion in the last two decades of what is clearly an Islamic version of American teleevangelism shows how pervasive the phenomenon has become. Perhaps no one exemplifies this development better than the Egyptian telepreacher, ʻAmr Khālid. Always clean-shaven and neatly dressed in fashionable Western suits, Khālid uses his talent for melodrama to "recount" in a mawkish, supplicant manner exemplary anecdotes of personal conduct from the life of early prominent Muslims. As he methodically works himself up to a tearful state, the studio audience, usually young men and women, appear mesmerized by the spectacle. Through his televised series, *wa-Nalqā al-Aḥibba* (Meeting the Beloved) widely available on DVD, ʻAmr Khālid has become a household name in much of the Arab world and beyond. The express objective of the series, as the blurb introducing each installment announces from the outset, is to imitate the "paradigmatic" personalities of the early Muslims. The spectacular success of this, and similar undertakings, measures accurately, I believe, the immense emotional and psychological investment in the idea of the Islamic personality and its staying power.

But if the prophetic ideal sets the upper limit of normative individuality in Arab/Islamic culture, and the idea of perfectibility motivates its teleology, self-discipline through, *inter alia*, education provides the means to that desideratum. What makes self-discipline mandatory, however, is a fundamental mistrust of the innate instincts and drives at the core of the biological self. It is in this sense that the Qur'ān reads references to the self as the source of evil. It is also significant in light of the foregoing discussion that this view finds its most direct expression in the chapter of Joseph, and in his own emphatic words about his own (normative?) self: "وماابرئ نفسي، ان النفس لأمارة بالسوء" (Qur'ān 12: 52; "Nor do I exonerate myself, for the self is indeed prone to command evil"). Interestingly, this generalization follows a direct appeal by Joseph to God to avert from him "the guile of women" lest he incline to them and transgress. (Qur'ān 12:32; "قال رب السجن احب الي مما يدعونني اليه والا تصرف عني كيدهن أصب إليهن وأكن من الجاهلين"). In this inimical capacity, the-self is both the enemy and the battleground. Hence, overcoming its "evil" inclinations occasions the greater of the two struggles in the words of the famous, though moot *ḥadīth*–prophetic tradition; (the other, lesser, struggle being war).[14] This typology of the self consigns the instinctual drives, especially sexual desire, to the lowest rungs of the personality gauge. Even when thus banished into obscurity, they must be kept in check, under vigilant surveillance. Mahfouz' *Cairene Trilogy* retains a memorable instance of the morbid effects this anxiety about the sexual drives can have on the individual, in this case 'Abd al-Mun'im, the grandson of Aḥmad 'Abd al-Jawād from his daughter Khadīja, and Kamāl's nephew.

The novel's abiding interest in all aspects of individuality brings it into direct, continuous, and often agonistic contact with these, and other, primary discourses of the self in the Egyptian national and cultural realms. What compounds the encounter still further is the common conviction that the novel's fictional characters mask referential types and representations of collective identity. Not only religious zealots and military desperados but also ordinary literary critics partake of this operative assumption. Thus, for example, the critic Durayd Yaḥyā al-Khawājā chastises Naguib Mahfouz for smearing "Egyptian intellectuals, Egyptian society, and authentic Arab culture in general" by fielding would-be-representative characters that are not true to authentic types in *Thartharah Fawq al-Nīl* (1966). Al-Khawājā asserts that he "knows that the reality of Egyptian society in particular, and Arab society in general, is not consonant with what the novel depicts." He blames the discrepancy entirely on Mahfouz' servile imitation of Western models.[15]

* * *

The foregoing canvassing of perimeters may suggest the nature and extent of the issues involved in the subject of individuality. For strictly procedural purposes, I will organize the various strands and discourses flowing therefrom under the two major categories of author and character. These broad, overarching concepts are seldom, if ever, fully separable as they often overlap and shade extensively into each other. Formally, this intimate association between author and character comes to the fore in autobiographical novels, where the protagonist often projects an idealized version of the (author's) self. As I noted earlier, no other aspect or issue of characterization has occupied Arab critics more than this question of the writer and his (reflexive) hero. In fact, the dissonant treatment of the nexus of issues associated with this question lies at the roots of an epistemological and aesthetic break between two generations of Egyptian writers: this time the generation of the novelists proper, that is, Yaḥyā Ḥaqqī, Naguib Mahfouz, 'Ādil Kāmil, and other realists, and the preceding generation of writers who never quite became novelists, for example, Ibrāhim 'Abd al-Qādir al-Māzinī, 'Abbās Maḥmūd al-'Aqqād, Tawfīq al-Ḥakīm, and Ṭāhā Ḥusayn.[16] As we shall see, a major cause of the indeterminacy of the latter's literary identity is their inability to distance themselves sufficiently from personal experience in order to recast the autobiographical material in aesthetically defensible novelistic form. For different reasons, the "personal" content of their writing about the self is often so homogenized as to flout the fundamental principles of autobiography: veracity and comprehensiveness.

The writer between Kamāl 'Abd al-Jawād and Ibrāhīm al-Kātib

The question of writing surfaces in a poignant scene in *The Cairene Trilogy*. Al-Sayyid Aḥmad summons his youngest son, Kamāl, to his presence one day, soon after Kamāl's graduation from secondary school, to "discuss" with him his plans for college. As usual in "conversations" with members of his household, the autocratic al-Sayyid is more apt to dictate than to discuss. Accordingly, he comes ready with his own predetermined ideas about what Kamāl should study: medicine or law. Barring these, the military or police academy, will do. Anything else, even commerce, would be incongruent with his self-image, of which Kamāl is but a species, albeit an awkward one. His surprise by Kamāl's choice of the Teachers Training College is thus shocking and incomprehensible. The father's implacable aversion to this choice registers the low esteem the teaching profession brooks in the public view, filtered here through al-Sayyid's peculiar mix of class bias, ignorance, and personal idiosyncrasy. He seems particularly indignant, for example, at the prospect of having his own son attend college gratis while he, al-Sayyid, underwrites the expenses of the son of his aide in the shop at law school.

For Kamāl the Teachers Training College is a means to an end. Neither the meager financial rewards nor the low social standing of the teaching profession has much to commend it otherwise. The line of reasoning he adopts in defense of his decision to attend this College is two-tiered. At the important, personal level, his choice speaks directly to the prerequisite qualifications of the writer, modulated here by the odd admixture of the young (autobiographical) protagonist in love. Ultimately, however, it is the curriculum of the Teachers Training College that exercises Kamāl's imagination with its promise of access to the secular canon of the Western humanities, mediated here exclusively by English, the language of the European occupier. To come into his own, to become himself, as both unique individual and writer, Kamāl deems it necessary to familiarize himself with the literary and intellectual traditions of the modern West. In this respect, the autobiographical dimension of the character shades into the historical referent, as Kamāl recapitulates a fundamental conviction of the first generation of Egyptian writers who launched what came to be known as the New School in Egyptian fiction in the 1920s. These writers, as we saw in Chapter 1, openly predicated the effective representation of modern Egyptian sensibility and experience on intimate familiarity with Western fictional models and techniques of representation.

The "canonical" works of Western culture and literature in Kamāl's personal library are thus meant to vouch for the promise of personality and literary sensibility and, beyond these, an eventual admission into the writerly profession.

All this obtains at the underlying level of Kamāl's reasoning. At the surface level, however, he presents matters quite differently to his incredulous father, in part out of filial devotion. He praises the teaching profession as noble and cites as evidence the high respect that advanced European societies accord teachers. More attuned to the harsh realities of contemporary Egypt, the father readily dismisses all this as mindless drivel and urges Kamāl to think "realistically." In despair, Kamāl falls back on his last line of defense and invokes the mediating status of teaching and writing as honored means of obtaining knowledge in Islamic culture.[17] In this vein, he presents writing as a continuation, rather than a break, with the tradition, and, knowing his father's partiality to the writer Muṣṭafā Luṭfī al-Manfalūṭī he cites this example to buttress his argument. In so doing, he appears less insincere than inconsistent. The evidence of sincerity abounds in his introspective reflections on al-Manfalūṭī's literary style as exemplary; the inconsistency is as much part of al-Manfalūṭī's composite makeup as it is of Kamāl's hopeless confusion of the experience of ardent love with the imaginative representation of that experience in literary form.

For all intents and purposes, al-Manfalūṭī represents an odd amalgam of anomalous personal and literary traits. The fact that he finds favor with both Kamāl and al-Sayyid, polar opposites in matters of literary and aesthetic taste, is a measure of his hybrid identity. This is precisely what makes him such a telling instance of the changing views about writing in Egypt during the first two decades of the twentieth century.

Evidently gifted and precocious, al-Manfalūṭī, like Ṭāhā Ḥusayn, was sent to al-Azhar at a tender age soon after he memorized the Qur'ān at the local *kuttāb* of his native village.[18] At the Azhar, however, he found himself attracted more to literary than to religious texts. In the introduction to his three-volume collection of short, anecdotal, expository pieces, *al-Naẓarāt* (Glances; 1910, 1912, and 1921 respectively) he describes some of the pains visited on him by fellow students and officials at al-Azhar on account of this predisposition to literature. Regarding literary pursuits heretical and literature the veritable domain of the devil, these inquisitorial vigilantes at al-Azhar felt thoroughly vindicated when, during surprise search raids, they seized a volume of poetry or literary prose hidden under a pillow or in a closet in his room.[19]

Whether al-Manfalūṭī's travails during his ten-year sojourn at al-Azhar were indeed as acute as he describes, or whether the description also contains a modicum of hyperbole, is of no serious consequence. Far more important is his use of the dramatized experience as a backdrop to his own development as a writer and the critical agency he assigns literature in the momentous task of reforming modern Arab/Islamic culture and identity. Faithful to the views of his teacher and mentor, Muḥammad 'Abdu, al-Manfalūṭī broaches the problematic of the literary through its direct bearing on religion. The combined effect of 'Abdu's teaching and al-Manfalūṭī's formulation on the relationship between Islam and imaginative literature goes much farther than any alternative, contemporary or subsequent, articulation.

Briefly, al-Manfalūṭī argues that the correct understanding of Islam not only tolerates but, in fact, presupposes and requires a fine literary sensibility and a thorough familiarity with the canonical texts of Arabic literature and literary criticism. Historically, he contends, the great Muslim scholars of old readily availed themselves of the linguistic and literary traditions of pre-Islamic and Islamic Arabic poetry while wrestling with the primary texts of Islam. To their present successors, these venerable scholars bequeathed a rich noetic heritage, which, through neglect of literary studies, contemporary shaykhs have all but fully squandered. The reasoning thus runs as follows: Ignorance of the ancillary traditions of Arabic literature vitiates religious scholarship and this, in turn, gradually erodes the very foundations of religious knowledge, thus leaving both scholarship and knowledge prey to superstition and chicanery. On the causal connection between the sorry state of Muslims and Islam in the modern world, and the historical agents thereof, al-Manfalūṭī minces no words: If the neglect of literary studies is a major cause of the decline of Islam, the benighted shaykhs of al-Azhar are the unwitting agents of that untoward development. To reverse the downward process and resurrect authentic, viable Islam, it is necessary to revive Islamic knowledge by rehabilitating Islamic scholarship. The incorporation of a substantial component of literary studies in the curriculum of al-Azhar is the first step in that direction.

Before literature can perform this vital task, however, it, itself, must be thoroughly reconstructed along untraditional lines to be able to nurture a different kind of literary sensibility. By this al-Manfalūṭī means primarily the general need to free Arabic literature from fatuous dependence on rhetorical embellishments and highfalutin style. This, more than any other flaw, he argues, has caused the decline of Arabic letters throughout the ages. Not even the paragons of classical Arabic poetry, al-Mutanabbī and Abū Tammām, were able to resist the seductive, but ultimately fatal appeal of rhetorical flair. Accordingly, a painstaking sifting of the literary canon becomes a virtual necessity if modern Arab literary sensibility is to escape the bleak fate of its predecessors. Instructed by his subjective criteria of eloquence, al-Manfalūṭī seems to have effected such a redaction of the canon to his own personal satisfaction. This intimacy with the "essentialized" canon enabled him to conjure up the life of the ancient Arabs directly, vividly, and fully—an imaginative feat to which he seems to have attached an intrinsic, existential/ideological, value incommensurate with its literary/aesthetic merit. In any event, as was amply clear to some of his more critical contemporaries, his own writing not only failed to demonstrate the validity of the discursive claims he made but, moreover, perpetrated the selfsame rhetorical faults he vehemently decried in others.[20]

Whatever one thinks of al-Manfalūṭī the writer, his phenomenal fame would have been inconceivable, even in his own lifetime, if it had rested exclusively on his literary merits. Rather, his genius seems to lie elsewhere; to wit, in his uncanny ability to project a totalized version of the writer's identity as a public persona and a champion of worthy causes. In this sense, his popularity indexes not only the literary taste of the contemporary Egyptian reading public but also the limits of that public's capacity and tolerance for change. Al-Manfalūṭī seems to have read that public mood accurately and to have calibrated his personal and literary gifts optimally to bend public opinion in his favor. The significance of his example to the changing paradigm of the writer can be assessed properly only within the historical context of Egypt during the three decades of his active writing career: roughly 1895–1924. By all accounts, this was a period of constant agitation for change and reorientation in all walks of Egyptian life, including literary expression. The direction of the desired change, however, was hotly contested on all sides. By far the strongest pull on the literary front toward the end of al-Manfalūṭī's life emanated from writers associated with the New School. The mounting presence of European cultural and literary models on the Egyptian scene, abetted, as these were, by the direct British colonial rule in Egypt, and especially the transcendent supremacy of English in the Egyptian educational system, significantly tilted the balance against the traditional modes of literary expression.

Both al-Manfalūṭī's fame during his life and its subsequent abatement since his death flow directly from the middle ground he consciously sought to occupy between perceived polarities in the discourse of identity. Mindful of his own birth to mixed Arab/Turkish parentage, al-Manfalūṭī seems to have elevated the hybridity emanating from his incidental birth to the status of constitutive principle of the writer's identity: as a mediator of differences. Thus, though he spent most of his life in Cairo as an influential columnist to the important newspapers of the time, and as a confidant of prominent leaders, such as Muḥammad ʻAbdu and Saʻd Zaghlūl, he nonetheless retained the mien and manners of his rural upbringing in upper Egypt. A "heretical" rebel at al-Azhar, his name was nonetheless inseparable in the public imagination from the quasi religious epithet "shaykh," as Aḥmad ʻAbd al-Jawād demonstrates in *The Trilogy*. He readily embraced and defended the reformist agenda of his mentor Muḥammad ʻAbdu, but disparaged Qāsim Amīn's revolutionary call for the liberation of women.[21] Similarly, he advocated a return to a pristine form of Arabic literary expression, and yet labored indefatigably to "adapt" into Arabic literary works that originated in European languages of which, to boot, he did not always have a sound command.

Generic indeterminacy seems to be a correlate of al-Manfalūṭī's version of the writer's hybrid identity. He wrote both poetry and prose, discursive and creative pieces, on topical, "philosophical," and social issues. In this respect, as in that of espousing the cause of his benefactors, and dispensing soothing homilies in a highly emotive, affective style, the profile al-Manfalūṭī projects in many ways reinscribes the traditional model of the Arab writer, the *kātib*. This affinity may also explain al-Manfalūṭī's nonchalant indifference to the fundamentals of translation in his "adaptation" or "Arabization" of European literary works, the "meaning" or "idea" of which was conveyed to him, in summary or paraphrases, by associates more conversant than himself with the original languages of these texts. Ideas, as classical Arab writers and critics often remind us, are public property, readily accessible to all. For them, as for al-Manfalūṭī, originality, as a marker of individuality, lay chiefly in stylistic virtuosity. In this inflection, generic indeterminacy virtually grants subjectivity a free range.

It is this combination of rhetorical eloquence, generic indeterminacy, and wide appeal that makes al-Manfalūṭī exemplary for impressionable Kamāl, as he ponders his writerly future in *The Trilogy*. If al-Manfalūṭī epitomized the Writer, the Qur'ān epitomized the Book. That Kamāl figures in, but never writes the contemplated book, even though he dabbles considerably in writing, is not surprising, and this is not only because the Qur'ān, being *sui generis*, is inimitable. Of course, to the extent that Kamāl is an autobiographical character, *his* failure to become such a writer is a prerequisite for the successful emergence of Mahfouz as a novelist. Similarly, the credibility of the autobiographical Kamāl as a fictional character measures the distance that separates him from Mahfouz and the extent of the writer's success in transmuting the personal and autobiographical into the fictional. From this and similar instances, such as the relation of Joyce's *Stephen Hero to A Portrait of the Artist as a Young Man*, we know that mastery of the formal techniques of the novel is causally and dialectically related to the psychological and emotional distance of the writer from his autobiographical subject, or former self. For Mahfouz at the time of writing *The Trilogy*, both Kamāl and al-Manfalūṭī are monuments of an outgrown past and aesthetic options transcended by the novel genre. In this reading, al-Manfalūṭī marks an end, more than a beginning in the annals of modern Arabic fiction. He represents one of the two last serious attempts to say the new in the language of the old, to project a modern sensibility in a traditional garb. The other is Ṭāhā Ḥusayn. Ultimately, neither al-Manfalūṭī's attempt to "Arabize" Western literary models, nor his other efforts to shore up indigenous identity from within, so to speak, yielded any lasting results. In retrospect, his enterprise appears more like a delaying action before immanent change than a viable alternative to it. The appeal of his purported synthesis of opposites, however, reenacts the familiar desideratum of modern Arab/Islamic culture, namely, to appropriate whatever is deemed desirable in the culture of the "Other," while retaining intact a simulacrum of indigenous identity. (There is another, more recondite tangent in the connection between Kamāl and al-Manfalūṭī: It concerns Kamāl's inordinately huge nose and al-Manfalūṭī's "translation" of Edmond Rostand's *Cyrano de Bergerac*.)

* * *

Curiously, the optimal subjectivity that flows from generic indeterminacy never quite eventuates in sustained autobiographical narratives in Arabic. On the contrary, the recognizably autobiographical often requires recasting in a fictional guise before it can gesture back toward its referential source. Naguib Mahfouz' *al-Marāyā* (1972; *Mirrors*, 1975) retains a compelling instance of this necessity; so do *hikāyāt ḥāratinā* (1975), and other works. Though sometimes dubbed "a novel," *al-Marāyā* is in fact more like a roster of the "who is who" in the life of the author, from childhood to the time of writing, the late 1960s. The vignettes are arranged in alphabetical order under fictitious names, and the "characters" are sketched in broad strokes, divested of any specific details that might reveal the true identity of the respective individuals. These anecdotal narratives refract a sense of the writer's personality, but hardly reenact, or even resemble, an account of a full life. Even so, until recently, this was as close as Mahfouz had come to writing an "autobiography"—an undertaking he, and others, deem virtually impossible under the present conditions of contemporary Arab culture.[22] The historical record bears him out: With the possible exception of Mohamed Choukri's *al-Khubz al-Ḥāfī* (1982; *For Bread Alone*, 1982) few Arab writers have come any closer to penning the autobiographical subject. Naturally, the phenomenon has occasioned a wide range of speculations, from von Grunebaum's mentalistic view, namely, that autobiography is categorically incompatible with Arab character, to Ṭāhā Ḥusayn's and Edwar Al-Kharrat's glib disregard for the fundamental, generic distinction between the autobiographical and the fictional.[23] Whatever its cause, this veritable taboo continues to constrain the representation of the self in modern Arab and Egyptian fiction. Many Arabic novels, in fact, bear a textual reminder of this inhibition. It often takes the form of a solemn disclaimer of any and all similarities that may obtain between represented events and characters in a novel and their (occluded) counterparts in reality. "The events, characters, and places of this novel are all fictitious; any resemblance they may bear to reality is entirely accidental," announces the typical epigraph of Bahaa Ṭaher's novel *Khālatī Ṣafiyya wal-Dayr* (1991; *Aunt Safiyya and the Monastery*, 1996).

* * *

By far the best known graduate of the Teachers Training College which Kamāl wishes to attend is Ibrahim 'Abd al-Qādir al-Māzinī. Like fictional Kamāl, al-Māzinī also becomes a teacher but, unlike him, he eventually eschews teaching to launch a hazardous, often turbulent, but ultimately brilliant writing career. A measure of his success can perhaps be gathered from the fact that he was able to live entirely off his writing, not a minor achievement in Egypt then, or now. Different explanations have been advanced to account for al-Māzinī's "failure" to become a novelist. Thus, while Mahfouz ascribes it to the relentless demands of humdrum journalism on the writer's time and creative energy, Muḥammad Mandūr locates the "deficiency" at a more fundamental level, namely, in al-Māzinī's inability to decenter the autobiographical subject that anchors much of his imaginative endeavor.[24] Preoccupation with the self, in its multiple valences: as the locus of experience, subject of introspection and interrogation, and perennial object of (re)presentation, literally defines al-Māzinī's style even as it delimits the range of his imagination. Here is how al-Māzinī himself foregrounds this hyper self-absorption in the "dedication" of his aptly titled book *Ibrahim al-Kātib* (1931; Ibrahim the Writer): "To the one for whom I live, and for whose sake I labor, who alone is the center of my voluntary and involuntary attention: to *myself*..." (emphasis added).

Though striking in its intensity, this ubiquitous psycho-thematic interest in the self is by no means entirely idiosyncratic. In fact, it appears to intersect and entwine at every phase of al-Māzinī's writing career with general trends and orientations obtaining on the larger Egyptian national scene. Without insisting on a direct causal relationship between similarities in the two domains, the compelling correspondence itself raises the possibility of reciprocal influence. This possibility becomes all the more cogent if we remember that al-Māzinī's writing career largely coincides with the interwar period: roughly 1914–1949. By all accounts, this is one of the most critical periods in the annals of modern Egyptian literature in general, and of fiction in particular, especially perhaps as regards the problematic of the individual and its proliferation across the various discourses of identity. Thus, for example, the obsessive repetition in al-Māzinī's quest for self-possession forcefully echoes the fierce political contestation for (re)defining and (re)possessing Egypt's national identity and destiny.

The pervasive repetition appears already in the titles of several of al-Māzinī's better known works, some of which allude playfully to his name, for example, *Ibrahim al-Kātib* (1931; Ibrahim the Writer), *Ibrahim al-Thānī* (1943; Ibrahim the Second); others allude to "his" life, for example, *Sabīl Ḥayāt* (1979; The Course of a Life), and *Qiṣṣat Ḥayat* (1971; The Story of a Life). Beneath this formal display lies a substantial record of a polemical and discursive endeavor to render into narrative form the elusive sense of al-Māzinī's self. Long ago the late Muḥammad Mandūr recognized this characteristic feature of al-Māzinī's work when he noted that everything al-Māzinī ever wrote revolves, in one way or another, around his own person and personality. As a consequence, surmises Mandūr, al-Māzinī was never able to fashion convincing fictional characters or, for that matter, to sustain narrative situations, or plots, on topics unrelated to him personally.[25] Constant digression is both an outcome and a mark of this highly subjective, unbounded mode of writing. And it is the flip side of endless repetition in al-Māzinī's work. The important "theoretical" proposition implicit in Mandūr's critique of al-Māzinī suggests that excessive preoccupation with the autobiographical subject is incompatible with the requirements of the novel genre. If this is true of al-Māzinī, it is even more so of al-'Aqqād, his intimate collaborator in the scathing attack on the literary old guard, especially the poet Aḥmad Shawqī and the writer al-Manfalūṭī.[26]

Further consequences flow from al-Māzinī's reflexive, expository mode of writing. In its sustained, inward turn, it collapses the idea of the self in general onto the writer's private self and proceeds to treat this latter as an ongoing writerly project. "This is not the story of *my* life, even though it contains many incidents thereof. It is, therefore, more appropriate to regard it the story of *a* life," writes al-Māzinī in the epigraph to *Qiṣṣat Ḥayat*, in typically equivocating manner (emphasis added). Paradoxically, al-Māzinī's constant harping on the "inferiority complexes" resulting from his physical "defects" and infirmities—his slight limp, short slim frame, bespectacled, haggard appearance—mutate into considerable assets in the course of writing. The combination of earning a living from writing, while also enjoying evident public respect—both of which al-Māzinī shared with his associate al-'Aqqād—may suggest that writing had become by that time a source of considerable cultural and even political empowerment. In the case of the intrepid al-'Aqqād, this sense of empowerment was to produce a rare instance of a lone writer mounting a public challenge not only to ministers and prime ministers but also to the very king of Egypt.[27]

How to explain this novelty, especially against the backdrop of the traditional dependence of the writer on the ruler in Arab culture—a dependence that often borders on abject subservience? Obviously literary qualifications, however extraordinary, cannot fully account for such a drastic departure from normative practice. Nor can the appeal to a mystique of singularity, that is, of preternatural individuals possessed of exceptionally strong personalities, although, as we shall see shortly, both considerations figure in the panoply. What necessitates a more satisfactory explanation is the fact that the phenomenon appears to have been fairly widespread, though perhaps not to the same degree of al-'Aqqād's temerity. Qāsim Amīn, 'Alī 'Abd al-Rāziq, Ṭāhā Ḥusayn, Ismā'īl Adham, 'Alī Shāhīn, Ibrahim al-Māzinī, and many others, partook in various degrees of this rugged individualism of the new literary personality type.

There is no doubt that the political culture of resistance to internal despotism and foreign occupation from the time of the 'Urābī uprising (1881–1882) onward, played a significant role in molding the political consciousness and nationalist identity of many Egyptians, including, perforce, writers. The strong imprint of such fervent patriots and fiery orators as Muṣṭafā Kāmil (d. 1908) and Sa'd Zaghlūl (d. 1927) is particularly evident in the combative streak characteristic of the public personality of so many writers of the interwar period. It is probably not accidental that the fiercest "literary battles" (*ma'ārik adabiyya*) of modern Arabic literature also unfold in Egypt during this very period. These battles were seldom limited to literary, artistic, or aesthetic concerns. Rather, under the rubric of literary conflict and change they advocated far-reaching cultural and epistemological change, especially in the hitherto neglected realm of the individual subject. The affinities among these seemingly disparate strands may be sinuous, but they are by no means fortuitous. It may be useful to interrogate them further in conjunction with two key terms that situate al-Māzinī's preoccupation with the autobiographical subject in the larger context of Egyptian literature and culture. These key terms are: the evolving concept of the writer, and the companion concept of literary generation.

The evolving concept of the writer, in slow motion since the publication of al-Ṭahṭāwī's pioneering work *Takhlīṣ al-Ibrīz fī Talkhīṣ Bārīs* (1834; The Golden Extract of Paris), goes into high gear during the interwar period. To recapitulate in broad strokes the major phases of this process, the following outline may suffice.

Formal education invariably functions as the engine that propels the movement for change. The direction of the change, at least as far as the writers are concerned, is practically uniform. As we have seen, the traditional "Islamic" educational system, beginning with the village *kuttāb* and ending with the Azhar, is often the immediate cause of the writer's alienation from the traditional constituents and patterns of identity. Exposure to, and eventual embrace of (Western) secular ideas, values, and norms often follow with predictable regularity. The acquisition of a European language, primarily French or English, literally furnishes the key to a curriculum and a library that, in due course, induce the inevitable psychological and intellectual (re)formation of individual consciousness and, ultimately, identity. Thus the liberal arts curriculum of the Teachers Training College that attracts fictional Kamāl in Mahfouz' *Cairene Trilogy* actually informs the literary sensibility of al-Māzinī, just as the selfsame Western literary canon, mediated through English, informs the sensibility of the autodidact al-'Aqqād and, of course, that of Mahfouz himself, among many other luminaries of modern Egyptian and Arabic literature.

This paradigmatic sequence plays itself out most graphically in the life of Ṭāhā Ḥusayn, except that in his case French, not English, was the agent of transformation and change. Alienated from both the *kuttāb* and the Azhar at a very young age, his alienation was further compounded by his blindness at the still younger age of four. How he overcame these formidable odds and went on to become perhaps the single most influential force in the history of modern Egyptian thought and culture is the very stuff of which legends of rugged individualism are made. But all that is common knowledge and need not detain us here. What deserves reiteration is the causal connection between the exposure to secular, specifically Western, modes of knowledge and the onset of individual consciousness that sets the triumphant march on its course. Prior to that encounter, the autobiographical protagonist of *al-Ayyām* shows no awareness of either consciousness or conscience. A disconcerting conclusion thus becomes inescapable: Inasmuch as it precludes the development of individual consciousness and conscience, the postulated trajectory of indigenous identity necessarily precludes the possibility of individuality. This conclusion bears paraphrasing in simpler, but more provocative terms: Ṭāhā Ḥusayn would not have been the (Egyptian) Ṭāhā Ḥusayn without the crucial input of Western thought and knowledge into his individual consciousness and personality.

It is important to remember, however, that the seminal narrative of the first volume of Ḥusayn's fictionalized autobiography, *al-Ayyām* (1929) was written against the public uproar occasioned by the publication of his highly controversial book *fīl-Shi'r al-Jāhilī* (1926; On Pre-Islamic Arabic Poetry). By 1929, the legal charges of blasphemy and sedition that were brought against the author, were in full swing. At one level, therefore, the narrative of *al-Ayyām* authorizes a discursive reading that indicts the traditional educational system and vindicates the grown up Ṭāhā Ḥusayn. That the thesis and argument of "On Pre-Islamic Poetry" are profoundly problematic is hardly in question. But that is less relevant to our purposes here than the constitution of the individual consciousness at work in it, even though the application of a thoroughgoing Cartesian skepticism to the very text of the Qur'ān, by a Sorbonne-educated former Azharite, hardly needs further elaboration.

Ṭāhā Ḥusayn was neither reticent nor apologetic about the "European" dimension of his highly complex, irreducibly composite identity. Instead, he sought to theorize his singularity into a general principle by redrawing the map of Egypt's cultural orbit. The crux of his argument in *mustaqbal al-thaqāfah fī miṣr* (1938; The Future of Culture in Egypt) is that in character, disposition, and culture, Egypt is more akin to Europe than it is to the "East." Although by "the East" Ṭāhā Ḥusayn meant primarily China, Japan, and India (as if these constitute a monolithic entity!), his thesis nonetheless implicitly elides the Arab/Islamic dimension of Egypt's national identity.[28] Geographic proximity to Europe seems to lend itself readily to this recurrent ideological attempt at (re)orientation, specially when packaged in the soothing nomenclature of a (re)invented and reified Mediterranean cultural space. Recently, not only the novelist Amitav Ghosh, but also the mightier European Union seems to have (re)discovered the topical relevance of S. D. Goitein's *Mediterranean Society*: the former in his novel *In An Antique Land* (1992), the later in the (1995) *EU–Mediterranean Partnership*.

What symbolic geography does to space, iconography does to time. Thus the choice of the image of the ancient Egyptian scribe as the emblem of the literary monthly *al-kātib al-miṣrī* (The Egyptian Writer, 1945–1948) which Ṭāhā Ḥusayn founded, and of which he was chief editor, bespeaks a cultural continuity between ancient and modern Egypt that is immune to "incongruent" cultural and historical interruptions. That this symbolic emphasis on the "Egyptianness" of the *Egyptian Writer* should coincide with the foundation of the Arab League in Cairo in 1945, may not be entirely accidental. For even as (official) Egypt was parading its Arab credentials as a fit home for the newly created framework of (nominal) Arab unity, the Pharaonic genealogy of the contemporary "Egyptian Writer" was being resurrected by Ṭāhā Ḥusayn to challenge that official version of Egyptian identity on the semiotic level of public discourse. The timing of this gesture is all the more curious as it comes at the tail end of the "Pharaonic trend" that was triggered by the discovery of the tomb of King *Tutankhamun* in 1922 and had lasted well into the 1930s. By the onset of the 1940s, however, the Pharaonic "spell" seems to have fully dissipated, for most Egyptians, at any rate. Witness Mahfouz' drastic decision to shelve the huge project he had underway, namely, to rewrite in narrative form the entire history of ancient Egypt in the manner of the historical *Trilogy* with which he had launched his novelistic career in the late 1930s.[29]

And yet, a fundamental incongruence that seems to originate in the deepest recesses of the writer's own literary disposition markedly vitiates the rigor of his grand vision of Egypt's "European" prospects. It concerns the register of Arabic Ḥusayn systematically used in his writing. No other writer in modern, and perhaps in all of Arabic literature, ever wrote in a style more reminiscent of the high Arabic of the Qur'ān and the other canonical texts of Islam than Ṭāhā Ḥusayn. As far as the novel is concerned, this inflexible, uniformly highbrow style, and the forceful personality it proclaims, are hardly compatible with the requirements of the novelistic imagination. It is not surprising, therefore, that none of Ṭāhā Ḥusayn's numerous narrative works ever crossed the threshold separating the novel proper from other forms of narrative.[30]

* * *

All the ingredients of strong individuality noted above obtain in grotesquely exaggerated proportions in the personality of the autodidact 'Abbās Maḥmūd al-'Aqqād. To mention but the most salient among these: an avid desire for knowledge, harnessed to an insatiable appetite for fame; an enabling familiarity (through English) with the basics of the Western canon; a sharp analytical mind, a penchant for the literary, and a passion for casuistry; a hefty share of the renowned Ṣa'īdī stubbornness, buttressed by a special aptitude for scurrility, and, an eager taste for controversy. As with Ṭāhā Ḥusayn and al-Māzinī, this (personality) mix jells against a progressively more propitious climate for political thinking on individual rights in Egypt. That progression culminated in the inscription of individual rights in the liberal constitution of 1923. While al-'Aqqād himself was among the first beneficiaries of this advance in political and legal thinking on the individual, his own writing and practice all but negate the universal foundations and applicability of this concept. As the poet Ṣalāḥ 'Abd al-Ṣabūr shows, al-'Aqqād's conception of individual rights all but confines the privilege to members of the self-appointed elite. It predicates the exercise of these rights, implicitly, on the acquisition of literary and intellectual abilities available only to a distinct minority in Egypt at the time. Al-'Aqqād thus has nothing but derision for democracy, which he dismisses as a way of legitimating the tyranny of the rabble, *al-dahmā'*—his favorite term for the common people, *demos*.[31]

By and large, al-'Aqqād's most significant, and perhaps most lasting, contribution to modern Arabic literature lies in his poignant critique of traditional literary sensibility and the norms and modes underpinning it. As it happened, this contribution originated in a collaborative effort with two associates, Ibrahim 'Abd al-Qādir al-Māzinī and 'Abd al-Raḥmān Shukrī. Together, the three waged a relentless battle against the reigning literary establishment in the name of the modern, of which individual experience and personal voice are primary attributes. Although, in retrospect, the attack appears unduly harsh and often *ad hominem*, at the time it had the salutary effect of destabilizing the prevalent literary aesthetic norms just enough to allow for greater experimentation with new literary forms that were deemed more amenable to the representation of modern experience. Both the collaborative spirit animating the concerted attack and the personal courage of the individuals involved in it are noteworthy, not least because the targets of the attack embodied literary authority at its official best. The collection of articles by al-'Aqqād and al-Māzinī that comprise *al-Dīwān* (1921) targeted the very symbols of the literary establishment in Egypt at the time: Sahwqī, "the prince of poets, and the poet of kings and princes," as his sobriquet announces, Ḥāfiẓ "poet of the Nile," and "the shaykh" Muṣṭafā Luṭfī al-Manfalūṭī. In many respects, the event marks an important threshold on the path of revolt in the name of literary innovation and reform.

The collaborative team work undertaken by members of what came to be known as the *Dīwān* school in modern Arabic poetry was paralleled elsewhere in fiction. As I mentioned earlier, in the early years of the twentieth century another group of Egyptian literati loosely formed what came to be known as the "New School." The sense of group solidarity animating these collective efforts also instructs the equally loose, yet enabling, concept of literary generation. But whereas the practitioners of the "new story" were unabashedly Francophone in education, taste, and sentiment, their counterparts in the *Dīwān* school were largely Anglophone. The differences between the two orientations were so pronounced as to warrant separate chapters in Ḥaqqī's account of the development of modern Egyptian fiction in *Fajr al-Qiṣṣa al-Miṣriyya*. And yet, the driving force behind both is identical, namely, the desire for a clean break with the traditional themes, forms, and tropes of Arabic literature, and the inauguration of a new beginning. Another point of similarity between the two is the conscious note of violence that permeates the language and discourse of this "literary" intent. Thus, the journal of the "New School" bore the subtitle: *Ṣaḥīfat al-Hadm wal-Binā'* (the journal of demolition and (re)construction). Likewise, the virulent attacks of al-'Aqqād on Shawqī, and of al-Māzinī on al-Manfalūṭī, bear the clear marks of figurative parricide. Each succeeding generation of Egyptian writers will partake, to one degree or another, of this generational animus. The antagonism often takes the form of a polemical disowning of the generation of the fathers, the adoption of an alternative genealogy, and a renewed assertion of the need and intention to start all over. This is as true of the Francophone school in relation to al-Muwayliḥī and the *Maqāma* genre, as it is of the Anglophone school in relation to al-Manfalūṭī, of Mahfouz' generation in relation to that of al-Māzinī, al-'Aqqād, and Ṭāhā Ḥusayn, and finally of the generation of the 1960s in relation to that of Mahfouz.

The task of constructing, or inventing, a fitting alternative genealogy engenders problematic by-products of its own. From the beginning of the twentieth century onward, another literary heritage, beside Arabic, and other styles and modalities than those obtaining there, become available to the new Egyptian writer. Even an Azharite like al-Manfalūṭī, who had no sufficient knowledge of any European language, nevertheless felt called upon to "adapt" European literary works into Arabic. In his case, however, this linguistic "inadequacy" permitted only an indirect encounter with the original texts, and this, in turn, allowed the Arabic "adapted" versions a semiautonomous existence, unencumbered by the disabling consciousness of imitation and the intractable problematics of mimicry. By contrast, writers of both the Francophone and the Anglophone schools, who had direct access to the original texts of the respective languages and literatures, wrote in full consciousness of the authority of their "adopted" European models and mentors, if not outright "masters."

On occasion, the inherent imbalance in the power relations between the two parties involved in this cross-cultural "translation" of the "Other" into the language of the self produces singularly untoward results. A case in point is the following example from al-'Aqqād's posthumously published volume of autobiographical fragments, *Anā* (1969; I). The instance harks back to the anecdote I cited earlier as evidence of the empowering agency of individualism vis-à-vis political power. Specifically, it arises from the thinly veiled insult al-'Aqqād had leveled at king Fu'ād of Egypt from the floor of the Egyptian parliament in early 1928. While he enjoyed parliamentary immunity, al-'Aqqād appeared invulnerable. But no sooner was the Parliament dissolved than charges of slander were brought against him and he was sentenced to a prison term of nine months.

Now, admittedly, incarceration is never pleasant, no matter under what conditions a prisoner is deprived of his or her freedom. But things are relative, even in prison. And by his own account, nothing of consequence ever happens to al-'Aqqād during his relatively short incarceration. He seems to have suffered none of the physical or mental torture, abuse, and humiliation routinely visited on political prisoners in many parts of the world. On the contrary, al-'Aqqād's prison experience seems to have been exceptionally mild, perhaps because he was accorded VIP treatment. What is more, he tells us that from the outset he found comfort in the company of his colleague, the satirical writer 'Alī Shāhīn, who had preceded him to prison for similar "offenses" against men of power. In prison, he eagerly assumed the role of guide to the newcomer.

No sooner does al-'Aqqād mention this Egyptian colleague, however, than he dubs him "my Virgil," that is, the one destined to lead the Egyptian reincarnation of Dante through the tortuous labyrinths of this Egyptian Purgatory! Given the uneventful nature of al-'Aqqād's prison experience, the only coupling the wide dissimilarity between Dante's text and al-'Aqqād's appropriation of it, is that of deliberate bathos or ironic juxtaposition. Neither, however, is anywhere in evidence. The only certain outcome of this insipid, singularly servile act of literary borrowing is the coining of the most awkward neologism in Arabic: *virgīlī*, that is, my Virgil. It goes without saying that such fatuous aping of the imaginative literature of the European "Other" cannot possibly impart to al-'Aqqād's trite prison experience the universal significance it covets.[32]

Still more important, however, is the inevitable effect of this predisposition to mimicry. The ready availability of the European master narrative to the writer's (pre)occupied memory all but renders the actual, circumstantial reality of prison life irrelevant to the interests of literary representation. With his gaze transfixed on the reified, "paradigmatic" European model of suffering, the actual suffering of Egyptian inmates simply pales in comparison and recedes into invisibility. In due course, recalling the banished circumstantial details of experience of ordinary Egyptians will be the task of the novel, not its antecedent, or even precursor, forms of narrative. In point of fact, the realistic depiction of prison life, in all its horrid ghastliness, will become possible only with the advent of the generation of the 1960s, many of whose members served extended periods of incarceration for political "offenses." To anticipate future developments, one of the most chilling scenes of sexual abuse in Arabic fiction occurs in Sonalla Ibrahim's often cited novella, *Tilk al-Rā'iḥa*, where the rape of a little boy in detention is depicted in graphic detail, but meets with total indifference by all, participants and observers alike.[33]

In al-Māzinī's case the problematic of "translating" the European "Other" takes a more subtle, but occasionally less benign form. Thus, for example, he berates al-Manfalūṭī for mentioning the names of some of his actual forebears in the autobiographical sketch embedded in the introduction to al-*Naẓarāt*. And on what authority does al-Māzinī's disallow this familiar feature of Arabic "autobiographical" narratives? Why, the German poet, Goethe, who is said to have left out of the account of his spiritual and intellectual development all references to his actual forebears, including the name of his own father![34] And yet, al-Māzinī seems to have had no qualms about the far more pernicious practice of rewriting and passing as his own texts he read in, or even translated from, English. This awkward mixture of dull aping and outright cribbing of the products of the colonizer's literary imagination, presumably in the process of revamping the Egyptian writer's indigenous identity, confounds discernment. But it may also be a logical outcome of the posture of an imagination recoiled onto itself.

One final note on the deliberate practice of contriving alternative literary genealogies warrants brief mention here. As a general rule, the immediate past of Arabic literature figures only negatively in the experience of these restive early literary generations. That is, it offers primarily models and examples to be avoided or, at best, challenged. This is not true of all epochs of Arabic literature. Al-Māzinī and al-'Aqqād, like Ṭāhā Ḥusayn and others, seem on occasion to have found sustaining affinities with fellow-rebel poets of earlier periods. The critical, creative interest these modern writers invested in such highly non-conformist poets as Ibn al-Rūmī, Bashshār ibn Burd, Abū Nuwās, and al-Ma'arrī, in a sense reclaims these problematic poets for modernity, and, at the same time, reinstates them as a legitimating genealogy for the modern writers themselves. Though highly selective, these acts of retrieval also help offset, if only partially, the rough-and-tumble manner in which the modern writers often appropriate Western literary techniques, forms, and modalities. Ultimately, however, both practices seem to be symptomatic of the lack of specialization so characteristic of much Arabic writing before the advent of the novel. The traditional Arab writer, in Ibn Khaldūn's words, "knows a little about every subject."[35]

* * *

Specialization and generic determinacy are the twin engines that ultimately propel the general concepts of *Kātib* and *Qiṣṣa*, writer and story, to their final destination as novelist and novel, respectively. The process remained tortuous and halting to the very end. And even then it did not conclude without a symbolically "decisive" battle between generations standing at opposite ends of the old–new spectrum. As chance would have it, al-'Aqqād himself spearheaded the futile attempt to impede the advent of the new genre. In retrospect, the incident in question may appear inconsequential, but its symbolic significance is unmistakable. In brief, a committee appointed to referee "Egyptian stories" for the King Fārūq Prize in 1942, on which al-'Aqqād served, deemed all the submitted samples inadequate, and decided to shelve the Prize for that year. Among the works submitted were two major novels in the new realistic mode: Mahfouz' *al-Sarāb* (1948; The Mirage) and 'Ādil Kāmil's *Millīm al-Akbar* (1944; Millim the Great).

While Mahfouz seems to have taken the slipshod gaffe in stride, its effect on 'Ādil Kāmil appears to have been far more serious and detrimental. He welcomed the opportunity to lash back at the committee's, especially al-'Aqqād's, ineptitude, and, concomitantly, to launch one of the most virulent polemical attacks on Arabic literature in toto. But the disappointment appears to have shaken his faith in the historical agency of the literary imagination and the transformative power of literature so badly that he practically gave up writing and all but disappeared from the literary scene after the publication of *Millīm al-Akbar*, in 1944.

Kāmil's argument, which was affixed as an introduction to the novel, invokes the familiar battle cry of every new generation, namely, the imperative to demolish the ossified values, norms, and conventions of the old guard before raising in their place the norms and conventions of the new(er) generation. A veritable treatise on the philosophy, ethics, and poetics of the literary, the argument is thoroughly and unabashedly informed by "authoritative" Western sources. It is obviously too involved and too elaborate to bear summarizing here, but the crux of its argument may suffice for our purposes.

Arabic literature, Kāmil argues, was never truly or sufficiently literary. The cause of this allegedly congenital and chronic deficiency is the paramount value Arab poets and critics have always attached to the verbal component of the literary expression. "How things are said" is far more pivotal to Arab taste and to the Arab conception of the literary, than "what is being said." Pressed to its (implicit) logical end, this thesis virtually reduces traditional Arab literary sensibility to something resembling a pathological infatuation with the sound of words. This innate bent, according to Kāmil, renders everything else, including meaning, a remote desideratum of the Arabic literary performance.

For the same reason, the purported richness of the Arabic language, specially in vocabulary, on account of which Arabic is often deemed superior to all other languages, spells poverty here. The phenomenon merely multiplies synonyms and antonyms without generating new meanings, or significant shades and nuances of meaning. Kāmil cites the numerous words for lion, among other examples, to illustrate this phenomenon.[36] What compounds this seemingly innate shortcoming of Arabic is the semireligious sanctity in which the language was invested from the outset. Among the pernicious effects of this development is the virtual freezing of Arabic in time, which, in turn, is said to have prevented it from evolving "naturally" to adapt to changing historical circumstances, like other, living languages.

Though grim, this diagnosis of the condition of Arabic literature is not without a silver lining. As can be expected, the hopeful note emanates from the transformative encounter with the modern West. 'Ādil Kāmil openly and emphatically predicates the prospects for positive change on the ability of modern Arabic literature to assimilate the historical lessons and precedents of Western literature. This process, he contends, is already well under way, as evidenced by the new kind of writing he, Mahfouz, and other like-minded Egyptian writers, are advancing. The novel, in this grand scheme of things, is assigned the dual role of harbinger and instrument of the desirable historical change, not only in Arabic literature, but also in the Arabic language, and Arab culture in general.

Neither the substance nor the tone of Kāmil's argument is beyond criticism; in fact, both strongly invite it. But that is not our concern here. Rather, it is to trace the permutations of the concept of the writer along the winding course it has traveled in tandem with the twin concepts of the individual and the novel. To that end, it would seem that the decisive move that signaled the successful conclusion of the long, gradual, and incremental process, is the de facto separation of the writer from the text, the historical author from the work of fiction. Quoting his favorite author, Somerset Maugham, Kāmil singles out this "self-detachment" of the author as the most crucial prerequisite of the acclimatization of the new genre in Arab culture. In a rare convergence of creative gifts reminiscent of Henry James and E. M. Forster, the legitimating theoretical underpinnings of the novel, and the actualization of the theory, coincide in Kāmil's *Millīm al-Akbar*.

Mahfouz' numerous, though scattered, and less systematic, pronouncements on the genesis of the Arabic novel fully corroborate Kāmil's conclusions, barring his polemics. Mahfouz leaves no doubt that he, Kāmil, Ḥaqqī, and other practitioners of the realist novel were engaged in creating a new literary genre in Arabic.[37] Their immediate predecessors "(Muḥammad Ḥusayn) Haykal, Ṭāha Husayn, and Tawfiq al-Ḥakīm wrote autobiographical works" Mahfouz notes, implying that the works in question: *Zaynab* (1914), *al-Ayyām* (first volume 1929), and *'Awdat al-Rūḥ* (1933), though remarkable in their own right and important milestones on the road to the novel, are not, properly speaking, novels. The categorical distinction between autobiographical accounts and genuine novels speaks directly to the question of generic determinacy, just as the formal separation of the writer from the narrative speaks to the fundamental distinction between the (Arab) writer, in the general sense mentioned earlier, and the novelist proper. The abstract concept of structure, and the more tangible features of plot and characters, now replace the writer, as the formal unifying principles in the text.

By and large, Mahfouz' presence towered over the landscape of the Arabic novel during the quarter of a century between 1945 and 1970. This preeminence was widely recognized in the Arab world long before he received the Nobel Prize for literature in 1988. In the wake of that momentous event, however, renewed worldwide interest in Mahfouz' work inevitably reasserted his prominence on the Egyptian literary scene with added force. These developments rendered still more precarious the standing of the younger generation of Egyptian writers, the generation of the sixties, already chafing in the shadow of the great writer. In a marked departure from the traditional trajectory of the conflict of generations, where the younger generation outgrows its predecessor and renders its work and norms obsolete, now it was the old writer who stood accused of stifling the creativity and growth of the younger generation.[38]

Clearly, this role reversal inverts the order of the oedipal (parricidal) plot that often furnishes a psychological subtext to the generational conflict. The reversal recasts the whole drama in the inverse terms of old (father) Cronos methodically annihilating his would-be successors. To stretch the mythic analogy a little further, no "Zeus" was anywhere in sight on the horizons of the Egyptian novel to dethrone old "Cronos" and free the younger generation from his thrall. But, as several critics have already shown, it is to the collective effort of the younger generation that one must look for evidence of continued innovation and experimentation in the Egyptian novel beyond the Mahfouzian paradigm. Before addressing this issue, however, let me draw brief attention to another aspect of the interplay between the evolving concepts of the individual and the writer as they crystallize in the example of Mahfouz.

Though outlandish, the analogy between the paragon of the Arabic novel and the chief Titan may still be permitted in the specific context of the antagonism between literary generations, even though it is singularly inconsonant with Mahfouz' personality and public demeanor. In stark contrast to al-'Aqqād, al-Māzinī, and Ṭāhā Ḥusayn, all of whom projected a strong sense of public personality that was also integral to their outlook and literary output, the eminently private, reserved, and elusive Mahfouz methodically cultivated a low-keyed, nonconfrontational public persona throughout his life. Mahfouz' lifelong service in the governmental bureaucracy, a veritable hatchery of Procrustean conformity, may have contributed its share to the mask of stoic placidity he always wears in public. But whether innate or acquired, the trait seems to have done much to deflect attention away from the writer's person and personality to his work. This, too, was to the detriment of the younger generation who found no easy target in the elusive Mahfouz on which to pin their anger, much less to elicit public sympathy, as was the case, for example, when the imperious al-'Aqqād rebuked the younger critic and writer Muḥammad Mandūr in public, only to have the gesture backfire and expedite the rise of Mandūr to a position of eminence that eventually eclipsed al-'Aqqād himself.

There thus seems to be a curious coincidence between certain types of literary sensibility and personality, on the one hand, and, on the other, the attitude to the novel at this juncture of its acclimatization in Egypt. The phenomenon consists of an apparent correlation between literary elitism, a strong sense of public personality, preoccupation with the autobiographical subject, and hostility or antipathy to the novel as a literary genre. What is particularly curious is that this hostility cuts across all other criteria of differentiation and makes strange bedfellows of arch enemies. Thus, we find in the anti-novel camp al-ʿAqqād, zealous advocate of the new, in the name of which he attacked Shawqī and Ḥāfiẓ in the epoch-making *al-Dīwān*, Muṣṭafā Ṣādiq al-Rāfiʿī, arch enemy of both the new and al-ʿAqqād, who waged his literary battle in the name of tradition under the banner of the Qur'ān,[39] and Tawfīq al-Ḥakīm, innovator, iconoclast, maverick, misogynist, and self-professed resident of the *Ivory tower*.[40]

Similarly, one wonders whether a causal relation exists between the preoccupation of al-Māzinī and Ṭāhā Ḥusayn with the autobiographical and their failure to become full-fledged novelists, or to write genuine autobiographies, for that matter. The question ultimately is whether preoccupation with the autobiographical subject, and the capacity to create nonautobiographical characters—a prerequisite of the novelistic imagination—are mutually exclusive? It would appear to be so in the present case, especially in light of the fact that antithetical traits do obtain in the personalities of Egyptian contemporaries of these writers who did outgrow the autobiographical limitations and went on to produce memorable fictional characters. Both Yaḥyā Ḥaqqī and ʿĀdil Kāmil, for example, partake equally of Mahfouz' self-effacing demeanor and distaste for the limelight. In fairness, one must situate the "shortcomings" of the older generation (of al-ʿAqqād, al-Māzinī, and Ḥusayn) in the right historical context. Unlike their successors who benefited from, and built on their pioneering work, these writers had to create, almost *ex-nihilo*, a working sense of individuality, against the entrenched general opposition to the personal, the mundane, and the real in Arabic literature.

* * *

Be that as it may, the emergence of the ordinary individual as a subject fit for literary representation is all but inconceivable outside the enabling matrix of realism. Literary realism, in turn, as Mahfouz notes, is causally linked to the relative social stability Egypt enjoyed during the two or three decades prior to the 1952 Revolution.[41] Mahfouz' major realist works, as we know, were written during the last decade of that period, including his magnum opus, *The Cairene Trilogy*. Open and steady access to the sources of knowledge, formally through the educational institutions, both religious and secular, and informally through the press, is a primary by-product of this stability. It is also a formative source of the Egyptian novel as we know it.

The forceful currents and thrusts that converge at the site of the realist novel in the mid-1940s diverge again in different directions in the late sixties. The close proximity of the Arab defeat in the 1967 war, and the death of President Nasser soon thereafter (1970), mark the late sixties as a moment of abysmal rupture and drift in every aspect of Egyptian life, including fiction. The informal grouping of a number of writers of the "sixties generation" around the literary periodical *Gallery 68* provides a convenient date for the formal placement of this generation in the chronological scheme. A more accurate date would be the publication of the first, though expurgated, edition of Sonalla Ibrahim's novella *Tilk al-Rā'iḥa* in 1966, not only because the novella marks a categorical departure from the Mahfouzian model, but also because it registers that conscious distinction in the form of a literary manifesto signed by the writer and a few prominent members of his generation and affixed as a blurb to the novella.[42] Apart from such conscious efforts to burke the Mahfouzian model, little else binds the members of this generation. Thus, while one critical study foregrounds this conclusion in its title and collapses it on the Arabic novel as a whole,[43] another classifies the motley of Egyptian fiction after Mahfouz into six different orientations, but lumps them together under the rubric of "new sensibility."[44] These and other available studies of the work of this generation, in both Arabic and English, make it unnecessary to rehearse the subject of literary generations any further here. Specific instances involving either the problematic of the writer, or that of generation, will be considered individually, as the context warrants. Since individuality is largely a function of characterization in fiction, it may be time to turn our attention to that major question now.

* * *

Of the numerous denunciations leveled against the novel by its detractors none matches that of Tawfīq al-Ḥakīm in graphic vividness. As late as 1948 he was still writing

> The difference between literature and the story [*sic*] is like that between the upper and the lower zones of the human (body). If the story depicts man in life, literature depicts thought in the life of man. For man is not merely a being that moves in the material world—which is what story writers are wont to call real life—but he is also, and foremost, a mind that traverses lofty intellectual universes.[45]

Aside from the persistent terminological confusion between story and novel, the above statement categorically reduces the real to the material, the material to the profane, and the profane to the base. Beyond the last register of this gliding scale lies the dreaded, and hence unspeakable, body in its physical, biological, and physiological actuality. By seeking to reclaim the body for literary representation, the "story" threatens to violate a long-standing taboo in modern Arab culture. And for that "offense" it forfeits its claim to literary status.

It is possible to trace the roots of this aversion to the literary representation of the body, eroticism, sexuality—in short, "obscenity"—in modern Arabic literature to Muḥammad 'Abdu's *expurgation* of the *Maqāmāt* of Badī' al-Zamān al-Hamadhānī in an edition that was first published in Beirut in 1889.[46] There is a poignant irony in this episode. 'Abdu turned his attention to the founder of this quintessential Arabic prose genre while in Beirut, where he had been exiled by the British, for his role in the 'Urābī uprising of 1881. That uprising sought to free

Egyptians from the yoke of the Turko-Circassian aristocracy in the Egyptian military, and to free Egypt from the incessant meddling of European powers, especially Great Britain, in its internal affairs. The "reformist" agenda of this great reformer sought to free Arabic literary style from the spurious accretions that had encumbered it during the long centuries of decline and decadence, but showed no awareness of the need to liberate the Arab literary imagination from the equally spurious prohibitions and constraints it had contracted during these same centuries. Thus, 'Abdu seems uncharacteristically tongue-tied in his attempt to explain why he deemed it necessary to excise an entire *Maqāma* (al-Shāmiyya), and to "expurgate" another (al-Ruṣāfiyya) from the work of a writer he exonerates of all offense and reveres enough to call "shaykh."[47] The times are different, he says, and what could be said at one time may become unspeakable at another.[48] With no more than a lame excuse, and a vague sense of personal discomfort at the explicit nature of the "suspect" material, does 'Abdu set here a *religious* precedent for the prohibition against the representation of the profane and the sensual in modern Arabic literature. It is important to note, however, that the precedent derives its force from the personal opinion of 'Abdu, not from his authority as a religious scholar. The distinction is significant because 'Abdu admits that he finds nothing intrinsically objectionable in al-Hamadhānī's text; only that it may be misconstrued and thus induce an unintended, and hence unwelcome, effect. Islamic law, as we shall see shortly, bears differently on the question of individuality.

To return briefly to al-Ḥakīm's statement, we note that the suppressed text in it gestures toward that tacit division of labor in Arab culture between the literary canon and its repressed other: the corpus of largely oral folk literature available in the vernacular. To that far off, subterranean region of the Arab literary imagination was the dreaded body consigned, and al-Ḥakīm would keep it there by delegitimating the very genre capable of "reclaiming" it for literary representation. By 1948, however, the realist novel had already established a firm foothold in Egypt and, through it, in modern Arab culture as a whole. An irreversible process had been set in motion, but the struggle of the new genre was hardly over. Though its logic is unmistakably bogus, al-Ḥakīm's demurral nonetheless furnishes a (pseudo) *philosophical* rationale for denying the novel legitimacy in modern Arab culture.

What may have appeared only virtual in 1948 became unbearably real in 1966 when the repressed body resurfaced with a vengeance in Egyptian fiction. The little drama in which the "historic" event unfolded is all the more noteworthy due to the unlikely identity of the actors destined to play it out. No two other individuals could be more antithetical to the image of the writer—as the embodiment of rugged individualism we encountered earlier in the strong personality type—than the two players in this little drama.

It all happened when the young, and rather frail and diffident Sonalla Ibrahim, barely out of a harrowing five-year-long political imprisonment (1959–1964), brought the slender manuscript of his first work *Tilk al-Rā'iḥa* to the attention of the equally frail and incomparably affable veteran writer, Yaḥyā Ḥaqqī—then editor of the literary magazine *al-Majalla*. Though on the whole impressed and sympathetic, the urbane Ḥaqqī was nonetheless put off by the "vulgarity" of certain passages in the novella. He found especially repulsive a scene in which the first person narrator/protagonist masturbates in his flat, in the midst of a severe writer's block, and then returns to the scene to inspect the outcome. Ḥaqqī's reaction indicates that he may have failed to grasp the scene's comic spoof on the standing motif of detective fiction, that is, the inevitable return of the "criminal" to the scene of the "crime," and even more so the implicit paralysis of the creative faculties of the writer, and the poignant symbolic equation of writing with masturbation under repressive political conditions. Equally lost on the great writer is the veiled allusion to Leopold Bloom's similar behavior in Joyce's *Ulysses*. The representation of Bloom's act, as is well known, was no less objectionable to the bourgeois sensibility of other literati in earlier times, at other places, including metropolitan New York. Trivial as the incident may be in both cases, it nonetheless reaffirms the novel's fundamental interest in the individual per se. Ḥaqqī's pronouncements on the question at hand contributed an *aesthetic* objection to the literary representation of the "obscene" in modern Egyptian fiction.

At the other end of the reception spectrum the secret police lay in wait. In contrast to the aesthete editor of *al-Majalla*, what mattered to the secret police was the expedient translation of the fictional into the autobiographical and the autobiographical into political gain. They caustically taunted the writer: Was the inability of the narrator to sleep with the prostitute in the text indicative of the author's own impotence?[49] Within Nasser's totalitarian conception of the nation, it seems, the painstakingly cultivated distinction between the autobiographical and the fictional was no more desirable than the distinction of any (dissenting) voice from that of the leader. The vocal debate that accompanied the evolution of the concept of the writer during the half century or so before the 1952 Revolution dissipates soon after it, giving way instead to cynical conformity or symbolic modes of opposition. After the Revolution the oppositional writer can be said to have gone underground: into the characters and, from the early 1960s on, steadily more into the interior spheres of imagined individuals. Narrative techniques of the stream of consciousness and interior monologue variety thus become central to the coding system of this formally symbolic and politically subversive fiction. Even then, as we have already seen, the writer was not always safe from the invasive reach of the secret police. Herein lies an example of the pervasive *political* constraint on the novelistic imagination.

* * *

The tacit assumption underlying the foregoing anecdotes is fairly transparent: Constraints on the representation of the body, in all its "unseemly" functions and capacities, circumscribe, to one degree or another, the mimetic illusion through which the novel summons into being credible fictional characters. In its own way, the concerted assault on the novel's imaginative interest in the body may be a displaced symptom of the pervasive state of denial subtending actual attitudes to sexuality, eroticism, and the body in modern Arab culture.[50] The concomitant overemphasis on the more abstract aspect of the individual, that is, "personality," in Arabic literature and Arab culture in general, may be a form of compensation for the absented body, which, paradoxically, the idea of personality helps to conceal or "absent" in the first place.

There is yet another constraint on the range of individuality that, perhaps more than any other, bedevils many a hapless character in Egyptian fiction. Kamāl, in Mahfouz' *Cairene Trilogy*, like Ḥamīda and 'Abbās in *Midaq Alley*, Zaynab in Haykal's *Zaynab*, and all the male characters in al-Ḥakīm's *'Awdat al-Rūḥ*, are among its direct victims. What makes this constraint exceptionally powerful is its coupling of class difference with (legalistic) religious considerations. In the literature of Islamic law it is known as *zawāj al-takāfu'* or *al-kafā'a*, that is, parity between the couple, or marriage of equals. According to most schools of law,[51] this is one of the few areas in which the father and family of a happily married woman retain the right to demand her separation from a husband they deem inferior to them in social or economic status. There is, in fact, a fairly detailed table that specifies the exchange value of personality traits according to a set criteria that span descent—where Arab Quraysh is accorded highest premium—race, color, class, trade, and intellectual abilities.[52]

The fictional depiction of the workings of this restriction on personal relations often mimics the even stranger contrivances of reality. The bizarre account of shaykh 'Alī Yūsuf's marriage to the daughter of shaykh al-Sādāt at the beginning of the twentieth century must have been in the back of Mahfouz' mind as he went about fashioning Kamāl's pained consciousness of the unbridgeable class difference between the merchant status of his father and that of 'Āida's aristocratic family. 'Alī Yūsuf's account vividly captures a characteristic predicament of the individual who, empowered by certain egalitarian features of the nascent Egyptian bourgeoisie, aspires to upward mobility, only to have that aspiration crudely checked by the built-in resistances to such mobility in Egypt's highly stratified society. Because it is paradigmatic of the fate of many characters who seek to break out of the social class, or station, in which they happen to be born, and because writing is the means used to effect that transformation, the "story" of 'Alī Yūsuf bears retelling in brief here.

As Aḥmad Bahā' al-Dīn relates it,[53] this is a quintessential Egyptian version of the rags to riches fairy tale. Born to a poor family in Upper Egypt, 'Alī Yūsuf left his village at a young age to study at al-Azhar. In Cairo, however, and much like so many of his real and fictional counterparts at the beginning of the twentieth century, he took to writing to newspapers and soon discovered the magic power of the written word. Before long he started publishing his own newspaper, *al-Mu'ayyad*, which espoused the nationalist cause and almost instantly became a leading newspaper in Egypt. Yūsuf crowned this spectacular success by founding a major political party under his own leadership. The wealth, prestige, and power he wielded as a result of this combined success was second to none in Egypt in 1904. That's when he decided to ask for the hand of Ṣafiyya, daughter of shaykh al-Sādāt, scion to one of the best known and wealthiest families of Egypt's religious aristocracy. The Sādāts—no relation to President Sadat, incidentally—claimed direct descent from the Prophet's daughter, Fāṭima.

Initially the father approved of the marriage, but, for no apparent reason, seems to have had second thoughts and thus balked and dragged his feet. Their fate in limbo for several years, the engaged couple finally decided to flout the shaykh's paternal authority and to marry in secret. Incensed at hearing the news of the event from the newspapers, al-Sādāt sued in the religious courts to have the marriage annulled on grounds of inequality between the bride and the bridegroom. The case riveted public attention for the duration of the trial, at the end of which the judge ruled in favor of the claimant, declared the marriage null and void on said grounds of "disparity," and ordered that the wife be returned to her father's house. She refused to comply with the ruling, and this act set in motion yet another bizarre chain of events, at the end of which, in a volte-face, al-Sādāt agreed to (re)marry his daughter to the same man he had just deemed unfit to be his son-in-law, and had the court's decision to prove it.

The twists and turns of this strange tale are indicative of the state of flux in the laws and conventions regulating matters of personal status in Egypt at the beginning of the twentieth century. Particularly curious is the legalistic reasoning that motivated the wide fluctuations in the fortunes of the protagonist—a veritable Randian individual in every respect. The fact that he was a self-made man who raised himself from abject poverty to impressive wealth militated against, not for him in the trial. For, wealth acquired through hard work was deemed not only inferior to inherited wealth, but also insufficient to wipe out the stigma of outgrown poverty. This is particularly true when the source of the wealth in question is menial work, such as writing and journalism. "Journalism," al-Sādāt's lawyer declared in court, "is not only a lowly profession, it is also prohibited in Islam because it thrives on eavesdropping, rumor mongering, and the disclosing of secrets, all of which are legally prohibited in Islamic law."[54]

Still, nothing in the foregoing quite prepares one for the extraordinary ending of the story. Thoroughly shaken by the humiliation visited on him on account of his humble origins, the rugged ʿAlī Yūsuf spent the last years of his life trying "to correct" this accident of birth in the wrong class. And he eventually succeeded, by renouncing his profession, giving up writing and political activism, and ultimately securing a certified pedigree attesting to his descent from noble ancestry. Incidentally, the happiness of the couple was the first casualty of this endless hassle to make, unmake, and remake a single individual.

ʿAlī Yūsuf died in 1913, one year before the publication of *Zaynab*, to which the author, Muḥammad Ḥusayn Haykal, declined to attach his real name, preferring instead to ascribe its authorship to "an Egyptian peasant"—*miṣrī fallāḥ*. Only in 1929, when the second edition came out, did Haykal openly acknowledge the work and affixed his name to it. Such was the low esteem in which writing in general was held; writing fiction was considered to be even lower. Echoes of this truism reverberate throughout the pages of Egyptian imaginative and discursive literature. Kamāl's anxiety in broaching the subject with his father in *The Trilogy* is symptomatic of this condition; so is al-Māzinī's "friendly" advice to Mahfouz "to stay away from realist fiction" if he, Mahfouz, wished to spare himself endless headache.[55]

While by no means exhaustive, the foregoing list of constraints may suggest the extent of the resistance the Egyptian novel has routinely encountered when broaching the contentious subject of the individual. On their part, and in the fluid context of the nation(state) in the process of formation, Egyptian novelists have only rarely been able to resist the temptation of enlisting fictional characters in the service of their particular reading of the nation. Consequently, characters are seldom permitted to exist in and for themselves, as unique individuals, in this fiction. That is, an added symbolic layer or dimension often inheres in the identity of "significant"—and signifying—characters. The Egyptian realist novel in particular, whether of the social or psychological variety, often utilizes a battery of linguistic and rhetorical means to embed in the narrative such coded "messages" as to make an ideological reading all but unavoidable. It is as much through the interpretation of these "embedded messages," as it is through explicit themes and plots, that the novel intervenes in the cultural discourse on identity in its multiple guises and configurations.

* * *

Like novelists everywhere, Egyptian novelists tend to reflect in their fiction—sometimes too directly, perhaps—the interests, concerns, and mores of the constituency, class, region, or professional milieu in which they happen to be raised and with which they are intimately familiar. This general observation often bears directly on questions of characterization. The major division between the city and the countryside, and urban and rural life styles, for instance, continues to be a viable criterion of imaginative and critical differentiation. Certain decisive actions and life-and-death choices in major Egyptian novels appear comprehensible only in terms of determinate personality types that inhere in characters by virtue of their association with one or another of these defining (extrinsic) criteria. The pervasive theme of honor killing and revenge in novels dramatizing characters from upper Egypt, for example, informs the tragic action of such masterpieces as Yaḥyā al-Ṭāhir 'Abdullāh's *al-Ṭawq wal-Isweira* (1975; The Ring and the Bracelet), Bahaa Ṭaher's *Khālatī Ṣafiyya wal-Dayr*, and the much earlier work of Ṭāhā Ḥusayn *Du'ā' al-Karawān* (1934; *The Call of the Curlew*, 1980), among many others. Similarly, at the opposite end, the cosmopolitan sophistication, suave casualness, and religious tolerance that distinguish many of Edwar Al-Kharrat's and Ibrahim Abdel Meguid's characters owe much to these writers' upbringing in cosmopolitan Alexandria. The small, concentric circles in which Mahfouz spent most of his life: the Jamāliyya quarter in old or Islamic Cairo, the 'Abbāsiyya in modern Cairo, the university, and the governmental bureaucracy, all fall within the perimeters of metropolitan Cairo. And they virtually limit his pool of characters accordingly. That is why one hardly finds any peasants, workers, soldiers, sailors, or nomads among Mahfouz' vast panoply of characters. By contrast, the works of such writers as Muḥammad Yūsuf al-Qa'īd and 'Abd al-Ḥakīm Qāsim primarily feature characters of peasant background, most of whom fall between the cracks of haphazard industrialization and random urbanization.[56]

The pressure emanating from this particularizing corner collides at the site of character formation with less tangible but equally forceful pressures originating elsewhere. From its inception, character in Egyptian fiction appears saddled with conflicting mandates: To intimate and animate actual, discrete individuals who are also, and simultaneously, representative of more general types and larger collectivities. The determined recourse to a uniform level of formal Arabic, even in dialogue, in the works of most Egyptian writers, including, or perhaps especially, Mahfouz, inevitably "rewrites" the specifically Egyptian in individual characters into the common (linguistic) idiom of literary Arabic that binds them and all literate Arabs in the act of literary representation.[57] An Egyptian character may be no less Arab when he speaks in the vernacular but he or she becomes a more pronounced one through recourse to the *fuṣḥā*, or formal Arabic. The intent of this linguistic choice is to render general and typical (Arab) what in the vernacular appears specifically local or parochial (Egyptian). While on the whole a workable *modus operandi* has obtained on this point, carrying the practice to an extreme can also disturb the delicate mimetic illusion on which it rests. Glaring examples of this possibility occur in many of Mahfouz' novels. To take just two examples from *Zuqāq al-Midaqq* consider the case of illiterate Ḥamīda, the impetuous "heroine" of the novel, using the correct grammatical case of the dual to say that combing her hair had brought out only two lice, *qamlatayn ithnatayn*; or when the equally illiterate wife of Kirsha uses singularly archaic and highly formal diction to describe her incorrigible husband, who would not desist from his shameful (homosexual) conduct, *lā yar'awī*.[58]

A craving for international recognition, impelled by the ultimate allure of the Nobel, exercised modern Egyptian and Arab literary imagination long before Mahfouz garnered the coveted Prize in 1988. How to impart to Arabic literature an international or universal dimension, has been an abiding preoccupation of Egyptian and Arab writers, poets, and critics all along. The continuous debate on this issue has often been conducted under the prescriptive slogan: *min al-maḥalliyya ilā al-'ālamiyya*, from the local to the universal or international. While it is impossible to gauge in concrete terms the effect of this pull on the actual production of characters in Egyptian fiction, there is no doubt about the direction of the pull. In this context *'ālamiyya*, universal or international standing, is merely a euphemism for Western recognition and approval. The steady migration of young Arab writers to the West in recent decades, like the concomitant phenomenon of writing about Arab experience in Western languages, to Western readers, is a logical outcome of that enduring pull.[59] At present, Ahdaf Soueif represents this trend better than any Egyptian writer residing abroad and writing on Egyptian experience in a foreign language.[60]

* * *

To recapitulate an overriding generalization, the inauguration of individuality in the Egyptian realist novel was fraught with fatal contradictions from the outset. For the common individual to whose birth the realist novel was a midwife proved impossible, when not stillborn. Death, defeat, and disappointment by far outstrip success and fulfillment in the narratives of the ordinary individuals one encounters in this fiction. This is generally true of all serious Egyptian novels, where even the ordinary ambitions of "common" individuals, such as love, marriage, decent livelihood, and a modicum of happiness, are routinely frustrated. While it is arguably true that such is indeed the case with most novels—the novel being a story in which something (always) goes drastically wrong!—in the Egyptian novel the fault line often arises from a fundamental incompatibility between the idea of the common individual and the prevalent socioeconomic cultural conditions. If we remember the pejorative reference routinely applied to common people as "the rabble"—*al-dahmā'*—by such elitist writers as al-'Aqqād, al-Rāfi'ī, al-Ḥakīm and others, it will not be difficult to surmise both the prescriptive nature of the novel's valorization of the individual and the concomitant pessimistic outlook concerning the individual's prospects in reality. Of the countless characters inhabiting Mahfouz' novels, for example, only a handful can be said to have survived the ravages of their (life-)stories, and none intact. The ratio is even lower in the works of Yūsuf Idrīs, Yūsuf al-Qa'īd, Sonalla Ibrahim, and most other Egyptian writers.

By far, the gravest danger to the artistic soundness of characters in Egyptian fiction stems from intrusive authorial ideology. It is through this indirect, but palpable ideological intervention that the writer reinsinuates himself in the text he had ostensibly relinquished to his characters. I will illustrate this potential with a few specific examples shortly. Here let me pursue a little further the historical trajectory of individuality in the postrealist phase of Egyptian fiction, which happens to coincide with the decade of the 1960s. More precisely, the beginning of this phase can perhaps be established with relative certainty in the publication of Mahfouz' novel *al-Liṣṣ wal-Kilāb* (1961; *The Thief and the Dogs*, 1984).

As many critics have noted, what distinguishes the half dozen or so novels Mahfouz published between 1961 and 1967 is the extensive recourse they make to techniques of the psychological or stream-of-consciousness novel. But what has gone unnoticed is the fact that, contrary to general practice and generic promise, these novels are more, not less, directly political than their counterparts of the earlier phase of social realism. This political "overdose" coincides with a marked recuperation of a sense of heroic individualism in these novels, beginning with *al-Liṣṣ wal-Kilāb*, where the disaffected protagonist, Sa'īd Mahrān, single-handedly takes on the sinister alliance between personal opportunism and political despotism. Against the danger of salacious conformity Mahfouz' fiction revives the concept of personality and character, in the moral and ethical sense, during this period. Thus, if sensual pleasure and an insatiable appetite for the good life identified the extroverted, largely apolitical al-Sayyid Aḥmad, ethical rectitude, personal geniality, altruism, and patriotic fervor characterize 'Āmir Wajdī, al-Sayyid's beleaguered, introverted, but defiant counterpart in *Miramār* (1967). In a sense, 'Āmir Wajdī serves an ideological function in relation to Mahfouz roughly analogous to al-Sayyid's psychological function in relation to Kamāl in my reading of *The Trilogy*. That is, 'Āmir Wajdī exists to "do" and think what Mahfouz can only imagine into fiction under the repressive conditions of Nasser's Egypt. Admittedly, this ideological reinvestment in personality produces a number of incongruities within Mahfouz' own work, and between him and the younger generations of Egyptian writers.

To begin with, Mahfouz seems to have reverted to a metaphysical view of personality quite at odds with his earlier, more or less material view of the subject. What makes the protagonists of these latter novels heroic is precisely the innate strength they all seem to possess, which enables them to rise above historical and personal circumstances to assert an absolute principle or value. A metaphysical moral essence seems to be posited at the inner core of these characters, is demonstrated by their actions, but is never interrogated or theorized. It obtains equally in Sa'īd Mahrān of *The Thief and the Dogs* (1961), as it does in 'Āmir Wajdī of *Miramār* (1967), and Anīs Zakī of *Thartharah fawq al-Nīl* (1966; *Adrift on the Nile*, 1993). The last case is particularly striking because Anīs Zakī, in addition to being an incurable skeptic, is a habitual hashish smoker who is rarely ever sober. Even so, when a moral imperative is infringed—in this case the hit-and-run accident in which the car, driven by a stoned driver, and carrying the band of revelers on an outing, fatally injures a peasant woman on a desert road near the pyramids—he rises to the occasion and puts absolute principle before everything else, including personal comfort and safety. He insists, against the collective will of his fellow addicts, to report the accident to the police.

It is in *Miramār*, however, that characterization assumes with exceptional clarity many of the qualities postulated earlier. 'Āmir Wajdī is the main prism through which characterization enlists the metaphysics and mystique of personality in the service of (authorial) ideology. As has already been noted, the strategic placement of his sections at the beginning and the end of the novel accords him obvious prominence. He literally has the first and the last word in the novel. His age serves a similar function. At the time of the novel's action, 1961–1962, he is said to be eighty years old. This puts all the major events and milestones of Egypt's long march towards national liberation and identity in modern history—from the 'Urābī uprising of 1881, to the Wafd-led revolution of 1919, and on to the Revolution of the Free Officers under Nasser's leadership in 1952—within the span of his own life. He in a sense sums up and incarnates in his person modern Egyptian patriotism. The positive valence of his name contributes to this carefully orchestrated valorization.

This symbolic transmutation of the personal into the ideological permeates all aspects of the plot, including interpersonal relations. Its manifestations must be read against the fierce political struggle brewing in the background over the right to represent Egypt. Thus, 'Āmir's "characteristic" geniality counts in his favor against his detractors. These, as we have seen, neatly divide into two groups: the regime's sycophants who crudely push him out of his lifelong journalistic career in Cairo, and the Azharite shaykhs who had condemned him to celibacy for dabbling in free thinking early on in his life. In the novel's moral economy the venality of the former and the rigidity of the latter appear all the worse for having maligned such a kind, gentle, impeccably patriotic, and devout man.

The full ideological measure of his cultivated geniality, however, crystallizes mostly through his relationship with the two female characters in the novel: Mariana, the Greek proprietress of the *pension*, and Zohra, the peasant girl who works as maid in the *pension*. Both women carry crucial symbolic significance in the novel: Mariana, a remnant of the once thriving Greek community of Alexandria stands metonymically for all the foreign communities with which the cosmopolitan city once bustled, before their summary expulsion in the aftermath of the 1956 Suez war; the young, beautiful peasant girl, Zohra, stands squarely for Egypt.

It is in this symbolic capacity that the "romantic" involvements of both women signify. Thus, the failed attempt at copulation between Mariana and the erstwhile feudal landlord Tolbat Marzūq, whose land had just been sequestered under the sweeping agrarian reforms of 1961, is implicitly ascribed to old age, but symbolically asserts the futility of trying to revive the defunct alliance between the indigenous Egyptian feudal aristocracy and foreign interests. As for Zohra, with the exception of 'Āmir Wajdī, all the male residents of the *pension*, including hoary Tolbat, entertain sexual fantasies of possessing her. Not altogether surprisingly, she falls for, but does not quite succumb to an opportunist who parrots the ideological slogans of the regime for selfish interests. Zohra, we learn, had fled her village and come to Alexandria in the nick of time to escape an impending forced marriage to a much older relative. Attractive, ambitious, strong-willed, and bent on improving her lot in life, Zohra, like Egypt, is singularly unschooled in the ways of distinguishing true from false lovers. What Zohra lacks in personal experience, Egypt lacks in democratic political practice, that is: free, informed choice. And since none of Zohra's contemporary suitors qualifies as a rightful lover/husband, the same holds for Egypt on the subtextual, political level of the symbolic narrative. In this casting 'Āmir Wajdī emerges as the only true friend of Zohra/Egypt, but one strictly limited by personal and historical circumstance to the role of moral guardian. It is important in this respect that neither Zohra nor Mariana speaks in her own voice, since neither has a section of her own in the text. Their narrative is thus filtered exclusively through the male characters, primarily 'Āmir Wajdī.

On one level, this formal feature appears consonant with the political import of the novel. Since women, like foreigners, are all but voiceless in modern Egyptian and Arab culture, denying them the right to self-representation in fiction merely mimics reality. But the logic of such an extrapolation should also preclude from representation "oppositional" figures like 'Āmir Wajdī himself, as well as most of the protagonists of Mahfouz' novels of the 1960s. Moreover, the very rationale of the interior monologue technique militates against such a mechanical subordination to normative or referential reality. One of the principal objectives of the inward turn of the psychological novel is precisely to skirt political and cultural constraints and taboos. It does so by ostensibly confining the purview of the narrative to the inner chambers of a character's private mind, so to speak.

Seen in this light, the decision to deny the female characters of *Miramār* a textual space from which they could speak on their own behalf seems to originate elsewhere. The frequent recurrence of similar instances in Mahfouz' fiction—indeed in the writing of most Egyptian and Arab male novelists—would tend to implicate gender in the phenomenon. A brief glance at Mahfouz' oeuvre, for example, suffices to show how schematically reductionist his representation of women is. On the whole, women tend to conform neatly to one or the other of two general types: the saintly, asexual woman (usually mother, sister, or a surrogate thereof), or the veritable whore, in potential, if not always in practice. The female characters of al-Sayyid's household in *The Trilogy*, including the maid, Umm Ḥanafī, like the mother in *Bidāya wa Nihāya* (1949; A Beginning and an End), Zohra in *Miramār*, and a few others, exemplify the former type; most of the rest—too numerous to list—exemplify the latter.

What is peculiar about the treatment of women, especially of the latter type, is Mahfouz' evident inability, or unwillingness, to accord them the minimal formal requirement of a fictional character: a full name. Many of them have little more than a first name and a readily available body to show for their contingent individuality:[61] If, as Freud says in *Totem and Taboo*, "a human being's name is a principal component in his person, perhaps a piece of his soul,"[62] the excision of part of these characters' names amounts to a form of spiritual and emotional mutilation. This principle seems to cut across gender in Mahfouz' fiction. No wonder some of these characters, like Ḥamīda and Zeiṭa in *Zuqāq al-Midaqq*, pay society back in similar coin: She turns prostitute and he makes a living by deforming perfectly healthy individuals so that they can beg to survive and pay him dues for "inflicting" on them enabling disabilities, if an oxymoron be allowed. Already adumbrated in the association of his name with chaos in the vernacular expression from which it is taken, *zeita wa zabalita*, the evident diabolic dimension of Zeita's character represents one of the most disturbing, but also profoundly insightful strokes of characterization in modern Arabic fiction.[63]

To return briefly to the question of female sexuality, it is next to impossible to find strong, sensible, yet sexually attractive and active female characters in Mahfouz' imaginative fiction. The only serious attempt to grapple with such a multidimensional female character proves more than it flouts the limitation. It concerns Haniyya, al-Sayyid's first wife, Yāsīn's mother in *The Cairene Trilogy*.

True to form, the account of her "personality" is fragmentary and filtered through the familiar male perspective, in this case a trilateral one involving the omniscient narrator, al-Sayyid, and Yāsīn. More than it illuminates *her* or relates *her* side of the story, the narrative depicts the unsettling effects her personality and conduct have on her "scandalized" former husband and estranged son. In rapid succession the pretty young woman moves through the stages of wife, mother, and divorcee, to end up in the permanent station of virtual slut. What triggers the unhappy sequence, we are told, is her refusal to put up with al-Sayyid's abusive behavior, which includes brutal beatings. A chain of ill-fated marriages and sexual liaisons punctuates the rest of her life until her early death, dejected and lonely. Both al-Sayyid and Yāsīn readily ascribe this ruinous outcome to the insatiable sexual appetites they impute to her. The narrator is somewhat more reserved in his judgment, going so far as to note the compelling similarities in sexual drives and passion between her and al-Sayyid. On the face of it, this would make her no more than al-Sayyid's female foil. And yet, nowhere does she receive any of the elaborate considerations the narrator concocts to mitigate al-Sayyid's libertine lifestyle and sexual excesses. In the overall typology of the novel, Haniyya's character remains ambivalent, baffling, and uncannily threatening, especially to al-Sayyid's inflated male ego, and to Yāsīn's irreparably damaged ego. In this regard, she is for Yāsīn what al-Sayyid is for Kamāl: a psychological complex as insurmountable as it is inescapable. What is surprising is that a sense of her tragic personality somehow survives the contortions of the male perspectives that mediate her identity, perhaps against authorial will and intentionality.

If the verdict on Haniyya's sexuality is not as unequivocal as the stringent terms of the female stereotype would seem to demand, this may be because she still stirs unresolved tensions in the psyche of the male characters who "define" her in the text, especially Yāsīn. In one of his numerous, obsessive, broodings on the subject of his troubled relation with her he coincidentally sums up the essence of the stereotype. The specific occasion is yet another marriage for mother Haniyya: "A woman. Yes, she is nothing but a woman… And every woman is a filthy curse. A woman takes to chastity only when adultery becomes unfeasible. Even my good stepmother (Amīna), God alone knows what she could have become were it not for my father!" (*Bayn al-Qaṣrayn*, p. 76). The sudden shift from the specific to the general, from a single woman to the female species as a whole, in Yāsīn's agitated rumination seems to gesture beyond the actual mother toward the archetype of the mother-prostitute. By its very nature, an archetype is all the more potent when its working in the psyche goes undetected by the individual's consciousness, as is often the case with Yāsīn.

The narrator neither confirms nor challenges Yāsīn's, and al-Sayyid's, stereotypical view of women here. Elsewhere, however, he comes close to corroborating the substance of the sweeping generalization. At one point in the seduction pageant in *Zuqāq al-Midaqq* the pimp, Faraj Ibrahim, says of Ḥamīda that she is "a whore by intuition"—عاهرة بالسليقة—(p. 195). Had this "insight" into Ḥamīda's character been left at that, it would have carried little truth value, given the suspect character of its source. Later on in the novel, however, the narrator lends it credence by reaffirming it on the basis of "objective" observation. She took so readily to the new life (of prostitution), he observes, that she fully justified her lover's hunch that "she is a whore by instinct"—عاهرة بالفطرة—(p. 254).

The revived interest in the heroic personality suppresses the gender agenda in Mahfouz' work in the 1960s, and with it the dominant female stereotype sketched earlier. No other character exemplifies this "paradigm shift" better than the prostitute Nūr of *al-Liṣṣ wal-Kilāb*. To be sure, the stereotype persists in the person of the hero's treacherous wife, Nabawiyya, whose offense is made all the more glaring by her name, which links her linguistically to the Prophet. But she plays only a minor, and decidedly subordinate role in comparison with Nūr, who embodies the essence of faithfulness in the novel. Though her love for Sa'īd remains unrequited, she remains faithful to him, sharing only her body, not her heart, with other men, during his marriage to Nabawiyya, and his subsequent imprisonment. When he runs afoul of the law anew, and becomes a fugitive from the police, she risks her life by giving him shelter.

The symbolism is too transparent here to warrant extensive elaboration. In the state of rife corruption and opportunism under Nasser's dictatorial rule the traditional value system is completely inverted and stands topsy-turvy: Wife (Nabawiyya) spells whore; professed revolutionary (Ra'ūf 'Alwān) spells opportunist; friend ('Aleish) spells traitor. By contrast, prostitute (Nūr) spells faith; thief (Sa'īd) spells hero; and police spells dogs.

The ideological intent behind this schematic clarity is not far to seek. Both materialize at the expense of the effectiveness of the interior monologue technique. Applied with adequate artistic skill and discretion, the technique is singularly apt to yield the kind of nuanced complexity and ambiguity of sense impressions and mental life that are otherwise inaccessible to external observation. The extent of the ideological transparency of Mahfouz' characters in these novels relates inversely to the artistic appeal and mimetic credibility of the characters. Without exception, they are singularly one-dimensional and shallow. Against the grain of the metaphor of depth and interiority implicit in interior monologue technique, the ideological investment yields psychologically less, not more, complex characters than did the more traditional narrative techniques of social realism in Mahfouz' fiction.

This incongruity between narrative technique and scant characterization may not be entirely the result of ideological import or authorial intent. It is just as likely to be the result of an incomplete assimilation of the broad range of the technique, on the one hand, and of the philosophical intellectual discourses of individuality, on the other. Mahfouz, we must remember, had to condense into the span of a few years the long centuries of experimentation with novelistic conventions and techniques in Europe. Moreover, what evolved there sequentially, where new narrative forms and styles replaced older ones in a timely, leisurely manner, was here thrust onto the consciousness of Mahfouz and his generation all at once, and often rather haphazardly. According to his own testimony, Mahfouz felt called upon to start writing Arabic novels and to transplant the genre in Arab culture even as he was being introduced to the artistic norms, techniques, and conventions of the European novel.[64]

To this formidable challenge we must add the absence of any serious philosophical or critical literature on the subject of the individual in Arabic, and the equally disabling absence of proper conditions for the emergence of what Ian Watt calls "homo economicus." If fictional Robinson Crusoe is inconceivable without the firm idea of the individual as homo economicus, most Egyptian fictional characters who seek to become such an individual fall between the cracks of stratified socioeconomic structures and perish, literally, in the process of trying to become self-sufficient individuals.

Mahfouz' resurrection of the heroic individual as the apotheosis of fixed, stable, personality traits, and a metaphysical core of selfhood, puts him at odds with the rest of his Egyptian fellow writers, especially those of the younger generations. His largely phallocentric view of sexuality puts him at even greater odds with the female writers among these. With a few exceptions, such as Yaḥyā al-Ṭāhir 'Abdallah and Bahaa Taher, in whose work the conventional idea of personality as a stable entity persists, the majority of post-Mahfouz Egyptian writers view personality as a contingent, fluid, and largely open-ended process. It is no accident perhaps that both 'Abdallah and Ṭāhir come from upper Egypt, as do most of their striking fictional characters. But unlike Mahfouz' metaphysical sources of personality, the origins of personality in upper Egyptian characters are deeply rooted in the traditions of the place. For this reason they also appear more convincingly tragic than Mahfouz' demonstrably ideological characters. Interestingly, as the examples of both 'Abdallah's *al-Ṭawq wal-Isweira* and Ṭāher's *Khālatī Ṣafiyya* show, women exemplify this type of tragically inflexible personality at least as forcefully as men. In fact, a closer scrutiny may reveal a deep-seated matriarchal streak at work in these novels.

Examples of the alternative conception of personality as a contingent entity abound in Egyptian fiction from the 1960s onward. By coincidence, one of the first outstanding novels to inaugurate the conceit was written about the same time Mahfouz was reviving the character of heroic individualism. Yūsuf Idrīs's *al-'Ayb* (1962; Shame) studies the effects of adverse social conditions on personal ethics, morality, and ultimately sense of identity. A newly graduated idealist woman joins the governmental bureaucracy in Cairo and shares an office with four male employees. Being one of the first Egyptian women to be admitted into public service, she presents a puzzling challenge to her curious office mates. Bribery, we soon learn, is the norm, rather than the exception in the daily routine of the office, and it is practiced openly. Her presence momentarily disrupts this routine and calls for an adjustment in the group's *modus operandi*. As she rebuffs endless attempts to engage her romantically, or to draw her into the ongoing bribery schemes, the twin forces of poverty and social conformity spring into action to rein in her idealism. The novel ends with her negotiating the "terms of surrender" in the form of a secret tryst with the most repulsive of her office mates, and a married man, to boot.

If Idrīs's *Shame* merely intimates the onset of the disintegration of personality in Egyptian fiction, several of Sonalla Ibrahim's novels take that inevitability as their point of departure. No Egyptian or Arab writer has examined this issue more thoroughly than Ibrahim. Already in *Tilk al-Rā'iḥa*, political repression emerges as the bane of individuality. The textual juxtaposition of the heroic and its antithesis brings this impression into sharp relief. Here narrative technique plays an inverse role to the one assigned to it in Mahfouz' novels of the 1960s. There is a hero in Ibrahim's piece, to be sure, and a formidable political one at that. But he is dead, and is recalled only in bits and pieces of memory scattered all over the text. From these interior monologue glimpses, we identify the historical figure behind the fragments as that of Shuhdī 'Aṭiyya al-Shāfi'ī, the secretary-general of the Egyptian communist party who died under torture in prison in 1960.[65]

Because there is no plot, nor any descriptive, omniscient, or circumstantial constitution of characters in the novella, its narrative defies the very concept of character. A pertinacious dwelling on the surface of objects and "events" systematically frustrates every expectation of causality and thwarts the illusion of depth, interiority, and predictability. There is no greater evidence for the dissolution of character and personality than the protagonist's inability to relate meaningfully to anything around him after his release from prison. Not only is he diminished as an individual, he is in fact reduced to an automaton who literally does nothing other than self-monitoring and self-censorship. Put under house arrest from sunset to sunrise, he observes the curfew with unfailing punctuality. What is more, he does so with little help from external reminders of time. And even though he appears incapable of engaging anything or anyone emotionally, intellectually, or politically, he nonetheless records every meaningless thing he does, says, or hears, possibly as an alibi of innocence. In other words, to himself, he is eternally on trial. Total withdrawal from the mere semblance of character, personality, and individuality thus undergird the narrative of identity in this short, but profoundly disturbing novella.

Not surprisingly, perhaps, both gender and sexuality figure negatively here. I have already mentioned the attempt of the secret police to exploit the incident of the protagonist's inability to sleep with the prostitute, for political purposes against the author. A recurrent ploy used to break the will of the (male) political detainees during interrogation was to torture them until they agreed to say "I am a woman."[66] Reversing gender roles under coercion, particularly the feminization of the masculine, and the consequent violation of the (male) body, preoccupy Ibrahim's attention in several subsequent novels. Both *al-Lajna* (1982; *The Committee*, 2001) and *Sharaf* (1997; Honor) explore this problematic at some length. *Sharaf*, in particular, subjects the view of personality as a stable, atemporal, or metaphysical essence to the stringent demands of exigency. This is particularly true of the common, unmistakably phallocentric predication of personality and personal identity on masculinity.

Like Sanā' in Idrīs's *al-'Ayb*, Sharaf's first act in the eponymous novel sets in motion the dynamic context of his transformation to an antithetical version of (him)self. At the age of twenty-one he unintentionally kills a gay English man who lures him into his lush apartment in a fashionable neighborhood of Cairo, drugs him, tries to seduce him, and when this fails, tries to rape him. As the drunk, aroused English man scurries to strip him, Sharaf grabs a bottle of whisky and smashes it on his head. The Englishman dies of his wounds the next day, and Sharaf is arrested on charge of murder and armed robbery. All his efforts to communicate to his interrogators what actually happened fall on deaf ears. Under torture, he finally admits to murder as charged. To secure this end, the police threaten not only to rape him, but also to rape his sister in his presence. The confession sets Sharaf on a prolonged journey into the entrails of the Egyptian prison system where his traditional view of individual identity is severely tested. He endures endless trials and punishments before he is finally broken, foregoes his masculine identity, and prepares to give in to his anticipating sexual assailants. The novel ends with him shaving his legs in preparation for the ultimate surrender.[67]

This skeletal summary hardly does justice to the complexity of the novel, but it suffices to suggest the poignant irony abiding therein. Sharaf ends up bargaining away his "honor," and consequently his personal identity in prison under immeasurably less advantageous conditions than he could have had outside it. In fact, his steadfast determination to protect his honor relates inversely to his bargaining power: The more determined he is, and the longer he tarries, the less he gets in return. He kills to save his honor, and ends up in detention; confesses to murder to save his sister's honor, and ends up condemning himself to a prolonged prison sentence; resists rape in prison, and ends up incurring additional punishments and deprivations, and so on until he foregoes all fixed notions of identity.

The chilling logic of this trap is self-evident: Under the prevalent socioeconomic terms of exchange, Sharaf, like Sanā', has no recourse to any countervailing alternatives. Moreover, both instances admit a metaphoric relation whereby the establishment in *al-'Ayb*, and the prison in *Sharaf*, stand metonymically for Egypt. The novels thus replicate under laboratory conditions the norms and rules of exchange operating in the society at large. *Sharaf* in particular appears typical of a trend in Egyptian fiction during the last two decades or so. As the Egyptian critic Sabry Hafez notes in a recent study, a major preoccupation of this fiction is to study the effects of the values of consumerism inaugurated by the open-door policies of President Sadat on the traditional value system of common Egyptians, especially among the underprivileged classes.[68] Sharaf's body, and more specifically his masculinity, furnish the site for exploring this pervasive system of rife commodification in Ibrahim's novel.

* * *

I want to conclude this chapter with a brief discussion of two pairs of fictional texts that symbolically bracket the twentieth century and recapitulate some of the major themes and issues I have been discussing, including the recurrent pattern I postulated at the outset of this study in Chapter 1. The first pair involves Muḥammad Ḥusayn Haykal's flawed but pioneering novel *Zaynab* (1914) and Muḥammad Yūsuf al-Qa'īd's novel *al-Ḥarb fī Barr Miṣr* (1978; *War in the Land of Egypt*, 1986); the second pair involves al-Manfalūṭī's story "al-Ḥijāb"

(1915; The Veil) and Hala El Badry's (Hāla al-Badrī) recent novel *Imra'a Mā* (2001; *A Certain Woman*, 2003).

Haykal, we remember, refrained from attaching his real name to the first edition of *Zaynab*, preferring, instead, to publish it under the sobriquet *miṣrī fallāḥ* (An Egyptian Peasant). Whatever Haykal's "real" reasons were, there is no doubt about the underlying intention to valorize the *fallāḥ* as the quintessential Egyptian. The word order in Arabic readily suggests that sense, which in English may be intimated by the alternative rendition "An Egyptian *and* a Peasant." At least on the symbolic level, this formal act foregrounds the peasant as apt author of his own narrative and thereby entitles him to self-representation. For better or for worse, the gesture irrevocably yokes the new genre of the novel to the problematic of Egyptian identity. As I have tried to show, all subsequent fictional works dealing with rural Egypt and the Egyptian peasantry, whether in the romantic or the realistic tradition, owe something to this ambiguous gesture.[69]

Yūsuf al-Qa'īd's novel *al-Ḥarb fi Barr Miṣr* sets out to debunk this rhetorical mystification of the reality of the *fallāḥ*. Its action unfolds against the historical backdrop of the Sadat era, especially Sadat's systematic recension of the Nasserist agrarian reforms that limited land holdings, and distributed small tracts of land to landless peasants. The "protagonist," *Miṣrī* (Egyptian), whose family depends on the favors of the *'umda* (village chief) for its survival, is compelled to enlist in the Egyptian army in lieu of the *'umda's* youngest son, on the eve of the 1973 Arab–Israeli war. An elaborate plot involving participants at various levels of the bureaucracy is hatched to effect this scheme of identity swapping. However, once recruited, the war breaks out, and *Miṣrī* volunteers to the front, where he serves heroically, and dies in battle. The question of his burial occasions further complications: Having served and died under the assumed identity of the *'umda's* (derelict) son, under what identity will he be buried? Here again ubiquitous favoritism springs into action and mysteriously rearranges the facts so as to indict *Miṣrī* for "trying to steal" the identity of his betters, presumably to advance his personal ambition. Until further notice, it is decreed, he will remain buried in an anonymous grave, his identity suspended. As if to underscore the problematic relation to Haykal's gesture, however, al-Qa'īd names *Miṣrī's* mother—what else?—*Fallāḥa*, Peasant.

On the discursive level, the "message" of the novel appears starkly clear: To be *Miṣrī* (Egyptian), and a patriotic one at that, when Egypt's national identity is in flux, does not augur well for the individual Egyptian. The novel thus continues to perform the critical task of mapping out the crucial terrain where the personal/individual and collective/national components of identity converge. But *al-Ḥarb fī Barr Miṣr* breaks new grounds by combining the techniques of investigative reporting and docufiction with those of more traditional modes of self-conscious fiction.[70] Thus, formally, the novel is divided into discrete sections, each narrated by a different narrator, in the manner of Mahfouz' *Miramār*. Also like Zohra of *Miramār*, the protagonist of this novel, Miṣrī, remains (understandably) voiceless.

His "story" is filtered piecemeal through the narratives of the other characters. In contradistinction from Mahfouz' characters, however, the narrators of al-Qa'īd's novel flout the illusion of verisimilitude, flaunt consciousness of their narrative roles, as they discuss these and the craft of storytelling openly in the text.

* * *

The gap between al-Manfalūṭī's relentlessly didactic, masculine, and authoritative story and El Badry's highly experimental, tentative, feminist novel measures the distance that the fictional representation of women, especially female sexuality as a register of individual identity, traversed in the course of the twentieth century. By the same token, the contrast between the two works suggests an even wider gap between the relative latitude of the novelistic imagination in this area and the austere constraints of historical reality. At the beginning of this chapter, I mentioned the increasingly more visible and more vocal role of what I called there teleevangelical Islamist preachers, citing the widespread popularity of 'Amr Khālid as an example. I will conclude the chapter by incorporating in my discussion of the two fictional texts mentioned here a related phenomenon that immensely complicates the task of the novel as an agent of historical change in contemporary modern Arab culture. The phenomenon in question concerns the status of the *niqāb*—usually a black veil that covers a woman's entire face, except for the eyes—a variant of the *burka* Afghani women had to wear in public under the Taliban. The rapid spread of the *niqāb* in various Arab countries, including Egypt, was the topic of the weekly program *lil-nisā' faqaṭ* (For Women Alone) on the Arab satellite al-Jazeera during the last week of September, 2004. I will return to this program after a brief discussion of al-Manfalūṭī's story, "*The Veil.*"

The story relates in broad strokes the "inevitable" fate of a European-educated Egyptian who advocates the unveiling of Egyptian women. Against the advice of his lifelong friend, the narrator, he puts his convictions to the test and allows his wife to unveil and to socialize with his male friends. Before long he discovers that to do so is to court disaster. He is called to the police station one night to learn that his wife and his "best" male friend had been caught in a compromising position. The shock paralyzes and ultimately kills him, but not before he renounces his "European" ideas about the veil and embraces the inevitability and desirability of the eternal segregation of the sexes.

The moral of the story is quite obvious: Woman, reduced here to the sexual dimension of her being, is what Yāsīn calls "a curse," and what is commonly known in Islamic law as "*'awra*," that is, body. In many Islamic vernaculars, however, the term often carries a pejorative connotation to mean "genitals." This is the sense the wife's "character" imparts in al-Manfalūṭī's story: If she is not a pliable sex object, she is a source of temptation. To guard against both, the veil and segregation of the sexes must be strictly enforced. The intended historical target of the fictional account, we surmise, is Qāsim Amīn, the staunch advocate of the liberation of women, whose book, bearing this very title, appeared in 1900 (*taḥrīr al-mar'a*). Al-Manfalūṭī's literary version of the reformist agenda of his master, Muḥammad 'Abdu, thus contains little promise of change in the status of women, much less in their traditionally designated (a)sexual roles.

What may have been a sufficient safeguard against such tragic consequences as al-Manfalūṭī depicts at the beginning of the twentieth century no longer seems so at the beginning of the twenty-first. The above mentioned program on al-Jazeera drew attention to a trend in several Arab countries, including Egypt, where the traditional veil—*ḥijāb*—was deemed inadequate, as it left the woman's face uncovered. Hence the increasing recourse in these countries to the more comprehensive *niqāb*. Al-Jazeera's program followed the uproar in various parts of the Arab world over the call of the Qaṭarī writer and activist Ḥiṣṣa al-'Iwaḍī to Qaṭarī women to shed the *niqāb* as a spurious innovation that dates no farther back in modern Arab culture than the 1970s. Al-'Iwaḍī's call, in turn, followed on the heels of another commotion at the American University in Cairo early in 2001 over the propriety/legality of wearing the *niqāb* during lectures and exams on campus. When a *niqāb*-wearing woman was prevented from entering campus, she sued the University, and the Egyptian courts ruled in her favor.[71] These incidents are reminiscent of the recurrent zigzags that have kept modern Arab culture at a virtual standstill in regard to all the crucial questions of modernity, including the right of women to appear, compete, and function on equal footing with men in the public spaces and institutions of the nation-state.

Against the alleged novelty of the *niqāb*—a view supported, incidentally, by abundant, sound scholarly evidence from Islamic law in all but the strict Ḥanbalī school and its modern derivative, the Wahhābī variant—its sole proponent on the program argued otherwise. Born and educated in Egypt, the Wahhābī theologian and legal director of the Qaṭarī ministry of religious endowments, Muwāfī Muḥammad al-'Azab, asserted that wearing the *niqāb* is obligatory not only on religious but also, implicitly, on national and patriotic grounds. In his view, the *niqāb* was lifted in Egypt and the rest of the Arab world at the beginning of the twentieth century as a result of a conspiracy against Islam hatched by Masonic circles and the World Zionist Organization. As "evidence" of this conspiracy, the origins of which hark all the way back to the founder of modern Egypt, Muḥammad 'Alī, al-'Azab cites the example of Hudā Sha'rāwī, an early pioneer of women's rights in Egypt.[72] Hudā's father, al-'Azab argued, was a well-known Free Mason, and that is why he began the assault on Islam in his own household, by removing the *niqāb* from the face of his daughter, Hudā.

I cite these instances to suggest the scope and intensity of the ongoing, and increasingly more strident, campaign to roll back whatever meager advances Arab women have made on the path to individual identity in the past century or so. For, on the semiotic plain of public discourse, the *niqāb* symbolically banishes individual women from public space by reassimilating the identifying facial characteristics of each into the amorphous collective identity of the female gender. It thus has the same leveling effect on the public persona of women as does the generalizing principle on individual species in Islamic painting.

Hala El Badry's novel was written, and must be read, against this increasingly more polarized background. In one fundamental respect, it is a novel of retrieval and reclamation. Written in the bold tradition of Alīfa Rif'at and, more recently, of Ahdaf Soueif and Aḥlām Mustaghānamī, it strives to reinstate female sexuality as a constitutive component of a woman's personal identity and to reinscribe it as an apt subject of literary representation. Let me illustrate the significance of this point through a brief comparison.

There is a telling contrast between Sonalla Ibrahīm's two novels, *Dhāt* and *Sharaf*, on the one hand, and Hala El Badry's novel, on the other, as regards the relation of title to trajectory or direction of action in these respective novels. Being personal names, the titles of Ibrahim's novels posit personal identity as a known quantity at the outset and then proceed to deconstruct that proposition in the text. Under the socioeconomic and political conditions of postcolonial Egypt neither selfhood (*Dhāt*), nor honor (*Sharaf*), is a tenable criterion of individual identity. Soon after her marriage, for example, Dhāt learns to transform her most intimate desires, especially the sexual ones, into fantasies, and to consign these exclusively to the inner recesses of her imagination. Eavesdropping from her bed on her husband and a neighbor as they watch pornographic videos—made widely available in Egypt thanks to the economic open-door policies of President Sadat—makes this retreat into inner fantasies that much easier. Similarly, Sharaf learns through successive ordeals in prison that the new conditions of consumerism render obsolete all notions of individual identity predicated on personal honor.

Imra'a Mā follows an inverse course: It proceeds from the anonymity of the title, *A Certain Woman*, to depict a unique, articulate, and multidimensional woman. Nāhid, the protagonist, is a new kind of Egyptian-Arab-Muslim woman: well-educated, professional, and fiercely independent. In addition, she is keenly attuned to her inner drives and desires, acknowledges them fully, and enlists this recognition in her struggle to become sole mistress of her body and mind. Thus, though married and sharing a bed with a husband from whom she is emotionally estranged, she withholds conjugal rights from him, lavishing these instead on her lover, the novelist, 'Umar. This obvious move aims to challenge the widely lopsided, traditional power relations between the sexes in marriage, especially the explicit religious ordinances that govern sexual duties.[73] But even as we read the novel against the immediate historical background sketched here and the implicit legal literature, we cannot fail to hear in it echoes of Qāsim Amīn's call for the liberation of women a century earlier.

El Badry's novel is also remarkably experimental in a postmodern sense. It uses the "metafictional" format of embedding a novel within a novel to juxtapose different layers of imagined and "lived" experience, or, in Genette's more technical terms, diegetic and extradiagetic levels of narration.[74] Admittedly, the ploy remains tentative, as the "core" narrative at the "diegetic" level is at best tenuous. But the format accomplishes a far more critical task: It refocuses attention on the historical role of the novelistic imagination to envision alternatives to what obtains by coercion or force of tradition in contemporary Arab culture. A brief mention of some of the main issues the novel thematizes may suggest this dialectic.

A love affair between a married man and father, 'Umar—a journalist and writer by profession, and a married woman and mother, Nāhid—an archeologist by profession, motivates the main course of events in the novel. Often hauntingly lyrical in style, the episodic narrative of "developments" in that relationship never quite yields a plot in any traditional sense. The interest of the novel lies elsewhere: in the sustained exploration of powerful emotions and acutely felt states of consciousness as these battle traditional roles and ideas of individual responsibility in the minds of the characters, especially the main protagonist, Nāhid. Echoes of the following cry, uttered at the beginning of a fragment entitled *Desire*, reverberate throughout the text. "Crushed between impotence and desire, I screamed: I want to be myself! I want to flee in body and soul" (p. 127). With a statue of mythic Pegasus close at hand to suggest desirable trajectories, Nāhid knows that under the social and cultural circumstances the only possible flight is inward, where the vital (re)sources of individual identity ultimately lie. Imaginative fiction, including 'Umar's ostensible novels, proves enabling in this pursuit. Nāhid routinely draws on novelistic techniques to negotiate "existential" difficulties she encounters on her journey through self-discovery and self-realization. Here, in Farouk Abdel Wahab's translation, is an example of this intricate interfacing of narrative levels, which happens to have the added merit of bearing directly on the question of characterization. The first person pronoun belongs to the heroine, Nāhid, who is on a short vacation in Greece. The book in question is 'Umar's largely autobiographical novel, *Maze*, which happens to be the title of the first chapter of *A Certain Woman*:

> Why did I take his book with me and what was I looking for? The smoke of anger dissipated like lines erased by the wind. When I voraciously began to read between the lines, knowing how he thought helped me figure out what he gave of himself to his characters. I know that an author gives each hero a little bit of their soul, making the characters and their contradictions, and their wavering between good and evil, a little more human. I may be mistaken about that, but I like to believe the idea. I got hold of a thread and stayed with it: the protagonist of his novel suffers in silence and displays bitter sarcasm and great self-esteem, very much like the author. I set up a trap of details that I knew about him and kept closing it on the minutiae of a world that I took to be his world. The more certain I became of my reading, the more deeply I was involved with him. I listened to the cells of his soul in the rhythm of the unspoken, in the words of the book, and I discovered that in his absence he was present at the very heart of my heart. I began to open the curtains in the secret pathways that we paved every time we met and dispersed the dark till he appeared before me. I see him. I am one with him.[75]
>
> (*A Certain Woman*, p. 13)

For similar purposes, El Badry orchestrates the physical and mental movements of her two major protagonists so as to incorporate in their personal narratives actual experiences of fellow Arab writers whose fictional works stirred up fierce controversy in Egypt at the time of the novel's action, the late 1990s. Specially notable in this regard is the reference to the Moroccan writer Mohamed Choukri and the Syrian writer Ḥaydar Ḥaydar, some of whose works were banned in Egypt at the time: the former on grounds of "obscenity," the latter of "blasphemy."[76] As we have seen, the charge of obscenity is often invoked by various authorities to absent the body, especially the female body, from public view, and to suppress whatever drives and desires may reside therein. Nāhid reflects poignantly on this obsession with the body as she watches her husband performing daily routines.

> I watch him from a distance, talking, acting, and making decisions calmly, confidently, proudly. I try to ascertain who he is? Can he be the same man who faces the wall (in bed) lest my fingers should accidentally touch certain parts of his body, deemed taboo? It never occurred to me that my own body had such a special sanctity. I see it as part of a natural design, bestowed on me by God, and cannot understand the mystery in which they shroud it, or the secret of the furtive effort to conceal it.
>
> (p. 131)

To demystify, even as it celebrates, the human body, especially of the female, is a major objective of the novel. It informs numerous introspections, many of which are explicitly sexual in nature, such as orgasm, penetration, wetness, and so on. The following example is particularly striking, not only because of its daring content, but also because it is ascribed by the woman writer to her male foil inside the text, the novelist 'Umar. It concerns the inviolable taboo of virginity.

Reflecting on the disarming frankness with which his Greco-Italian-Alexandrine wife, Magie, spoke about her sexual experiences with other men before their marriage, 'Umar ruminates

> I did not feel jealous, and asked myself, why? She, too, felt no shame, regret, or that she had violated any immutable, fundamental principles. Rather, she felt that her private experiences are her own prerogative in life. I must confess that her previous experience with other men delighted me. Which made me wonder about the eager preference of men in the East for an ignorant virgin, over an experienced woman.
>
> (p. 91)

Such thoughts may occasion little surprise, and much less controversy in secular cultures, where the rights of the individual to his or her body, including their sexual acts and preferences, are firmly enshrined in law and practice. Not so in Arab Islamic culture. To gauge the full measure of this bold leap in Egyptian fiction written in Arabic it may suffice to recall the fundamental fact that matters of personal status, such as marriage, divorce, inheritance, and so on, come under the purview of the religious, not the civil, authority in Egypt as in most Arab and Islamic countries. To engage in extramarital sex, as Nāhid and ‘Umar do, is to commit adultery, a punishable offense under Islamic law. Nāhid compounds her offense further by denying her husband his conjugal right to enjoy her body, while committing adultery with another man.

It is surely not without symbolic significance that El Badry's daring dramatization of this issue coincides with the antithetical treatment of the question by Muḥammad Kamāl Muṣṭafā, the imām of the mosque of Fuengirola, Costa del Sol, in Spain, whose case attracted international attention recently. As was widely reported in the electronic and print media, a Spanish court in Barcelona sentenced the Egyptian-born shaykh to a fifteen-month suspended sentence, and a monetary fine, on January 14, 2004, for "advocating" wife-beating as a legitimate disciplinary measure against a disobedient wife, *nāshiz*, in his book *The Woman in Islam*. Whatever one thinks of the book, the case, or the practice, there is no doubt that the principle itself inheres in the text of the Qur'ān (4: 33), and, as such, enjoys a broad consensus among Muslim scholars and jurisprudents. In his well-known collection of religious rulings on women, *Fatāwā al-Nisā'*, Ibn Taymiyya acknowledges as much.[77] The revolutionary implication of the fictional treatment of the subject stems from the exclusively personal moral code the novel sets up as an alternative to the explicit precepts that regulate sexuality in Islamic law. Nāhid's personal moral code predicates the sexual act on the sincerity and reciprocity of feeling between the two partners to the act. "It was only natural that I should not allow Muṣṭafā (the husband) to touch me after he became a stranger (to me). Yes, we are still married, but he is the Other now. I am ‘Umar's, and can't belong to two men at the same time" (p. 50). This obvious conflict notwithstanding, Nāhid continues to profess Islam with equal sincerity and conviction. Since Mahfouz' *Cairene Trilogy* (1956–1957) no Egyptian or Arab novel has raised this problematic more vividly or addressed it more cogently than *Imra'a Mā*.

Although much of the novel's criticism is directed against the pervasive constraints foisted on women in the name of religion or tradition, it is by no means oblivious to the sinister role of political oppression in its local and global manifestations. In fact, the novel valorizes the culture of political resistance openly by ascribing the onset of individual consciousness in the heroine to political activism in her student days. It was the internalization of the experience of political prisoners in solitary confinement, under dictatorial governments, that enabled her disciplined mind to cope with the relentless pressures of daily life as wife, mother, and professional, in the midst of utter uncertainty about the future (p. 35). The effects of the enriched uranium used by the American troops on the Iraqi people since the first Gulf War, and the continuing brutalization of the Palestinian people in the occupied territories by the Israeli army, share the space of the text with the intimate concerns of the characters' personal lives.

In many fundamental respects, therefore, *Imra'a Mā* embodies, and fosters, the enduring tradition of the Arabic novel as a subversive genre and champion of oppositional agendas. Nothing captures this quality better than the final scene in the novel which shows Magie, 'Umar's wife, burning the sheets of the manuscript of the "novel" within the actual novel we had just finished reading. She does so out of a misplaced outrage resulting from confusing the fictional imaginary with the autobiographical and the factual. In other words, she "reads" the story of her troubled relationship with 'Umar into the novel. In this brilliant move the novel simultaneously mocks the standing practice of reading Arabic fiction autobiographically and referentially,[78] and celebrates the staying power of the novel. Like the Phoenix, it arises again and again from its own ashes.

NOTES

1 A GENRE AT WAR: LITERARY FORM AND HISTORICAL AGENCY

1 The general consensus among literary critics and historians of the Arabic novel credits Muḥammad Ḥusayn Haykal's *Zaynab* (1914) with the honorific of the first Arabic novel. See, for example, 'Abd al-Muḥsin Ṭāhā Badr, *Taṭawwur al-Riwāya al-'Arabiyya Fī Miṣr* (Cairo: Dār al-Ma'ārif, 1968), p. 42; Ḥamdī Sakkūt, *The Egyptian Novel and Its Main Trends: From 1913 to 1952* (Cairo: The American University Press, 1971), pp. IIV ff.; Fatma Mousa Mahmoud, *The Arabic Novel in Egypt: 1914–1970* (Cairo: The General Egyptian Book Organization, 1973), p. 19. For a divergent genealogy of the Arabic novel see Matti Moosa, *The Origins of Modern Arabic Fiction* (Washington DC: Three Continents Press, 1983), especially p. 124 where Moosa credits Salīm al-Bustānī (1848–1884) with the honorific of "true father of the Arab short story and novel." In *Fīl-Riwāya al-'Arabiyya: 'Aṣr al-Tajmā'* (Beirut: Dār al-Shurūq, 1959) Fārūq Khurshīd provides yet another genealogy for modern Arabic fiction.

2 See, for example, Ḥusayn Fawzī, *Sindbād Fī Riḥlat al-Ḥayāt* (Cairo: Dār al-Ma'ārif, 1968), pp. 36, 38, where the term *Riwāya* is used to designate play, even though in other places in the same book Fawzī uses the term to designate novel, and sometimes even to distinguish it from *qiṣṣa*, that is, story. See, ibid., p. 73. A similar ambivalence seems to inform the titles of two important books on the subject: Muḥammad Yūsuf Najm, *al-Qiṣṣa fil-Adab al-'Arabī* (Beirut: The American University Press, 1961) and Yaḥyā Ḥaqqī, *Fajr al-Qiṣṣa al-Miṣriyya* (Cairo: al-Dār al-Qawmiyya lil-Ṭibā'a wal-Nashr, 1964) where the term *qiṣṣa* seems to designate both novel and short story. Shawqī 'Abd al-Ḥakīm ambiguates the term *Riwāya* still further by reviving its more general denotation of narrative. He calls his average-length novel (181 pages) *Aḥzān Nūḥ* (Cairo: al-Dār al-Qawmiyya lil-Ṭibā'a wal-Nashr, n.d.) a long Egyptian tale (or narrative): "riwāya miṣriyya ṭawīla." As late as 1983 Aḥmad Ṭāhir Ḥasanayn was still using the term "riwāya" for play. See his *Dawr al-Shāmiyyīn al-Muhājirīn ilā Miṣr fī l-Nahḍa al-Adabiyya al-Ḥadītha* (Damascus: Dār al-Wathba, 1993), p. 58. See also Badr, *Taṭawwur*, p. 212 passim, and Moosa, *Origins*, p. 24. For a recent discussion of this issue see Roger Allen, "Narrative Genres and Nomenclature: A Comparative Study," in *Journal of Arabic Literature*, XXIII (1992) pp. 208–214.

3 The attack on Mahfouz was widely reported in the Arab and international press and electronic media at the time. See, for example, the pictorial report in the Cairene weekly *Niṣf al-Dunyā*, No. 245 (November 23, 1994), pp. 21–40; *Ibdā'*, No. 11, (November 1994), pp. 1–58, and *al-Qāhira*, No. 157 (December 1995), pp. 30–86. On the larger phenomenon of recent religious intolerance and violence against unorthodox thinkers, scholars, and writers in Egypt see, in addition to the above,

Rose El Youssef, No. 3463 (October 24, 1994), which reports the existence of lists of targeted writers and describes in detail various plots to eliminate them as well as the *modus operandi* of recruiting potential assassins for that purpose. For a comprehensive discussion of censorship in Egypt between 1952 and 1981 see Marina Stagh, *The Limits of Freedom of Speech: Prose Literature and Prose Writers in Egypt Under Nasser and Sadat* (Stockholm: Almqvist & Wiksell International, 1993). See also *Index On Censorship*, No. 2 (1996), No. 3 (1996). For a partial list of targeted Algerian writers see John Erickson, *Islam and Postcolonial Narrative* (Cambridge: Cambridge University Press, 1998), note 5, p. 171. On the specific case of Naṣr Ḥāmid Abū Zayd see Mary Anne Weaver's "Letter From Cairo: Evolution By Stealth" in *The New Yorker* (June 8, 1998), pp. 38–48; *Rose El Youssef*, No. 3557 (August 12, 1996), and No.3558 (August 19, 1996).

4 See *al-Wafd* (January 7, 11, and especially 14, 1999); *al-Ahram Weekly* (January 3, 1999), p. 5; *al-Hayat* (February 4, 1999), p. 17. On March 2, 1999, the *Associated Press* reported that the book was banned and withdrawn from the curricula of the American University in Cairo on orders of the minister of higher education, Mufīd Shihāb, who had told Parliament the day before that the book "contains indecency."

5 Tharwat 'Ukāshah served twice as minister of culture under Nasser between 1959–1962 and 1966–1970.

6 There are two different English translations of *Awlād Ḥāratinā*. The first, by Philip Stewart, is *Children of Gebelawi* (London: Heinemann, 1981); the second, by Peter Theroux, is titled *Children of Our Alley* (New York: Doubleday, 1996).

7 Fu'ād Zakariyyā, "kayf nufakkir fī azmat al-thaqāfa," *Al-'Arabī*, No. 255 (Kuwait: February, 1980); later included in Fu'ād Zakariyyā, *Khiṭāb ilā al-'Aql al-'Arabī* (Kuwait: Kitāb al-'Arabī, 1987), pp. 13–22.

8 To name only a few of the numerous books dealing with "the crisis" in one realm or another of modern Arab culture, the following may suffice: Abdallah Laroui, *The Crisis of the Arab Intellectual: Traditionalism or Historicism* (Berkeley and Los Angeles: University of California Press, 1976; French original 1974); Mahdī 'Āmil, *Azmat al-Ḥaḍāra aw Azmat al-Burjuwāziyya al-'Arabiyya?* (Beirut: Dār al-Fārābī, 1974, second printing); Nu'mān 'Āshūr, *Azmat Akhlāq* (Cairo: al-Hay'a al-Miṣriyya al-'Āmma lil-Kitāb, 1976); 'Abd al-Fattāḥ Khaḍr, *Azmat al-'Ilm fil-'Ālam al-'Arabī* (al-Riyāḍ: 1981); 'Abd al-Laṭīf Ḥamza, *Azmat al-Ḍamīr al-Ṣaḥafī* (Cairo: Dār al-Fikr al-'Arabī, 1960); Fu'ād al-Bīṭār, *Azmat al-Dīmuqraṭiyya fil-'Ālam al-Ārabī* (Beirut: Dār Beirut, 1981); Muḥammad 'Imāra, *Azmat al-Fikr al-Islāmī al-Mu'āṣir* (Cairo: Dār al-Sharq al-Awsaṭ lil-Nashr, 1990); Fārūq 'Abd al-Salam, *Azmat al-Ḥukm fil-'Ālam al-Islāmī* (Cairo: Maktab Qaylūb lil-Ṭab' wal-Nashr, 1981); Fatḥī Ghānim, *Azmat al-Islām Ma' al-Siyāsa* (Cairo: Kitāb al-Yawm, 1998); Ghālī Shukrī, *Azmat al-Jins fil-qiṣṣa al-'Arabiyya* (Cairo: al-Hay'a al-Miṣriyya al-'Āmma lil-Ta'līf wal-Nashr, 1971); Muḥammad Marzūqī, *Azmat al-Khiṭāb al-Siyāsī al-'Arabī* (Cairo: al-Muntadā al-'Arabī lil-Dirāsāt wal-Nashr, 1994); Samīr Amīn, *Azmat al-Mujtama' al-'Arabī* (Cairo: Dār al-Mustaqbal al-'Arabī, 1985); Muḥammad Ḥasanayn Haykal, *Azmat al-Muthaqqafīn* (Cairo: al-Sharika al-'Arabiyya al-Muttaḥida lil-Tawzī', 1961); 'Abd al-'Azīz al-Maqāliḥ, *Azmat al-Qaṣīda al-'Arabiyya* (Beirut: Dār al-Ādāb, 1985).

9 For a representative sample of Arab writings in other languages see the special issue of *Alif*, "The Hybrid Text: Arab Creative Authors Writing in Foreign Languages," No. 20 (Cairo: The American University, 2000). For a historical survey of earlier generations of Arab writers, see Geoffrey P. Nash, *The Arab Writer in English: Arab Themes in a Metropolitan Language 1908–1958* (Sussex: Academic Press, 1998). Jenine Abboushi Dallal draws attention to some of the untoward consequences of this phenomenon in her article, "The Perils of Occidentalism," *Times Literary Supplement* (April 24, 1998).

10 The first American edition of *Ulysses* appeared in 1934, after judge John M. Woolsey lifted the ban on it. His ruling on the case brought by the United States of America against the book was prefixed to that edition and to all subsequent American editions. See James Joyce, *Ulysses* (New York: Random House, Inc., 1934). For censorship in Canada see, *Forbidden Passages: Writings Banned in Canada* (Pittsburgh and San Francisco: Cleis Press, Inc., 1995).

11 For a good general mapping of the inter-relation among novel–culture–nation see Benedict Anderson, *Imagined Communities* (London and New York: Verso, 1983), Homi K. Bhabha, ed. *Nation and Narration* (London and New York: Routledge, 1990) and *The Location of Culture* (London and New York: Routledge, 1994), Timothy Brennan, *Salman Rushdie and the Third World* (London: Macmillan, 1989), R. S. Pathar, ed. *Quest for Identity in Indian English Writing* (New Delhi: Bahri Publications, 1992); Gerry Smyth, *The Novel and the Nation: Studies in the New Irish Fiction* (London and Chicago: Pluto Press, 1997); David Lloyd, *Anomalous States: Irish Writing and the Post-Colonial Moment* (Durham: Duke University Press, 1993), especially the last chapter "Violence and the Constitution of the Novel." For a discussion of the role of fiction in promoting national identity in Latin America, see Doris Sommer, "Irresistible Romance: The Foundational Fictions of Latin America" in *Nation and Narration*, pp. 71–98. See also there James Snead's article "European Pedigrees/African Contagions: Nationality, Narrative, and Community in Tutuola, Achebe, and Reed," pp. 231–249. Miriam Cooke discusses some of these issues in relation to Lebanon in her article "Reimagining Lebanon," in V. Y. Mudembe, ed. *Nations, Identities, Cultures* (Durham: Duke University Press, 1995) pp. 1075–1102. The Greek novel and modern Greek literature in general show an equally abiding concern with questions of national identity. See, for example, Gregory Jusdanis, *Belated Modernity and Aesthetic Culture: Inventing National Literature* (Minneapolis and London: University of Minnesota Press, 1991). 'Izz al-Dīn Ibrāhīm and others examine aspects of national identity in modern Arabic literature. See 'Izz al-Dīn Ibrāhīm, ed. *al-Huwiyya al-Qawmiyya fil-Adab al-'Arabī al-Mu'āṣir* (Cairo: Jāmi'at al-Duwal al-'Arabiyya, 1999).

12 Salman Rushdie, *Midnight's Children* (London: Jonathan Cape Ltd, 1980; Penguin edition, 1981); Frederick Jameson, "Third World Literature in the Era of Multinational Capitalism," in *Social Text*, 15 (Fall 1986), pp. 65–88. For a critique of Jameson's view see Aijaz Ahmed, *In Theory* (London and New York: Verso, 1992), chapter 3 "Jameson's Rhetoric of Otherness and the 'National Allegory'," pp. 95–122.

13 See Benedict Anderson, *Imagined Communities*, pp. 26 ff.

14 Mahfouz addresses this question directly when he says: "literature, it seems to me, is a revolt against, rather than a reflection of reality. All there is to it is that this revolt may take a direct, revolutionary form, as in modernist literature, or it may assume the guise of manifest reality after effecting in it, secretly, all the necessary changes." Naguib Mahfouz, *Ataḥaddath Ilaykum* (Beirut: Dār al-'Awda, 1977), p. 18.

15 The case for the role of foreign influences on the development of the major genres of modern Arabic literature has been repeatedly made by various scholars. See, for example, Luwīs 'Awaḍ, *al-Mu'aththirāt al-Ajnabiyya fil-Adab al-'Arabī al-Ḥadīth* (Cairo: Ma'had al-Dirāsāt al-'Arabiyya al-'Āliya, Vol. 1, 1962, Vol. 2, 1966); Matti Moosa, *The Origins of Modern Arabic Fiction*, especially chapters I–IV, pp. 7–92; Muḥammad Yūsuf Najm, *al-Masraḥiyya fī al-Adab al-'Arabī al-Ḥadīth: 1847–1914* (Beirut: Dār al-Thaqāfa, 1956); Jacob Landau, *Studies in the Arab Theatre and Cinema* (Philadelphia: University of Pennsylvania Press, 1958).

16 In the classic studies of the novel the question of verisimilitude is invariably subsumed under the rubric of realism which, of course, figures prominently in these studies. In addition to Eric Auerbach's *Mimesis: The Representation of Reality in Western Literature* (Princeton: Princeton University Press, 1953) and George Lukacs'

several works on realism, for example, *Realism in our Time* (New York: Harper Torchbooks, 1964), *Studies in European Realism* (New York: The Universal Library, 1964), *Essays On European Realism*, ed. Rodney Livingstone (London: Lawrence and Wishart Ltd., 1980; MIT edition, 1981), see F. W. J. Hemmings, ed. *The Age of Realism* (Middlesex: Penguin Books, 1974), Ian Watt, *The Rise of the Novel* (Berkeley and Los Angeles: University of California Press, 1957), especially chapter 1 "Realism and the Novel Form"; David Lodge, *Language of Fiction* (New York: Columbia University Press, 1966); Robert Alter, *The Invention of Hebrew Prose: Modern Fiction and the Language of Realism* (Seattle and London: University of Washington Press, 1988).

17 According to 'Abd al-Muḥsin Ṭāhā Badr the educational incentive informed the didactic strand of fiction writing during the formative phase of the Arabic novel. See *Taṭawwur al-Riwāya al-'Arabiyya al-Ḥadītha Fī Miṣr 1870–1938*, pp. 49–115. It is presumably for this transformative power of imaginative fiction that Muḥammad 'Abdu approved of, and encouraged, the writing of novels. Many of the laws governing basic freedoms of thought and expression in contemporary Western societies owe their origins to literary interventions in the legal domain. See, for example, Richard A. Posner, *Law and Literature: A Misunderstood Relation* (Cambridge: Harvard University Press, 1988) and Charles Rembar, *The End of Obscenity* (New York: Harper and Row Publishers, 1968). For discussions of the authoritarian exercise of power in the Arab world see Fu'ād Zakariyyā, *Khiṭāb ilā al-'Aql al-'Arabī*, pp. 80–83; Hishām Sharābī, *Neopatriarchy: A Theory of Distorted Change in Arab Society* (New York: Oxford University Press, 1988); Ṣādiq Jalāl al-Aẓm, *Dhihniyyat al-Taḥrīm* (London: Riad El-Rayyes Books Ltd, 1992); Elizabeth Picard, "Arab Military in Politics: From Revolutionary Plot to Authoritarian State," in Giacomo Luciani, ed. *The Arab State* (Berkeley and Los Angeles: University of California Press, 1990) pp. 189–219. Readers familiar with Mahfouz' *Cairene Trilogy* will readily recognize in the household of Aḥmad 'Abd al-Jawād a paradigmatic representation of authoritarian practice on the microcosmic level of the nuclear family. We will see later how the novel subverts that authority even as it displays its awesome power.

18 Several scholars and critics have alluded to the formative influence of Tawfīq al-Ḥakīm's novel *'Awdat al-Rūḥ* on Nasser. To begin with, there is Nasser's telling autograph of his *Falsafat al-Thawra* (1954) presented to al-Ḥakīm in the following words: "to the reviver of literature, Mr. Tawfīq al-Ḥakīm, with the ardent request that he revive the spirit once again after the Revolution." Quoted in Tawfīq al-Ḥakīm, *Ṣafaḥāt min al-Tārīkh al-Adabī* (Cairo: Dār al-Ma'ārif bi-Miṣr, 1975), p. 154. Ghālī Shukrī quotes Nasser as having said, in the process of defending al-Ḥakīm against a public charge of plagiarism, that he [Nasser] "learned revolution from al-Ḥakīm's novel *'Awdat al-Rūḥ*." See *al-Qāhira*, No. 157 (December 1995), p. 64. Aḥmad Muḥammad 'Aṭiyya identifies the prominent critic Rushdī Ṣāliḥ as the source of this charge against al-Ḥakīm. See *Tawfīq al-Ḥakīm al-Lāmuntamī* (Cairo: Dār al-Mawqif al-'Arabī, 2nd edition, 1984), p. 108. 'Aṭiyya adds further that Nasser went on in that same week to proffer on the writer the prestigious award Medal of the Republic: First Order, "which is restricted to heads of state." ibid. The Russian biographer of Nasser, A. Agaryshev, relates a similar anecdote whereby Nasser's direct intervention on behalf of his "favorite writer" saved al-Ḥakīm from being dismissed from his position as director of Dār al-Kutub. "This writer had a tremendous influence on me," Nasser is quoted to have said to the minister who brought to his attention al-Ḥakīm's unsatisfactory performance at Dār al-Kutub. See A. Agaryshev, *Jamāl 'Abd al-Nāṣir*, tr. Sāmī 'Imāra (Moscow: Dār al-Taqaddum, 1983), p. 101; 'Aṭiyya, *Tawfīq*, p. 107. Vera Micheles Dean cites another example of the influence of literary works on Nasser's political thinking and relates this motif to the larger quest for national identity. She writes: "Egypt has been trying to slough off outside influences, and to get back to

the roots of its own 'Egyptianism', which brings back memories of great cultural glories and military prowess. Premier Nasser expressed this attitude in a speech of March 29, 1955, when he said, invoking the Italian playwright, Pirandello, 'Egypt is in search of a national personality.' This search for its identity, which takes the form of vigorous assertiveness, explains much of Egypt's policy at home and abroad." *The Nature of the Non-Western World* (New York: Mentor Books, 1957), p. 57.

19 Studies on *al-Nahḍa* and its effects on various aspects of modern Arab thought, culture, literature, and identity abound in Arabic. For a representative sample of primary sources and critical discussions see: Muḥammad Kāmil al-Khaṭīb, *al-Iṣlāḥ wa al-Nahḍa* (Damascus: Manshūrāt Wizārat al-Ma'ārif, 1992) 2 volumes; 'Abd al-'Azīz al-Dūrī, *al-Takwīn al-Tārīkhī li l-Umma al-'Arabiyya: Dirāsa fī al-Hawiyya wa al-Wa'y* (Beirut: Markaz Dirāsāt al-Waḥda al-'Arabiyya, 1984); Jābir 'Aṣfūr, *Hawāmish 'Alā Daftar al-Tanwīr* (Kuwait: Dār Su'ād al-Ṣabāḥ, 1994); Salāma Mūsā, *Mā Hiya al-Nahḍa* (Beirut: Maktabat al-Ma'ārif, 1962); 'Alī Umlīl, *al-Iṣlāḥiyya al-'Arabiyya wa al-Dawla al-Waṭaniyya* (Beirut: Dār al-Tanwīr, 1985); Anwar 'Abd al-Malik, *al-Ibdā' wa al-Mashrū' al-Ḥaḍārī* (Cairo: Dār al-Hilāl, 1991); Ḥasan Ḥanafī, *al-Turāth wa al-Tajdīd: Mawqifunā min al-Turāth al-Qadīm* (Cairo: al-Markaz al-'Arabī lil-Baḥth wa al-Nashr, 1980); Burhān Ghalyūn, *al-Wa'y al-Dhātī* (al-Dār al-Bayḍā': Manshūrāt 'Uyūn, 1987); Muwaffaq Zurayq, *Nahḍa am Taghrīb: Qirā'a Thaqāfiyya-Siyāsiyya li-'Ittijāhāt Marḥalat al-Nahḍa min Manẓūr al-Hawiyya* (Beirut: al-Manāra, 1996). This is in addition to the well-known classic works on the subject, for example, George Antonius, *The Arab Awakening* (New York: C. P. Putnam's Sons, 1946); Albert Hourani, *Arabic Thought in the Liberal Age: 1798–1939* (Cambridge: Cambridge University Press, 1962); Ibrāhīm Abū-Lughud, *Arab Rediscovery of Europe* (Princeton: Princeton University Press, 1963); Hishām Sharābī, *Arab Intellectuals and the West: The Formative Years, 1875–1914* (Baltimore and London: The Johns Hopkins Press, 1970).

20 Anwar El Sadat, *In Search of Identity* (New York: Harper and Row, 1978). The Arabic version of Sadat's autobiography appeared under the title: *al-Baḥth 'an al-Dhāt: Qiṣṣat Ḥayātī* (Cairo: al-Maktab al-Miṣrī al-Ḥadīth, 1978). Concerning Sadat's reference to himself as Pharaoh, see Aḥmad Bahā' al-Dīn, *Muḥawarātī ma' al-Sādāt* (Cairo: Dār al-Hilāl, n.d.) p. 64, and Muḥammad Ḥasanayn Haykal, *Kharīf al-Ghaḍab* (Beirut: Sharikat al-Maṭbū'āt lil-Tawzī' wal-Nashr, 1982, 13th printing, 1986) p. 189. In both accounts Sādāt includes Nasser with himself as "the last two great Pharaohs of Egypt." In *Keeping Faith* former president Carter echoes this point, only more circumspectly: "I always had the impression," he writes, "that he [Sadat] looked on himself as inheriting the mantle of authority from the great pharaohs and was convinced that he was a man of destiny." Jimmy Carter, *Keeping Faith: Memoirs of a President* (Toronto and New York: Bantam Books, 1982) p. 328.

21 Northrop Frye, *The Educated Imagination* (Bloomington and London: Indiana University Press, 1964), p. 55.

22 Madan Sarup, *Identity, Culture and the Postmodern World* (Athens: The University of Georgia Press, 1996), p. 1.

23 The inherent interest of the novel in individuality was firmly established by Ian Watt in his classic study *The Rise of the Novel* (Berkeley and Los Angeles: University of California Press, 1957). See especially Chapter Three "Robinson Crusoe, Individualism and the Novel") pp. 60–92. See also Michael McKeon, *The Origins of the English Novel* 1600–1740 (Baltimore and London: The Johns Hopkins University Press, 1987), especially chapter 3 "Histories of the Individual," pp. 90–130. For the role of the novel in defining and abetting nationalist consciousness see references in note 6 above. The philosophical literature about identity, selfhood, and individuality in Western languages is enormous.To cite only three major studies, Charles Taylor, *Sources of the Self: The Making of the Modern Identity* (Cambridge: Harvard

University Press, 1989), Thomas C. Heller, Morton Sosna, and David E. Wellbery, eds *Reconstructing Individualism: Autonomy, Individuality, and the Self in Western Thought* (Stanford: Stanford University Press, 1986), and Gerald N. Izenberg, *Impossible Individuality: Romanticism, Revolution, and the Origins of Modern Selfhood, 1787–1802* (Princeton: Princeton University Press, 1992).

24 Individuals in novels of course appear as fictional characters. They often have to be reprocessed mentally before they can be experienced as ontologically anterior to the fictional roles in which they are cast. In his pioneering book on the novel E. M. Forster devoted two out of nine chapters to what he calls "people." See *Aspects of the Novel* (New York: Harcourt, Brace & World, Inc., 1927). See also W. J. Harvey, *Character and the Novel* (Ithaca and New York: Cornell University Press, 1965), and John V. Knapp, ed., *Literary Character* (Lanham, New York and London: University Press of America, Inc., 1993). For a discussion of the counter tradition in modernist fiction, where the human referent of fictional characters is replaced by a linguistic referent, see Christine Brooke-Rose, "The Dissolution of Character in the Novel," in *Reconstructing Individuality*, pp. 184–196. Catherine Gallagher discusses some of the crucial philosophical and epistemological issues involved in the representation of fictional characters in "Nobody's Story: Gender, Property, and the Rise of the Novel," *Modern Language Quarterly*, 53, No. 3 (September 1992), pp. 263–278, and "George Eliot: Immanent Victorian," *Proceedings of the British Academy*, Vol. 94 (1997), pp. 157–172.

25 Hilary Kilpatrick problematizes this very issue in her article "The Arabic novel: A Single Tradition?" *Journal of Arabic Literature*, Vol. V (1974), pp. 93–107.

26 Flaubert evokes this mystique in a letter to his mother from Alexandria on November 17, 1849: "When we were two hours out from the coast of Egypt I went into the bow with the chief quartermaster and saw the seraglio of Abbas Pasha like a black dome on the blue of the Mediterranean. The sun was bearing down on it. I had my first sight of the Orient through, or rather in, a glowing light that was like melting silver on the sea." Francis Steegmuller, tr. and ed., *Flaubert in Egypt* (Chicago: Academy Chicago Limited Edition, 1979), p. 28. In *Miṣr fī 'Uyūn al-Ghurabā'* (Egypt in the Eyes of Foreigners) (Cairo: al-Hay'a al-Miṣriyya al-'Amma, 1984) Tharwat 'Ukāshah traces aspects of this morbid European fascination with Egypt from Napoleon's boyhood dreams to recent times. For the impression that the "East," particularly Lebanon, left on three prominent European "travelers" (Lamartine, Nerval, and Flaubert) see Hudā 'Adrā, *Thalāth Riḥlāt ilā al-Sharq* (Beirut: Dār al-Ḥusaynī lil-Ṭibā'a wal-Nashr, 1994).

27 Ḥasan al-'Aṭṭār's famous *maqāma* was appended to Jalāl al-Dīn al-Suyūṭī's collection of *maqāmāt*. See *Hādhih al-Maqāmāt al-Suyūṭiyya -Mudhayyala bi Maqāmat Ḥasan al-'Aṭṭār* (Cairo: Ṭab' Ḥajar, 1275 H, 1858/9 CE).

28 In *al-Tārīkh wal-Mu'arrikhūn fī Miṣr fil-Qarn al-Tāsi' 'Ashar* (Port Said: Maktabat al-Thaqāfa al-Dīniyya, 2000) p. 35, Jamāl al-Dīn al-Shayyāl quotes al-Jabarti's account of shaykh Ismā'īl al-Khashshab's apparent infatuation with several members of the entourage of French scholars who accompanied Napoleon to Egypt. Al-Khashshab is said to have composed poems in praise of the beauty of one of these scholars, to whom the Azharite shaykh seems to have taken a special liking. The two are said to have exchanged visits frequently. This is most likely the referential backdrop of al-'Aṭṭār's "fictional" rendition in his famous *maqāma*, "*fil Firinsīs*."

For an insightful discussion of al-'Attar's "*maqāma*," see Shaden M. Tageldin, "On the -I- and Its Dismantlings: Hasan al-'Attar's Anti-History of the French Seduction of Egypt, 1798–1799," in "Disarming Words: Reading (Post)Colonial Egypt's Double Bond to Europe" (PhD dissertation, University of California, Berkeley, 2004), pp. 57–127.

29 Jalāl al-Dīn al-Ṣuyūṭī, *Rashf al-Zalāl Min al-Siḥr al-Ḥalāl* (Beirut: al-Intishār al-'Arabī, 1997).

30 On the "sexualization" of cultural relations between East and West, see George Ṭarabīshī, *Sharq wa-Gharb; Rujūla wa-Unūtha* (Beirut: Dār al-Ṭalī'a, 1977).

31 Bayram al-Tūnisī, *al-Sayyid wa-Imra'atuh fī Bārīs* (Beirut and Sayda: al-Mataba'a al-'Ariyya, n.d.).

32 Although he was born and raised in Alexandria, al-Tūnisī was considered "a foreigner" by the British colonial administration in Egypt, and was thrown out of the country several times in his life for writing anticolonial poetry. Because of his Tunisian descent, he qualified for French "protection," and thus spent most of his prolonged periods of exile in either Tunisia or Paris. His literary works, however, are completely identified with his residence and experience in Egypt. In fact, like Luwīs 'Awaḍ before him, the Egyptian writer Maḥmūd al-Sa'danī considers al-Tūnisī one of the two supreme poets in the Egyptian vernacular. Curiously, the other poet, Ḥusayn Shafīq al-Miṣrī, is also of foreign origin, in this case Turkish. See Maḥmūd al-Sa'danī, *al-Ẓurafā'* (Beirut: Dār al-'Awda, 1974) p. 72. Luwīs 'Awaḍ's appreciation of al-Tūnisī as "the supreme poet of Egypt" originally appeared in the introduction to 'Awaḍ's only collection of poems, *Plutoland*, in 1947, as quoted in Rajā' al-Naqqāsh, *al-In'izaliyyūn fī Miṣr* (Cairo: al-Hay'a al-Miṣriyya al-Āmma lil-Kitāb, 1996), p. 76. After the 1952 Revolution, al-Tūnisī was "granted" full Egyptian citizenship (in 1954), and was awarded highest national honors and prizes in subsequent years. For a comprehensive discussion of al-Tūnisī's remarkable life and works see Marilyn Booth, *Bayram al-Tunisi's Egypt: Social Criticism and Narrative Strategies* (Exeter: Ithaca Press, 1990).

33 Abbas Kelidar puts this matter succinctly: "Throughout the nineteenth century and the early part of the twentieth, Cairo was the center of the intellectual output which dominated the cultural climate of the Arab countries. The printing press made it possible for writers, journalists, and publicists from different parts of the Arab world to reach a wider readership. It consolidated their solidarity; and brought the intellectuals recognition as precursors of modern ideas. They served as the catalyst for the emergence of new concepts, the revival of older notions on the reorganization of society, the state, and the individual's position, as well as the nature of his relationship with both." See his article "Shaykh 'Alī Yūsuf: Egyptian Journalist and Islamic Nationalist," in Marwan R. Buheiry, ed. *Intellectual Life in the Arab East, 1890–1939* (Beirut: Center for Arab and Middle East Studies, American University, 1981), p. 10. See also Ilyās Abū Shabaka, *Rawābiṭ al-Fikr wal-Rūḥ Bayn al-'Arab wal-Faranja* (Beirut: Manshūrāt Dār al-Makshūf, 2nd printing, 1945), pp. 52, 79.

34 See Badr, *Taṭawwur*, pp. 29–32 passim; Moosa, *Origins*, p. 19 passim; Aḥmad Ṭāhir Ḥasanayn, *Dawr al-Shāmiyyīn*, especially pp. 49–55; Abū Shabaka, *Rawābiṭ*, pp. 52, 79.

35 See Rif'at al-Sa'īd, *Thalāthat Lubnāniyyīn fil-Qāhira* (Beirut: Dār al-Ṭalī'a, 1973); Shimon Ballas, *al-Adab al-'Arabī wal-Taḥdīth al-Fikrī* (Germany: Manshūrāt al-Jamal, 1993), pp. 11–37; In *Layāli Saṭīḥ* (Cairo: al-Dār al-Qawmiyya lil-Ṭibā'a wal-Nashr, 1964, originally published in 1906), p. 10, Ḥāfiẓ Ibrāhīm draws attention to the remarkable role the Syrian emigrés played in spreading the Arabic language. So do many other writers and critics. See a sample and discussion of such views in Aḥmad Ṭāhir Ḥasanayn, *Dawr al-Shāmiyyīn*. In *Rawābiṭ*, Ilyās Abū Shabaka notes that many Syrian and Lebanese intellectuals and literati followed Ibrāhīm Pasha to Egypt when he was forcibly evicted from Syria by the European powers in 1840. During his brief reign in Syria, Ibrāhīm had cultivated the Christians of Syria and Lebanon in his attempt to lay the foundations of an Arab state comprising Egypt and the Arab East (pp. 51–52).

36 Although this is the correct orthography of the name, strictly speaking, it is commonly mispronounced as "Abd al-Jawwād." See, for example, Rasheed El-Enany, *Naguib Mahfouz: The Pursuit of Meaning* (London and New York: Routledge, 1993), pp. 5, 6 ff.

37 See Naguib Mahfouz, *Qaṣr al-Shawq* (Cairo: Maṭba'at Miṣr, 1957), pp. 407–408. Unless otherwise indicated, all citations from, and references to the Arabic versions of Mahfouz' works are to the uniform editions of Maktabat Miṣr, which has exclusive rights to publishing Mahfouz' works in Egypt. Page numbers follow the citations in parentheses.

38 Muṣṭafā Bayyūmī, *al-Fukāha 'ind Naguib Mahfouz* (Humor in the Works of Naguib Mahfouz), (Cairo: al-Sharika al-Miṣriyya al-'Ālamiyya lil-Nashr-Longman, 1994).

39 'Abbas Maḥmūd al-'Aqqād, *Muṭāla'āt fil-Kutub wal-Ḥayāt* (Beirut: Dār al-Kitāb al-'Arabī, 1966, 3rd printing), p. 315; originally published in *al-Balāgh* March 17, 1924.

"ولقد كان الدكتور (شبلي شميل) يقول بالحرف "فضونا من غلبتكم يا ادباتية، يا اولاد الكلب!"
وتقول الانسة مي "كان للادباء ان يسألوه: قلمك يقول اننا اولاد القرد وصوتك يقول اننا ابناء
الكلب، فاي الوجهين جدنا؟"

40 Rajā' al-Naqqāsh, *Naguib Mahfouz: Ṣafaḥāt min Mudhakkirātih wa-Aḍwā' Jadīda 'alā Adabih wa-Ḥayātih* (Cairo: Markaz al-Ahrām lil-Tarjama wal-Nashr, 1998) p. 21.

41 Suhayr al-Qalamāwī makes this very point in defense of the use of the *'āmmiyya* in Tawfīq al-Ḥakīm's *'Awdat al-Rūḥ*. See Aḥmad Ibrāhīm al-Hawwārī, *al-Fikra al-'Arabiyya fī Awdat al-Rūḥ* (Cairo: Dār al-Ma'ārif, 1983), p. 118. The question of linguistic diglossia, and its ramifications for modern Arabic literature, have been hotly debated by Arab and non-Arab writers, intellectuals, and scholars for over a century. Opinions on this issue tend to be stark and categorical. To cite just one example, Ibrāhīm 'Abd al-Qādir al-Māzinī had a diametrically opposite view from that of Suhayr al-Qalamāwī on *Awdat al-Rūḥ*. See *al-Fikra*, p. 96. As late as April 2000, Shawqī Dayf was still calling the Egyptian dialect "a corrupt version of the *fuṣḥā*" and "a transient phenomenon." See the transcript of his lecture before the Arabic Language Academy, of which he was the standing president at the time, in *al-Kutub: Wujuhāt Naẓar*, Vol. 2, No. 16 (May 2000), pp. 52–55. For a thorough discussion of the history of the question in Egypt see Naffūsa Zakariyyā Sa'īd, *Tārīkh al-Da'wa ilā al-'Āmiyya fī Miṣr* (Cairo: Dār al-Ma'ārif, 1954), and Yūsuf al-Shārūnī, "Lughat al-Ḥiwār bayn al-'Āmiyya wal-Fuṣḥā," in *al-Majalla* (Cairo) No. 67 (August 1962), pp. 40–54. An inkling of Mahfouz' view on the matter can be found in Naqqāsh, *Naguib Mahfouz: Ṣafaḥāt*, p. 62; Naguib Mahfouz, *Ataḥaddath Ilaykum* (Beirut: Dār al-'Awda, 1977), pp. 48, 61 ff.

42 Sasson Somekh, *Genre and Language in Modern Arabic Literature* (Wiesbaden: Otto Harrassowitz, 1991), especially pp. 3–35. For a critique of Somekh's view see Muḥammad Ṣiddīq, "Partial Theory: A Review of Sasson Somekh's *Genre and Language in Modern Arabic Literature*," *Al-'Arabiyya* 25 (1992), pp. 97–105.

43 *Ṣabāḥ al-Khayr*, No. 6 (February 16, 1956), p. 50, cited in al-Shārūnī, "Lughat al-Ḥiwār," p. 46.

44 The well-known theoretician and advocate of Arab nationalism Sāṭi' al-Ḥuṣrī singles out Arabic as the major unifying factor in this ideology. For a discussion of this matter see, Walid Kazziha, "Another Reading into al-Ḥuṣarī's [*sic*] Concept of Arab Nationalism," in Marwan al-Beheiry, ed. *Intellectual Life in the Arab East, 1890–1939*, pp. 160–163. See also Abū Khaldūn Sāṭi' al-Ḥuṣrī, *fil-Lugha wal-Adab wa 'Alāqatihima bil-Qawmiyya* (Beirut: Markaz Dirāsāt al-Waḥda al-'Arabiyya, 1958, 1985), pp. 29–50.

The role of formal Arabic as a unifying national factor recurs with increasing assertiveness in the polemical articles of another prominent Lebanese Christian writer who never immigrated to Egypt, Mārūn 'Abbūd. See *fil-Mukhtabar* (Lebanon-Ḥarīṣā: al-Maṭba'a al-Būlusiyya, 1952), pp. 28, 51, and especially pp. 71–72 where 'Abbūd mentions his impassioned appeal to Ṭal'at Ḥarb to "blot out this anarchy," that is, the use of the vernacular in Egyptian plays. Al-Māzinī assigns the *fuṣḥā* a similar task and advocates harnessing the aesthetic appeal of fiction to reviving the *fuṣḥā* further. See Hawwārī, *al-Fikra*, p. 96.

45 Aḥmad Ṭāhir Ḥasanayn, *Dawr al-Shāmiyyīn*, p. 49.

46 Ḥāfiẓ Ibrāhīm, *Layālī Saṭīḥ*, p. 7.

47 The last two lines of Ibrāhīm's poem run as follows:

فيا ايها الشيخ الجليل تحية　　ويا ايها القصر المنيف تجلدا
لئن غاب هذا الليث عنك لعلة　　لقد لبثت اثاره فيك شهدا

48 Mahfouz discusses this dual image of the West openly in his conversations with Rajā' al-Naqqāsh, *Naguib Mahfouz: Ṣafaḥāt*, pp. 64–66. See also Muḥammad 'Ābid al-Jābirī, *Al-Mas'ala al-Thaqāfiyya* (Beirut: Markaz Dirāsāt al-Waḥda al-'Arabiyya, 1994), especially pp. 75 ff.

49 Muḥammad Ḥasanayn Haykal's testimony can be found in *Rose El Youssef*, No. 3463 (October 31, 1994), pp. 39–40.

50 The names of the three members of the committee appointed by al-Azhar to look into this matter were not made public at the time and they remained anonymous until recently. 'Alī al-Jawharī identifies the three as Shaykh Muḥammad al-Ghazālī, Shaykh Aḥmad al-Sharbīṣī, and Shaykh Muḥammad Abū Zahra; see 'Alī al-Jawharī, *Ḍajīj Awlād Ḥaratinā* (Cairo: Dār al-Hudā, 1994), p. 55. According to Ghālī Shukrī, it was al-Ghazālī who wrote the report of the committee, a version of which was delivered orally to President Nasser. See Ghālī Shukrī, "Naguib Mahfouz fī Khaṭṭ al-Muwājaha," *al-Qāhira*, No. 157 (December 1995), p. 68.

51 Naguib Mahfouz, *Awlād Ḥāratinā* in *al-A'māl al-Kāmilahl* (Beirut: al-Maktaba al-'Ilmiyya al-Jadīda, n.d.), Vol. 6.

52 While most critics acknowledge the primary allegorical nature of the novel, some have attempted to interpret it "realistically" as a critique of social injustice and authoritarian practices in Egypt and the rest of the Arab world. See Jareer Abu Haydar, "Awlād Ḥāratinā by Naguib Mahfouz: An Event in the Arab World," in *Journal of Arabic Literature*, Vol. 16 (1985), pp. 119–131. Ghālī Shukrī basically echoes this argument but goes a little further and reads the novel as a political indictment of Nasser and his regime. In support of his dubious interpretation Shukrī cites the view of Tharwat Abāẓa who also denies the allegorical representation of religious subject matter in the novel. See Ghālī Shukrī, *al-Qāhira*, pp. 30–86. Until the late seventies, Mahfouz himself seems to have been in agreement with the allegorical interpretation of the work. See Philip Stewart's Introduction to his translation of the novel, *Children of Gebalawī* (London: Heinemann, 1981), p. VII. This is not to suggest, however, that the allegorical interpretation is necessarily incompatible with the novel's realistic character or social message. Realism is as innate to the novel as the critique of social injustice is to all religions. By contrast, restricting interpretation to these obvious levels suppresses the powerful symbolism that undergirds everything else in the novel.

53 See 'Abd al-Ḥamīd Kishk, *Kalimatunā fil-Radd 'Alā Awlād Ḥāratinā* (Cairo: al-Mukhtār al-Islāmīlil-Ṭab' wal-Nashr wal-Tawzī', 1989), pp. 94–109; al-Jawharī, *Ḍajīj*, pp. 15–23.

54 Naguib Mahfouz has often described as "painful" and "horrible" the struggle he endured while trying to choose between philosophy and literature. According to him, 1936 was the decisive year in which the conflict was finally settled in favor of creative writing. See Rajā' al-Naqqāsh, *Naguib Mahfouz: Ṣafaḥāt*, p. 53; Gamal Al-Ghitani, *Naguib Mahfouz Yatadhakkar*, pp. 25–27.

55 Stewart, *Chrildern of Gebalawī*.

56 See Walter Kaufmann, *Nietzsche* (Princeton: Princeton University Press, 1968, 1974), pp. 76 ff.

57 References and allusions to Nietzsche, Marx, Freud, Bergson, and other major Western philosophers abound in Mahfouz' works. It is also relevant to note in this

connection the appearance of 'Abd al-Raḥmān Badawī's book on Nietzsche in 1937. On the whole, the two decades of the 1920s and 1930s produced the most serious "philosophical" and secular challenges to orthodox religious, political, and social thought. The wave of atheism that swept Egypt during the 1930s is symptomatic of this intellectual climate and fervor.

58 For an insightful analysis of the problematic agenda of three generations of Arab/ Islamic reformers, see Shukrī 'Ayyād, *al-Adab fī 'Ālam Mutaghayyir* (Cairo: al-Hay'a al-Miṣriyya al-'Āmma lil-Ta'līf wal-Nashr, 1971), especially pp. 9–20, but also thereafter. See also Muḥammad 'Ābid al-Jābirī, *al-Mas'ala al-Thaqāfiyya*, pp. 75, 76.

59 In point of fact, as Walter Kaufmann shows, Nietzsche's statement laments, rather than celebrates, the "killing" of God by the scientific and technological advances of European civilization. See Kaufmann, *Nietzsche*, p. 96. A similar note of forlorn nostalgia begins to haunt 'Arafa, Jabalāwī's grandson and "killer," in *Awlād* as soon as he realizes the finality of his act and the permanent departure of "the old man."

60 See Muṣṭafā Muḥammad Ramaḍān, *Dawr al-Azhar fil-Ḥayāt al-Miṣriyya Ibbān al-Ḥamla al-Faransiyya wa Maṭla' al-Qarn al-Tāsi' 'Ashar* (Cairo: Maṭba'at al-Jabalāwī, 1986). I discuss at greater length the role of al-Azhar in Egypt's national struggles for independence from foreign rule in Chapter 3.

61 Muḥammad Jalāl Kishk, *Wa-Dakhalt al-Khayl al-Azhar* (Cairo: Dār al-Ma'ārif, 1978), p. 7.

62 See Kamāl 'Abd al-Laṭīf, *Mafāhīm Multabisa fil-Fikr al-'Arabī al-Mu'āṣir* (Beirut: Dār al-Ṭalī'a, 1992); Nissim Rejwan, *Arabs Face the Modern World: Religious, Cultural, and Political Responses to the West* (Gainsville: University Press of Florida, 1998).

63 Chapter 24 of Part Two of *'Awdat al-Rūḥ* postulates the convergence of the myth of Osiris and the emergence of Sa'd Zaghlūl as the modern reincarnation of that myth. The explicit reference to Sa'd Zaghlūl was considered by al-Māzinī a major artistic defect in the novel. See al-Hawwārī, *al-Fikra*, p. 99.

64 See Tawfīq al-Ḥakīm, *Taḥt Shams al-Fikr* (Cairo: Maktabat al-Ādāb, 1938), especially pp. 57–72. See also Aḥmad Ibrāhīm al-Hawwārī, *al-Fikra*, pp. 40–41 ff.

65 Bayly Winder, tr. *The Return of Consciousness* (New York and London: New York University Press, 1985).

66 For a critique of al-Ḥakīm's shifting views about Egypt's national identity, see Muḥammad 'Awda, *al-Wa'y al-Mafqūd* (Cairo: al-Qāhira lil-Thaqāfa al-'Arabiyya, 1975), and Rajā' al-Naqqāsh, *al-In'izaliyyūn fī Miṣr* (Cairo: al-Hay'a al-Miṣriyya al-Āmma lil-Kitāb, 1996). The essays comprising the latter book were originally published separately in 1978. Even the habitually reserved and circumspect Mahfouz finds the volte-face of his lifelong friend, al-Ḥakīm, about Nasser and the Nasserist regime unconscionable. See Naqqāsh, *Naguib Mahfouz: Ṣafaḥāt*, pp. 247–248.

67 Naqqāsh, *Naguib Mahfouz: Ṣafaḥāt*, pp. 134 ff.

68 On the mutations of the question of religion in the various Egyptian constitutions since 1923 see Chapter 3.

69 See Mukhliṣ al-Ṣayyādī, *al-Azhar wa Mashārī' Taṭwīrih: 1872–1970* (Beirut: Dār al-Rāshid, 1992), especially chapters 4 and 5, which deal with the reforms carried out during the Nasser era.

70 Mahfouz relates in an interview with the Egyptian critic, 'Abd al-Raḥmān Abū 'Awf, that Sadat made this remark about *Bidāya wa Nihāya* directly to him. See, *al-Idhā'a wal-Tilifizyon* (December 20, 1986), p. 13.

71 For 'Āmir's threats against Mahfouz on account of *Tharthara Fawq al-Nīl* see Rajā' al-Naqqāsh, *Naguib Mahfouz: Ṣafaḥāt*, pp. 130–131. *Tharthara* was translated into English by Frances Liardet under the title *Adrift on the Nile* (New York: Doubleday, 1993).

72 Ghālī Shukrī, "Naguib Mahfouz fī Khaṭṭ al-Muwājaha," *al-Qāhira*, p. 48.

73 Mahfouz makes no secret of his morbid "anxiety" over the implications of the more transparent among his politically symbolic works. For an instructive example of this condition see Naqqāsh, *Naguib Mahfouz: Ṣafaḥāt*, pp. 129–130.

74 Ibid., p. 133.

75 Mahfouz has often asserted the centrality of politics to his imaginative fiction. Thus, for example, he tells Gamal Al-Ghitani "politics permeates everything I write. You may find (among my works) a story without love, or any other subject, but never without politics, because politics is at the center of our thinking. Even *Awlād Ḥāratinā*, which you might describe as a metaphysical novel, you will find the struggle over the religious endowments." Ghitani, *Naguib Mahfouz Yatadhakkar*, p. 78.

76 'Awaḍ b. Muḥammad al-Qarnī, *al-Ḥadātha fī Mīzān al-Islam*, (Riyāḍ: Dār 'Ālam al-Kutub lil-Nashr wal-Tawzī', 1988). The first issue of the monthly *al-Nāqid* (July 1988) published the entire text of the tape, including the names of the blacklisted writers, pp. 31–46.

77 Adūnīs' views on his own poetry, and on Arabic poetics in general, have received considerable attention. See, for example, his *Zaman al-Shi'r* (Beirut: Dār al-'Awda, 1972), and *al-Shi'riyya al-'Arabiyya* (Beirut: Dār al-Ādab, 1985), tr. Catherine Cobham, *An Introduction to Arab Poetics* (Austin: University of Texas Press, 1990); M. M. Badawi, *A Critical Introduction to Modern Arabic Poetry* (Cambridge: Cambridge University Press, 1975), especially pp. 231–241; Mounah A. Khouri, *Studies in Contemporary Arabic Poetry and Criticism* (Piedmont: Jahan Book Co., 1987), especially chapter 1 "A Critique of Adonis's Perspectives on Arabic Literature and Culture."

There is an extensive literature on the question of *Ḥadātha* and *Aṣāla*, and the relationship between the two, in Arabic, much of which, unfortunately, tends to be polemical in nature. See, for example, 'Abd al-'Aẓīm Ibrāhīm al-Miṭ'anī, *al-Ḥadātha Saraṭān al-'Aṣr* (Cairo: Maktabat Wahba, 1994). For more scholarly discussions, see Munāf Manṣūr, *'Aqliyyat al-Ḥadātha al-'Arabiyya: al-Baḥth 'an al-Bu'd al-Thālith* (Beirut: Maktabat Ṣādir, 1986); *al-Islām wal-Ḥadātha*, a special issue of *Mawāqif* (London: Dar al Saqi, 1990).

78 This Ḥadīth appears in slightly different variations in the sources. The following version from Jalāl al-Dīn al-Suyūṭī's *al-Amr bil-Ittibā' wal-Nahy 'an al-Ibtidā'* (Dammām: Dār Ibn al-Qayyim, 1990), p. 33, enjoys extensive and authoritative documentation:

"اوصيكم بتقوى الله والسمع والطاعة وان كان عبدا حبشيا، فانه من يعش منكم بعدي فسيرى
اختلافا كثيرا، فعليكم بسنتي وسنة الخلفاء الراشدين المهديين، تمسكوا بها وعضوا عليها بالنواجد،
واياكم ومحدثات الامور، فان كل محدثة بدعة وكل بدعة ضلالة."

See also there, p. 67, "innovation is more pleasing to Satan than disobedience: the latter can be forgiven, but not the former."

"البدعة احب الى ابليس من المعصية، المعصية يتاب منها، والبدعة لا يتاب منها"

79 *Al-Nāqid*, ibid.

80 I discuss this phenomenon at some length in Chapter 3.

81 See 'Abbās Maḥmūd al-'Aqqād, *Fī Baytī* (Saida-Beirut: Manshūrāt al-Maktaba al-'Aṣriyya, n.d. first published in 1945), pp. 33–36.

82 Ibid., p. 36.

83 Al-Rāfi'i's low opinion of "the story" was expressed most emphatically in a letter he published in *al-Risāla*, No. 48 (June 4, 1934), under the title "the philosophy of the story and why I shun it," quoted in Muḥsin Jāsim al-Mūsawī, *al-Riwāya al-'Arabiyya: al-Nash'a wal-Taḥawwul* (Baghdad: Manshūrāt Maktabat al-Taḥrīr, 1986), p. 51.

84 'Ādil Kāmil, *Millīm al-Akbar* (Cairo: Maktabat Miṣr, 1944), pp. 3–128.

85 Muṣṭafā al-Shak'a, *Badī' al-Zamān al-Hamadhānī: Rā'id al-Qiṣṣa wal-Maqāla al-Ṣaḥafiyya* (Cairo: Maktabat al-Qāhira al-Ḥadītha, 1959).

86 Muḥammad Rushdī Ḥasan, *Athar al-Maqāma fi Nash'at al-Qiṣṣa al-Miṣriyya al-Ḥadītha* (Cairo: al-Hay'a al-Miṣriyya al-'Āmma lil-Kitab, 1974).
87 Fārūq Khurshīd, *Fil-Riwāya al-'Arabiyya: 'Aṣr al-Tajmī'* (Beirut: Dār al-Shurūq, 1982, 3rd edition).
88 See *al-Ḥayat*, November 28, 1990, for a summary of Al Ghitani's views on the "sixteen centuries of Arabic narrative art." For the views of Sabry Hafez on this matter see, *The Genesis of Modern Arabic Fiction*. See also Yusuf al-Shārūnī, *Ma'al-Riwāya* (Cairo: al-Hay'a al-Miṣriyya al-'Āmma lil-Kitāb, 1984).
89 See 'Abd al-Muḥsin Ṭāhā Badr, *Taṭawwur al-Riwāya*; Matti Moosa, *The Origins of the Arabic Novel.*
90 Yaḥyā Ḥaqqī, *Fajr al-Qiṣṣa al-Miṣriyya* (Cairo: al-Hay'a al-Miṣriyya al-'Āmma lil-Kitāb, 1997). All citation in the text are taken from this edition.
91 Ḥusayn Fawzī, *Sindbād Fi Riḥlat al-Ḥayāt* (Cairo: Dār al-Ma'ārif, 1968), p. 56.
92 See Ṣonalla Ibrahim's introduction to the 1986 complete edition of *Tilk al-Rā'iḥa* (Cairo: Dār Shuhdī, 1986), p. 6.
93 Ḥaqqī, *Fajr al-Qiṣṣa*, p. 21.
94 Ibid., pp. 22–23.
95 Ibid., p. 21
96 Ibid., pp. 21–22.
97 Muḥsin Jāsim al-Mṣsawī, *al-Istishrāq fil-Fikr al-'Arabī* (Beirut: al-Mu'assasa al-'Arabiyya lil-Dirāsāt wal-Nashr, 1993).
98 Quoted in Timothy Brennan, *Salman Rushdie and the Third World* (London: Macmillan, 1989), p. 47.
99 Ihab Hassan, "Globalism and Its Discontents: Notes of a Wandering Scholar," *Profession* (1999), p. 99. I thank Shaden Tageldin for bringing this article to my attention.
100 "What holds for Egypt holds for the rest of Muslim Arabs everywhere," writes Nessim Rejwan in *Arabs Face the Modern World* (Florida: University Press of Florida, 1998), p. 4.

2 TANGENTS OF IDENTITY: THE POETICS OF SPACE IN THE EGYPTIAN NOVEL

1 Egypt's formal name and form of government, like its borders, changed several times in the course of the country's modern history. In the twentieth century alone it changed from a state headed by a Khideve under nominal Ottoman suzerainty, to one headed by a Sultan, then a king, under British rule, before it became a fully independent republic in 1956. In a further permutation during this latest republican phase the name changed to that of the United Arab Republic in 1958, in recognition of the union between Egypt and Syria (1958–1961), only to be changed again to that of the Arab Republic of Egypt a few years after the collapse of the short-lived union. Mahfouz considers the exclusion of Egypt's name, *Miṣr*, in the United Arab Republic one of Nasser's unforgivable sins. See Naguib Mahfouz, *Amām al-'Arsh* (Cairo: Maktabat Miṣr, 1983), pp. 193, 195. See also Muḥammad Salamāwī *Ḥiwārāt ma' Naguib Mahfouz* (Beirut: Dār al-Shurūq, 1997).
2 Article Two of the UN Charter states: "All Members shall refrain in their international relations from the threat or use of force against the territorial integrity or political independence of any state, or in any other manner inconsistent with the Purposes of the United Nations." See also Nazih N. Ayubi, *Over-stating the Arab State: Politics and Society in the Middle East* (London and New York: I. B. Rauris Publishers, 1995).
3 For a good examination of the subject of borders in modern Latin American literature see D. Emily Hicks, *Border Writing: The Multidimensional Text* (Minneapolis and Oxford: University of Minnesota Press, 1991). For a discussion of the issue of borders

in the context of "nation-states" in the Arab world see Ayubi, *Over-stating the Arab State*, especially chapter 4 "The Arab State: Territorial or Pan-Arabist?" pp. 135–163. See also Giacomo Luciani, *The Arab State* (Berkeley and Los Angeles: University of California Press, 1990).

4 See Ayubi, *Over-stating the Arab State*, ch. 3 "State Formation in the Modern Era: the Colonial/Indigenous Mix," pp. 86–134.

5 Israel Gershoni and James P. Jankowski, *Egypt, Islam, and the Arabs: The Search for Egyptian Nationhood* (New York and Oxford: Oxford University Press, 1986), pp. 6–7.

6 Yūnān Labīb Rizq, *Ṭābā: Qaḍiyyat al-ʻAṣr* (Cairo: Markaz al-Ahrām lil-Tarjama wal-Nashr, 1989), p. 7. See also Fatḥī Raḍwān "Ṭābā Bayn al-Tārīkh wal-Siyāsa," *al-Hilāl* (July 1986), pp. 44–48.

7 Rizq, *Ṭābā*, p. 325.

8 See Fatḥī Raḍwān, *Muṣṭafā Kāmil* (Cairo: Dār al-Maʻārif bi-Miṣr, 1974), p. 46.

9 Muḥammad Ḥusayn Haykal, *Zaynab* (Cairo: Kitāb al-Hilāl, 1953, 3rd edition), p. 11.

10 Ibid., p. 8. Curiously, at the beginning of the century the law profession was not held in much higher esteem, if at all, than that of fiction wirting in Egypt. Aḥmad Bahā' al-Dīn relates that a lawyer was commonly called a *safīh*, that is, a stupid, insolent fellow. According to Bahā' al-Dīn it took the exemplary personality and stature of someone like Saʻd Zaghlūl to rehabilitate the profession. See Aḥmad Bahā' al-Dīn, *Ayyām lahā Tārīkh* (Cairo: Dār al-Shurūq, 1985, 2nd edition), p. 104.

11 ʻAbd al-Raḥmān al-Rāfiʻī, *ʻAṣr Ismāʻīl* (Cairo: Maktabat al-Nahḍa al-Miṣriyya, 1932; 2nd edition, 1948), Vol. 1, p. 7.

12 Ibid., p. 5.

13 Ibid., p. 106.

14 Ibid., pp. 105–106.

15 The terms "imagined communities" and "enframed colsures" are borrowed, respectively, from Benedict Anderson's *Imagined Cummunities* (London and New York: Verso, 1983) and Timothy Mitchell's *Colonizing Egypt* (Berkeley: University of California Press, 1988).

16 See Roger Allen, *The Arabic Novel: An Historical and Critical Introduction* (Syracuse: Syracuse University Press, 1982), especially chapter III, "The Period of Maturity," pp. 46–86.

17 In the lengthy introduction to his English translation of *Ḥadīth* Roger Allen treats many crucial historical, biographical, textual, and literary issues associated with the production, interpretation, and overall significance of this important work. See Roger Allen, *A Period of Time* (Oxford: Middle East Center, 1992).

18 Al-Afghānī's encomium is contained in a letter addressed to the author, which appears as a preface to the second edition of the book.

19 For a discussion of Al-Ghitani's use of this traditional genre of Arabic historical writing, see Samia Mehrez, *Egyptian Writers Between History and Fiction* (Cairo: The American University in Cairo Press, 1994), especially chapter three, "Re-Writing the City: the Case of Khitat al-Ghitani," pp. 58–77.

20 Ibid., p. 105.

21 Allen, *The Arabic Novel*, pp. 13–14.

22 Tawfīq al-Ḥakīm, *ʻAwdat al-Rūḥ* (Beirut: Dār al-Kitāb al-Lubnānī, 1974), pp. 3–4.

23 Raymond Williams, *The Country and the City* (Oxford: Oxford University Press, 1973).

24 Made perhaps more widespread by the title of Tawfīq al-Ḥakīm's popular work *Yawmiyyāt Nā'ib fil-Aryāf* (Cairo: lajnat al-ta'lif wal-tarjama wal-nashr, 1937).

25 See El-Said Badawi and Martin Hinds, *A Dictionary of Egyptian Arabic* (Beirut: Maktabat Lubnan, 1986), under *rīf*, and *bandar*.

26 See Khairiya El-Bishlawi, "Frantic for Laughs," *Al-Ahram Weekly* (January 27–February 2, 2000).

27 See Al Kharrat's foreword to *Writing the Self: Autobiographical Writing in Modern Arabic Literature*, eds, Robin Ostle, Ed de Moor, and Stefan Wild (London: Saqi Books, 1998) pp. 14 ff.
28 Yaḥyā Ḥaqqī, *Fajr*, p. 15.
29 See the Introduction to M. M. Badawi's translation of *Qindīl Umm Hāshim* (*The Saint's Lamp*) (Leiden: Brill, 1973).
30 Franco Moretti, *Atlas of the European Novel 1800–1900* (London and New York: Verso, 1998), p. 100.
31 Ṣalāḥ Faḍl, *Ta'thīr al-Thaqāfa al-Islāmiyya fil-Kūmīdya al-Il'ilāhiyya li Dāntī* (Cairo: Mu'assasat Mukhtār lil-Nashr wal-Tawzī', 1993; The Influence of Islamic Culture on Dante's Divine Comedy).
32 See Rajā' al-Naqqsh, *Naguib Mahfouz: Ṣafaḥāt*, p. 35.
33 Naguib Mahfouz, *Ataḥddath Ilaykum*, p. 29.
34 This is as true of *Khān al-Khalīlī* (Cairo: Maktabat Miṣr, 1946) as it is of the three parts of *The Trilogy*: *Bayn al-Qaṣrayn* (Cairo: Maktabat Miṣr, 1956) *Palace Walk*, tn. William Maynard Hutchins and Olive E. Kenny (New York: Doubleday, 1990); *Qaṣr al-Shawq* (Cairo: Maktabat Miṣr, 1957) *Palace of Desire*, tr. William Maynard Hutchins, Lorne M. Kenny, and Olive E. Kenny (New York: Doubleday, 1991); and *al-Sukkariyya* (Cairo: Maktabat Miṣr, 1957) *Sugar Street*, tr. William Maynard Hutchins and Angele Botros Samaan (New York: Doubleday, 1992).
35 Cafes figure as prominently in Mahfouz' life as they do in his fiction. It is not surprising therefore that he should single out the cafe as one of the three major sources of inspiration in his writing; the other two being his job in the government bureaucracy and the traditional neighborhood or alley, *ḥāra*. See, for example, Rajā' al-Naqqsh, *Naguib Mahfouz: Ṣafaḥāt*, p. 46.
36 Quoted in Derk Gregory "The Rumour of Cairo: the City of the Arabian Nights and 'Paris-on-the-Nile'" (p. 19) a paper delivered at a symposium on "Cairo during the nineteenth century" held at at UC Berkeley on October 29, 1999.
37 S. M. Stern writes "I should like to suggest that one of the most essential characteristics of the Islamic city is the looseness of its structure, the absence of corporate municipal institutions." "The Constitution of the Islamic City," in *The Islamic City: A Colloquium*, ed. A. H. Hourani and S. M. Stern (Oxford and Philadelphia: Burno Cassirer and University of Pennsylvania Press, 1970), p. 26.
38 Ervin Y. Galantay, "Islamic Identity and the Metropolis: Continuity and Conflict," in Abdulaziz Y. Saqqaf, ed. *The Middle East City: Ancient Traditions Confront a Modern World* (New York: Paragon House Publishers, 1987), p. 9.
39 Lawrence Durrell, *The Aexandria Quartet* (London: Faber and Faber, 1962). All quotations are from this one-volume edition; page numbers follow the quotation in parentheses.
40 Edwar Al Kharrat, *Iskandariyyatī* (Cairo and Alexandria: Dār wa Maṭābi' al-Mustaqbal, 1994), pp. 6–14.
41 Ibid.
42 Ibid., p. 6.
43 Ibid., pp. 5–6.
44 For a discussion of these issues see Magda al-Nowaihi, "Memory and Imagination in Edwar Al Kharrat's Turābuhā Za'farān," *Journal of Arabic Literature*, Vol. XXV (1994), pp. 34–57.
45 Al Kharrat elaborates his views on the theory and practice of narrative in different places in his works. A good representative sample can be found in the collection of essays, *al-Ḥasāsiyya al-Jadīda: Maqālāt fil-Ẓāhira al-Riwā'iyya* (Beirut: Dār al-Ādāb, 1993).
46 The identity of the narrator overlaps considerably, but does not completely coincide with that of the writer in Al Kharrat's work. For a discussion of the relation between

the two, especially the subtle distinctions between them, see al-Nowaihi, "Memory and Imagination," pp. 52–57.

47 Al-Nowaihi writes: "Thus certain images, by virtue of their frequent recurrence and their placement in key parts in the narrative, become symbols, framing the text and anchoring it. The most recurrent of these images are those of open spaces, of what may be called 'primitive immensities'—the sky and birds in flight, and the sea and its shore," ibid., p. 42.

48 For example, in *Turābuhā Za'farān*, pp. 10, 12, 16, 18, 29, 33, 34, 37, 38, 41, 65, and so on. Similarly, the first line of *Yā Banāt Iskandariyya*, reads: "as if I am entering through the narrow door directly to the dark stone stair-case in the house of Jullanār alley," p. 9. See also, pp. 13, 14, 25, 32, 42, 43, 48, 54, 68, 75, and so on.

49 Al Kharrat makes several references to Keats in these works, which suggests a possible romantic influence on him as regards the definition of beauty. See, for example, *Yā Banāt Iskandariyya*, p. 57. The last image of chapter three in that work is highly reminiscent of Keats' *Ode To A Grecian Urn*. It reads: "To whom is the smoke of this desolate sacrifice raised? Who will accept it? And whom will it please? Or will it be rejected and returned to the youth as he is stepping into manhood, his foot lifted across time, never to land?" p. 58.

50 Homi K. Bhabha, ed. *Nation and Narration* (London and New York: Routledge, 1990), p. 294.

51 'Abd al-Raḥmān al-Rāfi'ī, *'ASr Ismā'īl* (Cairo: Maktabat al-Nahḍa al-Miṣriyya, 1932, 2nd edition, 1948), Vol. 1, pp. 5 ff.

52 Muṣṭafā Muḥammad Ramaḍān, *Dawr al-Azhar fil-Ḥayat al-Miṣriyya Ibbān al-Ḥamla al-Faransiyya* (Cairo: Maṭba'at al-Jabalāwī, 1986), pp. 139, 150, 192 ff.

53 'Abbās Maḥmūd al-'Aqqād, *Sa'd Zaghlūl* (Cairo: Maṭba'at Ḥijāzī, 1936), p. 499.

54 'Abd al-Raḥmān Munīf links the emergence of the novel causally to the complexity of urban experience and life in the city. See *al-Kātib wal-Manfā: Humūm al-Riwāya al-'Arabiyya* (Beirut: al-Mu'assasa al-'Arabiyya lil-Dirāsāt wal-Nashr, 1994), p. 36.

55 Ibid.

56 See Sonalla Ibrahim's introduction to the 1986 edition of *Tilk al-Rā'ḥa* (Cairo: Dār Shuhdī, 1986), pp. 9–10.

57 John Waterberry, *Egypt: Burdens of the Past/Options for the Future* (Bloomington and London: Indiana University Press, 1978), p. 314.

58 J. Christopher Herold, *Napoleon in Egypt* (London: Hamish Hamilton, 1962), p. 10. The question of "ill-treatment" comes up in Napoleon's proclamation, ibid., p. 69.

59 Waterbury, ibid., p. 316.

60 See 'Abd al-Muḥsin Ṭāhā Badr, *al-Riwā'ī wal-Arḍ* (Cairo: Dār al-Ma'ārif, 1983).

61 Ibid., p. 58.

62 Ibid.

63 Ibid., p. 63.

64 Raymond Williams, *The Country and the City*, pp. 35 ff.

65 This xenophobia finds its most compelling example in the treatment of Muṣṭafā Sa'īd by the native residents of the Sudanese village in which he settles after his return from Europe in Al Tayeb Saleh's novel, *Season of Migration to the North*.

66 These connections are not always clearly differentiated in the narrative. Inasmuch as they involve the first person narrator and the heroine, they benefit from the intimacy and protection that accrue from his exclusive control of the narrative point of view. Beyond the structural (and possibly autobiographical) bearings, what narrative, political, or moral value attach to the abortive "sexual" encounters beween the narrator and Waṣīfa, especially given the site at which they occur? In the absence of any textual interpretive clues, or further substantive development, these truncated episodes remain indeterminate and do not cohere with any of the recognizable structures of meaning in the novel. This indeterminacy is symptomatic, and may indeed be a result

of a larger problem which Badr identified as al-Sharqāwī's failure to stabilize the status of his first person narrator in the narrative.

67 Badr, *al-Riwā'ī*, p. 131.

68 Fatḥī Ghānim, *al-Jabal* (Cairo: Rose El Youssef, 1959).

69 'Abd al-Ḥakīm Qāsim, *Ayyām al-Insān al-Sab'a* (Cairo: Kitābāt Jadīda, 1969).

3 DIVINING IDENTITIES: RELIGION AND THE EGYPTIAN NOVEL

1 Fatḥ Raḍwān, *Dawr al-'Amā'im fī Tārīkh Miṣr al-Ḥadīth* (Cairo: al-Zahrā', 1982; The Role of the Turbaned (Shaykhs) in Modern Egyptian History), p. 15.

اذا تأمل الانسان في تاريخ مصر الحديث، منذ بدأ، حتى اللحظة التي نكتب فيها هذه السطور، (١٩٨٢)، ظهرت له حقيقة غريبة، وهي ان مصر الحديثة، صاغها وصورها والهمها بالفكر، ودعاها الى العمل، ورسم لها طريق النهضة، شيوخ لم يتخلوا عن العمامة، ولا عن الجبة والقفطان، وحرصوا على اصول الحياة القديمة في الدار وفي خارج الدار، فأكلوا وشربوا، وتبادلوا احاديث الأنس، على النسق الذي حرص عليه وتابعه آباؤهم واجدادهم، وان هؤلاء الشيوخ، على شدة حرصهم على سالف العادات، وقديم المناهج، كانوا قادة حركات تجديد، ورواد نهضات تحرر، وناثري بذور ثورة، وطليعة عهد جديد. وأنهم ثاروا وتمردوا، واصطدموا بقوى اكبر منهم، ولكنهم لم يتزلزلوا ولم يتخلوا عن رسالتهم، ولم يداخلهم الخوف، او يتسرب اليهم العور بالنقص.

2 See, for example: 'Ābid Tawfīq al-Hāshimī, *al-Wajīz fil-Adab al-Islāmī al-Mu'āṣir wa-Tārīkhuh* (Beirut: Mu'assasat al-Risāla, 2000). This four-volume "work" consists of brief biographical entries and a sample of works by Muslim authors who wrote in the "traditional Arab/Islāmic styles and were, therefore, shunned by critics and readers weaned on the new, imported genres: the novel, theatre, and short story," Vol. 1, p. 8; Naguib al-Kaylānī, *Āfāq al-Adab al-Islāmī* (Beirut: Mu'assasat al-Risāla, 1985); Ṣābir 'Abd al-Dāyim, *al-Adab al-Islāmī Bayn al-Naẓariyya wal-Taṭbīq* (Zaqāzīq: Dār al-Arqam, 1990); Aḥmad Muḥammad 'Alī, *al-Adab al-Islāmī Ḍarūra* (Cairo: Dār al-Ṣaḥwa, 1991); Ma'mūn Farīz Jarrār, *Khaṣā'is al-Qiṣṣa al-Islāmiyya* (Jadda: Dār al-Manāra, 1988); Muḥammad Ḥasan Burayghash, *fil-Adab al-Islāmī al-Mu'āṣir: Dirāsa wa-Taṭbīq* (Beirut: Mu'assasat al-Risāla, 1998); *Naḥw Adab Islāmī: al-Qiṣṣa al-Islāmiyya al-Mu'āṣira* ('Ammān: Dār al-Bashīr, 1992).

3 *Ḥadīth* was first serialized in *Miṣbāḥ al-Sharq* in 1898–1899 before it appeared in book form in 1907. For more details see Roger Allen, *A Period of Time*.

4 Some scholars have since questioned the sincerity of this "recanting," especially on the part of Muḥammad Ḥusayn Haykal and Ṭāhā Ḥusayn. See Al-Sayyid Aḥmad Faraj, *Judhūr al-'ilmāniyya* (Manṣūra: Dār al-Wafā', 1985), p. 81. A public display of this ambivalence is captured in Laṭīfa al-Zayyāt's *Ḥamlat Taftīsh: Awrāq Shakhṣiyya* (Cairo: Dār al-Hilāl, 1992), p. 96, where she relates that during Ṭāhā Ḥusayn's funeral on October 16, 1973 the patriotic slogan "*bilādī, bilādī*" (homeland, homeland) suddenly changed at one point to the Islāmic cry "lā ilāh illā allāh" (there is no God but Allah).

5 Officially, Sayyid Quṭb was sent by the Egyptian government to the United States to study educational systems there with a view to reforming the education system of Egypt along similar lines. Since by 1948 he was already a well-known public figure and a highly visible Islamic activist, the decision to send him to America on such a vague assignment raises more questions than it answers. For a discussion of this matter see 'Ādil Ḥammūda, *Sayyid Quṭb min al-Qarya ilā al-Mishnaqa* (Cairo: Sīnā lil-Nashr, 1987; Sayyid Quṭb: From the Village to the Gallows), especially pp. 79–101.

6 Ṣāfīnāz Kāẓim, *Rūmantīkiyyāt* (Cairo: Dār al-Hilāl, 1970), pp. 28–29 ff. According to his own "confessions," Muṣṭafā Maḥmūd was a confessed atheist for nearly a quarter

of a century. In fact, he is said to have founded an "association of atheists" at the age of twelve. He cites an egregious example of superstition perpetrated on him and other children by a charlatan shaykh as the source of his disenchantment with traditional Islām and his subsequent embrace of atheism. See Maḥmūd Fawzī, *I'tirāfāt Muṣṭafā Maḥmūd* (Cairo: Dār al-Nashr Hātiyyih, 1991), pp. 26 ff.

7 Ṣāfīnāz Kāẓim, *'An al-Sijn wal-Ḥurriyya* (Cairo: al-Zahrā' lil-I'lām, 1986) pp. 33 ff.

8 See Fu'ād Zakariyyā, *al-Ṣaḥwa al-Islāmiyya fī Mīzān al-'Aql* (Cairo: al-Fikr al-Mu'āṣir, 2nd edition, 1987).

9 Ghālī Shukrī, *al-Thawra al-Muḍāḍḍa fī Miṣr* (Beirut: Dār al-Ṭalī'a lil-Ṭibā'a wal-Nashr, 1978). The English version of this book is titled *Egypt: Portrait of a President 1971–1980: Counter Revolution in Egypt* (London: Zed Press, 1981).

10 Martin Smith and Lowell Bergman, "Saudi Time Bomb," *Frontline*, PBS, 2001. See also William Dalrymple, "The Truth About Muslims," *New York Review of Books* (November 4, 2004), especially p. 34, where Dalrymple writes:

> It is true that just as there have been some strands of Christian thinking that have always been deeply hostile to Islam, so within Islam there have been schools of thought that have always harbored a deep hostility toward Christians, Jews, and other non-Islamic religions and civilizations, notably the Wahhabi and Salafi schools dominant in modern Saudi Arabia. Until this century, however, the Wahhabis were a theological movements of only localized significance and were widely regarded by most Muslims as an alien sect bordering on infidelity—kufr. It is the oil wealth of modern Saudi Arabia that has allowed the Wahhabis to spread their narrow-minded and intolerant brand of Islam, notably by the funding of extremist Wahhabi, Salafi, and Deobandi madrasas across the Islamic world since the mid-1970, with the disasterous results we see today.

11 This approach ultimately rests on a prophetic tradition, *ḥadīth*, that exists in slightly different versions, but to the same epistemological/ethical effect, namely, that "wisdom/ knowledge belongs to the believer by right, therefore to find it is to retrieve it"; الحكمة ضالة المؤمن حيثما وجدها ثقفها.

12 'Abd al-Ṣabūr Shāhīn, *Qiṣṣat Abū Zayd wa-inḥisār al-'ilmāniyya fī Jāmi'at al-Qāhira* (al-Riyāḍ: al-Nāshirūn al-'Arab, n.d.).

13 For an excellent discussion of the symbolic ramifications of the attempt on Mahfouz' life to the discourse of the nation, see Hosam Aboul-Ela, "The Writer Becomes Text: Naguib Mahfouz and State Nationalism in Egypt," *Biography*, Vol. 27, No. 2 (Spring 2004).

14 It is common knowledge now that many of the major concepts in Sayyid Quṭb's views on political Islām are in fact borrowed from the work of Abū al-A'lā al-Mawdūdī; hence the quotation marks around "theorizing." This is particularly true of the key concepts of *takfīr*, *hijra*, and *jihād*, which correspond to the three major stages in the trajectory of militant Islām in Egypt during the second half of the twentieth century, namely: the declaration of both society and government in Egypt, as in most Muslim countries, un-Islāmic; the necessity of withdrawing from both momentarily in order to regroup and reorganize for fighting them; and, finally, the waging of armed struggle against them until they revert to true Islām by surrendering all sovereignty, *ḥākimiyya*, exclusively to Allāh. See Ḥammūda, *Sayyid*, pp. 131–146 ff. In *al-Ikhwān al-Muslimūn: wal-Tanẓīm al-Sirrī* (Cairo: Roz al-Yūsuf, 1982), p. 214, 'Abd al-'Aẓīm Ramaḍān shows that it was Ṣāliḥ 'Ashmāwī who first used these key concepts in an article published in 1954 in *al-Da'wa*, of which Sayyid Quṭb was chief editor.

Since literature on political Islam in English has become widely available in recent times, I will mention here only two major books that deal with the subject, especially as it bears on Sayyid Quṭb. These are: John E. Esposito, ed. *Voices of Resurgent Islam*

(New York and Oxford: Oxford University Press, 1983), and Ibrahim M. Abu-Rabi', *Intellectual Origins of Islamic Resurgence in the Modern Arab World* (Albany: State University of New York Press, 1996).

15 Ḥammūda, *Sayyid*, p. 34.

16 Ibid., p. 56.

17 Sulaymān Fayyāḍ, "Taḥawwulāt Kātib: Sayyid Quṭb bayn al-Naqd al-Adabī wa-Jāhiliyyat al-Qarn al-'Ishrīn," *al-Hilāl* (September 1986), p. 65. See also 'Alī Shalash, *al-Tamarrud 'alā al-Adab: Dirāsa fī Tajribat Sayyid Quṭb* (Beirut: Dār al-Shurūq, 1994).

18 Sayyid Quṭb, *Kutub wa-Shakhṣiyyāt* (Beirut: Dār al-Shurūq, n.d.), p. 159.

19 In the aforesaid article, the writer Sulaymān Fayyāḍ asserts that soon after the 1952 Revolution Sayyid Quṭ showed him pictures of himself with several of the Free Officers, including Nasser, in his flat in Ḥilwān, a southern suburb of greater Cairo. On that occasion, according to Fayyāḍ, Sayyid Quṭb even pointed to the tree under which the officers used to sit to plot the takeover. See, Fayyāḍ, "Taḥawwulāt," pp. 62–63. See also Ḥammūda, *Sayyid*, pp. 107–108.

20 Ḥammūda, *Sayyid*, p. 35.

21 See 'Abd al-'Azīz Sharaf, *Adab al-Sīra al-Dhātiyya* (Cairo: Longman, 1992), p. 63.

22 See Khayrī Shalabī, *Muḥākamat Ṭāhā Ḥusayn* (Cairo: Dār wa-Maṭābi' al-Mustaqbal, 1994).

23 This is a main theme, for example, of Timothy Mitchell's book *Colonising Egypt* (Berkeley and Los Angeles: University of California Press, 1988).

24 Fatḥī Raḍwān, *Dawr al-'Amā'im fī Tārīkh Miṣr al-Ḥadīth*, p. 53.

25 I deal with this issue more extensively in "Deconstructing the Saint's Lamp," *Journal of Arabic literature*, Vol. XVII (1986), pp. 126–145.

26 See Ḥaqqī, *Qindīl*, p. 18 ff., and p. 53 for the night of visitation.

27 See Abū al-Walīd Muḥammad ibn Aḥmad al-Azraqī, *Akhbār Makka* (Beirut: Dār al-Andalus, 1969, 3rd edition), p. 88. The following summary version of al-Azraqī's account in English is by Emel Esin, *Mecca the Blessed; Madinah the Radiant* (New York: Crown Publishing, Inc., 1963), p. 35. I wish to thank my colleague, Hamid Algar, for bringing this translation to my attention.

> At the height of their power, the Jurhum became neglectful of their duties as keepers of the Ka'bah. Far from maintaining peace in the sacred precinct, the temple guardians began to steal from the pilgrims the gifts they brought to the sanctuary. Some young men attempted to rob the Ka'bah of its treasures. They posted a guard at each of its four corners, while a fifth tried to climb into the roofless building from above. He, however, was struck dead before he could enter, and the others fled in terror.
>
> A woman called Nailah and her lover Isaf, who had made a tryst within the precincts of the Ka'bah, were turned to stone. The reigning Mudad, who viewed these profanations with indignation and alarm, ordered that the petrified bodies of Nailah and Isaf should be placed as a warning to other potential sinners on the hill of Safa and Marwah, where Hagar had once searched for water. He was afraid that these acts of sacrilege might bring down the judgment of God upon the Jurhum. Indeed, it seemed that his fears were justified, for the waters of the miraculous Zamzam well began to sink, and at length dried up.

28 It is perhaps for this reason that neither has been translated into English, so many years after the writer received the Nobel Prize for Literature (1988).

29 In 1937 Ismā'īl Adham published a short article titled "limādhā Anā Mulḥid" (Why I am an Atheist), which he later printed in a pamphlet and distributed openly in Cairo.

For a critique of this article see Vol. 3 of Adham's collected works, ed. Aḥmad Ibrāhīm al-Hawwārī, *al-Mu'allafāt al-Kāmila lil-Duktor Ismā'īl Aḥmad Adham: Qaḍāyā wa-Munāqashāt* (Cairo: Dār al-Ma'ārif, 1986), pp. 92–118. Though by no means original, Adham's views appear typical of the general climate that induced similar antireligious sentiments and attitudes in Sayyid Quṭb, Muṣṭafā Maḥmūd, and other Egyptians, actual and fictional alike.

30 For an excellent discussion of Islamic banking, see Ibrahim Warde, *Islamic Finance in the Global Economy* (Edinburgh: Edinburgh University Press, 2000).

31 See Muḥammad Ṣiddīq, "Ishkāliyyat al-Ma'rifa fil-Riwāya al-'Arabiyya," *Mawāqif*, 70–71 (Winter–Spring 1993), pp. 152 ff.

32 For the turbulent history of reform at al-Azhar see 'Abd al-Muta'āl al-Ṣa'īdī, *Tārīkh al-Iṣlāḥ fil-Azhar wa-Ṣafaḥāt min al-Jihād fil-Iṣlāḥ* (Cairo: Maṭba'at al-I'timād, n.d.); A. Chris Eccel, *Egypt, Islam, and Social Change: Al-Azhar in Conflict and Accommodation* (Berlin: Klaus Schwarz, 1984).

33 See, for example, Adolf Grunbaum, *The Foundations of Psychoanalysis: A Philosophical Critique* (Berkeley: University of California Press, 1984); and Frederick Crews, *Out of My System: Psychoanalysis, Ideology, and Critical Method* (New York: Oxford University Press, 1975).

In this chapter, I have used the following symbols to refer to different volumes of the Arabic edition of *The Cairnere Trilogy* B—volume 1, Q—volume 2, and S—volume 3. The numbers following these symbols within parentheses indicate the relevant page numbers.

34 See George Ṭarabīshī, *'Uqdat Ūdīb fil-Riwāya al-'Arabiyya* (Beirut: Dār al-Ṭalī'a lil-Ṭibā'a wal-Nashr, 1982).

35 Frederick Crews, ed. *Psychoanalysis and Literary Process* (Cambridge: Winthrop Publishers, Inc., 1970), p. 15. Crews has since completely renounced psychoanalysis. That fact notwithstanding, the general principle he enunciates here is still eminently applicable to literary texts that invite a psychoanalytic interpretation. The way out of the implicit tautology "psychoanalytic interpretation best explains psychoanalytic texts" must go through, not circumvent, the psychoanalytic entanglement, whatever one thinks of the general validity, or lack thereof, of psychoanalysis as a whole.

36 This is the drift of Edward Said's review article "Good Bye to Mahfouz," in the *London Review of Books* (December 8, 1988), pp. 10–11.

37 Mahfouz himself has commented extensively on this affinity, though, as is his wont on all personal and autobiographical matters, always obliquely. In Al Ghitani's *Naguib Mahfouz Yatadhakkar*, for example, he admits that "a significant part of myself went into *The Trilogy* and that is represented by Kamāl 'Abd al-Jawād.... Kamāl's crisis is my crisis, and a considerable part of his suffering echoes mine; hence my love and nostalgia for *The Trilogy*," p. 68. Elsewhere, he seems less willing to own up to the implicit emotional identification and to limit the similarity with Kamāl exclusively to the intellectual aspect. See, for example, Mahfouz, *Ataḥaddath Ilaykum*, pp. 79, 84 ff.

38 Otto Rank, *The Incest Theme in Literature and Legend*, tr. Gregory C. Richter (Baltimore and London: The Johns Hopkins University Press, 1992), p. 94.

39 In answer to a pointed question by Alfred Faraj about "the unconvincing and unnecessary death" of some of his heroes, such as 'Ā'isha's family, Mahfouz seems unable to muster more than the feeble "explanation" that in fiction, as in life, death is sometimes completely arbitrary. See *Ataḥaddath Ilaykum*, p. 149.

40 Mahfouz comments briefly on the God-like quality of the type represented by Aḥmad 'Abd al-Jawād in *Ataḥaddath Ilaykum*, p. 175.

41 I use this transliteration rather than the strict alternative 'Ā'ida for two reasons. First, it corresponds to the actual transcription of the name in the text, namely, عايدة "not عائدة. Second, it is closer to the spelling of Verdi's Aida, which resonates in the background of the fully Europeanized Egyptian beloved.

42 See El-Said Badawi and Martin Hinds, *A Dictionary of Egyptian Arabic*, s.v. ء ب ل.

43 Nūr al-Sharīf himself related this anecdote on Ṣafā' Abū al-Su'ūd's program "*Sā'at Ṣafā*" on *al-Jazeera* (June 26, 2003). The program, in two segments, dealt with the achievement of Naguib Mahfouz.

44 Sigmund Freud, "A special Type of Choice of Object Made by Men: Contributions to the Psychology of Love I," in *The Standard Edition of the Complete Psychological Works of Sigmund Freud* (London: The Hogarth Press, 1957), Vol. XI, pp. 163–176; and "On the Universal Tendency to Debasement in the Sphere of Love: Contributions to the Psychology of Love II," ibid., pp. 177–190.

45 Sūra 42, *al-Shūra*, Āya 10. The translation used here is A. J. Arberry's, *The Koran Interpreted* (Toronto: The Macmillan Company, 1969, third printing), Vol. 2, p. 193.

46 See Judith Butler, *The Psychic Life of Power: Theories in Subjection* (Stanford: Stanford University Press, 1997). The various chapters of this book address from different perspectives and through different genealogies in Western thought the following overarching question: "How does the subjection of desire require and institute the desire *for* subjection?" (emphasis in the original) p. 19. Particularly germane to the issue under consideration is the following elaboration: "In Freud and Nietzsche, a prohibition on action or expression is said to turn 'the drive' back on itself, fabricating an internal sphere, the condition for self-inspection and reflexivity. The drive turning back upon itself becomes the precipitating condition of subject formation, a primary longing in recoil that is traced in Hegel's view of the unhappy consciousness as well. Whether the doubling back upon itself is performed by the primary longings, desire, or drives, it produces in each instance a psychic habit of self-beratement, one that is consolidated over time as conscience," p. 22.

Butler's (re)formulations have not gone unchallenged in the field. See, for example, Molly Anne Rothenberg and Joseph Valente "Identification Trouble in Butler's Queer Theory," in *Gender and Psychoanalysis* (2001), Vol. 6, No. 2, pp. 183–208.

47 Slavoj Zizek, *Looking Awry: An Introduction to Jacques Lacan Through Popular Culture* (Cambridge: MIT, 1991, 7th printing, 1997), p. 24.

48 It is instructive that Mahfouz embeds this chracterization of Kamāl "as a prototype of the Eastern man who is lost between East and West" within a hypothetical project for a novel (within the novel). See *al-Sukkariyya*, p. 191.

49 Translating *waṭanī* as *patriotic* instead of *nationalist* maintains the fine distinction between the pair *Qawmiyya* (nationalism) and *waṭaniyya* (patriotism). The passage quoted from Riyāḍ Qaldas' discourse seems to bear this out by reserving the term *Qawmiyya* for the more inclusive affiliation with the nation. Arthur Goldschmidt, Jr, however, translates al-Ḥizb al-Waṭanī as the National Party. See Arthur Goldschmidt, Jr, *Modern Egypt: The Formation of a Nation-State* (Boulder: Westview Press, 1988), pp. 50 ff.

50 Fahmī Huwaydī, "Aḥdāth al-Kushḥ: How? Why? And Wither?" *Al-Kutub: Wujuhāt Naẓar*, Vol. 2, No. 13 (February 2000), pp. 24–31. See also Otto F. A. Meinardus, *Coptic Saints and Pilgrimages* (Cairo: The American University Press, 2002), p. 28.

51 Huwaydī, Ibid., p. 24:

المصادفة لا تخلو من مفارقة لها دلالتها الجديرة بالانتباه . فقد دخلت مصر الى القرن العشرين وبوادر النفور والشقاق بين المسلمين والاقباط فيها تلوح في الافق، ثم ودعته وقد تحول ذلك النفور الى اشتباك واقتتال في عمق الصعيد، الامر الذي يعني اننا لم نتقدم على صعيد الوحدة الوطنية، بل ربما نكون قد تراجعناعدة خطوات الى الوراء .

52 Mīlād Ḥannā, *Miṣr li-Kull al-Miṣriyyīn* (Cairo: Markiz Ibn Khaldūn, 1993), pp. 54 ff.

53 Maḥmūd Ḥilmī, *Dustūrunā al-Jadīd* (Cairo: Dār al-Fikr al-'Arabī, 1973), p. 146.

54 Ibid., p. 128.

55 Ibid., p. 152.

56 Ibid., p. 155.
57 Ḥannā, *Miṣūr li-Kull al-Miṣriyyīn*, pp. 48–53.
58 Ḥilmī, *Dustūrunā*, p. 200.
59 Ḥannā, *Miṣr li-Kull al-Miṣriyyīn*, p. 66.
60 Ibid.
61 On this point the unrelenting logic of the novel seems to run counter to historical evidence. For, historically, many prominent Christians, in Egypt and elsewhere in the Arab world, often expressed cultural affinity with Islām even as they upheld their Christian faith. This is as true of the Syrian Michel ʻAflaq, founder of the Baʻth party, as it is of the Egyptian Copt Makram ʻUbayd who coined the phrase: "Chrisianity is my religion, Islām is my homeland." More recently the late Coptic scholar Ghālī Shukrī argued further that Eastern Christianity has always felt more at home in the context of Islām than anywhere else, and that, in fact, "it forms an integral part of Islāmic civilization." See Ghālī Shukī, *Thaqāfat al-Niẓām al-ʻAshwāʼī* (Cairo: Kitāb al-Ahalī, 1994), pp. 55 ff., and *al-Aqbāṭ fi Waṭan Mutaghayyir* (Cairo: Kitāb al-Ahālī, 1990).
62 The writings of Yūsuf al-Qarḍāwī, perhaps the most prominent of contemporary orthodox Muslim scholars, exemplify this impasse. See his *Ghayr al-Muslimīn fil-Mujtamaʻ al-Islāmī* (Cairo: Maktabat Wahba, 1977; Non-Muslims in Islamic Society), and *Bayyināt al-Ḥall al-Islāmī wa-Shubuhāt al-ʻIlmāniyyīn wal-Mutagharribīn* (Beirut: Mu'assasat al-Risāla, 1988; Certainties of the Islamic Solution, Uncertainties of the Secularists and the Westernized).
63 Arthur Goldschmidt, Jr, *Modern Egypt*, p. 60.
64 Ṭāriq al-Bishrī *al-Ḥaraka al-Siyasiyya fi Miṣr: 1945–1952* (Cairo: al-Hay'a al-Miṣriyya al-ʻĀmma lil-Kitab, 1972), p. 44.
65 According to Mahfouz, *The Trilogy* was completed in April 1952, a few months before the Revolution (July 23, 1952). See Naguib Mahfouz, *Ataḥddath Ilaykum*, p. 91.
66 Bahaa Taher, a leading figure of the so-called 1960s generation, elaborates on this point in the preface to his remarkable novel *Khālatī Ṣafiyya wal-Dayr* (Cairo: Dār al-Hilāl, 1991), pp. 24 ff.
67 See Otto F. A. Meinardus, *Monks and Monasteries of the Egyptian Deserts* (Cairo: American University in Cairo Press, 1989, revised edition).
68 In Egypt, as elsewhere in the Arab world, the question of building new and renovating old churches is still subject to the Ottoman humāyūnī (imperial) decree of 1856. See Ḥannā, *Miṣr li-Kull al-Miṣriyyīn*, p. 58, pp. 195–203.
69 Ibid., p. 92.
70 See, for example, Ibrahim Abdel Meguid, *Lā 'Aḥad Yanām fil-Iskandariyya* (Cairo: Dār al-Hilāl, 1996), pp. 120, 124 ff.; Farouk Abdel Wahab, tr. *No One Sleeps in Alexandria* (Cairo: American University in Cairo Press, 1999).
71 Abdel Meguid, *Lā 'Aḥad.*, p. 390; Abdel Wahab, *No One Sleeps*, p. 395.

4 QUESTIONABLE SUBJECTS: INDIVIDUALITY, REPRESENTATION, AND THE EGYPTIAN NOVEL

1 For a sample of the extensive literature on the individual and individuality in English see notes 22 and 23 to Chapter 1.
2 Matti Moosa asserts that *Robinson Crusoe* was the first English novel to have been translated into Arabic. See *The Origins of the Modern Arabic Fiction*, p. 72.
3 See George Ṭarabīshī, *al-Riwāʼī wa-Baṭaluh* (Beirut: Dār al-Ādāb, 1995); Aḥmad Muḥammad ʻAṭiyya, *al-Baṭal al-Thawrī fil-Riwāya al-ʻArabiyya al-Ḥadītha* (Damascus: Manshūrāt Wizārat al-Thaqāfa wal-Irshād al-Qawmī, 1977); Muḥyī al-Dīn Ṣubḥī, *al-Baṭal fī Maʼzaq* (Damascus: Manshūrāt Ittiḥād al-Kuttāb al-ʻArab, 1979).

4 For the legal charge against Chahine's film *al-Muhājir*, see *Rose El Youssef*, No. 3464 (October 31, 1994), p. 30. For a discussion of the film, and the case, see 'Iṣām Zakariyyā "Min Yūsuf al-Injīl wal-Qur'ān ilā Yūsuf Shāhīn," *Rose El Youssef*, No. 3461 (October 10, 1994), pp. 64–67.

5 Mahfouz relates the anecdote in which Sadat expressed this sentiment directly to him. See the interview with 'Abd al-Raḥmān Abū 'Awf, "Naguib Mahfouz fī 'Īd Mīlādih al-Sab'īn," "*Majallat al-Idhā'a wal-Tilifizion*" (December 20, 1986), p. 13. Samia Mehrez cites and discusses many similar instances of censorship and intimidation of writers in the first chapter of her book *Egyptian Writers between History and Fiction*, pp. 17–38.

6 See Muḥammad 'Alī al-Ābūnī, ed. *Mukhtaṣar Tafsir ibn Kathīr* (Beirut: Dār al-Qur'ān al-Karīm, 1981, 8th edition), p. 246, for the conflicting accounts concerning the substance or referent of what Joseph "saw" that deflected his attention from the pining Zulaykha and made him desist from consummating the liaison with her. Ibn Kathīr's brief summary of the views of earlier commentators on this episode leaves no doubt about the considerable unease it has always occasioned. In marked contrast, Ṭabāṭabā'ī's commentary is refreshingly direct and unabashedly honest. It not only acknowledges the erotic nature of Joseph's inclination to Zulaykha but considers this entirely normal under the circumstances: Joseph being a handsome young man, barely come of age, alone with a pretty and influential woman who desires him, and so on. To my mind, this explicit recognition of Joseph's humanity, and his innate susceptibility to the weakness of the flesh, renders the *'iṣma* (inerrancy) of the prophet more, not less, powerful when it transpires. While it re-consigns the *'iṣma* in the divine will, rather than in the prophet's own being, it also makes the divine intervention immeasurably more dramatic. See Muḥammad Ḥusayn al-Ṭabāṭabā'ī', *al-Mīzān fī Tafsīr al-Qur'ān* (Tehran: Dār al-Kutub al-Islāmiyya, 1976, 3rd edition), Vol. 11, pp. 134–137. I wish to thank my colleague, Hamid Algar, for bringing this commentary to my attention.

7 A. J. Arberry, *The Koran Interpreted*, p. 256.

8 Abdullah Yusuf Ali, *The Holy Qur'ān: Text, Translation, and Commentary* (Beirut: Dār al-'Arabiyya lil-Ṭibā'a wal-Nashr wal-Tawzī', 1968), p. 558.

9 This assertion recurs numerous times in different forms and contexts in the Qur'ān. The most relevant to our discussion are those addressed by beleaguered prophets, including Muḥammad, to their incredulous contemporaries who hold the prophets' humanity, and the limitations abiding therein, against their claim to prophethood. The implicit charge of falsehood is predicated on the proposition that prophethood entails superhuman or supernatural abilities. See, for example, Qur'ān: 14: 10; 18: 109; 41: 5.

10 Qur'ān, 33: 20.

11 These are: Qur'ān 60: 3, and 60: 5: "لقد كانت لكم اسوة حسنة في ابراهيم والذين معه؛ "لقد كان لكم فيهم اسوة حسنة لمن كان يرجو الله" respectively.

12 Yūsuf al-Qarḍāwī, *al-Tarbiya al-Islāmiyya wa-Madrasat Ḥasan al-Bannā* (Cairo: Maktabat Wahba, 1979; Islamic Education and the "School" of Hasan al-Banna).

13 See 'Ā'isha 'Abd al-Raḥmān (Bint al-Shāṭi'), *al-Shakhṣiyya al-Islāmiyya: Dirāsa Qur'āniyya* (Beirut: Dār al-'Ilm lil-Malāyīn, 1973). For a historical survey of the permutations of the concept of man in Arab/Islamic gnosis see 'Abd al-Raḥmān Badawī, *al-Insān al-Kāmil fil-Islām* (Kuwait: Wikālat al-Maṭbū'āt, 1976, 2nd edition).

14 See the *Encyclopedia of Islam, New Edition*, Vol. 2 (Leden: E. J. Brill, 1965) q.v. Djihād. Ibn Taymiyya, as we saw earlier, disputes the authenticity of this *ḥadīth*.

15 Durayd Yaḥyā al-Khawājā, *Ishkāliyyat al-Wāqi' wal-Taḥawwulāt al-Jadīda fil-Riwāya al-'Arabiyya* (Damascus: Ittiḥad al-Kuttāb al-'Arab, 2000), pp. 20–21. The following brief quote may suggest the general tenor of the argument:

"الرواية كاملة تولدت تولدا غير عربي الى حد ما" ص٢٠؛ " انا اعرف حقيقة اجملتمع المصري بخاصة
والعربي بعامة ليس على هذه الصورة" "انا لا انكر على محفوظ الروائي الكبير تطوره ابدا، بل

انكر استخدامه هذا التطور في اعطاء مثل هذه الصورة المشوهة عن المثقف المصري الحشاش بكل قطاعاته" ٢١: "والمرحلة المتدهورة التي يعيشها الغرب، لا نعيشها نحن بحال! ان التراث الحضاري العربي ، وافكاره متميزة تميزا عجيبا عن اي فكر اخر وهو عندما يأخذ، نراه كانه يعطي، انه موهبة ما زالت تبعث بشرارتها الاولى الاصيلة بالرغم مما اصابها من نكبات."٢٢

16 For the generic ambivalence of Ṭāhā Ḥusayn's major work, *al-Ayyām*, see Ghālī Shukrī, *Mādhā Yabqā min Ṭāhā Ḥusayn*? (Beirut: Dār al-Mutawassiṭ lil-Nashr wal-Tawzī', 1974), pp. 47–48. Muḥammad Mandūr reaches a similar conclusion about the ambivalence of al-Māzinī's works. See his *Ibrāhīm al-Māzinī* (Cairo: Maṭba'at Nahḍat Miṣr, 1954), pp. 68–69. Na'mān 'Āshūr holds a similar view of al-'Aqqād's only "novel," *Sāra*. See Aḥmad Ibrāhīm al-Hawwārī, *Maṣādir Naqd al-Riwāya fil-Adab al-'Arabī al-Ḥadīth fī Miṣr*, p. 42. Mahfouz, who often acknowledges indebtedness to his predecessors, from al-Muwayliḥī and al-Manfalūṭī to al-Māzinī, al-'Aqqād, and especially Tawfīq al-Ḥakīm, considers their works precursors of the novel. See, for example, al-Naqqāsh, *Naguib Mahfouz: Ṣafaḥāt*, pp. 69–78.

17 There are numerous popular sayings in praise of knowledge in Arabic, most of which are ascribed to the Prophet, for example, "seek knowledge from the cradle to the grave," "seek knowledge even if it be in (distant) China," "the ink of the scholars is dearer to God than the blood of martyrs," and so on.

18 Muḥammad Abū al-Anwār, *Muṣṭafā Luṭfī al-Manfalūṭī: Ḥayātuh wa-Adabuh* (Cairo: Maktabat al-Shabāb, 1981), Vol. 1, p. 28.

19 Muṣṭafā Luṣfī al-Manfalūṭī, *al-Naẓarāt* (Beirut: Dār al-Thaqāfa, n.d.), pp. 10–11 ff. Initially these pieces were published separately between 1907–1921 in *al-Mu'ayyad*. See Matti Moosa, *The Origins of Modern Arabic Fiction*, p. 85.

20 Particularly scathing was the criticism of al-Māzinī and al-'Aqqād in *al-Dīwān* (Cairo: al-Sha'b, 1972, 3rd edition), pp. 80–114; and that of Ṭāhā Ḥusayn in several political dailies. Admittedly, this criticism was not entirely objective or literary in nature as it had an obvious political agenda. In the third volume of his autobiographical *al-Ayyām* Ṭāhā Ḥusayn acknowledges this much openly.

21 In *al-Ḥijāb* (The Veil), one of the "stories" included in the collection *al-'Abarāt* (Tears) al-Manfalūṭṭī outrightly condemns the call for the unveiling "*sufūr*" of women. See *al-'Abarāt* (Cairo: Maṭba'at al-Istiqāma, 1952, 14th edition), pp. 49–70.

22 Mahfouz, *Ataḥaddath Ilaykum*, p. 82; al-Naqqāsh, *Naguib Mahfouz: Ṣafaḥat*, pp. 100–101.

23 Von Gurnebaum's view of the "psychological inhibition" against autobiography in Arabic is cited in Robin Ostle's "Introduction" to *Writing the Self*, p. 19. Al Kharrat's view appears in the "Foreword" to this anthology, "Random Variations on an Autobiographical Theme," pp. 9–17.

24 For Mahfouz' view of al-Māzinī's talent and predicament see al-Naqqāsh, *Naguib Mahfouz: Ṣafaḥāt*, pp. 74–75.

25 Mandūr, *Ibrāhīm al-Māzinī*, pp. 69–70.

26 *Al-Dīwān*, ibid.

27 For details of al-'Aqqād's insult to king Fu'ād see: 'Abbās Maḥmūd al-'Aqqād, *Anā* (Beirut: Dār al-Kitāb al-'Arabī, 1969), p. 158, note 1. It is true that al-'Aqqād was a member of the Egyptian parliament when he issued this "challenge" to the King, but that fact seems completely incidental to his personality. His public attacks on the immeasurably more formidable person of Sa'd Zaghlūl attest to this conclusion.

28 Sayyid Quṭb wrote several critical reviews of Ṭāhā Ḥusayn's influential book, *Mustaqbal al-Thaqāfa fī Miṣr* (1938). These reviews were later collected and published by a Saudi publishing company in a small book bearing the same title. See Sayyid Quṭb, *Mustaqbal al-Thaqāfa fī Miṣr* (Jadda: al-Dār al-Sa'ūdiyya lil-Nashr wal-Tawzī', 1969).

29 Al Ghitani, *Naguib Mahfouz Yatadhakkar*, pp. 43–44.
30 Ṣalāḥ 'Abd al-Ṣabūr, *Mādhā Yabqā Minhum lil-Tārīkh* (Cairo: al-Hay'a al-Miṣriyya al-'Āmma lil-Kitāb, 1997; first published in 1968), pp. 14–15.
31 Ibid., pp. 53–54. It may be relevant to note in connection with this elitist attitude of al-'Aqqād that his first choice of a career was to become a "military commander." See al-'Aqqād, *Fī Baytī*, p. d.
32 Al-'Aqqād, *Anā*, pp. 157–166.
33 Sonalla Ibrahim, *Tilk al-Rā'iḥa*, pp. 26–27.
34 *Al-Dīwān*, p. 82.
35 Ibn Khaldūn, *al-Muqaddima* (Beirut: Dār Iḥyā' al-Turāth al-'Arabī, n.d. 4th edition), p. 553. In Franz Rosenthal's translation the phrase reads as follows: (the writer is one who) "has some knowledge of every science." See *Ibn Khaldūn: The Muqaddimah* (Princeton: Princeton University Press: The Bollingen Series, 1967), p. 438. In fact, this definition of the *adīb* predates Ibn Khaldūn by at least six centuries. A version of it already exists in *al-Kāmil* of the ninth century al-Mubarrad. See Muḥammad 'Abd al-Ḥalīm 'Abd-Allāh, *Liqā' bayn Jīlayn*, p. 15.
36 'Ādil Kāmil, *Millīm al-Akbar*, p. 75.
37 Rajā' al-Naqqāsh, *Naguib Mahfouz: Ṣafaḥāt*, p. 154; Munīf, *al-Kātib wal-Manfā*, p. 93.
38 'Abdullāh Abū Hayf, *al-Qiṣṣa al-'Arabiyya al-Ḥadītha wal-Gharb* (Damascus: Manshūrāt Ittiḥād al-Kuttāb al-'Arab, 1994), p. 192.
39 Muṣṭafā Ṣādiq al-Rāfi'ī, *Fī Ẓilāl al-Qur'ān: al-Ma'raka bayn al-Qadīm wal-Jadīd* (Cairo: Maṭba'at al-Istiqāma, 1956, 4th edition).
40 This is the title of a book by al-Ḥakīm, *Min al-Burj al-'Ājiyy* (1941).
41 Naguib Mahfouz, *Ataḥaddath Ilaykum*, p. 71.
42 Sonalla Ibrahim, "The Experience of a Generation," in *Index on Censorship*. See also Samia Mehrez, *Egyptian Writers*, pp. 39–57.
43 Muḥsin Jāsim al-Mūsawī, *Infirāṭ al-'Iqd al-Muqaddas: Mun'aṭafāt al-Riwāya al-'Arabiyya ba'd Mahfouz* (Cairo: al-Hay'a al-Miṣriyya al-'Āmma lil-Kitāb, 1999; Dissolution of the Holy Bond: Turns of the Arab Novel after Mahfouz).
44 Edwar Al Kharrat, *al-Ḥasāsiyya al-Jadīda: Maqālāt fil-Ẓāhira al-Qaṣaṣiyya* (Beirut: Dār al-Ādāb, 1993), especially pp. 13–23.
45 Quoted in Muḥsin Jāsim al-Mūsawī, *Infirāṭ al-'Iqd*, p. 33.
46 See Muḥammad 'Abdu's introduction to *Maqāmāt Badī' al-Zamān al-Hamadhānī* (Beirut: Dār al-Mashriq, 1889; sixth printing, 1964), p. 2.
47 Ibid.
48 Ibid.
49 Sonalla Ibrahim, *Tilk al-Rā'iḥa*, p. 6.
50 Critical attention to the problematic subjects of sexuality and the body in Arab/Islamic culture and literature has been steadily increasing in the last few decades. The following is but a sample of this literature. Abdelwahab Bouhdiba, *Sexuality in Islam*, translated from the French by Alan Sheridan (London, Boston, Melbourne and Henley: Routledge and Kegan Paul, 1985); Roger Allen, Hilary Kilpatrick, and Ed de Moor, eds, *Love and Sexuality in Modern Arabic Literature* (London: Saqi Books, 1995); Leila Ahmed, *Women and Gender in Islam: Historical Roots of a Modern Debate* (New Haven and London: Yale University Press, 1992) Fatna A. Sabbah (Fatima Mernissi), *Women in the Muslim Unconscious* (New York: Pergamon Press, 1984, translated from the French by Mary Jo Lakeland); Fatima Mernissi, *The Veil and the Male Elite: A Feminist Interpretation of Women's Rights in Islam* (Reading, Massachusetts: Addison-Wesley Publishing Company, Inc., 1987, tr. Mary Jo Lakeland); Fedwa Malti-Douglas, *Woman's Body, Woman's Word: Gender and Discourse in Arab-Islamic Writing* (Princeton: Princeton University Press, 1991); Marilyn Booth, "Framing the Imaginary: Conditions of Literary Production in Egypt," *Peuples Méditerraneens*, No. 77 (October 1996), pp. 131–153.

51 Among the four Sunnī schools of law only the Mālikī disregards the criterion of *kafā'a* in marriage.
52 See 'Abd al-Raḥmān al-Jazīrī, *Kitāb al-Fiqh 'Alā al-Madhāhib al-Arba'a* (Beirut: Dār al-Irshād, n.d.), Vol. 4, pp. 54–62. See also Amira El Azhary Sonbol, ed. *Women, the Family, and Divorce Laws in Islamic History* (Syracuse: Syracuse University Press, 1996), especially pp. 246–256.
53 Aḥmad Bahā' al-Dīn, *Ayyām lahā Tārīkh* (Cairo and Beirut: Dār al-Shurūq, 2nd edition, 1985), pp. 49–66.
54 Ibid., p. 61.
55 Al-Naqqāsh, *Naguib Mahfouz: Ṣafaḥāt*, p. 75.
56 See Muḥammad 'Abd al-Ghanī Ḥasan, *al-Fallāḥ fil-Adab al-'Arabī* (Cairo: Dār al-Qalam, 1965); Timothy Mitchell, "The Invention and Reinvention of the Egyptian Peasant," *International Journal of Middle Eastern Studies*, Vol. 22 (May 1990), pp. 129–150. Al-'Aqqād, as was noted earlier, ascribes much of Sa'd Zaghlūl's charisma and appeal to his peasant background. "Sa'd was the best leader of Egypt because he was a peasant in a nation of peasants." Al-'Aqqād, *Sa'd Zaghlūl*, p. 499.
57 Mahfouz relates a telling incident about this point. When the Lebanese film *Bayyā' al-Khawātim* (The Rings Vendor) of Fairuz was shown in Cairo, subtitles in the *fuṣḥā* (literary Arabic) were added to mediate the Lebanese dialect used in the film to the Egyptian spectators. See al-Naqqāsh, *Naguib Mahfouz: Ṣafaḥāt*, p. 62.
58 *Zuqāq al-Midaqq*, pp. 25 and 90, respectively.
59 Jenine Abboushi Dallal, "*The Perils of Occidentalism*."
60 Both of Ahdaf Soueif's major novels, so far, illustrate this trend. These are: *In the Eye of the Sun* (New York: Vintage International, 1992), and *The Map of Love* (New York: Anchor Books, 1999). For a precis of Soueif's background, education, and writing see Pascale Ghazaleh, "Ahdaf Soueif: Different Readings," *Al-Ahram Weekly On-Line* (November 8–14, 2001), pp. 1–6.
61 Thus Jalīla, Zubayda, Zannūba, Haniyya, and 'Aṭiyya, of *The Trilogy*, Ḥamīda, and Ḥusniyya (the baker) of *Midaq Alley*, Nūr and Nabawiyya, of the *The Thief and the the Dogs*, and so on. Truncated names seem also to reflect a class dimension in Mahfouz' work. Thus, for example, the characters of *Zuqāq al-Midaqq* divide into two major categories in respect of their names: The propertied and well to do characters have full names, the poorer ones have only truncated names or nonsensical nicknames. Thus, Raḍwān al-Ḥusaynī, Salīm 'Alwān, Saniyya 'Afīfī, and even the pimp Faraj Ibrāhīm, represent the former; Zeiṭa, Ja'dah, 'amm Kāmil, Ḥamīda, and Ḥusniyya represent the latter.
62 Quoted in Justin Kaplan and Anne Bernays, *The Language of Names* (New York: Simon & Schuster, 1997), p. 15.
63 I discuss this issue at greater length in "The Problematic of Knowledge in the Arabic Novel—اشكالية المعرفة في الرواية العربية" *Mawāqif*, 70–71 (Winter–Spring 1993), pp. 144–163, especially pp. 150–155.
64 Naguib Mahfouz, *Ataḥaddath Ilaykum*, p. 20.
65 See Rif'at al-Sa'īd, *al-Jarīma* (Cairo: Dār Shuhdī lil-Nashr, 1984) for the details of the death of Shudī 'Aṭiyya al-Shāfi'ī.
66 See transcript of the testimony of Ibrāhīm Fu'ād al-Mānāstrilī in Rif'at al-Sa'īd, *al-Jarīma*, pp. 146, 156. A similar scene of torture, followed by a command to say "I am a woman," occurs in al-Sharqāwī's novel, *Al-Arḍ* (1954), p. 260. There, however, the torture is carried out by agents of the notorious government of Ismā'īl Ṣidqī in the 1930s.
67 In outline and some crucial details the plot of *Sharaf* resembles Maḥmūd al-Mas'adī's story "*Sayyid Elḥelewa*." See *al-Walad al-Shaqī fil-Sijn* (Cairo: Akhbār al-Yawm, 1990).

68 See Sabry Hafez "*Jamāliyyāt al-Riwāya al-Jadīda: al-Qaṭī'a al-Ma'rifiyya wal-Naz'a al-Muḍāḍḍa lil-Ghinā'iyya*—Aesthetics of the New Novel: Epistemological Rupture and Anti-Lyrical Poetics," *Alif*, Vol. 21, pp. 184–246.

69 See note 56 above.

70 See Robert Alter, *Partial Magic: The Novel As A Self-Concious Genre* (Berkeley, Los Angeles, and London: University of California Press, 1975).

71 See Soha Abdelaty's report "Should Freedom Have Limits?," *Al-Ahram Weekly On-line* (December 13–19, 2001). See also Philip Smucker's report "A Veil Drapes Cairo Campus in Controversy," *The Christian Science Monitor* (January 17, 2001).

72 See *Mudhakkirāt Hudā Sha'rāwī : Rā'idat al-Mar'a al-'Arabiyya al-Ḥadītha* (Cairo: Dār al-Hilāl, 1981).

73 In *Fatāwā al-Nisā'*, Ibn Taymiyya affirms the right of a man "to discipline" his wife in case of *nushūz*, disobedience, when he calls her to bed. See *Fatāwā al-Nisā'* (Beirut: Dār al-Arqam, n.d.) pp. 186–187. Ibn Taymiyya leaves no doubt that "disciplining" includes "beating," and cites the relevant Qur'ānic verse in support of his view, "al-Nisā' " (Women), 34; in Araberry's *The Koran Interpreted*, 4: 35–40.

74 For "metafiction" see Patricia Waugh, *Metafiction* (London: Methuen, 1983). For a discussion of "diegesis" and its multiple derivatives see Gerard Genette, *Narrative Discourse: An Essay in Method* (tr. Jane E. Lewin, Ithaca: Cornell University Press, 1980), pp. 227–234.

75 Hāla al-Badrī, *Imra'a Mā* (Cairo: Dār al-Hilāl, 2001; *A Certain Woman*, tr. Farouk Abdel Wahab, Cairo: American University Press, 2003), p. 13.

76 For a comprehensive discussion of the controversy over Ḥaydar's novel, *Walīma li-A'shāb al-Baḥr* and the general climate of restrictive censorship in Egypt see Sabry Hafez, "The Novel, Politics, and Islam," *New Left Review*, Vol. 5 (September–October 2000), pp. 117–141.

77 Ibn Taymiyya, *Fatāwā al-Nisā'*, p. 186.

78 It was precisely of such risks that al-Māzinī tried to warn the young practitioner of realistic fiction, Naguib Mahfouz, over six decades ago. See al-Naqqāsh, *Naguib Mahfouz: Ṣafaḥāt*, p. 75.

INDEX

For Product Safety Concerns and Information please contact our EU representative GPSR@taylorandfrancis.com
Taylor & Francis Verlag GmbH, Kaufingerstraße 24, 80331 München, Germany

www.ingramcontent.com/pod-product-compliance
Lightning Source LLC
Chambersburg PA
CBHW071513110726
47908CB00003B/827

* 9 7 8 0 4 1 5 5 9 7 4 3 2 *